LISTEN   SECOND BRIEF EDITION

LISTEN

SECOND BRIEF EDITION

JOSEPH KERMAN

University of California, Berkeley

WITH VIVIAN KERMAN

WORTH PUBLISHERS

Listen: Second Brief Edition

Copyright © 1992, 1987, 1980, 1976, 1972 by Joseph Kerman

Printed in the United States of America

Library of Congress Catalog Card No. 91–66159

ISBN: 0–87901–517–9 (Case edition)

ISBN: 0–87901–549–7 (Paperback edition)

Printing: 3 4—95 94 93

Development editor: Barbara Curialle Gerr

Design: Malcolm Grear Designers

Art director: George Touloumes

Production editor: Carolyn Viola-John

Production supervisor: Sarah Segal

Layout: Patricia Lawson

Picture Editor: Elaine Bernstein

Composition: New England Typographic Service, Inc.

Music typesetting: A-R Editions, Inc.

Printing and binding: R. R. Donnelley & Sons Company

Cover: Assemblage by Starr Ockenga

Cover illustration credits: Excerpt from George Crumb's *Black Angels* © 1972 by C.F. Peters Corporation. Used by permission; Kyrie (detail), © Austrian National Library; Ella Fitzgerald at the Cafe Society, New York (detail), 1951 © Charles Peterson; Opening Night (detail), 1989. © Winnie Klotz/The Metropolitan Opera Guild; Zubin Mehta conducting the New York Philharmonic in Central Park (detail), July 8, 1983. © Bereswill/ New York Newsday; Open air concert (detail). © Stockman/International Stock Photo.

Music, literary, and illustration credits begin on page 426 and constitute a continuation of the copyright page.

Worth Publishers

33 Irving Place

New York, New York 10003

Preface

Some years ago we prepared the first brief version of our larger textbook LIS-TEN (now in its third edition) to meet the needs of one-semester and one-quarter courses for students with no training in "classical" music and with little previous exposure to it. This new edition—LISTEN: SECOND BRIEF EDITION—is the first to be accompanied by CD (compact disc) recordings, in addition to cassettes and LPs. It also includes a much expanded chapter on American music.

More about that in just a moment. For those unacquainted with the LIS-TEN texts, we should first say briefly that our emphasis has always been on music, rather than on theory, history, or listening techniques in the abstract. As far as possible, theoretical and historical materials are introduced not for their own sake, and not for the sake of memorization, but in order to help convey the aesthetic qualities of actual musical works to which students *listen*. We also attempt to place music in its cultural context—at least partly for practical reasons. People who find careful listening difficult or abstract often get excited by the concept of music in relation to painting, literature, ideas, and historical events. Learning about such relationships can lead them to listen more intensely and fruitfully. With this in mind, we precede the main coverage of Baroque, Classical, Romantic, and twentieth-century music with chapters summarizing the culture of the times, especially as this involves music. These introductory chapters (Chapters 8, 11, 15, and 19) also include concise accounts of the musical styles of the era, so that they furnish background of two kinds—cultural and stylistic—for listening to specific pieces of music that are discussed in the chapters that follow.

We think that instructors and students will welcome the expanded chapter on American music of the twentieth century, Chapter 21, now the book's longest. After a brief introduction to earlier American music, we attempt to coordinate "vernacular" music—blues, jazz, and show music—with the developing concert tradition, treating Gershwin and Bernstein as "crossover" figures. Another brief treatment of rock, music videos, and rap should serve to orient students to the background and context of the popular music of their own time. We debated whether to include some rock numbers —perhaps some rock classics—on the recording set, and concluded that given limited recording time it made more sense to treat early blues and jazz in some depth (four numbers are included) rather than provide students with what they already know and probably already own.

We grappled once again in this edition with questions of coverage: how much time and emphasis should be devoted to music of the so-called standard repertory (now sometimes called the Eurocentric canon) and how much to "early music" and music of the twentieth century? We believe that this text will work for instructors who feel a special sense of commitment to any one of these broad areas. Our main emphasis is indeed on the standard repertory —once again, on practical grounds: only so much can be accomplished in a short time, and we are convinced that students learn more from the presentation of a limited amount of material in some depth than from overambitious surveys. A strong argument can be made that introductory courses in music should introduce students to the good music they are most likely to hear.

So we want to stress that Unit II, *Early Music: An Overview,* is *strictly optional* in the book's sequence. Since some courses will omit Unit II altogether, nothing in the book depends on having read it. Those who start with Unit III (*The Eighteenth Century*) will not have to skip back for explanations of continuo texture, recitative, fugue, and so on. On the other hand, for those who wish to include selections of early music without teaching the entire unit, the fairly modest amount of prose in Unit II should prove manageable as a general orientation for the music chosen.

The following pedagogical features of LISTEN: SECOND BRIEF EDITION should help students with varying backgrounds and exposure to music to develop their listening skills and their appreciation of music:

> Rather than starting directly with the elements of music, the book opens with an "Overture"—an immediate listening experience that instructors can use at the very beginning of the course. Debussy's *Fêtes* is traced through simply, in what is now sometimes called a "phenomenological" fashion. The emphasis is on direct listening impressions rather than terminology—though en route some basic technical terms are slipped in, terms that will be introduced more formally in Chapters 2, 3, and 4.

Instructors often like to work out a special presentation in the first week to break the ice and introduce students directly to the subject matter (and keep them from wandering off in the direction of other courses). Our "Overture" offers a brief ice-breaker that students should enjoy, a learning experience that instructors can build on to motivate and engage them.

> Between the short chapters in Unit I, *Fundamentals,* there are optional "interludes" covering special material: "The Science of Sound," "Musical Notation," and "Musical Instruments." These interludes can be assigned whole or in part whenever needed, or they can be omitted without loss of continuity.

> We have further refined our format for tabular Listening Charts, which have received very positive response. When CDs are used with the charts, students can follow the timings directly on the CD timer; and if the CD player includes the indexing function (most do), students can move rapidly from one major point in the music to another. When cassettes are used, digital stopwatches will be helpful; however, the prose material on the charts— along with the miniature music examples, for those with some reading knowledge of music—make the charts easy enough to use without the timings. The numbers on the left of the charts give index points for the location in the three-CD set (in red) and the six-CD set (in black).

> Biographical sketches of the main composers are included before their music is discussed. (We thought it was time to include biographies of Clara Schumann and Fanny Mendelssohn along with Robert and Felix.) Once again, the format developed here is distinctive: the biographies and portraits are clearly set off from the main text, and easy-to-read lists of chief works are provided for study purposes or reference.

> Of the 69 compositions discussed in the text, 67 appear on the accompanying set of six CD or cassette recordings, in whole or in part (e.g., one movement of a symphony). Much effort has been devoted to finding the very best possible performances for this set—performances which we think are likely to interest, excite, and captivate the listener. Quite a number of students, we predict, will keep listening to these recordings long after the course is over. Needless to say, all the works that have Listening Charts are included on the recordings; the discussions and the Listening Charts were fashioned with these recordings in mind.

For those instructors who do not have time to cover as much of the book or who prefer that students have access to a less expensive listening package, there are also sets of three CDs and three cassettes. These smaller sets of recordings include twenty-four compositions, twenty-two of them with Listening Charts. Each Listening Chart notes the location of the work in the sets of three or six CDs or cassettes.

> Other features include time charts of the lives of composers and other important figures, the glossary, and supplements:

> A Study Guide (by Greg Grove of Butte College) has been written to guide students as they read each chapter of this textbook and listen to each musical work with a Listening Chart. Questions are provided that help students to test their understanding of the key ideas and terms in each chapter. Textbook page numbers are given so that students can refer back to the book for answers and additional reading.

> The Instructor's Resource Manual (by Robert M. Greenberg, San Francisco Conservatory of Music, revised by Mark Harbold, Elmhurst College) contains a number of resources to aid instructors: chapter objectives and major listening objectives for each chapter; teaching suggestions; and additional listening suggestions, with listening charts.

> The Test Bank (by Julie Brye, University of Kansas) contains over thirteen hundred multiple-choice questions and over five hundred short essay questions that test the listening selections, musical terms, facts, theory, and concepts presented in the textbook.

Many "intro" and music appreciation instructors have taken the time to tell us of their needs and their experiences with the previous edition, and to review draft chapters of this revision and give us the benefit of their advice. Their responses—ranging from brisk red pencillings to detailed arguments about matters of pedagogical and historical principle—have been wonderfully supportive and nicely critical. In addition to users of our longer text, LISTEN, who over the years have given us suggestions for abbreviating it, and those who advised us and reviewed the first Brief Edition, we wish to thank those whose help with this edition has been most valuable:

Hugh Albee, *Palm Beach Community College*
Jeanne Marie Belfy, *Boise State University*

Roger L. Briscoe, *Raritan Valley Community College*
Julie Brye, *University of Kansas*
William K. Burns, *Seton Hall University*
Nancy L. Davis, *Lorain County Community College*
Mark DeBellis, *Columbia University*
Craig De Wilde, *University of California at Santa Barbara*
David P. Doerksen, *University of Oregon*
David M. Edris, *Peru State College*
Stephen G. Gates, *University of Arkansas*
Mark Harbold, *Elmhurst College*
Steven Johnson, *Brigham Young University*
Ronald J. Klimko, *University of Idaho*
Steven Kreinberg, *Temple University*
Bruce Mayhall, *University of Nevada, Reno*
William R. Rudolph, *Burlington County College*
K. Robert Schwarz, *Brooklyn College*

Thanks also to Greg Salmon of the University of California, Berkeley, Music Department for specific editorial assistance. Professor Philip Brett, a friend in need, interrupted a crowded recording session to make the Dufay recording for Chapter 6.

We feel that writing about music should evoke (however faintly) the artistic qualities of its subject matter, and we feel that it ought to be read from pages that are aesthetically appealing, too. The first brief LISTEN won a merit award at the New York Book Show, and Pat Appleton of Malcolm Grear Designers has refined this design for LISTEN: SECOND BRIEF EDITION. She has made a book that is beautiful in itself, and also functions beautifully: the second color works wonders to clarify diagrams, music examples, and listening charts, and the generous use of full-color gatherings allows the artwork to be integrated vividly into the text, rather than stuck on cosmetically. Warm thanks also to George Touloumes, the miracle man who implements this design, and to our immediate co-workers at Worth Publishers, who this time around are all accomplished musicians: editor Barbara Curialle Gerr (vocals, keyboards), art consultant Elaine Bernstein (lyric coloratura soprano), and master trouble shooter Tom Gay (piano).

Berkeley, California
November 1991

JOSEPH KERMAN
VIVIAN KERMAN

Contents in Brief

Contents

Unit I

Fundamentals

The introductory unit of this book, Unit I covers musical fundamentals and their standard terminology. Chapter 1 of this unit will introduce us at once to a piece of music, Festivals, *by Claude Debussy. Chapter 2, "The Elements of Music," takes up pitch, dynamics, tone color, beat, meter, and rhythm. Chapter 3, "The Structures of Music," deals with melody, harmony, and other combinations of the basic elements already discussed. Chapter 4 carries the discussion one stage further, to a consideration of musical style and musical form.*

Listening

The basic activity that leads to the love of music and to its understanding— to what is sometimes called "music appreciation"—is listening to particular pieces of music again and again. Such, at least, is the premise underlying this book. The following pages are filled mostly with discussions of musical compositions—symphonies, concertos, songs, and operas—that people have found more and more rewarding as they have listened to them repeatedly. These discussions are intended to clarify the contents of the works and their aesthetic qualities: what goes on in the music and how it affects us.

It should be apparent that the kind of understanding involved here is not the same required in, say, the study of physics. We do not need to understand concepts such as velocity, force, and energy in the same way we would if we were going to use them in working out problems or conducting lab experiments. That kind of hands-on knowledge of music is necessary only for a music professional—for a composer or a performer; it is not necessary for a nonprofessional listener.

Our goals here are different. Listeners need to understand musical concepts and know musical terms in order to grasp more clearly what they already hear in music. Analyzing things, pinpointing things, even simply using the right names for things, makes us more sharply aware of them. Sometimes, too, this process of analysis, pinpointing, and naming can actually assist listening. We become aware of some aspects of the music only after they have been pointed out. And sharper awareness contributes to greater appreciation of music as well as all the other arts.

Since our emphasis is on listening to music, that is where we start. Before defining such concepts as pitch, meter, and so on, we will get to know a major piece of music—our "overture." Starting with an actual work of art, rather than a set of definitions, may also help us get through the fundamentals more smoothly. The work exemplifies concepts that will be explained later.

Some readers will already know many of the terms that will be mentioned in Chapter 1 as they listen to this music; those who do not should not attempt to memorize them at this point. All the terminology will be explained more fully in the later chapters. Even short of complete understanding, a reader with some basic familiarity with musical terms, gained directly from an interesting, attractive musical composition, should find the terminology of music less abstract and mysterious, more immediate and alive.

Chapter 1

Overture

Listen, then, to *Festivals (Fêtes),* an orchestral work written in 1899 by the French composer Claude Debussy. It is not, to be sure, an actual overture, that is, the orchestral number designed to introduce and set the mood for a stage play or an opera—such as Felix Mendelssohn's overture to Shakespeare's *Midsummer Night's Dream,* or Leonard Bernstein's overture to his musical *Candide.* Debussy wrote it as part 2 of a three-part composition for orchestra and chorus that he called *Nocturnes,* meaning "night pieces." But *Festivals* will do nicely as an introduction to our subject.

First, let's just listen to it through.

It starts with a highly rhythmic section that is exceedingly rich in orchestral sounds; various fragments of melody dash in and out in an exhilarating fashion. Suddenly this music stops, and we hear a strange march in the distance. It comes closer and closer; the music gets very loud, then gets soft again when the original rhythmic music returns (less of it, though, than was heard originally). Rather surprisingly, in view of all the energy that the music has been registering, the last minute or so consists of a drawn-out dying-down process. Tantalizing fragments of the earlier melodies and the march melody are heard, as the rhythms deconstruct and fade. There is one hushed cymbal clash, and the piece is over.

Claude Debussy

Does that description correspond to anything you experienced while Debussy's music was playing, in fact? Does the piece grab you, does anything about it intrigue you—would you care to hear it again? If the answer is "no," skip to page 10. (You might also like to arrange a conference with your instructor.) If the answer is "yes," rewind the cassette, or track the CD back, and listen again. Read on.

The Music Begins   You'll hear a number of things more clearly the second time around. For example, *Festivals* begins with a tiny introductory section— a short pulsation in the orchestra. Loud chords are played in a lively rhythm; they have no melody, just a pulse or a beat. When a fast-moving, up-and-down melody slips in, played by some woodwind instruments, the pulsation quiets down. You can still hear it, however, continuing softly back of the melody.

beats:
1   2
ta-ke-te ta——ke
ta-ke-te ta——ke
ta-ke-te ta——ke
ta-ke-te ta——ke

Rhythmic pulsations of this kind can be counted out to nonsense syllables such as, for example, *ta* and *ke*. The present pulsation counts in brisk "*ta*-ke-te ta—ke" patterns.

The terminology for rhythm will be developed later. Behind the "*ta*-ke-te ta—ke" rhythm is a simple recurring meter, a **duple meter** generated by the regular alternation of one strong beat ("*ta*") and one weak beat ("ta").

The melody hardly has time to rush up and down again before an irregular blast from the trumpets threatens to throw the beat off completely. But instead of that, regular pulsation is resumed—pulsation of a somewhat new kind. It prepares us for the return of the fast melody, this time played by different woodwind instruments.

When the melody is played the first time, the woodwind instrument that sounds most clearly is the clarinet; the second time it is the oboe. The oboe has a sharper, more pungent sound.

The term for quality of sound is **tone color,** or **timbre;** what distinguishes the oboe from the clarinet is its characteristic tone color.

And this time something happens to the end of the melody. A short fragment of it is picked up by high stringed instruments and repeated obsessively—all the while getting louder and louder, as low instruments surge up below. This really *does* throw the beat off . . . and the music grinds to a halt. A pompous fanfare sounds on the brass instruments.

This big sound collapses completely. Nothing remains but a low, expectant drum roll, a drum roll that *lacks any beat.* You could not beat your way through this drum roll (or feel a beat through it) if you tried to, neither at the original lively pace nor at the slower pace of the fanfare.

What has happened to the momentum? Debussy picks it up again with a splendid upward swish on two orchestral harps, leading to the next section of music.

A small fragment of melody that is isolated and repeated many times in a composition is called a **motive** (sometimes spelled *motif*). Repeating motives in various ways is an important technique for extending long pieces of music and providing them with interest and significance. Here Debussy's obsessive repetition of a motive seems to unnerve the music and force it to a halt.

The technical term for the speed of music (more precisely, the rate of the beats) is **tempo;** the brass fanfare has slowed the tempo down for a moment. To indicate that a note has no fixed tempo—no discrete number of beats—the composer marks it with a sign called a **fermata.** This means that the note is held longer than its normal time as counted in the regular beats.

A Second Beginning   Another pulsation is heard, followed by the same melody scurrying up and down . . . and the two elements are repeated. We can't help but be reminded of the opening music. Debussy seems to be starting the piece up a second time. This time he is not going to allow anything to halt the forward motion; indeed, the music sounds more solid than before. The pulsation is longer and has a new, sly quality to it, and the melody has acquired an attractive new turn at the end.

> The ending fragment of a melody is called the **cadence.** Cadences are an important feature in music because of the way they punctuate music's constant flow. Here, the new cadence acquired by the little melody makes it seem more like a melody than it did before.
>
> We have already heard this melody several times, and we will hear it again as the music continues. It turns out to be one of the main musical building blocks used by Debussy to put his piece together. Melodies and motives that perform this function are called **themes;** this melody is one of the main themes of *Festivals.*

In the music that follows, the listener is struck by ever-new sounds coming from all regions of the orchestra, lasting for only a second or two, and then giving way to other sounds. It would be impossible to mention all the instruments and novel combinations of instruments that Debussy brings in here. The impression is of a veritable kaleidoscope of sound, almost an overload, but a fascinating one.

One thing stands out: another pulsation, played by a co-ordinated group of brass instruments, which forces the rhythm into threes. From now on the music has to be counted in steady three-beat patterns for a considerable time.

```
beats:
1          2        3
ta-ke-te ta——ke  ta——ke
ta-ke-te ta——ke  ta——ke
```

> These brass instruments are French horns—more mellow than trumpets when played quietly, more throaty or hooty when played loudly (as here). The meter of *Festivals* has now changed from duple meter to **triple meter**, in which one strong beat ("*ta*") alternates with two weak beats ("ta   ta").

Presently a new, slower melody is presented by the oboe—its sustained notes stand out well against the pulsing in the background. There's a nice, slightly "funky" swing to the music now; this highly active piece seems to be settling down into something more relaxed and tuneful. We catch another new melody in the strings, with waltzlike lilt. The two new melodies alternate several times.

But suddenly they collapse. What remains is a new pulsing rhythm, a last spasm of all the motor energy that has been supporting the two melodies. Rushing to a climax, the music rapidly gets louder; then very abruptly it *stops.*

> **Dynamics** is the technical term for the volume of sound—its loudness or softness. In this part of *Festivals*, dynamics are marked on the score as follows: *p* (*piano*, meaning soft), **cresc.** (*crescendo*, which means gradually getting louder), and finally *ff* (*fortissimo*—very loud. *Forte*, or *f*, means loud).

Stop   The stop is infinitesimally brief. Yet it is decisive, for nearly everything changes at this point. The music quiets down and loses all vestige of melody. Pulse there is, very definitely; but the pulsation is more mechanical than before—and a great deal longer. It is presented in a drastically simple way, without any of the previous *ta*-ke-te rhythms.

```
beats:
1  2   1  2   1  2
ta  ta  ta  ta  ta  ta
```

We spoke of the intricate, iridescent quality of the earlier music. By comparison, what happens now is plain, one-dimensional, even monolithic. This is true even after a weird and wonderful march is introduced by distant-sounding trumpets. (An extraordinary contrast—who would have predicted *that*?) The effect of great distance is achieved by the use of <u>mutes</u>—cone-shaped objects wedged into the flared part of the trumpets, blocking the sound and distorting it in a striking way.

> **Texture** is a term used for the "weave" of music, for the blending together of various elements heard at the same time. The march is said to have a homophonic texture, or to be in **homophony,** because the trumpets playing it are coordinated or synchronized: they play simple chords. (*Homo* is the Greek prefix meaning "same," as in "homogeneous.")
> A **chord** is simply a musical sound consisting of two or more pitches sounding at the same time.

A Distant March   The march sounds steady and simple compared with any of the melodies heard before. It goes on for some time without interruption, and it comprises two similar sections which clearly complement one another. This march melody is something most people could learn to sing (in contrast, perhaps, to the other melodies in *Festivals*).

Next, the entire march appears a *second time*—higher and on different instruments, to be sure, but the same sounds, rhythms, chords.

> The second time, the last part of the march comes in the massed French horns, answered by high woodwinds—an especially solemn and impressive effect.
> A melody of some length, divided into sections that go together as in the march melody, can be called a **tune.** Clearly defined sections in tunes are called **phrases.** We often feel a sense of "balance" between the phrases of a tune, as is the case here.

The march is getting closer. More and more instruments are joining in. Our adrenalin level shoots up when the snare drum enters; it prepares a *third appearance* of the same music, played by the brass at maximum volume and capped by cymbal clashes. And we are astonished to hear the fast up-and-down melody of the opening, played at the same time as the march melody. It no longer sounds skittery but, rather, ecstatic and triumphant.

The loudness and the cymbals, and the charge we get from experiencing these two quite different melodies simultaneously—all this brings the third appearance of the march to a tremendous climax.

And Debussy manages to intensify the climax by one more notch, as the brass blares an emphatic new figure. Then the original music, which had stopped suddenly prior to the march, starts up again no less suddenly.

> Where the march and the up-and-down melody are heard simultaneously, the music is said to be in a **polyphonic** texture. (*Poly* means "many," as in "polygamist" and "polytechnic.") We have heard polyphonic textures before in *Festivals*, but never anything as striking as the combination of these two very different-sounding melodies.

Mardi Gras in New Orleans

Return to the Original Music The volume has dropped, and we identify the original music at once from its rhythms and its approximate melodic forms, even though what we are hearing now is not identical to anything we heard previously. Soon a passionate new melody emerges in the high strings, briefly. Trumpets deliver a loud flash of the march music, in a somewhat frantic, compressed version.

Return to the "Second Beginning" The trumpet figure was a signal. Debussy now returns to the music of his "Second Beginning," which had been led up to by the dramatic pause and the harp passage, near the beginning of the piece. And this music returns almost identically. (The orchestration is a little thicker.) We hear the same pulsation we heard before, and we hear the original up-and-down melody with its catchy cadence.

> For listeners, there is usually a sense of satisfaction in coming back, after new musical material, to music that we remember from before. This satisfaction of recognition, as it might be called, is an effect gained from the apprehension of musical form. **Form**—the "shape" of music in time—depends to a large extent on the way we recognize repetitions and reinterpretations of musical themes and sections.

The Music Runs Down This heading tries to match the impression Debussy creates soon after the feeling of "return" to his second beginning. The music up to now has seemed endlessly effervescent, but now it dries up, fragments, and virtually disintegrates.

The process starts with a rumbling, muttering sound in low instruments, while the brilliant darting rhythms and melodies begin to come apart. They collapse into isolated sounds and wisps of melody above the rumble. The muttering continues, until Debussy finds a way to deenergize his music even further—by gradually slowing it down. In the new, slow tempo, a new motive emerges with a new melancholy flavor.

A strange mood, for a piece called *Festivals*! Repeated several times by the oboe and bassoon, the melancholy motive, too, sounds like a fragment of something . . . but of what? We never figure out. The rumble begins again, a little faster, with just a few semicoherent sounds above it, and then a single barely audible cymbal stroke. Then silence. The music is over. The vision is at an end.

> Does the quiet cymbal stroke remind you of the shattering cymbal strokes at the climax of the march? If so, that is another effect of musical form, of a more subtle and poetic kind. A blatant, forceful sound has been transformed in your imagination into a mild, ghostly memory.

Listening Charts

In this book, the musical compositions that we study most carefully are accompanied by graphic listening charts or summaries, which have been designed to guide you through the music and remind you of the main points made about it in the text. The first of these charts appears on page 9.

Read down the page on the listening chart while listening. Note that it is not necessary to read music to use these charts. Even people who think they are tone-deaf (there's no such condition) can follow the music and the charts with the help of the timings in the left-hand margin, which correspond to the performance of Debussy's *Festivals* on the CD/cassette/LP set accompanying *Listen.* CD index points are also indicated on the chart. The red index numbers refer to the three-CD set, the black to the six-CD set. For the benefit of those who *can* read or follow music, the charts in subsequent chapters include a brief notation of the main themes, directly across from the timing indication and the reference.

Words, Music, Images   The word *vision* at the end of the description of *Festivals*, on page 7, is worth a moment's thought. A vision is something that we see, yet the word was used in a description of music—which is an art of sounds, not of sights.

The usage may seem natural enough in this age of music videos. However, the idea that music *necessarily* goes together with pictures or images would be hard to maintain. Certainly the arts can sometimes be combined, but sometimes they also ought to be granted their own private spaces. Music isn't usually piped into art museums, and certain kinds of music deserve to be listened to without the distraction of visions or pictorial fantasies.

But this cannot be true of *Festivals*. The words *nocturnes* and *festivals* are in our minds as we listen to it, and those words suggest visual images. The first idea that will occur to anyone in connection with night is darkness, which determines what one does or doesn't see, rather than what one hears. And to think about festivals taking place at night is to think about ways of seeing: lanterns, torches, flares. Debussy knew this when he wrote those words in his score. In a very real sense, the words and the visual images they suggest are a component of Debussy's music—a component, at least, of the aesthetic effect that he was interested in projecting.

Stimulated by those words, and by the dynamic, dramatic character of the music, we are likely to summon up in our mind's eye not just an image but a changing image. . . . *Groups of revelers at a Mardi Gras celebration, or something of the sort, mingling on the streets of a town at nighttime. There is a group of hectic, nonstop dancers, and some others, each with their own music; they meet, greet each other, and pass each other by.*

A military band, far in the distance—its banal march music distorted and transfigured by the magic spell of Carnival . . .

The music gets closer and closer. When the band catches up with us in a narrow street, we're almost deafened by the sound echoing off the masonry. What ricochets off the masonry is, weirdly, not the march but the original hectic dance music.

The band vanishes, the revelry resumes. Night is speeding on. The merrymakers wander off to a distant part of town—we hear them only faintly. It must be nearly dawn before they finally pack up. The cymbal player from the military band, it seems, has joined them. . . .

Fanciful? No more fanciful than Debussy's fabulously imaginative score. Music has been called the supreme product of human fancy. Enjoy it.

LISTENING CHART NUMBER 1

3 Cassette 1A-1/3 CD 1-1
6 Cassette 1A-1/6 CD 1-1

Debussy, *Festivals (Fêtes),* from *Three Nocturnes*

6 min. 17 sec.

	0.00	**The Music Begins**	A pulsation begins in the high instruments.
			The music is in **duple meter,** with two regularly alternating beats: one strong beat, one weak.
	0.04		A short, fast melody is heard, running up and down, played by woodwinds.
	0.17		Same melody, repeated
			With a new **tone color** (played by different woodwind instruments)
	0.23		Buildup: repetitions of a fragment of the original melody
			A small musical figure is called a **motive.**
	0.35		Slowdown: loud trumpet fanfare, drum roll
			The speed, or **tempo,** of the music changes momentarily.
1.2 1.2	0.46	**A Second Beginning**	Another kind of pulsation, then the fast melody again
			Music that is heard again and again in a piece is called its **theme,** or one of its themes. The theme now has a new ending, or **cadence.**
	1.03		French horn figure
			The meter changes to **triple meter**—one strong beat and two weak beats.
	1.22		New melody, oboe
1.3 1.3	1.40		New, lilting melody, strings
	2.18		Buildup
			An increase in music's **dynamics** (volume) is called **crescendo.**
	2.35	**Stop**	
1.4 1.4	2.36	**A Distant March**	A steady pulsation—a little slower
	2.51		March melody, distant trumpets: first time
			The march is played with chords—a **homophonic texture.**
	3.04		(Second part of the March)
			The march consists of two similar segments, or **phrases.**
	3.18		March: second time, louder
1.5 1.5	3.42		March, third time, louder yet, with the original fast theme played simultaneously
			A texture with two or more melodies sounding simultaneously is called **polyphonic.**
	4.04		Climax—new figure in brass
1.6 1.6	4.10	**Return to the Original Music**—approximately	
			The satisfaction of recognizing that we have returned to something familiar is one consequence of the musical **form** of *Festivals.*
	4.23		New, passionate theme in the strings
	4.33		A rapid flash of the march music (trumpets)
	4.38	**Return to the "Second Beginning"**—almost literally	
1.7 1.7	5.10	**The Music Runs Down**	"Rumbling" effect
	5.35		Slowdown: new motive (oboe)
	5.59		The original tempo is resumed; the rumbling, again
	6.13		Quiet cymbal clash

INTERLUDE 1: The Science of Sound

Sound—more exactly, musical sound—was one of the first phenomena to be investigated scientifically in the Western world. Only astronomy goes back further; and of these two ancient scientific subjects, astronomy was at a certain disadvantage in that it does not allow for direct experimentation, as the study of musical sound does. Only later were mechanics, light, chemistry, and medicine studied in a truly scientific manner.

Acoustics in Ancient Greece

The pathbreaking investigations into the nature of sound are credited to the Greek mathematician-philosopher Pythagoras, who lived before 500 B.C. He is also famous for his theorem about right-angled triangles ($a^2 + b^2 = c^2$). Pythagoras discovered or codified numerical facts about the sounds produced by plucking strings. If we pluck a taut string, it gives out a certain pitch (that is, a sound at a certain level of "highness" or "lowness"). Then if we pinch the string exactly in the middle and pluck the half-length string, the new pitch is exactly an octave (see page 13) higher.

Another way of saying this is that string lengths in the ratio 2:1 produce pitches that sound one octave apart. Strings in other simple numerical ratios—such as 2:3, 3:4, 4:5, 8:9—produce all the other pitches of the diatonic scale, the ancient Greek name for what is now the white-note scale on a piano keyboard.

Pythagoras's experiments were repeated and discussed with great admiration and interest for more than two thousand years after his death. In the Middle Ages, they formed the basis of the university curriculum in both music and mathematics. Perhaps, after all, there is something to the popular view that musical and mathematical talents go together.

Modern Acoustics

What the Greeks did not know—what was not grasped until the sixteenth century—was how sound is actually produced. Sound results from very small, very rapid vibrations that are set up in certain objects or bodies—taut strings, gongs, bells, discs, and columns of air enclosed in tubes—and transmitted through the air. One complete vibration is called a *cycle*.

The human ear can detect a considerable range of these vibrations, from around 20 cycles per second up to around 20,000. What sounds to us like an "average" musical sound—for instance, the A that is used to tune up at the beginning of a symphony concert—has a frequency of 440 cycles per second.

Properties of Sound

Three basic properties of sound are frequency, timbre, and volume. As we shall see, these scientific terms correspond to the musical terms *pitch, tone color,* and *dynamics,* respectively.

> **Frequency** refers to the speed or rate of the vibrations in a sound-producing body. The higher the frequency, the higher the sound; and the shorter the length of the vibrating body, the higher the frequency. A piccolo sounds higher than a trombone because it encloses a shorter tube of vibrating air. If you blow across the top of a bottle as you fill it up with water, the sound becomes higher as the column of air above the water becomes shorter.

The phenomenon of octaves has to do with the remarkable fact that strings and other sound-producing bodies tend to vibrate not only along their full length, but also simultaneously in halves, quarters, eighths, and so on. These fractional vibrations are called *partials* or *overtones*. The sound of the overtones is much softer than that of the main note; when a string is plucked, or played with a bow, one can scarcely hear the overtones. But when a second string half the length of the first string vibrates, it also reinforces the half-length overtone of the first string. The ear receives this as a kind of duplication.

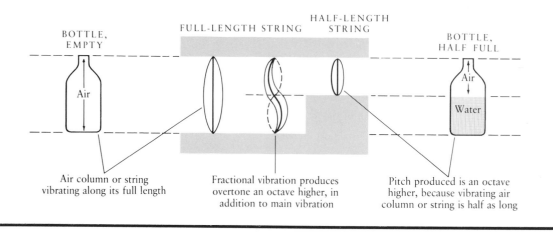

Air column or string vibrating along its full length

Fractional vibration produces overtone an octave higher, in addition to main vibration

Pitch produced is an octave higher, because vibrating air column or string is half as long

The piano hammer has just struck one of the piano's strings, which can be seen vibrating laterally while the other strings are still. To the right, a simulated picture of a guitar string vibrating in partials (in fractions of its length, rather than over its entire length).

> The **timbre** or quality of sound, also called tone "color," depends on the amount and proportion of the overtones. In a flute, the air column vibrates strongly along its total length and not much in halves or quarters, so there are few overtones. Violin strings, on the other hand, vibrate simultaneously in many subsegments, so that violin sound is rich in overtones. This is what accounts for the relatively thin, "white" tone color of the flute and the warm, rich tone color of the violin.

> The **volume** or degree of loudness of sound depends on the amplitude of the vibration, on how far or hard the string or air column vibrates. For example, in a guitar, volume depends on how many sixteenths or thirty-seconds of an inch the string flares out when you pluck it. The frequency does not change, but the harder you pluck, the louder the sound.

Players of wind instruments control volume by the wind pressure that they produce by blowing. It is no accident that loudness in music is associated with force and exertion.

The Synthesizer

Unlike most traditional musical instruments, which are powered largely by human force or breath, the sound synthesizer works through purely electronic means. A synthesizer may consist of any of three basic elements: (1) a network of electronic oscillators, amplifiers, speakers, and other mechanisms to produce and manipulate sound;

(2) a device to select the pitches and determine the type and quality of sound to be produced—generally a keyboard for the pitches, and controls for tone colors; (3) a computer or microchip to translate those instructions into sound vibrations.

The actual production of electronic sound is a complicated affair. The oscillator produces pure tones by combining two electrical currents whose vibrations are at slightly different frequencies; the ear hears this small difference as a specific pitch. Several such tones are added together to give a richer, more interesting timbre to the sound, which is then amplified and broadcast through speakers.

But the heart of any synthesizer is its computer. The first synthesizers were developed in the 1950s; these were cumbersome instruments, requiring bulky rats' nests of circuitry and producing only the most rudimentary sounds. The synthesizers used in the 1960s, such as the Moog synthesizer, were divided into more manageable components and then hooked up to keyboards. With the microchip revolution of the 1970s and 1980s, the synthesizer has become easier and cheaper to use and the music-making abilities of Casios and Yamahas continue to grow more sophisticated.

Most of us are familiar with synthesizers (as electronic pianos and organs) through their use in the performance of rock music. Synthesizers are also valuable to composers, for with such instruments they can now exert precise control over almost all musical elements and almost all aspects of sound production.

Chapter 2

The Elements of Music

We begin with the three basic properties of musical sound—pitch, dynamics, and tone color. Since the pitches used in music are assembled in scales, scales are discussed next. Then a number of concepts are introduced having to do with music in time: rhythm, beats, meter, and tempo.

1 Pitch

We instinctively hear some sounds as high, others as low—and we accept almost as instinctively the adjectives *high* and *low* to describe the sounds in question, though their appropriateness is by no means obvious. The quality of highness or lowness of sound is called **pitch.**

Sound is produced by very fast, very small vibrations in taut strings, gongs, bells, columns of air in pipes, and other objects, as we saw in Interlude 1. The pitch of a sound is determined by the speed of vibration; the scientific measurement of pitch is simply a rate (or frequency) of so many vibrations per second. When at the beginning of a rehearsal an orchestra tunes to "A 440," that means that the pitch A has a frequency of 440 vibrations per second.

Pitch figures centrally in the whole notion of music. If sound lacked this quality, we would have no melodies or tunes, and even motorcycles and police sirens would sound much the same. But of course road noises, even though they do have pitch, are not the normal material of music. This is not because they are too loud or too ugly but because they are too indefinite. Usually, if sounds are to be used in music, their pitch must be focused, rather than blurred or indefinite as it is in low or high noises.

There are some musical instruments with indefinite pitch, such as the bass drum and cymbals, but they can't carry the tune.

Our experience of pitch is gained very early; babies only a few hours old respond to human voices, and they soon distinguish between high and low ones. They are most responsive to high pitches, naturally—these are in their mothers' pitch range. At the other end of life, it is the highest frequencies that old people find they cannot hear. Shown at right is the range of pitches that seems most normal to us, since they are those spoken or sung by men and women. (For those who are not familiar with musical notation for pitch, it is explained on pages 25–29.)

NORMAL
VOICE RANGES
as in a chorus

Intervals: The Octave

The difference, or distance, between any two pitches is called an **interval.** Of the many different intervals used in music, one has a special character that makes it particularly important.

This is the **octave.** If a series of successive pitches is sounded, one after another—say, the white keys on the piano—there comes a point at which the pitch seems in some sense to "duplicate" an earlier pitch. This new pitch does not sound identical to the old one, but somehow the two sounds are very similar. They blend extremely well; they almost seem to melt into each other.

When men and women sing together, they instinctively sing in octaves, duplicating each other's singing an octave or two apart. If you asked them, they would all say they are singing "the same tune," and only the most sophisticated of them would think of adding "at different octave levels."

As a result of the phenomenon of octaves, the full continuous range of pitches that exists in nature (and that is covered, for example, by a siren starting very low and going up higher and higher until it can no longer be heard) falls into a series of "duplicating" segments. About ten of these octave segments are audible. Most voices and instruments have ranges of around two to three octaves; a large pipe organ covers all ten; a piano covers about seven. Two octaves are shown in the upper diagram on page 15.

2 Dynamics

The second basic property of musical sound is its loudness or softness—its volume of sound, or **dynamics.**

Musicians use Italian terms to describe dynamics, because in the period when these terms began to be used regularly, Italy dominated the musical scene in Europe. The two main categories are simply loud *(forte)* and soft

Choral singing, the route by which millions of people come to know and love music

(piano). However, these can be made to refer to a considerable range of dynamics by expanding to "very loud" or "very soft" and by adding the Italian word for "medium," *mezzo:*

pianissimo	*piano*	*mezzo piano*	*mezzo forte*	*forte*	*fortissimo*
pp	**p**	**mp**	**mf**	**f**	**ff**
very soft	soft	medium soft	medium loud	loud	very loud

Sometimes changes in dynamics are sudden *(subito),* and sometimes they are gradual—a quiet passage may swell into a loud one, or a powerful blare fade into quietness. Below are the terms for changing dynamics and their notational signs (sometimes called "hairpins"):

crescendo (**cresc.**)

decrescendo (**decresc.**)
or *diminuendo* (**dim.**)

gradually getting louder

gradually getting softer

"The first, most beautiful, and most widely used of all the sources of music—the human voice": soprano Maria Callas, who all but revolutionized opera singing (and acting) in the 1950s, at the Metropolitan Opera

3 Tone Color

The individual notes in music, whether loud or soft, differ in general *quality* of sound, depending on the instruments or voices that produce them. **Tone color,** or **timbre,** is the term for this quality.

Tone colors are almost impossible to describe, let alone indicate in musical notation; about the best one can do is use imprecise adjectives such as bright, warm, harsh, hollow, or brassy. Yet tone color is one of the most immediately and easily recognized musical elements. Many people who cannot carry a tune can distinguish the sounds of various instruments. Even without being able to identify instruments by name, everyone can hear the difference between the smooth, rich sound of violins, the bright sound of trumpets, and the thump of drums. The most distinctive tone color of all, however, belongs to the first, most beautiful, and most widely used of all the sources of music—the human voice.

Musical instruments are the subject of Interlude 3. It is amazing how many different devices have been invented in all societies to produce the different tone colors that people have wanted for their music. And the search goes on in the new spheres of sound opened up by electronic and computer technology (see Chapter 19).

4 Scales

Music, as we noted above, generally does not make use of the total continuous range of sound that exists in nature, but draws on only a limited number of fixed pitches in each octave segment. These pitches can be assembled in a collection called a **scale.** In effect, a scale is the pool of pitches available for the making of music.

Which exact pitches make up a scale, and how many in each octave, differ from culture to culture. Twelve pitches have been fixed for most of the music we know. Five were once used in Japan, as many as twenty-four have been used in Arab countries, and Western Europe originally used seven.

The Diatonic Scale

The set of seven pitches originally used in Western music is called the **diatonic scale.** Dating from ancient Greek times, it is still in use today. When the first of the seven pitches is repeated at a higher duplicating pitch, the total is eight—hence the name *octave,* meaning "eight span."

Anyone who knows the series *do re mi fa sol la ti do* is at home with the diatonic scale. You can count out the octave for yourself starting with the first *do* as *one* and ending with the second *do* as *eight.* The set of white notes on the piano (or other) keyboard constitutes this scale. Shown below is a keyboard and diatonic scale notes running through two octaves.

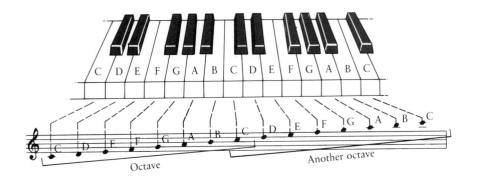

The Chromatic Scale

The diatonic scale was the basic scale of Western music. At a later period, five more pitches were added between certain of the seven members of the diatonic scale, making a total of twelve. This is the **chromatic scale,** represented by the complete set of white and black notes on a keyboard.

The earliest European keyboards had only the seven white notes in each octave, since all music used only the seven-note diatonic scale, as shown above. The fact that the black notes occupy a secondary position physically on today's keyboards—they are thinner, and set back—reminds us that these pitches were originally regarded as secondary insertions within the diatonic scale. Black notes were introduced for the extra pitches.

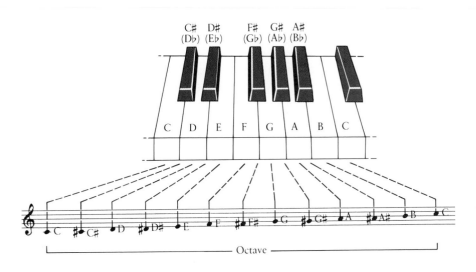

In musical notation, these extra pitches required the introduction of sharps and flats to indicate them. The pitches of the diatonic scale are marked on the lines and spaces of the staff; there are no positions in between, so symbols such as those shown to the right were employed. B♭ stands for B flat, the pitch inserted between A and B; C♯ stands for C sharp, the pitch between C and D, and so on.

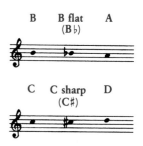

Scales and Instruments

Until fairly recently, Western music used the twelve pitches of the chromatic scale, duplicated through all the octaves, and in principle no other pitches. Features of many instruments are designed to produce these particular pitches exactly: frets on guitars, carefully measured holes in flutes, and the tuned sets of strings of harps and pianos.

Other instruments, such as the violin and the slide trombone, have a more continuous range of pitches available to them (as does a police siren or the human voice). In mastering these instruments, one of the first tasks is learning to pick out exactly the right pitches. This is called *playing in tune;* singing in tune is a matter of constant concern for vocalists, too.

It is true that many instrumentalists and all singers regularly perform certain notes slightly out of tune for important and legitimate artistic effects. "Blue" notes in jazz are an example. The fact remains that these "off" pitches are only small, temporary deviations from the main pitches of the scale—the same twelve pitches that, on instruments such as the piano, are absolutely fixed.

Half Steps and Whole Steps

As previously noted, the difference, or distance, between any two pitches is called the interval between them. Look at the chromatic scale on page 15, where the interval of an octave between low C and high C is marked with a bracket. Besides the octave, eleven other intervals exist between C and the other notes of the scale.

For our present purposes, only two more intervals need be specified:

> The smallest interval is the **half step,** or semitone, which is the distance between any two successive notes of the chromatic scale. ("Step" is a name for small intervals.) On a keyboard, a half step is the interval between the closest adjacent notes. The distance from E to F is a half step; so is the distance from F to F sharp (F♯), G to A flat (A♭), and so on.

Probably because the half step is the smallest interval in regular use, it is also the smallest that most people can "hear" and identify. Many tunes, such as "The Battle Hymn of the Republic," end with two half steps, one half step going down and then the same one going up again ("His truth is *march-ing on*").

> The **whole step,** or whole tone, is equivalent to two half steps: D to E, E to F♯, F♯ to G♯, and so on. "Three Blind Mice" starts with two whole steps, going down.

The chromatic scale consists exclusively of half steps. Therefore, this scale can be described as "symmetrical," in the sense that one can start on any of its pitches and move by half steps up or down the scale with exactly the same effect as if one started anywhere else. The diatonic scale is *not* symmetrical in this sense. It includes both half steps (two of them) and whole steps (five). Between B and C and between E and F, the interval is a half step, but between the other pairs of adjacent notes the interval is twice as big—a whole step.

Music is made out of these scales, and the diatonic and chromatic scales differ in the intervals between their constituent pitches; hence the importance of intervals. In the diagram below, the two scales are lined up in order to show the differences in their interval structure.

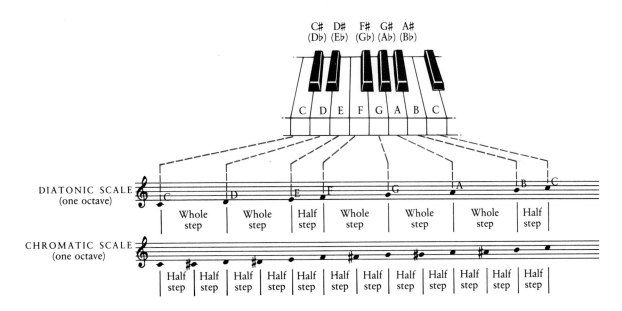

5 Rhythm

So far we have been discussing sound and its qualities in the abstract, without any reference to the fact that pitches, tone colors, and dynamics are perceived over periods of time and that they rarely stay the same for very long. As we now go on to discuss sounds as they are arranged into time patterns, we get a little closer to actual music. **Rhythm,** in the most general sense, is the term referring to the whole time aspect of music.

Beat

One way to approach the question of time in music is to ask first how musical time is measured. The answer is in **beats.** Listening to a marching band, we can't fail to sense a regular recurrence of short time units, which serve as a steady background for more complicated time patterns. We can easily beat time to the music by waving a hand or tapping a foot, which is basically the same thing that conductors do with their batons or big-drum players do with their drumsticks. What is being waved or tapped or conducted or thumped is the music's beat.

We can appreciate the importance of beats as a measurement of time if we think a little about the process of musical composition. Composers have to manipulate and manage the element of time, as well as scales, harmonies, instrumentation, and so on. They may be said to control time, just as painters control space in two dimensions and architects and sculptors control space in three. And measurement is a necessary preliminary to control; only by surveying land can you tell where your neighbor's lot begins so that you can determine where to put in a fence. Only by measuring and then controlling time can composers determine when to apply this or that artistic effect.

The beat: there are times when the drummers in a band do little more than bang it out.

Accent

Ordinary clock time is measured in seconds, and musical time is measured in beats. There is, however, an all-important difference between a clock ticking, as a way of measuring out spans of time, and a drum beating time. Mechanically produced ticks all sound exactly the same, but it is virtually impossible to beat time without making some of the beats more emphatic than others. This is called giving the beat an **accent.**

The natural way to beat time is to alternate accented ("strong") and unaccented ("weak") beats in a simple pattern such as ONE *two*, ONE *two*, ONE *two* or ONE *two three*, ONE *two three*, ONE *two three*. To beat time, then, is not only to measure it but also to organize it, at least in this simple two- or three-beat way. This is why a drum is a musical instrument and a clock is not.

Accents are not always indicated in musical notation, since in many types of music they are simply taken for granted. However, when composers want a particularly strong accent—something out of the ordinary—they put the sign > above or below a note. Thus, a pattern of alternating very strong and weak beats can be indicated as shown to the right. An even stronger accent can be indicated by the mark **sfz** or **sf,** short for *sforzando,* the Italian word for "forced."

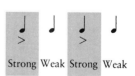

Strong Weak Strong Weak

Meter

Any recurring pattern of strong and weak beats, such as we have already referred to and illustrated above, is called a **meter.** Meter is a strong/weak pattern repeated again and again to form a continuous steady pulse.

Each occurrence of this repeated pattern, consisting of a principal strong beat and one or more weaker beats, is called a **measure,** or **bar.** In musical notation, measures are indicated by vertical lines called **bar lines.** The meter indicated schematically on page 18 would be represented as shown to the right.

There are just two basic kinds of simple meter in use, duple meter and triple meter, plus a third, compound meter, which really amounts to a combination of the other two.

> *Duple Meter* In duple meter—shown above—the beats are grouped in twos (ONE *two,* ONE *two,* or else ONE *two* three *four,* ONE *two* three *four*). Duple meter is probably most familiar from marches, which almost always use it in deference to the human anatomy (LEFT *right,* LEFT *right*).

> *Triple Meter* In triple meter the beats are grouped in threes (ONE *two three,* ONE *two three*). Triple meter happens to be the meter of two of our national songs, "America" and "The Star-Spangled Banner." "America" ("My Country, 'Tis of Thee") starts on the first, strong beat of the triple meter; "The Star-Spangled Banner" starts on the third, weak beat.

Experiments with more complicated meters, with groups of five beats, seven beats, and so on, can be found as early as the sixteenth century and increasingly in more modern times, but have never entered into common use.

> *Compound Meter* This meter consists of a certain number of *main* beats, each subdivided into three *subsidiary* beats. The most common type of compound meter has two main beats subdivided into a total of six (ONE *two three,* four *five six*). On the highest level it amounts to a kind of duple meter, but it is classified as compound meter when each of the two main beats is broken down into three smaller ones.

Examples of compound meter are afforded by the familiar rounds "Row, Row, Row Your Boat" and "Three Blind Mice." In each of these, we start out by beating a moderately slow ONE *two,* ONE *two* ("ROW, *row,* ROW *your* BOAT . . . ," "THREE *blind* MICE . . ."), but by the time we get to "Merrily, merrily" or "cut off their tails with a," the basic two beats are each subdivided into three faster ones, for a total of six.

What is the difference between one measure of this kind of compound meter (ONE *two three* four *five six*) and two measures of triple meter (ONE *two three,* ONE *two three*)? Not much, usually. The composer wants the "four" beat accented more strongly than the five and the six, but not as strongly as the "one." It is always possible to beat compound-meter measures as two measures each of triple meter, but the result is likely to be too heavy and fussy or, if the music is fast, too frantic.

Rhythm and Rhythms

We have already said that, in its most general sense, the term *rhythm* refers to the whole time aspect of music. In a more specific sense, **rhythms** refer to the particular arrangements of long and short notes in melodies or other musical passages.

In most Western music, duple, triple, or compound meter serves as the regular background against which one perceives the actual rhythms, which are almost always much more complicated. As the rhythm now coincides with the meter, then goes its own way, all kinds of variety, tension, and excitement can result. Indeed, it is the interaction of rhythm and meter that supplies much of music's vitality. Meter is background, rhythm foreground.

Musical notation has developed a conventional system of signs (see pages 24–25) to indicate the relative durations, or lengths, of various notes; combining various signs is the way of indicating rhythms. Below are examples of well-known tunes in duple, triple, and compound meters. Notice from the shading (even better, sing the tunes to yourself and *hear*) how sometimes the rhythm corresponds with the meter and sometimes departs from it. The shading indicates passages of rhythm-meter correspondence:

Syncopation

One way of obtaining an interesting effect in music is to displace the accents in a foreground *rhythm* away from their normal beats in the background *meter*. This is called **syncopation**. For example, the accents in duple meter can be displaced so that the accents go *one* TWO, *one* TWO, *one* TWO instead of the normal ONE *two*, ONE *two*. Or a syncopation can occur in just a single measure within a longer passage:

Notice the especially strong accent the composer has indicated by the *sf* mark—and notice where it comes: not on the normally accented beat 1 but on beat 2. This is syncopation. Here is an example in triple meter:

J. Strauss, Jr.,
Blue Danube Waltz

three **ONE** two **THREE** (one) **TWO** three **ONE** two three **ONE** two three **ONE** . . .

Syncopation is often associated with jazz, where it is especially important, but a certain amount of syncopation occurs in nearly all music.

Metrical and Nonmetrical Music

Marches and dances, which exist in order to stimulate body motion, always emphasize the meter in a strong, obvious way. Most popular music has a heavy beat, too, because meter gives rise to a very basic emotional response. The beat is front and center in the music of many non-Western cultures, too, such as that of Javanese orchestras (gamelans) and African drum ensembles. All this music may be characterized as strongly metrical.

In other kinds of music, meter is not always emphasized, or even explicitly beaten out at all, in back of the rhythm. It does not need to be, for the listener can almost always feel it under the surface. People will even imagine they hear a simple duple or triple meter in the steady dripping of a faucet or

An early printed edition of Gregorian chant. Lacking fixed rhythm, this music has no bar lines; vertical strokes on the staff mark off sections of music, not bars. Notice the four-line staff and square notes as compared to today's five-line staff and round note shapes.

the ticking of a clock. The psychological reason for this probably lies in the fact that simple repetitive patterns of stress/unstress underlie so many of our basic life functions: the heartbeat, breathing, walking, as well as more obvious activities, such as dancing and marching.

Still other kinds of music are nonmetrical or only loosely metrical. Such is the earliest surviving music in the Western tradition, the Gregorian chant of the early Middle Ages. The indefinite rhythm of Gregorian chant, constantly fluctuating and devoid of sharp accents, can mystify or fascinate modern listeners at a first hearing. At the other end of history, some radical music of the present century has been produced by strictly random means—and you can't beat time to this music, either.

6 Tempo

The discussion so far has referred to the *relative* duration of sounds—some twice as long as others, and so on—but nothing has been said yet about their *absolute* duration, fast or slow, in fractions of a second. **Tempo** takes account of this. It is the term for the speed of music. In metrical music, the tempo is the rate at which the basic, regular beats of the meter follow one another.

Tempo can be expressed quantitatively by such indications as ♩ = 60, meaning 60 quarter-note beats per minute. Such indications are **metronome marks,** named after the metronome, a mechanical or electrical device that ticks out beats at any desired tempo. Metronome 100 is an average easy march tempo; 42 is very slow, and 160 is very fast.

Tempo Indications

When composers give directions for tempo, however, they usually prefer general terms. Rather than freezing the music's speed by means of a metronome mark, they prefer to leave some latitude for different performers, different acoustical conditions in concert halls, and so on. Like the indications for dynamics, the conventional terms for tempo are Italian:

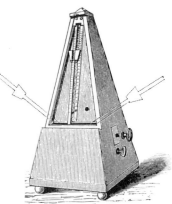

An early metronome owned by Beethoven, who was a friend of the inventor, Johannes Maelzel

COMMON TEMPO INDICATIONS

adagio: slow
andante: on the slow side, but not too slow
moderato: moderate tempo
allegretto: on the fast side, but not too fast
allegro: fast
presto: very fast

LESS COMMON TEMPO INDICATIONS

lento, largo, grave: slow, very slow
larghetto: somewhat faster than *largo*
andantino: somewhat faster than *andante*
vivace, vivo: lively
molto allegro: faster than *allegro*
prestissimo: very fast indeed

In their original meaning, many of these Italian words refer not to speed itself but rather to a mood, action, or quality that can be associated with tempo only in a general way. Thus, *vivace* is close to our "vivacious," and *andante,* derived from the common Italian word for "go," might be translated as "going along steadily."

Other terms indicate irregularities of tempo and tempo changes:

accelerando (*accel.*)   gradually getting faster
ritardando (*rit.*) or *rallentando* (*rall.*) gradually getting slower
più lento, più allegro   slower, faster
⌒ (fermata symbol)   a hold of indefinite length on a certain note
                          or rest, which in effect suspends the tempo

The most important terms to remember are those listed under "common tempo indications" above. When they appear at the top of a symphony movement or the like, they usually constitute its only heading or title. People refer to the "Andante" of Beethoven's Fifth Symphony, meaning a certain movement of the symphony (the second), which is to be played at an *andante* tempo.

7 Pitch and Time: Two Dimensions of Music

We started our discussion of musical fundamentals with the properties of sound: pitch, dynamics, and tone color. Next, aspects of music in time were studied: rhythm, beats, meter, and tempo. We are now ready to put sound and time together, as it were, in order to consider melody, and then harmony and counterpoint.

For this purpose, it may be helpful to think of pitch and time as the two main dimensions or "coordinates" of music. A graph with pitch reading up and down on the vertical axis, and time running from left to right on the horizontal axis, can help in the conceptualization of music, just as a graph with food prices and time as coordinates can help us keep track of changing grocery bills from month to month.

In fact, such a pitch/time graph comes quite close to musical notation. In musical notation, low and high notes are positioned on a sort of grid made up of rows of horizontal lines crossed with occasional verticals. The horizontals mark off pitch, from low to high; the verticals mark off fractions of time (compare the months on the price index):

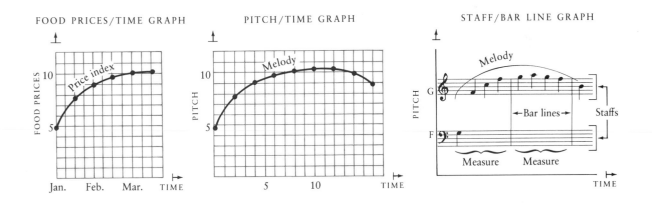

To see how this concept can be put to use, consider a melody—that is, a series of notes of various pitches following one another in time. They can be plotted on the pitch/time graph with dots, as in the middle diagram above. The pitch of each note (its "highness" or "lowness") is indicated by its placement up or down, and its position in time is indicated by its placement from left to right. In actual musical notation, the big dots (noteheads) of a melody are "plotted" on the notation grid in much the same way (see the right-hand diagram).

And melody is the first musical structure that we will go on to discuss in Chapter 3.

INTERLUDE 2: **Musical Notation**

This section explains musical notation, the notation in notes and rests of rhythm, meter, and pitch. Readers with some musical experience will probably skip these pages, or at most skim them for review purposes, but others will come to this material new.

Notes and Rests

The longest note in common use today is called a whole note. A half note lasts for half the time of a whole note. A quarter note lasts for a quarter of the time of a whole note, an eighth note for an eighth of the time, and so on.

This is the notation for the various notes:

Whole	Half	Quarter	Eighth	Sixteenth
note	note	note	note	note

The eighth note is distinguished from the quarter by a curl on the top called a *flag* (because it resembles a pennant). The sixteenth note has two flags, the thirty-second note has three, and so on.

There is another way of writing the eighth and sixteenth notes:

or

In this example, the flags have been starched up, as it were, and joined together to form thick, straight lines called *beams*. This merely makes them easier to read and to group into beats; the notational change is purely cosmetic, and does not change the time value of any of the notes.

Multiple beams have the same effect as multiple flags. These are thirty-second notes: , and these are sixty-fourth notes: .

Rests   To make rhythms, composers use not only sounds but also short silences called *rests* (because the players rest —or at least catch their breath). The diagram below

shows, to the left, the relation between note values and, to the right, the relation between rests, which are equivalent in duration to their corresponding notes. Compare the whole- and half-note rests: a slug beneath or atop one of the lines.

The eighth and sixteenth rests have their own sort of flags. As with notes, more flags can be added to rests, with each flag cutting the time value in half. Thus, three flags on a rest ( ) would make it a thirty-second rest, and four flags ( ) would make it a sixty-fourth.

Rhythmic Notation

Beyond the notation of basic notes and rests, a number of other conventions are necessary to indicate the combining of notes and rests into actual rhythms.

Dotted Notes and Dotted Rhythms   A dot placed after a note or a rest lengthens its time value by 50 percent. Thus putting a dot after a quarter note makes its duration equal to a quarter plus an eighth: ♩. = ♩ + ♪ In a similar way, a dotted eighth rest equals an eighth plus a sixteenth: ⁊· = ⁊ + ⁊ Even the simplest of tunes, such as "America," make use of the dot convention.

A dotted rhythm is one consisting of dotted (long) notes alternating with short ones: ♩. ♫♩. ♫ or ♫. ♫ ♫. ♫ The lively, lilting quality of dotted rhythm is characteristic of the folk music of certain nations, such as Scotland:

Gin a body   meet a body   Comin' thro' the rye

Ties   Two notes of the same pitch can be connected by means of a curved line called a *tie*. This means they are played continuously, as though they were one note of the combined duration. Any number of notes of the same pitch can be tied together, so that this notational device can serve to indicate a pitch of very long duration.

Ties

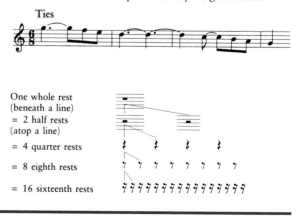

One whole note	
= 2 half notes	
= 4 quarter notes	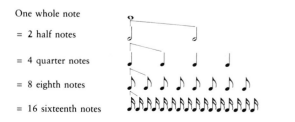
= 8 eighth notes	
= 16 sixteenth notes	

One whole rest (beneath a line)	
= 2 half rests (atop a line)	
= 4 quarter rests	
= 8 eighth rests	
= 16 sixteenth rests	

The same sort of curved line is also used to connect notes that are *not* of the same pitch. In this case it means simply that they are to be played smoothly *(legato)*. These curved lines are called *slurs*.

Slurs: legato

To indicate that notes are to be played in a detached fashion *(staccato)*, dots are placed above or below them.

Staccato dots

Triplets Three notes bracketed together and marked with a 3 (♪ ♪ ♪) are called a *triplet*. This indicates that they are to be played one-third faster than usual, so that the three notes take exactly the same time that would normally be taken by two. A quarter-note triplet has the same duration as two ordinary quarter notes: ♩ ♩ ♩ = ♩ ♩ ; an eighth-note triplet equals two eighths: ♪ ♪ ♪ = ♪ ♪ ; and so on.

The convention is occasionally extended to groups of five notes, seven notes, etc. For an example, see page 262.

Meter: Measures and Bar Lines A *measure* (or *bar*) is the basic time unit chosen for a piece of music, corresponding to the meter of the piece (see page 19). As we saw earlier, measures are marked in musical notation by vertical *bar lines*. Each measure covers the same time span. In the following example, the time span covered by each measure is one whole note, which is equivalent to two half notes (measure 1), or four quarter notes (measure 2), or eight eighth notes (measures 3 and 4).

Time signature
Measures

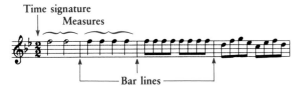

— Bar lines —

Time Signatures In the example above, the meter is indicated by means of a *time signature*. Time signatures are printed on the staffs at the beginning of all pieces of music; they are not repeated on later staffs. (If the meter changes later in the piece, however, a new time signature is put in at that point, as in the music example on page 306.)

In spite of appearances, time signatures are not fractions. The top digit shows *how many beats* are in each measure. If there are to be two beats in the measure, the top digit will be 2; if there are to be three beats, it will be 3; and so on. The bottom digit shows *what kind of note* represents a beat. If the bottom digit is 2, the beat is represented by a half note; if by 4, by a quarter note; if 8, by an eighth note, and so on.

In the example above, the 2 at the top indicates there are two beats in each measure (duple meter), and the 2 at the bottom indicates that the beats are half-note beats. This time signature is often indicated by a half-circle with a line through it: ¢

Pitch Notation
The letter names A B C D E F G are assigned to the original seven pitches of the diatonic scale. Then the letters are used over and over again for pitches in the duplicating octaves. The octaves can be distinguished by prime marks such as A′, A″, and so on; another, more approximate system designates the C in one octave "high C," that two octaves below "low C," and the one in the octave in between "middle C." Middle C is the comfortable note that nearly any man, woman, or child can sing and that can be played by the great majority of instruments. On the piano, it lies in the middle of the keyboard, right under the maker's name.

The Staff: Ledger Lines For the notation of pitch, notes are placed on a set of five parallel lines called a *staff*. The notes can be put on the lines of the staff, in the spaces between them, or right at the top or bottom of the staff:

In addition, more notes can be added by extending the staff above or below with additional short lines called *ledger lines*. Ledger lines are used just like ordinary staff lines; they simply extend the staff up or down when necessary. A staff with two ledger lines below it and two above it can include enough notes for two octaves and more, which is enough for almost any melody:

Clefs Nothing has been said so far about which pitch each position on the staff represents. To clue us in to precise pitches, signs called *clefs* (French for "key" or "clue") are placed at the beginning of each staff. Clefs calibrate the staff: that is, they connect one of the five lines of the staff to a specific pitch. Then the other lines and spaces of the staff are read in reference to this fixed point.

Thus in the treble clef, or G clef (𝄞), the spiral in the middle of the antique capital G curves around line 2, counting up from the bottom of the staff. Line 2, then, is the line for the pitch G—to be precise, the first G above middle C.

In the bass clef or F clef (𝄢), the two dots straddle line 4 (counting from the bottom). The pitch F goes on this line—the first F below middle C. Adjacent lines and spaces on the staff have adjacent letter names, so we can place all the other pitches on the staff in relation to the fixed points marked by the clefs.

Here is how the pitches are located on the staffs marked by the treble and bass clefs:

There are other clefs, but these two are the most common, especially when they are used in conjunction, for between them they accommodate the maximum span of pitches without overlapping. The treble and bass clef staffs fit together as shown below in Figure 1.

One useful fact is that middle C lies on a ledger line between the two staffs. Remember that, even when just one staff is used, middle C is always to be found on one ledger line *below* the treble clef staff or on one ledger line *above* the bass clef staff.

The notation for the pitch A in six different octaves, requiring the two staffs and a good number of ledger lines, is shown in Figure 2.

Sharps and Flats; Naturals   The pitches produced by the black keys on the piano are not given letter names of their own. (This is a consequence of the way they arose in history; see page 16.) Nor do they get their own individual lines or spaces on the staffs. The pitch in between A and B is called either A sharp (A♯), meaning higher than A, or B flat (B♭), meaning lower than B.

Figure 1

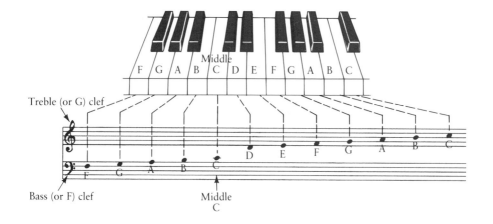

Figure 2

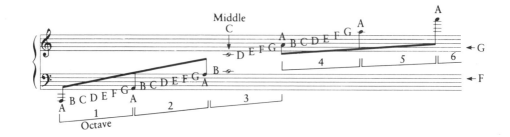

A Table containing the value of every Note, according to the value of the Moodes or signes.

⅓ ◊	⅔ ◊	· ◊	⅙ ◊	½ ◊	⅔ ◊	1 ◊	1 ◊
2	2	2	2	2	2	3	3
1 ◊	1 ◊	1 ◊	1 ◊	1 ◊	1 ◊	3 ◊	3 ◊
3	3	2	2	3	2	3	2
3 ☐	3 ☐	2 ☐	2 ☐	3 ☐	2 ☐	9 ☐	6 ☐
3	2	3	2	2	2	2	2.
9 ☐	6 ☐	6 ☐	4 ☐	6 ☐	4 ☐	18 ☐	12 ☐
3	2	2	2	2	2	2	2
27 ☐	12 ☐	12 ☐	8 ☐	12 ☐	8 ☐	36 ☐	24 ☐
O3	C3	O2	C2	O	C	O⊙	¢

ter (A♮) to show this. The following example shows G sharp being canceled by a natural sign:

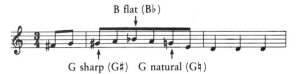

G sharp (G♯)   G natural (G♮)

Key Signatures   In musical notation, it is a convention that a sharp or flat placed before a note will also affect any later appearance of that same note *in the same measure*—but not in the next measure. However, provision is also made for specifying that certain sharps or flats are to be applied throughout an entire piece, in every measure, and in every octave. Such sharps and flats are indicated on the staffs at the very beginning of the piece, even prior to the time signature, and at the beginning of each staff thereafter. They constitute the *key signature:*

is equivalent to:

Which of these two names is used depends partly on convenience, partly on convention, and partly on theoretical considerations that do not concern us here. If a pitch is regarded as A♯, it appears in the same position on the staff as A, but with a sharp sign before it. If it is thought of as B♭, it will be placed on the staff in the B position with a flat sign before it.

In either case, the same pitch is being represented in two different ways. The other black notes can be notated in the same two ways: for instance, the pitch between C and D can be either C♯ or D♭, and so on.

The original pitches of the diatonic scale, played on the white keys of the piano, are called "natural." If it is necessary to cancel a sharp or a flat within a measure and to indicate that the natural note should be played instead, the natural sign is placed before a note (♮ ♩) or after a let-

Scores   Music for a melody instrument such as a violin or a trumpet is written on one staff; keyboard instruments require two—one staff for the right hand, another staff for the left hand. Music for two or more voices or instruments, choirs, bands, and orchestras is written in *scores*. In scores, each instrument and voice that has its own independent music gets one staff. Simultaneously sounding notes and measure lines are aligned vertically. There are a number of conventional rules for the vertical ordering of instrument staffs in a score, but in general the high-

sounding instruments go on top, the low ones on the bottom.

Shown below is a page from the original score for Mozart's "Jupiter" Symphony. Shown opposite is a page from a modern printed version of the score, with arrows pointing to the various details of notation that have been explained above. Notice that, in Mozart's day, the violins and violas were written at the top of the score, above the wind instruments. Today they are written below, as on the facing page.

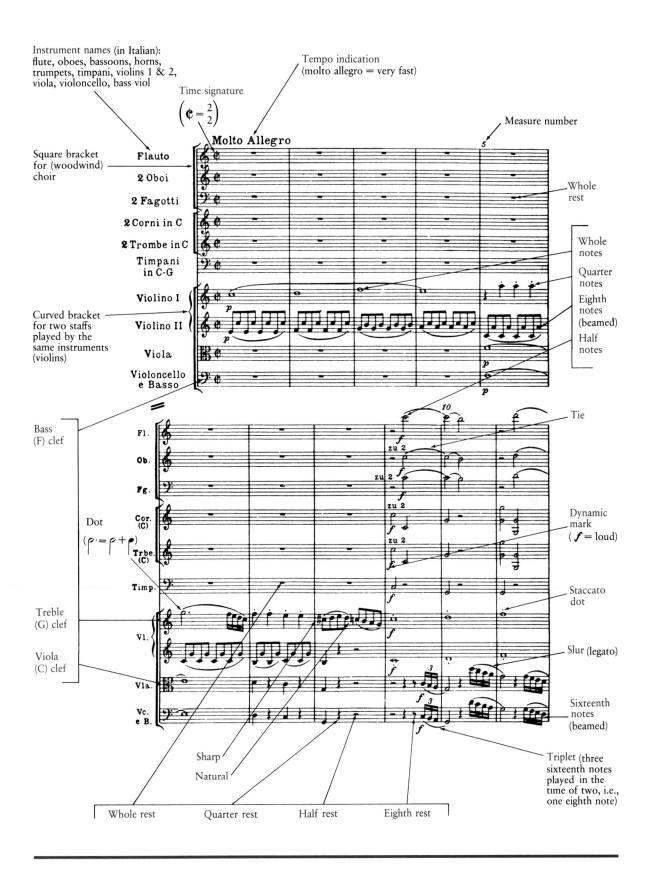

Chapter 3

The Structures of Music

In this chapter we take up musical concepts that combine the basic elements discussed in Chapter 2. In actual music, pitch, rhythm, tone color, and dynamics are never experienced in isolation from one another, and for that matter single pitches, single rhythms, and so on are very seldom experienced one at a time. Music consists of simple and complex "structures" built from these elements.

1 Melody

As we have seen, successive pitches can be plotted on a pitch/time graph as a rising and falling line. When a coherent succession of pitches is played or sung in a certain rhythm, the result is called a **melody,** and indeed musicians very commonly speak of "melodic line" (or simply "line") in this connection.

Just as an actual line in a drawing can possess character—can strike the viewer as forceful, graceful, or tentative—so can a melodic line. A melody in which each note is higher than the last can seem to soar; a low note or a low passage can feel like a setback; a long series of repeated notes on the same pitch can seem to wait ominously. The listener develops a real interest in how the line of a satisfactory melody is going to come out. In such a melody, the succession of notes seems to hold together as a meaningful, interesting unit.

Interesting, and emotional; of all the structures of music, melody is the one that moves people the most, that seems to evoke human sentiment most directly. The familiar melodies of folksongs and popular songs "register" simple qualities of feeling instantly and strongly. These qualities vary widely: romantic in "Yesterday," martial in "Dixie," mournful in "St. Louis Blues," extroverted and cheerful in "Happy Birthday to You."

Blues singer

Tunes

The most familiar type of melody is a **tune**—a simple, easily singable, catchy melody such as a folksong or a dance. In this book the word *tune* will be reserved for this use. A tune is a special kind of melody. *Melody* is a term that includes tunes, but also much else.

"The Star-Spangled Banner," a tune that everyone knows, can be used to illustrate the general characteristics of tunes.

> *Division into Phrases* Tunes fall naturally into smaller sections, called **phrases.** This is, in fact, true of all melodies, but with tunes the division into phrases is especially clear and sharp.

In tunes with words (that is, songs), the musical phrases typically coincide with the poetic lines. And since most lines in a song lyric end with a rhyming word and a punctuation mark, these features also serve to emphasize the musical phrase divisions. These two rhyming lines mark two musical phrases:

And the rockets' red **glare** [*comma*]
The bombs bursting in **air** [*comma*]

Singing a song one has to breathe—and one tends to breathe at the ends of phrases. You may not need to breathe after the first phrase of "The Star-Spangled Banner," but you had better not wait any longer than the second:

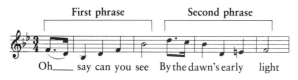

> *Balance between Phrases* In many tunes, all the phrases are two, four, or eight measures long. (Measures, or bars, are the basic time units of music; see page 19.) Blues tunes, for example, typically consist of three four-bar phrases; hence the term *twelve-bar blues.*

Almost all the phrases of "The Star-Spangled Banner" are two measures long. But one phrase broadens out to four measures, with a fine effect: "Oh say, does that star-spangled banner yet wave . . . ." One doesn't want to breathe in the middle of this long phrase.

Other phrase lengths, besides two, four, and eight measures, can certainly occur in a tune and make for a welcome contrast. For a good tune, the main requirement is that we sense a balance between the phrases, in terms of phrase lengths and in other terms, too, so that taken together the phrases add up to a well-proportioned whole.

> *Parallelism and Contrast* Balance between phrases of a tune can be strengthened by means of both melodic and rhythmic *parallelism.* There are many possible shades of parallelism between two phrases. Sometimes phrases are exactly parallel except for the words (for example "Oh say, can you see" and "Whose broad stripes and bright stars"). Sometimes they have the same rhythm but different pitches ("Oh say, can you see," "By the dawn's early light").

Sometimes phrases have the same general *pattern* of pitches, but one phrase is slightly higher or lower than the other ("And the rockets' red glare," "The bombs bursting in air"). **Sequence** is the technical name for this device. Such duplication of a phrase at two or more different pitch levels occurs frequently in music, and is a special hallmark of certain musical styles.

Composers also take care to make certain phrases *contrast* with their neighbors—one phrase short, another long, for example, or one phrase low, another high (perhaps even *too* high, at "O'er the land of the free . . ."). A tune containing some parallel phrases and some contrasting ones will seem to have logic, or coherence, and yet will avoid monotony.

> *Climax and Cadence* A good tune has *form.* It has a clear, purposeful beginning, a feeling of action in the middle, and a firm sense of winding down and concluding at the end.

A highly imaginative picture of Francis Scott Key composing "The Star-Spangled Banner." In fact, Key wrote only the words; later, his new poem—with its fine rousing climax on "land of the *free*"—was adapted to an older melody.

Nearly every tune has a distinct high point, either a single high note or a high passage, which its earlier portions seem to be heading toward. This is usually referred to as the **climax**. A melodic climax is typically the emotional climax, too; feelings rise as the voice soars. The climax of our national anthem highlights what was felt to be the most important word in it—"free."

Then the later part of the tune relaxes from this climax, until it reaches a very conclusive stopping place at the end. Emotionally, this is a point of relaxation and great satisfaction. In a less conclusive way, the music also stops at earlier points in the tune—or, if it does not fully stop, at least it seems to pause. The term for one of these stopping or pausing places is **cadence**.

Cadences can be made with all possible shades of finality about them. "And the home of the brave" is a very final-sounding cadence; "That our flag was still there" is an interim-sounding one. The art of making cadences, indeed, is one of the most subtle and basic processes in all of musical composition.

Motives

Much music exists that does not consist of tunes—music that people probably do not sing much but that they evidently enjoy anyhow. Neither the longer, more ambitious rock numbers nor symphonies and other concert pieces consist exclusively of tunes, though they almost always have tunes or melodies or melodic fragments embedded in them.

Such musical fragments are called **motives**. A motive is shorter than a tune, shorter even than a phrase in a tune. It can be as short as two or three notes—just long enough so that its rhythmic and/or melodic character is easily remembered and easily recognized when it comes again. Probably the most famous motive in all music is the *da da da **da*** motive of Beethoven's Fifth Symphony.

Listening to music built out of motives is rather different from listening to tunes. The experience is less direct and immediate, but it is more diverse and broad ranging, and it has more varied emotional potential. With music of this kind, we first recognize a motive and then lose it, as something else is played. We wait for it to come back; when it does, it may be turned into a tune or be presented in some other way that heightens its effect.

Motives are less interesting for their own sake, then, than for what happens to them. In listening to music that features motives, the listening experience focuses not on the unfolding of phrases, one directly after another in a relatively short span of time as in a tune, but rather on the way things are "worked out" over a longer span.

Themes

The term **theme** is the most general term for the basic subject matter of a piece of music. *Theme* is another word for "topic": the themes or topics of a political speech are the main points that the politician elaborates, enlarges, and develops. The composer of a symphony or a fugue treats themes in somewhat the same way.

Themes vary in length and characteristics, depending on the type of music. For example, the themes of fast symphony movements are typically short motives of the type described above. The theme of the first movement of Beethoven's Fifth Symphony consists of the famous motive presented twice in sequence (that is, at two different pitch levels: see page 227). On the other hand, in the musical form known as theme and variations, the themes can be full tunes, often taken from actual songs or dances. Beethoven ended his Third Symphony with a theme and variations in which the theme is a favorite ballet tune he had written a few years before.

2 Texture

Texture is the term used to refer to the blend of the various sounds and melodic lines occurring simultaneously in a piece of music. The word is adopted from textiles, where it refers to the weave of the various threads—loose or tight, even or mixed. A cloth such as tweed, for instance, leaves the different threads clearly visible. In fine silk, the weave is so tight and smooth that the individual constituent threads are hard to detect.

Looking back to the pitch/time graph on page 23, we can see that it is possible to plot more than one melody on it. Melody exists in the "horizontal dimension" of music. Texture is perceived in the "vertical dimension."

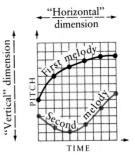

The term for the simplest texture of all, a single unaccompanied melody, is **monophony.** Monophony may be compared to a single thread spun out in a line and bending up and down. Simple as this texture is, some very sophisticated monophonic music has been written, just as artists such as Pablo Picasso have done wonderful things with line drawings.

A line drawing by Pablo Picasso—illustration for music by Igor Stravinsky, *Ragtime.* A drawing such as this can be compared with single-line melody in music (monophony).

Polyphony

When two or more melodies are played or sung simultaneously, the texture is described as *polyphonic.* In **polyphony,** the melodies are felt to be independent and of approximately equal interest. The whole is more than the sum of the parts, however; the play of the melodies against one another makes for the possibility of greater richness and interest than if they were played singly. This is the case in Debussy's *Festivals,* for example, when the fast "festival" theme is heard in combination with the march melody.

Another term frequently applied to polyphonic texture is *contrapuntal.* This comes from the word **counterpoint,** the technique of writing melodies so that they fit together in a satisfactory way. Strictly speaking, polyphony refers to the texture itself and counterpoint to the technique of producing the texture—one *studies* counterpoint in order to *produce* polyphony—but in practice the two terms tend to be used interchangeably.

Imitation

Two types of polyphony, or counterpoint, should be distinguished. **Imitative polyphony** occurs when the various lines sounding together use the same or quite similar melodies, but at staggered time intervals, with one coming in shortly after another. Imitative polyphony is often simply called *imitation.* Anyone who has ever sung a round such as "Row, Row, Row Your Boat" or "Frère Jacques" has helped to produce imitative polyphony:

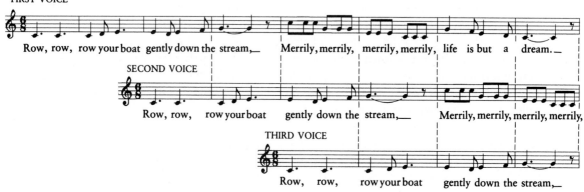

Nonimitative polyphony occurs when the melodies are essentially different from one another. A familiar kind occurs in traditional jazz when the trumpet, clarinet, trombone, and other instruments are each improvising on their own simultaneously. Each instrument has its own interest and its own melodic integrity, and each has its own kind of melody suited to the nature of the particular instrument. Listening to contrapuntal music of this kind, our attention shunts rapidly (and happily) back and forth from one instrument to another.

Combining "Old Folks at Home" and "Humoresque" produces nonimitative polyphony that might never have occurred to the composers Stephen Foster and Antonín Dvořák:

On the basis of the musical concept of "melodic line," the following graphs can be drawn to represent imitative and nonimitative polyphony, respectively. Below each graph is the same polyphony in standard musical notation:

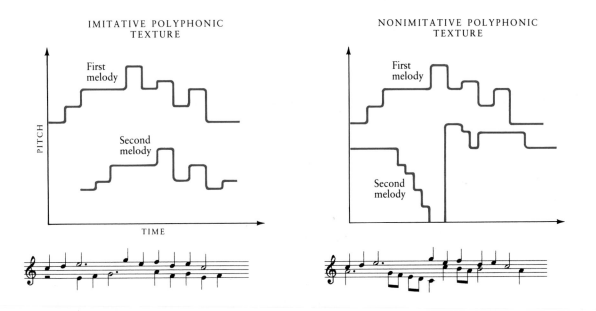

Homophony

When there is only one melody of real interest and it is combined with other sounds that are clearly less important, the texture is called **homophonic** or (more loosely) *harmonic*. The subsidiary sounds form the "accompaniment." A folk singer or blues singer singing and playing a guitar is spinning a simple homophonic texture, tune and accompaniment:

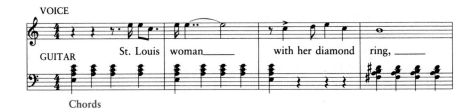

The folk singer uses a number of standard groupings of simultaneous pitches, or <u>chords</u>, that practice has shown will work well in combination. Imaginative guitar players will also discover nonstandard chords and unexpected successions of chords in order to enrich their accompaniments.

The folk song is said to be **harmonized** when it is provided with subsidiary chords in this manner. Hymns offer another example of music in a simple homophonic texture: usually each note of the melody is underpinned by a single chord. Such harmonizing can be done either by the organist or by the choir, with the various voices contributing the notes that make up the chords. The sopranos sing the hymn tune.

Diagramed below is a simple homophonic texture, in which the accompanying instruments or voices generally move simultaneously with the main melody. Each move creates a chord. Compare this diagram with the ones on the previous page.

HOMOPHONIC TEXTURE

Harmony

Any melody can be harmonized in many ways using different chords, and the overall effect of the music depends to a great extent on the nature of these chords, or the <u>harmony</u> in general. This is especially true of music of the last 250 years, which is the most familiar. We can instinctively sense the difference in harmony between Mozart and Mahler or between New Orleans jazz and rock, though the differences are exceptionally difficult to characterize, except in technical language.

Usually the first thing musicians learn, beyond their instruments, is harmony. They are taught how to construct correct chords and how to connect them effectively. The study of harmony can be defined as the study of chord structures in both the vertical and horizontal dimensions of musical space-time.

Consonance and Dissonance

A pair of terms used in discussions of harmony is **consonance** and **dissonance,** meaning (roughly speaking) chords that sound at rest and those that sound tense, respectively. *Discord* is another term for dissonance. These qualities depend on the kind of intervals (see page 13) that are sounding simultaneously to make up these chords. Octaves, for example, are the most consonant of intervals, whereas half steps are among the most dissonant.

In nonmusical parlance, "discord" implies something unpleasant; discordant human relationships are to be avoided. But music does not avoid dissonance in its technical meaning, for a little discord supplies the subtle tensions that are essential to make music flow along. A dissonant chord leaves the listener with a feeling of expectation; it requires a consonant chord following it to complete the gesture, and to make the music come to a point of stability. Without dissonance, music would be like food without salt or spices.

Cadences—the ends of pieces of music—are almost always helped by the use of dissonance. Movement from tension (dissonance) to rest (consonance) contributes centrally to a sense of finality and satisfaction.

Indeed, the real point about dissonant harmony is that we instinctively expect its feeling of tension to relax, or **resolve,** into the calm of consonance. Composers use both in conjunction, deriving artistic effects from the contrast between the two.

3 Key and Mode

In Chapter 2, a *scale* was defined as the collection of pitches taken by convention to be available for music making—the twelve pitches of the chromatic scale into which the octave is divided for Western music, the five pitches of Japanese music, or whatever. Such a definition is rather abstract, however. How is music actually made from these scales? Are all the pitches treated equally? We can get less abstract as we inquire into the actual mechanics of melody building.

Tonality

The basic fact about melody building is a simple one: melodies nearly always give the sense of focusing around a single "home" pitch that feels more important than all the others. Often this is *do* in the *do re mi fa sol la ti do* scale. This pitch feels fundamental, and on it the melody seems to come to rest most naturally. The other notes in the melody all sound close or remote, dissonant or consonant, in reference to the fundamental note, and some of them may actually seem to "lean" or "lead" toward it.

This homing instinct that we sense in melodies can be referred to in the most general terms as the feeling of **tonality**. The music in question is described as **tonal**. The "home" pitch (*do*) is called the *tonic pitch,* or simply the **tonic**.

The easy way to identify the tonic is to sing the whole melody through, for the ending note is almost invariably *it*. Thus "The Star-Spangled Banner" ends on its tonic, *do,* and it also includes the tonic in two different octaves as its first two accented notes ("Oh, *say* can you *see*"). An entire piece of music, as well as just a short melody, can give this feeling of focusing on a home pitch and wanting to end there.

Mode: Major and Minor

We have been speaking of *do* as the most usual tonic pitch. However, many melodies are built around *la* as the tonic. The term for these different ways of organizing (or centering) the diatonic scale is **modality**; the different "home" pitches are said to determine different **modes** of music.

The **major mode** is the diatonic scale with the tonic pitch C, and the **minor mode** is the diatonic scale with the tonic pitch A. Music in both these modes is familiar to us from countless well-known melodies. In any church (or shopping mall) at Christmas time, we can hear major- and minor-mode carols back to back: "Joy to the World!" (major) and "God Rest Ye Merry, Gentlemen" (minor), "Silent Night" (major), and "What Child Is This?" (minor).

What is the operative distinction between the major and minor modes? Remember that, in the diatonic scale, some of the intervals between successive pitches are half steps and some are whole steps, and they come in an irregular order (see page 16). Hence, whichever note is chosen as tonic entails a different order of steps up or down when we start moving away from "home." If the tonic is C (major mode), the upward order goes whole step–whole step–half step, and so on. If the tonic is A (minor mode), the upward order goes whole step–half step–whole step (see the right margin).

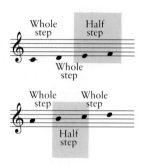

As a result of this consistency, all major-mode melodies resemble one another in melodic character, coloration, and mood. So do all minor-mode melodies, and they are subtly different from major ones.

The diagram below shows how the modes are derived from the diatonic scale. It should be mentioned that music in both modes can, under certain conditions, include some notes—sharps and flats—other than those shown below. But the notes shown are the basic components of the modes. Once again, the real point to remember about the major and minor modes is that the intervals in each are arranged differently in reference to the tonic.

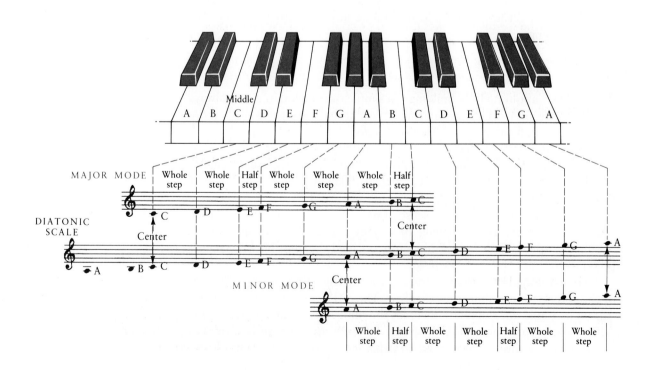

Is it fair to represent the major and minor modes by comedy and tragedy masks? Yes, but only in a very general sense—there are many, many exceptions.

Hearing the Major and Minor Modes

The two modes differ from each other mainly in their third and sixth notes. The third note, for example, is four half steps higher than the tonic in the major mode, whereas it is only three half steps higher in the minor. The diagram on page 38 helps us to see how these modes are dissimilar and why one is called major (larger) and the other minor (smaller).

Actually *hearing* modality—that is, recognizing the distinction between music in one mode or the other—is something that comes easily to some people, less easily to others. As a consequence of the interval differences described above, music in the minor mode tends to sound more subdued than music in the major. It seems clouded, by comparison with the major. It is often said that the major mode sounds cheerful and the minor sounds sad, and this is true enough in a general way; but there are many exceptions, and in any case people have different ideas about what constitutes "sadness" and "cheerfulness" in pieces of music.

To learn to distinguish the major and minor modes requires attentive comparative listening. The following well-known tunes are in the minor mode: "Joshua Fit the Battle of Jericho," "Summertime," "We Three Kings of Orient Are," and "When Johnny Comes Marching Home." Singing them through, we come to recognize the characteristic minor-mode sound involving the third note up from the tonic at the final cadence:

Compare this with the third note up from the tonic at the end of major-mode songs such as "Happy Birthday to You," "Row, Row, Row Your Boat," "The Star-Spangled Banner," and many others. It sounds brighter:

Keys

Mode and key are concepts that are often confused. Let us see if we can keep them clear.

We have discussed the derivation of the major and minor modes from the original diatonic or white-note scale, with their tonics, or "home" notes, C and A, respectively. At the piano, if you try the experiment of using any of the other white notes as tonic—D, E, F, G, or B—you will find that in each case, if you stick to white notes, the arrangement of intervals is different from that of either the major or the minor mode. The scales you play will sound wrong.

If you use the whole twelve-note *chromatic* scale, however—the black notes as well as the white—you can construct both the major and the minor modes starting from any note at all. Whichever note you choose as tonic, starting from there you can pick out the correct sequence of half steps and whole steps. (This is because the chromatic scale is "symmetrical"—it includes all possible half steps, and therefore all possible whole steps.) If C is the starting point, the major mode comes out all on the white notes; if the same mode is started from D, two black notes are required; and so on.

Thanks to the chromatic scale, then, many positions are possible for the major and minor modes. These different positions are called **keys.** If the major mode is positioned on C, the music is said to be in the key of C major, or just in C major. If it is positioned on D, the key is D major. Likewise we have the keys of C minor, C-sharp major, C-sharp minor, D minor, and—since there are twelve pitches in the chromatic scale—a grand total of twenty-four major and minor keys. Some examples are shown below.

If you're having trouble figuring out steps and intervals, you're not the first. For centuries, choirboys were taught music with the "Guidonian Hand," a memory device named after its inventor, the monk Guido of Arezzo (c. 991–c. 1033).

This already hints at the important artistic resource that composers discovered: the possibility of changing from one key to another. Changing keys during a composition is called **modulation.** Starting from C, the most frequent modulations are from C major to G major, F major, and A minor; but the less frequent ones sound more mysterious or dramatic. Note that a simple change of mode, as from C major to C minor, is not a modulation.

Distinguishing Mode and Key

Between the two modes, the difference can be described as internal. As has already been emphasized, in each mode the pitches form their own special set of intervals with one another and with the tonic. A comparison of the half steps on the diagram on page 38 for C major and A minor will show where the two modes differ.

Between two keys, on the other hand, the difference amounts only to the positioning of the whole set of pitches, taken as a group. The half steps for C major and A major all come in the same relative positions.

As for actually *hearing* keys—that is, recognizing the different keys and the modulations between them—for some people this presents an even greater problem than hearing modality, though to others it comes more easily. The latter are the fortunate ones born with absolute pitch or perfect pitch, the innate faculty of identifying pitches the way most people can identify colors. However, this is not the great boon of nature that it is sometimes believed to be. The important thing is not to be able to identify keys in themselves, but rather to be able to tell when keys change. For modulation, a change of key, leads to a change in mood; modulation is a resource that composers have made much of, in respect to tonality. And we can hear *changes* of tonality in large compositions, that is, changes of the tonic or "home" note, whether or not we were born with absolute pitch.

Indeed, we hear such changes instinctively in shorter compositions. If you know Cole Porter's "Night and Day," you know the exciting switch in mood that comes at the words

> Night and *day—under the hide of me,*
> *There's an Oh, such a hungry yearning, burning inside of me.*

This is the direct result of a sudden modulation. In "Deck the Halls," an agreeable little emotional lift is caused by a modulation at the end of the segment "Don we now our gay apparel, *Fa la la, la la la, la la la.*"

Two deep convictions we have about music are inherited from the nineteenth century: that music is composed by special great geniuses, and that music arose "naturally" among the simple people who constitute one's nation or ethnic group. This depiction of "The Birth of Folk Song" is by a nineteenth-century Hungarian painter.

INTERLUDE 3: **Musical Instruments**

Different voices and different instruments produce different tone colors, or timbres. Over the course of history and over the entire world, an enormous number of devices have been invented for making music, and the range of tone colors they can produce is almost endless.

This section will provide a listing, a brief description, and illustrations of the main instruments of Western music, with special emphasis on those found in the symphony orchestra. Afterward we will take a brief look at some musical instruments from India, Indonesia, South America, and Africa. It is interesting to see how these non-Western instruments are related to more familiar ones.

Instruments of the Orchestra

Musical instruments can be categorized into four groups: *stringed instruments* or *strings, woodwinds, brass,* and *percussion.* Musical sound, as we saw in Interlude 1, is caused by rapid vibrations. Each of the four groups of instruments produces sound vibrations in its own distinct way.

Stringed Instruments   These are instruments that have their sound produced by taut strings. The strings are always attached to a "sound box," a hollow box containing a body of air that resonates (that is, vibrates along with the strings) so as to amplify the string sound.

The strings themselves can be played with a bow, as with the violin and other orchestral strings; the *bow* is strung tightly with horsehair, which is coated with rosin so that the bow grips the strings. Or else the strings can be plucked, as on the guitar, using either the hand or a small pick. Strings can be plucked on bowed stringed instruments, too, for special effects.

The Violin and Its Family   The **violin,** one of the most versatile of instruments, is often considered to be the most beautiful of all that are used in Western music. Its large range covers alto and soprano registers and many higher notes. As a solo instrument, it can play incisively or delicately, and it excels in both brilliant and songlike music. Violinists also play chords by bowing two or more of the four strings at once, or nearly so.

The violin is an excellent ensemble instrument; and it blends especially well with other violins. An orchestra violin section, made up of ten or more instruments playing together, can produce a strong yet sensitive, flexible tone. Hence the orchestra has traditionally relied on strings as a solid foundation for its composite sound.

Like most other instruments, violins come in *families,* that is, in several sizes with different pitch ranges. Very young children learn the violin on miniature instruments that fit their small hands. These small violins are seldom used except for teaching purposes, whereas the larger members of the violin family are basic to the orchestra.

Violin

> The **viola** is the tenor-range instrument, several inches larger than a violin. The viola has a throaty quality in its lowest range, from middle C down an octave, yet it fits especially smoothly into accompaniment textures. When it plays in its high register, the instrument's tone is powerful and intense.

> The **cello,** short for *violoncello,* is the bass of the violin family. This large instrument is played between the legs. Unlike the viola, the cello has a rich, gorgeous sound in its low register. It is a favorite solo instrument, as well as an indispensable member of the orchestra.

Bass Viol   Also called **string bass, double bass,** or just **bass,** this deep instrument is used to back up the violin family in the orchestra. (However, in various details of construction the bass viol differs from members of the violin family; the bass viol actually belongs to another, older stringed instrument family, the *viols.*)

Played with a bow, the bass viol provides a splendid deep support for orchestral sound. But unlike the cello, it is not favored as a solo instrument. The bass viol is often (in jazz, nearly always) plucked to give an especially vibrant kind of accent and to emphasize the meter.

Harp   Harps are plucked stringed instruments with one string for each pitch available. The modern orchestral harp is a large instrument with forty-seven strings covering a range of six and a half octaves. A pedal mechanism allows the playing of chromatic (black-key) as well as diatonic (white-key) pitches.

In most orchestral music, the swishing, watery quality of the harp is treated as a striking occasional effect rather than as a regular thing.

Woodwind Instruments   As the name indicates, woodwind instruments were formerly made of wood and some still are; but today certain woodwinds are made of metal. Sound in these instruments is created by setting up vibrations in the column of air in a tube.

Of the main woodwind instruments, *flutes, clarinets,* and *oboes* have approximately the same range; all three are used in the orchestra because each has a quite distinct tone quality, and composers can obtain a variety of effects from them. With a little practice, it is not hard to learn to recognize and appreciate the different sounds of these woodwinds.

The Flute and Its Family   The **flute** is a long cylinder, held horizontally, in which the player sets the air vibrating by blowing through a side hole. The flute is the most agile of the woodwind instruments and also the gentlest. It nonetheless stands out clearly in the orchestra when played in its higher register.

> The **piccolo,** the small, highest member of the flute family, adds special sparkle to band and orchestral music.

> The **alto flute** and **bass flute**—larger flutes—are less frequently employed.

Harp

Rehearsal at the summer music school in Aspen, Colorado: a violin, a cello, and a viola (note the slightly bigger size)

Flute

> The **recorder,** a different variety of flute, is blown not at the side of the tube but through a mouthpiece at the end. Used in older orchestral music, the recorder was superseded by the horizontal, or "transverse," flute because the latter was more powerful and flexible. However, recorders have made a spectacular comeback for modern performances of old music using reconstructed period instruments. The instrument is also popular (in various family sizes) among musical amateurs today. It is fairly easy to learn and fun to play.

Clarinet   The **clarinet** is a slightly conical tube made, usually, of ebony. The air column is not made to vibrate directly by blowing into the tube, as with the flute. The way the player gets sound is by blowing on a reed—a small piece of cane—in much the same way as we can blow on a blade of grass held taut between the fingers. The vibrating reed activates the vibration of the air in the clarinet itself.

The clarinet developed later than instruments of the flute and oboe types. Thus the six *Brandenburg* Concertos of Johann Sebastian Bach, which feature all the important instruments used in the early eighteenth century, do not include the clarinet.

Compared to the flute, clarinet sound is richer and more flexible, more like the human voice. The clarinet is capable of warm, mellow tones and quite strident, shrill ones; it has an especially intriguing quality in its low register, below middle C.

The small **E-flat clarinet** and the large **bass clarinet** are family members with a place in the modern orchestra. The tube of the latter instrument is so long that it has to be bent up, like a saxophone.

Oboe   The **oboe** also uses a reed, like the clarinet, but it is a double reed—two reeds lashed together so that the air must be forced between them. (Playing the oboe is hard work.) This kind of reed gives the oboe its clearly focused, crisply clean, and sometimes plaintive sound.

The **English horn** is a larger, lower oboe, descending into the viola range. (Scores often give the French equivalent, *cor anglais;* in either language, the name is wildly deceptive, since the instrument is not a horn but an oboe, and it has nothing to do with England.)

Bassoon   The **bassoon** is a low (cello-range) instrument with a double reed and other characteristics similar to the oboe's. It looks somewhat bizarre: the long tube is bent double, and the reed has to be linked to the instrument by a long, narrow pipe. Of all the double-reed woodwinds, the bassoon is the most varied in expression, ranging from the mournful to the comical.

The **contrabassoon** or **double bassoon** is a very large member of the bassoon family, equivalent in range to the bass viol.

Clarinet

Saxophone The saxophone is the outstanding case in the history of music of the successful invention of a new instrument family. Its inventor, the Belgian instrument maker Adolphe Sax, also developed saxhorns and other instruments. Introduced around 1840 as a band instrument, the saxophone (or "sax") is occasionally added to the modern orchestra, but it really came into its own in jazz.

Saxophones are close to clarinets in the way they produce their sound. The reeds are similar, but the saxophone tube is made of brass. This makes their tone even more mellow than the clarinet's, but at the same time more forceful. The long saxophone tube has a characteristic bent shape and flaring "bell," as its opening is called.

Most common are the **alto saxophone** and the **tenor saxophone,** but the big family also includes *bass, baritone, soprano,* and even *contrabass* (very low) and *sopranino* (very high) members. The two smallest instruments are not bent; they look like clarinets, except for the metal, and sound quite similar.

Brass Instruments The brass instruments are the loudest of all the wind instruments because of the unusual way their sound is produced. The player blows into a small cup-shaped mouthpiece of metal, and this makes the player's lips vibrate. The lip vibration activates vibration of the air in the brass tube.

All brass instruments have long tubes, and almost always these are coiled in one way or another—something that is easy to do with the soft metal they are made from.

Oboe

Bassoon (with a clarinet in the background)

Alto saxophone

The trombones with their horizontal slides, and the sousaphones with their dramatic bells, make a striking navy band picture

Trumpet   The **trumpet,** highest of the main brass instruments, has a bright, strong, piercing tone that provides the ultimate excitement in band and orchestral music alike. The pitch is controlled by three pistons or valves that connect auxiliary tubes with the main tube or disconnect them, so as to lengthen or shorten the vibrating air column.

French Horn   The **French horn** has a lower, mellower, "thicker" tone than the trumpet. It is capable of mysterious, romantic sounds when played softly; played loudly, it can sound like a trombone. Chords played by several French horns in harmony have an especially sumptuous tone.

Trombone   The **tenor trombone** and the **bass trombone** are also pitched lower than the trumpet. The pitch is controlled by a sliding mechanism (thus the term "slide trombone"), rather than a valve or piston, as in the trumpet and French horn.

   Less bright and martial in tone than the trumpet, the trombone can produce a surprising variety of sounds, ranging from an almost vocal quality in its high register to a hard, powerful blare in the low register.

Tuba   The **bass tuba** is typically used as a foundation for the trombone group in an orchestra. It is less flexible than other brass instruments, and like most other deep bass instruments it is not favored for solo work.

Other Brass Instruments   All the brass instruments described so far are staples of both the orchestra and the band. Many other brass instruments (and even whole families of instruments) have been invented for band use and have then sometimes found their way into the orchestra.

Among these are the *cornet* and the *flügelhorn,* which resemble the trumpet, the *euphonium, baritone horn,* and *saxhorn,* which are somewhere between the French horn and the tuba, and the *sousaphone,* a handsome type of bass tuba named after the great American bandmaster and march composer, John Philip Sousa.

Finally there is the *bugle.* This simple trumpetlike instrument is limited in the pitches it can play because it has no piston or valve mechanism. Buglers play "Taps" and military fanfares and not much else.

The way buglers get different pitches is by "overblowing," that is, by blowing harder into the mouthpiece so as to get partials (see page 10). Overblowing is, indeed, an important resource of trumpets and many other brass instruments.

French horn

Percussion Instruments Instruments in this category produce sound by being struck (or sometimes rattled, as with the South American maraca). Some percussion instruments, such as drums and gongs, have no fixed pitch, just a striking tone color. Other percussion instruments, such as the xylophone and vibraphone, have a whole series of wooden or metal elements tuned to regular scales.

Timpani The **timpani** (or *kettledrums*) are large hemispherical drums that can be tuned precisely to certain low pitches. They are used in groups of two or more. As with most drums, players can obtain different sounds from the timpani by using different kinds of drumsticks, tapping at different places on the drumhead, and so on.

Timpani are tuned by tightening the drum head by means of screws set around the rim. During a concert, one can often see the timpani player, when there are rests in the music, leaning over the drums, tapping them quietly to hear whether the tuning is just right. Also available is a pedal mechanism to retune the timpani instantaneously.

Since they are tuned to precise pitches, timpani are the most widely used percussion instruments in the orchestra. They have the effect of "cementing" loud sounds when the whole orchestra plays; they are also often played in conjunction with the trumpets.

Glockenspiel, Xylophone, Marimba, Vibraphone, Celesta, Tubular Bells These are all "scale" instruments, consisting of whole sets of metal or wooden bars or plates played with sticks or hammers. While they add unforgettable special sound effects to many compositions, they are not usually heard consistently throughout a piece, as the timpani are. They differ in their materials:

> The *glockenspiel* has small steel bars. It is a high instrument with a bright, penetrating sound.

> The *xylophone* has hardwood plates or slats. It plays as high as the glockenspiel but also lower, and it has a drier, sharper tone.

> The *marimba*, an instrument of African and South American origins, is like a xylophone with tubular resonators for each note. They make the tone much more mellow.

> And the *vibraphone* has metal plates, like a glockenspiel with a large range, and is furnished with a controllable electric resonating device. This gives the "vibes" a flexible, funky quality unlike that of any other instrument.

> Like the glockenspiel, the *celesta* has steel bars, but its sound is more delicate and silvery. This instrument, unlike the others in this section, is not played directly by a

Timpani

Cymbals

percussionist wielding hammers or sticks. The hammers are activated from a keyboard; a celesta looks like a miniature piano.

> *Tubular bells* or *chimes* are hanging tubes that are struck with a big mallet. They sound like church bells.

Unpitched Percussion Instruments In the category of percussion instruments without a fixed pitch, the following are the most frequently found in the orchestra:

> The *triangle*—a simple metal triangle—gives out a bright tinkle when struck.

> *Cymbals* are concave metal plates, from a few inches to several feet in diameter. In orchestral music, large cymbals are traditionally used in pairs. Clapped together, they support forceful moments in the music with a grand clashing sound.

> The *gong* usually employed in the orchestra is a large one with a low, often sinister quality.

> The *snare drum, tenor drum,* and *bass drum* are among the unpitched drums used in the orchestra.

The Orchestra The orchestra has changed over the centuries just as greatly as orchestral music has. Bach's orchestra in the early 1700s was about a fifth of the size of the orchestra required by ambitious composers today. (See pages 120, 169, and 246 for charts showing the makeup of the orchestra at various historical periods.)

So today's symphony orchestra is a fluid group. Eighty musicians or more will be on the regular roster, but some of them sit out some of the pieces on almost every pro-

gram. And free-lancers have to be engaged for many special compositions in which composers have imaginatively expanded the orchestra for their own expressive purposes. A typical large orchestra today includes:

> *Strings:* about thirty to thirty-six violinists, twelve violists, ten to twelve cellists, and eight double basses.

> *Woodwinds:* two flutes and a piccolo, two clarinets and a bass clarinet, two oboes and an English horn, two bassoons and a contrabassoon.

> *Brass:* two trumpets, four French horns, two trombones, and one tuba.

> *Percussion:* one to four players, who between them manage the timpani and all the other percussion instruments, moving from one to the other. For unlike the violins, for example, the percussion instruments seldom have to be played continuously throughout a piece. If a composition uses a great deal of percussion—and many modern compositions do—more players will be needed. The percussionists in such a piece move like dancers in a complicated ballet.

There are several seating plans for orchestras; which is chosen depends on at least two factors. The conductor judges which arrangement makes the best sound in the particular hall. And some conductors feel they can control the orchestra better with one arrangement, some with another. One such seating plan is shown opposite.

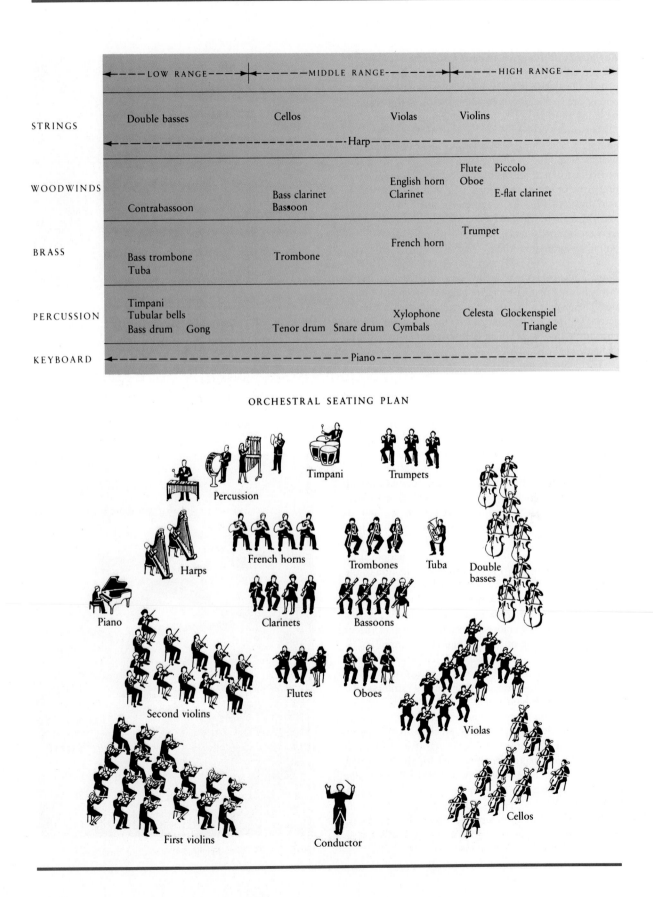

	— LOW RANGE —	— MIDDLE RANGE —	— HIGH RANGE —
STRINGS	Double basses	Cellos	Violas Violins
	←———————————————— Harp ————————————————→		
WOODWINDS	Contrabassoon	Bass clarinet Bassoon	English horn Flute Piccolo Clarinet Oboe E-flat clarinet
BRASS	Bass trombone Tuba	Trombone	French horn Trumpet
PERCUSSION	Timpani Tubular bells Bass drum Gong	Tenor drum Snare drum	Xylophone Celesta Glockenspiel Cymbals Triangle
KEYBOARD	←———————————————— Piano ————————————————→		

ORCHESTRAL SEATING PLAN

Keyboard and Plucked Stringed Instruments   Notice in the preceding chart that most orchestras today include a pianist. The piano is a relatively new addition to the symphony orchestra. In earlier times, the orchestra regularly included another keyboard instrument, the harpsichord.

The great advantage of keyboard instruments, of course, is that they can play chords and full harmony as well as melodies. One can play a whole piece on a keyboard instrument without requiring an accompanist, or orchestra, or any other musicians at all. Consequently the solo music that has been written for piano, harpsichord, and organ is much more extensive than (accompanied) solo music for other instruments—more extensive, and ultimately more important.

Piano   The **piano** may seem like a very familiar instrument, but not many people are familiar with all its subtleties. The piano's tuned strings are struck by felt hammers, activated from the keyboard. It is the activating mechanism, or *action,* over which the most ingenuity has been expended.

The hammers must strike the string and then fall back at once, while a felt damper simultaneously touches the string to stop the sound crisply. And all this must be done so fast that the pianist can play repeated notes as fast as the hand can move. Also, all possible shades of loudness and softness must lie ready under the player's fingers. This dynamic capability is what gave the piano its name: "piano" is short for *pianoforte,* meaning "soft-loud."

In the nineteenth century, the piano became *the* solo instrument. The list of great virtuoso pianists who were also major composers extends from Frédéric Chopin to Sergei Rachmaninoff. At the same time, every middle-class household had a piano. Obligatory piano lessons served (and still serve) for millions of young people as either an unwelcome chore or a magical introduction to the world of music.

Harpsichord   The **harpsichord** is an ancient keyboard instrument that has enjoyed a healthy revival in recent years for the playing of Baroque music, in particular.

Like the piano, the harpsichord has a set of tuned strings activated from a keyboard. The action is much simpler, however—instead of hammers striking the strings, little quills pluck them. This means, first, that the tone is brittle and pingy. Second, it means that the player cannot vary dynamics; a string plucked, in this way, always sounds the same.

Harpsichord makers compensated for this limitation in dynamics by adding one or two further sets of louder strings controlled by an extra keyboard. The sets of strings could be coupled so as to produce a louder, grander sound than any set played separately. Ultimately, the harpsichord was replaced by the "soft-loud" instrument, the piano.

A fantastically ornamented Victorian square piano

An elaborately painted eighteenth-century harpsichord

Despite its brittle tone and lack of dynamic flexibility, the harpsichord can be a wonderfully expressive instrument. Good harpsichord playing requires, first and foremost, great rhythmic subtlety. Also, little trills and other ornaments add an expressive dimension that is not possible on the piano.

Clavichord   The **clavichord** is another ancient keyboard instrument, small, private, with an even simpler action than the harpsichord's. The strings are struck with small pieces of metal. The clavichord has a very quiet, sensitive sound—so quiet that it cannot be heard across a big room, let alone in the concert hall.

Organ   The pipe **organ** has many sets of tuned pipes through which a complicated wind system blows air, again activated from a keyboard. The pipes have different tone colors; a large organ is capable of an almost orchestral variety of sound. Most organs have, in fact, more than one keyboard to control different sets of the pipes. There is also a pedal board—a short, big keyboard on the floor, played with the feet—to control the lowest pipes.

Each set of tuned pipes is called a *stop;* a moderate-sized organ has forty–fifty stops, but much bigger ones exist. (The biggest organ on record, at Atlantic City, has 1477 stops, for a total of 33,112 pipes.) Called "the king of instruments," the pipe organ is certainly the largest of them. Organs need their size and power in order to provide enough sound to fill the large spaces of churches and cathedrals on a suitably grand scale.

Electronic Keyboard Instruments   For many today, "keyboard" or "organ" means an electronic instrument. Electronic church organs were made as early as the 1920s, and have been perfected since, but almost all church organists prefer the old-style pipe instruments. The synthesizers of today can simulate the sound of organs, pianos, and harpsichords. Today's electronic pianos look like acoustic ones and sound quite like them, though the "feel" is rather different. They cost a great deal less.

Modern concert music, from the 1960s on, has made occasional use of electronic keyboards. On the whole, however, synthesizers have been used more to compose concert music than to play it.

A five-manual organ. The round knobs are *stops* (or *stop knobs*); the player pulls them out to change the sets of pipes that sound.

Banjo

Plucked Stringed Instruments   Plucked stringed instruments figure much less in art music of the West than in Asian countries such as India and Japan. One exception is the orchestral harp, mentioned on page 43. The acoustic **guitar,** the **mandolin,** and the **banjo** are used very widely in Western popular music, only occasionally in orchestras or other concert-music groups.

An early plucked stringed instrument, the **lute,** was of major importance in earlier times. There is a significant body of solo lute music dating from the sixteenth and seventeenth centuries. One of the most beautiful-looking of instruments, the lute sounds rather like a gentle guitar. Unlike the guitar, the lute has a rounded back, and its peg box bends back at a right angle to the fingerboard.

Like keyboard instruments, plucked stringed instruments have been revolutionized by electronic technology. The **electric guitars** of rock music have not (not yet?) found their way into concert music.

Lute

An international array of beautifully decorated instruments, displayed on a mirror: (1) Chinese *pipa,* a lute-type instrument; (2) sitar, the best-known instrument of India, another member of the large lute family; (3) German hunting horn, made of porcelain; (4) French guitar, with marquetry (wood inlay), c. 1650; (5) a very early violin (sixteenth century); (6) simple ivory horn from Burma

Instruments of the World   This is not the place for a comprehensive discussion of the myriad musical instruments found outside the West. We can only make one or two points about them; the accompanying illustrations will have to do the rest.

The first important point is that the four basic types of instruments that we have identified in Western music (strings, woodwinds, brass, and percussion) are found throughout the world. So are the subtypes—plucked and bowed stringed instruments, flutes and reeds, percussion instruments with fixed pitch and percussion without fixed pitch. Prehistoric prototypes for most of these instrument categories have been discovered in excavations in Africa and Asia. Today some nations or cultures have all these types and subtypes; others lack some of them.

It can be fascinating to hear, examine, or even look at a picture of an unfamiliar instrument and realize that it represents a version of something we know well at home. Thus the big-bellied Peruvian peasant instrument illustrated on page 54 is (to us) a strange-shaped harp.

A second important point concerns the strengths and weaknesses of Western music. The West has been strong on technology, and therefore electronic and keyboard instruments have been developed mainly in Europe, America, and Asian countries that have adopted Western technology, notably Japan. Technology has also perfected violin-type and most wind instruments. Western music excels in these varieties. On the other hand, the West has no monopoly on fine plucked string instruments, and it is unusually weak in percussion.

Far Eastern countries have rich bodies of music for various plucked instruments. Notable among these are the Indian **sitar** and the Japanese **koto.** These instruments are very highly refined, and many of them are beautifully decorated.

Among the Senufo people of West Africa, drumming marks initiation into successive age classes.

North Indian *sgra-syan,* a long-necked instrument of the lute type

A Peruvian orchestra featuring mandolin, harp, violin, and *quena*—an instrument like the recorder, the inside of which is burned out and specially carved to refine the tone quality

As for percussion instruments, "chime"-type instruments flourish particularly in Indonesia. The Indonesian orchestra, the **gamelan,** does not use string instruments as a foundation for its sound, as the Western orchestra does. The basic sound of the gamelan is that of a remarkable variety of wood, bronze, and bamboo instruments of the xylophone variety.

The development of drums has proceeded particularly well in Africa. The drums in a Western orchestra (or rock group) can only seem crude by comparison with an African drum ensemble. The sophisticated drumming techniques, and the care lavished on the construction and decoration of the instruments themselves, correspond to the importance of drum music to African peoples. Drumming conveys messages, represents deities, and plays a central role in virtually all rituals.

Korean *ajaeng,* a bowed instrument resembling the more familiar Japanese *koto,* a long, graceful box strung with strings that are plucked rather than bowed

Part of a Balinese gamelan; the characteristic chime-type instruments are in the back, drummers and cymbal players in front.

Indian girl playing a *vina*, a lute-type instrument similar to the sitar

North Indian musicians: the *shahnai* is an instrument of the oboe type, and the *naghara* are small kettle-drums, like timpani

Chapter 4

Musical Form and Musical Style

Form is a general word with a long list of dictionary definitions. As applied to the arts, *form* is an important concept that refers to the shape, arrangement, relationship, or organization of the various elements. In poetry, for example, the elements of form are words, phrases, meters, rhymes, and stanzas; in painting, they are lines, colors, shapes, and so on.

Form in art has a good deal to do with its emotional quality; form is not a merely intellectual matter, even though it may be that some artists and art scholars treat it in too abstract a way. But the emotional "click" that we get at the end of a sonnet, where the accumulated meanings of the words come together with the final rhyme, is an effect to which form—sonnet form—contributes. Similarly, when at the end of a symphony a previously heard melody comes back with new orchestration and new harmonies, the special feeling this gives us emerges from a flood of memory; we remember it from before, in its earlier version. That effect, too, is created by musical form.

1 Form in Music

In music, the elements of form are those we have already discussed: rhythm, dynamics, tone color, melody, tonality, and texture. The organization of a musical work of some length is carried out largely by means of repetitions of themes, rhythms, tone colors, and textures, and by extended contrasts and balances among these elements. The repetitions may be strict or free (that is, exact or with some variation). The contrasts may be of many different kinds, conveying many different kinds of feeling.

In this book we shall be speaking about musical form a good deal. Over the centuries, composers of Western music have been much concerned with producing long or relatively long pieces of music, such as masses, fugues, symphonies, and operas. Everyone knows that music can easily make a nice effect for a minute or two. But how does it extend itself—and hold the listener's interest—for ten minutes, half an hour, or two full hours?

This is the function of musical form. Rarely have composers thought of music as a continuous stream, like Muzak, which listeners can hook into absentmindedly at will, enjoying or ignoring what they hear. Rather, composers have designed their music as a specific sound experience in a definite time span, with a beginning, middle, and end, and often with subtle routes between.

Musical form can be defined as the significant relationship between these beginnings, middles, and ends. And the true importance of form is that those relationships contribute to the emotional effect of music.

The Role of Memory

Form is a major factor in all the arts. However, musical form is not strictly comparable to form in any of the other arts. The special factor with music is the crucial importance of memory—and of anticipation, which is something like the reverse of memory. (The main talent involved in an "ear for music," in fact, is memory.) In grasping musical form, we are continuously putting together in our minds—or, rather, in our emotional experience—what we are hearing right now in the piece, what we heard earlier, and what we feel we have been led to expect to hear later.

On a simple level, no one has any trouble exerting memory and anticipation in order to appreciate musical form in a short tune, such as "The Star-Spangled Banner." The various phrases of a tune, with their repetitions, parallel features, contrasts, climax, cadences, and so on, provide a microcosm of musical form in larger pieces.

For in a way, a large-scale composition such as a symphony is an expanded, articulated tune, and its form is experienced in basically the same way. To be sure, a symphony requires more commitment from the listener— more attention and more time—than a tune does. Composers are aware of the potential difficulty here, and they exaggerate their musical effects accordingly. In other words, the larger the piece, the more strongly the composer is likely to help the memory along by emphasizing those features of repetition and contrast that determine the musical form.

Form in painting: a madonna by Raphael Sanzio (1483–1520), built out of two cunningly nested triangles. To balance the boys at the left, the Virgin faces slightly to the right, her extended foot "echoing" their bare flesh. On a larger scale, the activity at the left is matched by a steeper landscape.

Musical Forms

Like the words *rhythm* and *melody,* the word *form* has its general meaning and its more specific one. "Rhythm" refers to the whole time aspect of music, but "*a* rhythm" refers to the particular temporal and accented pattern of a specific musical passage. "Form" in general refers to the organization of elements in a musical work, but "*a* form" refers to one of the many standardized patterns or arrangements that composers have used over the centuries.

Forms in this sense are sometimes called "outer forms." In most periods, artists in all media have tended to employ them, for their fixed elements are always general enough to allow for many possibilities of organization on the detailed level. Hence the quality and feeling of works in the same outer form can vary greatly—or, to put it another way, works adhering to a common "outer form" also have an individual "inner form" of their own. Indeed, the interplay of the two can be an important factor in the aesthetic effect.

> In poetry, the simplest example is a poem in several parallel stanzas. Each stanza has the same outer form, but the poet varies the way the thought fits into the form and builds the total poem accordingly. For example, in the poem shown here, whose stanzas are in an *a b a b* rhyme form (some of the *a* rhymes being "half-rhymes"), the verbal phrases or thought units fit differently into each four-line stanza. The four lines of stanza 1 divide two and two, stanza 2 three and one, and stanza 3 one and three.

Also, in stanza 3, the *b* rhyme of the outer form is nearly eclipsed by an unexpected rhyming word in the middle of line 3, "old." This makes a unique, tense inner form, for "old" in line 4 resonates with "old" in line 3 more than with "told" in line 2. "Old" is a central concept in this poem.

> For an example from architecture, consider the ground plans of churches shown at the bottom of this page and the next (relatively thin walls are indicated by lines, and heavy masonry columns, and so on, by black areas). All Christian churches traditionally follow the same outer form, in that they are built in the shape of a cross, and all are supposed to face Jerusalem—that is, east, for churches in Europe or America. But the ground plans show how widely the architectural inner forms have ranged; a cross can be fitted into a circle, into a double cross, and many other shapes. We can imagine how different the space in these different cross-shaped churches would feel, if we were actually in them.

A Girl's Song

I went out alone
To sing a song or two,
My fancy on a man,
And you know who.

Another came in sight
That on a stick relied
To hold himself upright;
I sat and cried.

And that was all my song—
When everything is told,
Saw I an old man young
Or young man old?

—W. B. Yeats

San Vitale, Ravenna, c. 530–548

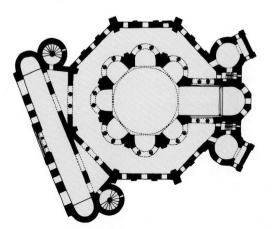

San Lorenzo, Florence, 1418–1446

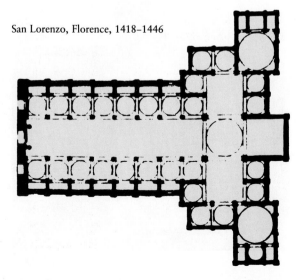

Musical forms, as standardized patterns, are conventionally expressed by letters. Two basic factors create musical form: *repetition* and *contrast*. In a form that is diagrammed **A B A,** the element of repetition is **A** and the element of contrast is **B.** Some sort of theme or other musical section is presented at the beginning (**A**), then another section (**B**) is presented that contrasts with the first, then the first one returns (**A**). If **A** returns with significant modification or variation, this is conventionally indicated by a prime mark: **A B A′**.

Such letter schemes are useful mainly for indicating repetitions and "returns"; they are less helpful with the contrasts, for a letter is utterly uncommunicative as to the nature of the contrast. Is section **B** in a different mode? In a different key? Does it present material radically different in rhythm, melody, texture, or tone color? Any or all of these resources of contrast? It must be said, too, that returns such as **A′** in an **A B A′** form can also feel very different from one another. One return can sound exciting, another inexorable, another tricky, while yet another can give a sense of relief.

So identifying musical "outer forms" is just a preliminary step in music appreciation. Getting the letters right is a necessary process of orientation, true, but there is much more to music than the way it fits into forms. The real point—the artistic point—about great music is the way composers refine, modify, and personalize those forms for their own expressive purposes.

Musical Genres

It is not uncommon to hear symphonies, string quartets, operas, and oratorios referred to as "musical forms." This is loose terminology, however, that is best avoided in the interests of clarity. For symphonies and other long works can be composed in different forms—that is, their internal orders or organizations can be of different kinds. Thus, the last movement of Joseph Haydn's Symphony No. 88 is in rondo form, whereas the last movement of the *Fantastic* Symphony by Hector Berlioz follows no standard form whatsoever. (We shall be listening to both these symphonies later.)

The best term for these general categories of music is *genre* (pronounced *zhahn*-ruh), borrowed from French. A genre is determined partly by style (a fugue is always contrapuntal), partly by function (a mass is usually written to be sung at a service), and partly by the performing forces (a quartet is for four singers or instrumentalists). We shall define and discuss all the important musical genres later in this book.

Salisbury Cathedral, 1220–1284

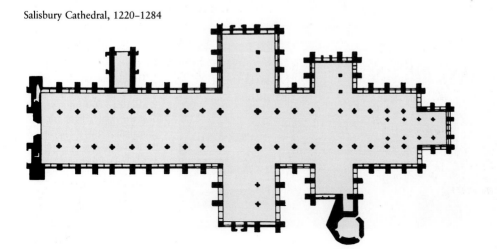
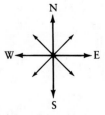

2 Musical Style

Style, like *form*, is another of those broad, general words—general but very necessary. The style of a tennis player is the particular way he or she reaches up for the serve, swings, follows through on the forehand, hits the ball deep or short, and so on. A life-style means the whole combination of things one does and doesn't do: the food one eats, the way one dresses and talks, one's habits of thought and feeling.

The style of a work of art, similarly, is the combination of qualities that make it distinctive. Musical styles can be discussed in terms of the basic elements of music we have already described. One composer's style may favor jagged rhythms, simple harmonies, and tunes to the exclusion of all other types of melody. Another composer may exhibit a highly refined preference for certain kinds of tone color; still another may concentrate on a particular form; and so on. The type of emotional expression a composer cultivates is also an important determinant of musical style.

One can speak of the life-style of a generation as well as the life-style of a particular person. Similarly, in music a distinction can be made between the style of a particular composer and the style of a historical period. For example, to a large extent George Frideric Handel's manner of writing falls within the broader limits of the Baroque style of his day. But some features of Handel's style are unique, and perhaps it is those features that embody his musical genius.

Musical Style and Life-Style

In any historical period or place, the musical style must bear some relation to the life-style in general; this seems self-evident. Perhaps the point is clearest of all with popular music, where distinct (and distinctly different) worlds are evoked by heavy-metal rock, folk, rap, and country-western music, to say nothing of the popular styles of past generations, such as 1960s rock-and-roll or 1930s swing. With older styles of music, too, everybody recognizes in a general way that they relate to total cultural situations, though how this works in detail is not well understood.

The central, contrasting unit of this building seems almost to flow into the unit at the right. The musical analogy would be to an interesting **A B A′** form, in which **A** comes back after **B** in an expanded version (**A′**), and that version includes some new rhythm or instrument that we first heard during **B**.

Even *where* people listen to music reflects their lifestyle. This open-air concert is at the Hatch Shell in Boston.

However, we can at least suggest some of these relationships for the music of various historical periods. For each period, the following chapters will sketch some aspects of the culture, history, and life-style of the time. We shall briefly outline the musical style in general terms and, wherever possible, suggest correlations. Then the musical style will be examined in more detail through individual composers and individual pieces of their music.

These individual pieces are our chief concern, of course—not history, or culture, or concepts about musical styles in general. This point may be worth stressing, now that the fundamentals of music have all been laid out in a more or less abstract way. In the last analysis, learning basic musical concepts and their terminology is valuable insofar as it focuses and sharpens the listening process. This book is called *Listen,* and it rests on the belief that the love of music depends first and foremost on careful listening to particular pieces. We experience these pieces for their own sake, not because they are "good examples" of some musical style, form, or genre, or because they are "typical" of some historical period.

But we *are* interested the other way around—in what history and style can tell us that illuminates music. If a glimpse into the culture of a certain historical period can shed light on its musical style, fine, for the more background that can be built up for the appreciation of art, the better. Certainly understanding the musical style in general terms can contribute to an appreciation of particular pieces of music written in that style. The general reflects upon the particular. It may seem paradoxical, then, but in this indirect way, history too can help us to *listen.*

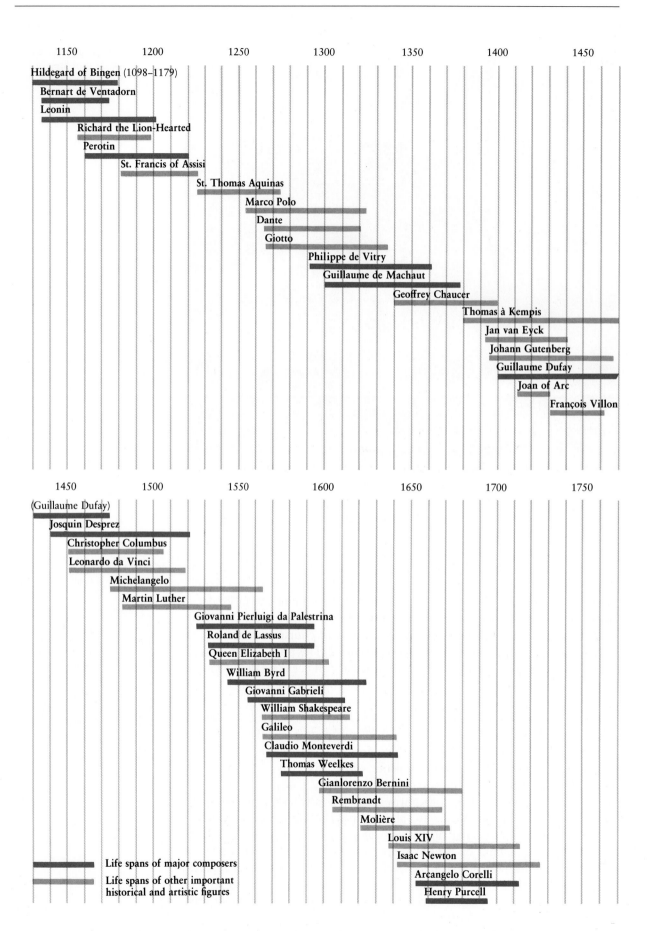

1150 1200 1250 1300 1350 1400 1450

Hildegard of Bingen (1098–1179)
Bernart de Ventadorn
Leonin
Richard the Lion-Hearted
Perotin
St. Francis of Assisi
St. Thomas Aquinas
Marco Polo
Dante
Giotto
Philippe de Vitry
Guillaume de Machaut
Geoffrey Chaucer
Thomas à Kempis
Jan van Eyck
Johann Gutenberg
Guillaume Dufay
Joan of Arc
François Villon

1450 1500 1550 1600 1650 1700 1750

(Guillaume Dufay)
Josquin Desprez
Christopher Columbus
Leonardo da Vinci
Michelangelo
Martin Luther
Giovanni Pierluigi da Palestrina
Roland de Lassus
Queen Elizabeth I
William Byrd
Giovanni Gabrieli
William Shakespeare
Galileo
Claudio Monteverdi
Thomas Weelkes
Gianlorenzo Bernini
Rembrandt
Molière
Louis XIV
Isaac Newton
Arcangelo Corelli
Henry Purcell

Life spans of major composers
Life spans of other important
historical and artistic figures

Unit II

Early Music: An Overview

Western art music extends from the great corpus of Gregorian chant, assembled around the year A.D. *600, to electronic compositions that were programmed yesterday and today. One does not have to be a specialist to have some feeling for the sheer scope, variety, and almost bewildering richness of all this music. Some of it was developed to sustain Christianity through centuries of barbarism, some to glorify powerful monarchs such as Queen Elizabeth I and Louis XIV; some is produced for the recording studios of the modern world. The field ranges from the music of Josquin Desprez—a contemporary of Leonardo da Vinci, Josquin is sometimes said to be the first great composer—through music by familiar masters such as Bach and Beethoven, to music by a former conductor of the New York Philharmonic, Pierre Boulez, who now runs a big state-of-the-art laboratory for sound research in Paris. All of this is music that has fascinated, moved, and inspired humanity.*

Certainly there is too much here to "cover" in a single semester or quarter course—too much, that is, if one is going to do more than skim the music, picking up a few frantic facts and figures about it without really listening. It cannot be said often enough that listening to particular pieces again and again is the basic activity that leads to the love of music and to its understanding. A galloping survey does justice to none of the world's significant music. In acknowledgment of this fact, the essential coverage of this book begins in Unit III with the music of Bach and Handel, who are the first composers with a long-standing place in the "standard repertory" of concert music. This term refers to a large but not limitless body of music from which concert artists and conductors usually draw their programs.

As an optional introduction to all this, Unit II presents a brief overview of music before the eighteenth century. Although "early music"—music of the medieval, Renaissance, and early Baroque periods—is seldom performed at the usual concerts, it is becoming more and more familiar largely through recordings. Once regarded as an esoteric taste, music of these distant eras now attracts a growing number of devotees.

How Did Early Music Sound?

There is a special problem about early music, a problem that is less trouble-some with music of more recent times: although we have the scores of early music, often we do not have a very clear idea of how it actually sounded.

One reason for this is that musical instruments have changed enor-mously over the centuries. Archaic instruments have survived in an imperfect condition, and trying to determine how they sounded is an uncertain busi-ness. One can make modern reconstructions of ancient instruments, but to reconstruct ancient playing is much more speculative. As for singing, who can imagine what style of singing was practiced in a cathedral choir of the late Middle Ages, just to take one example? Language itself has changed so much since that time that it is hard enough even to read a fourteenth-century English poet such as Geoffrey Chaucer, let alone imagine how the words he wrote were pronounced. A modern American might be completely baffled by the way those words were actually sung.

What is more, composers of early music never indicated the tempo and seldom specified the instrumental or vocal forces they anticipated for their music. They did not generally specify whether a single singer or a whole choir was to perform a particular voice part. Consequently it has taken gen-erations of patient research and experiment to "reconstruct," as it were, the probable sound of various kinds of early music. This is one of the most important tasks of musicology, the scholarly study of music.

The recordings of early music accompanying this book have been care-fully chosen to represent the most modern and sensitive research in these matters, but in terms of performance sound, these recordings are all edu-cated guesses. One should beware, in any case, of confident claims of "authenticity" in historical performance. Some guesses are better educated (and more artistic) than others, but there is much that we can never know about the sound of early music.

From an unusual series of medieval portraits—24 portraits of Minnesingers: Heinrich Frauenlob (Henry Praiselady), with his impressive band of jongleurs, and Walther von der Vogelweide (Walter of the Aviary–note his heraldic device), greatest of the Minnesinger poets.

2 Music at Court

Over the long span of the Middle Ages, the kings and barons gained political power at the expense of the Church. They also assumed leadership in artistic matters as well. The princely courts joined the monasteries and cathedrals as major supporters of music in the late Middle Ages.

Troubadour and Trouvère Songs

Large groups of court songs have been preserved from the twelfth and thirteenth centuries, the Age of Chivalry. The noble poet-composers of these songs—who also performed the songs themselves—were called **troubadours** in the south of France, **trouvères** in the north, and **Minnesingers** in Germany and Austria (*Minne* means ideal or chivalric love).

These poets wrote crusaders' songs, laments for dead princes, and especially songs in praise of their ladies—or complaints about their ladies' coldness. One interesting poetic type was the *alba*, the "dawn song" of a knight's companion who has kept watch all night and now warns him to leave his lady's bed before the castle awakes. Another was the *pastourelle,* a (typically unsuccessful) seduction dialogue between a knight on horseback and a country maid.

These songs bear the names of knights and princes, and even some kings, among them the most famous of all chivalric heroes, Richard I of England, "the Lion-Hearted." Troubadour society (but not trouvère society) also allowed for women troubadours, such as Countess Beatriz of Dia, Maria di Ventadorn, and many others.

Perhaps some troubadours and trouvères wrote the words only, leaving the music to be composed by *jongleurs,* the popular musicians of the time. The music is relatively simple—just a tune, in most cases, with no indication of any accompaniment. But when the jongleurs played instruments while they or the troubadours sang, perhaps they also improvised simple polyphony.

BERNART DE VENTADORN (c. 1135–1194)   6 Cassette 1A-3/6 CD 1-3
Troubadour song, "La dousa votz"

Bernart was one of the finest troubadour poets and probably the most important musically; other troubadour and trouvère songs were derived from some of his pieces. Originally of humble background, he came to serve the powerful Queen Eleanor of Aquitaine, wife of Henry II of England.

Like many troubadour songs, "La dousa votz" contains several stanzas in **a a′ b** form. It is in the G (Myxolydian) mode:

La dou-sa votz ai au-zi - da   Del ro-sin-ho- let sau - va-tge   Et es m'in sel cor sal-hi - da   Si que tot lo   co-si - rer

The performance on the recording stresses "secular" aspects of Bernart's song, including an imaginative reconstruction of a possible instrumental accompaniment to it. It sounds far removed indeed from the spiritual atmosphere of Hildegard of Bingen.

The language the troubadours spoke and wrote was Provençal, now almost obsolete. It combines elements from old French and old Spanish.

TEXT: Bernart de Ventadorn, "La dousa votz"

(STANZA 1)

La dousa votz ai auzida	I have heard the sweet voice
Del rosinholet sauvatge	Of the woodland nightingale
Et es m'insel cor salhida	And it has sprung up in my heart
Si que tot lo cosirer	So that all the cares
E'ls mals traihz qu'amors me dona,	And the unhappy betrayals love gives me
M'adousa e m'asazona.	Are softened and sweetened;
Et auria'm be mester	And I would be well served
L'autrui joi al meu damnatge....	By another's joy in my sorrow.

(STANZA 2)

Ben est totz om d'avol vida	In truth, every man falls short in life
C'a joi non son estatge ...	Who does not set his state toward joy ...

(STANZA 4)

Pois tan es vas me falhida,	Since she is so false to me,
Aisi lais so senhoratge,	I now quit her service,
E no volh que'm s'aizida,	And I don't want her to come near me,
Ni ja mais parlar no'n quer;	Nor even wish to speak to her;
Mas pero qui m'en razona,	But yet, if someone tells me of her,
La paraula m'en es bona,	Such talk still delights me,
E m'en esjau volonter,	And I willingly enjoy it,
E'm n'alegre mo coratge.	And my heart is made glad.

(one more stanza)

The Estampie

There also survive a few—a very few—dances from the same court circles that produced the chivalric trouvère repertory. Called **estampies,** they are unassuming one-line pieces in which the same or similar musical phrases are repeated many times in varied forms. (This suggests that these estampies may have been written-down jongleur improvisations.) Estampies are marked by lively and insistent rhythms in triple or compound meter. Modern performers often add a touch of spice with the help of percussion instruments.

This is a modest beginning to the long and important history of European dance music. We shall pick it up again in the next chapter.

Dance with fife and tabor
(small flute and drum)

3 The Evolution of Polyphony

Polyphony—the simultaneous combination of two or more melodies—must have arisen in early Europe because its inhabitants took pleasure in the sensuous quality of music. They must have enjoyed the rich sound of intertwining melodic lines and of the resulting harmony. Many cultures all over the world have developed some kind of improvised polyphony, polyphony that people can make up on the spot without complicated training. In America today, many people can "sing in thirds" without written-out music. This is a type of improvised polyphony.

But we only know about early European polyphony from its manifestations within the Church (for, once again, all we know about very early music comes from the writing of monks and other clerics). And within the Church, the sensuous aspect of polyphony had to be rationalized away. Polyphony was seen as a way of embellishing Gregorian chants—that is, as yet another way of enhancing the all-important services.

Organum

The earliest type of polyphony is called **organum.** First described in theoretical treatises around A.D. 900, actual "live" organum has survived in musical notation from around 1000. Organum consists of a traditional plainchant melody to which a composer-singer-improviser has added another melody, or counterpoint, sung simultaneously to the same words.

It is a famous unresolved question whether the name *organum* implies that early polyphony was accompanied by the organ. Certainly organs existed in those days. Winchester Abbey in England boasted a particularly splendid instrument with four hundred pipes and twenty-six bellows. This question aside, the history of organum between around 1000 and 1200 provides a fascinating record of growing artistic ambition and technical invention. A number of steps can be traced:

> Originally, each individual note of the chant was accompanied by a single note in the counterpoint; the two melodies moved along together with the same distance, or interval, between them. The rhythm of this early organum was the free rhythm of Gregorian chant.

> Soon the counterpoint was treated more independently—it would sometimes go up when the chant went down, and vice versa.

> Next, the counterpoint began to include several notes at the same time as each single chant note. The embellishment process was growing richer. As more and more notes were crowded in, making richer and richer melodies, the single chant notes were slowed down to surprisingly long drones.

> The next step was a radical one. Two counterpoints were added to the chant—which required much more skill from the composer, since the second counterpoint had to fit both the chant and also the first counterpoint.

> Equally radical was the idea of introducing definite rhythms controlled by meter. First the counterpoints and then the chant itself were set in lively rhythms. Fragments of the chant, too, were sometimes isolated and repeated many times, one after another.

Organum of this highly developed kind flourished at the Cathedral of Notre Dame in Paris, which was built slowly over the period 1163–1235. The names of some composers of the so-called Notre Dame school are recorded:

Notre Dame Cathedral in Paris: the two great front towers, the south rose (round) window, the spire, and the apse supported by flying buttresses—the great engineering feat that allowed Gothic architects to build unprecedentedly high buildings, which seem to reach up to heaven itself

Leonin and his follower Perotin (called "the Great"). Perotin astonished thirteenth-century Paris by producing impressive organa for as many as four simultaneous voices.

PEROTIN (c. 1200)   6 Cassette 1A-4/6 CD 1-4
Organum on the plainchant "Alleluia: Nativitas" (part)

For the birthday of the Virgin Mary—a big day at Notre Dame cathedral—Perotin wrote an organum adding two "free" counterpoints to one of the prescribed Mass plainchants. The chant is first sung in Gregorian fashion:

The whole chant lasts much longer, but this "Alleluia" section is the most important part—it comes back twice before the chant is over—and the most beautiful. Notice how the music rouses itself on the syllable *lu*, then springs up higher yet in the second phrase. This melodic climax is balanced by a tranquil "low climax" in the third phrase. After this (relative) excitement, the melody's last phrase stays within a calm range of four notes.

Then the organum starts. The higher voices first add a strange, static harmony—which starts to sway, as it were, when the voices intertwine in various rhythms of the kind shown at the right of this page. They are singing no words, just vocalizing the syllables *al—le—lu—ia*. Originally meandering and mysterious, these rhythmicized voices gain strength and clarity; by the end they are sounding jubilant and positively triumphant.

And what is going on underneath these ecstatic, rhythmicized voices? Listen carefully to the lowest of the voices, and you will hear long sustained tones. Notes 1 and 2 of the "Alleluia" chant shown above are each slowed down to amazingly long drones. Then notes 3 to 13 plod along in a slow regular rhythm (with a little break after note 8). Note 14 is another long drone:

But even if one hears these sustained notes or drones, one cannot recognize them as an actual melody, not at that speed—and not with the distractions offered by the counterpoints. The plainchant is an abstract basis for the ecstatic upper-voice melodies, the main focus of interest in this music.

4 Later Medieval Polyphony

The most significant thing that happened to polyphonic music in the thirteenth century was its gradual distancing from Church services. The "bottom
line" was still Gregorian chant, but this was now handled more abstractly.
For example, composers would now set only a fragment of chant and repeat
it several times in different arbitrary rhythms, as we saw in the "Alleluia:
Nativitas" organum.

In another radical development, the upper lines were now given their
own words. This sort of polyphony is no longer an organum but a **motet,**
from the French word *mot* ("word"). At first, motets were set to sacred
poems in Latin, then to sacred poems in French. Later, when some motets
used French love poems for texts, it is clear that a Church genre has been
taken over by the courts. Some motets even included bits of actual trouvère
songs; but almost all motets were still based on Gregorian chant.

Small portative (portable)
organ, an instrument that
was very popular in the later
Middle Ages

Ars Nova

After 1300 the technical development of polyphony reached new heights of
sophistication. Composers and music theorists of the time began to speak of
an *ars nova,* a "new art," or "new technique." The music of the Notre Dame
school was now regarded as "ancient art," *ars antiqua.*

Some historians have compared the fourteenth century with the twentieth, for it was a time of the break-up of traditions—an age of anxiety, cor-
ruption, and worse. The Black Death carried away an estimated 75 million
people, at a time when the papacy had been thrown out of Rome and two
rival popes claimed the allegiance of European Christendom. The motet grew
increasingly secular, intricate, and even convoluted, like the painting, architecture, and poetry of the time.

The new intricacy of the motet was mainly in the area of rhythm. The
composers of the *ars antiqua* had introduced rhythm and meter into
organum and the motet, as we have seen; the composers of the *ars nova* carried their innovations much further. Rhythm seems to have obsessed them.
They superimposed complex rhythmic patterns in the various voices so as to
produce extraordinarily complex combinations. We have to go all the way up
to 1950 to find anything like the dizzy rhythms of the advanced "new music"
of 1400.

The leading composers, Philippe de Vitry (1291–1361) and Guillaume de
Machaut (c. 1300–1377), were both churchmen—Vitry ended his life as a
bishop—but they were political churchmen in the service of the courts of
France and Luxembourg. Machaut was also the greatest French poet of his
time, admired (and imitated) by his younger English contemporary, Geoffrey
Chaucer.

GUILLAUME DE MACHAUT (c. 1300–1377)
Motet, "Quant en moy"

6 Cassette 1A-5/6 CD 1-5

Following tradition, Machaut based this motet on a repeated fragment of plainchant, taken from the Eastertide services. On the recording, it is played on a viol, an early bowed stringed instrument.

Above this, he wrote two faster counterpoints set to love poetry (very artificial and elegant poetry, in both form and content: see below). To the medieval mind, there was nothing sacrilegious about such a combination of sacred and secular elements. Notice the exceedingly complicated rhythm of these upper voices, the nervous, hyperelegant way in which they utter the words, and the spiky harmonies they produce in combination:

Quant en moi vint premièrement Amours, si tres doucette-ment Me vost mon cuer enamourer Que d'un regard

As the voices stop abruptly, rest, and start up again, they create an intriguing texture—perforated, glittering, asymmetrical. To make things even more intricate, the two singers actually sing two different poems simultaneously.

Each of these poems contains several stanzas with the same syllable counts and rhyme schemes, but Machaut (unlike a troubadour composer such as Bernart) does not repeat the same melodies for each stanza. A more esoteric system of repetition is at work. Successive stanzas are set to entirely different melodies in each voice—but these melodies have basically *the same overall rhythms,* complex patterns of over eighty notes in the soprano, forty notes in the tenor.

This technique of writing successive lengthy passages in identical rhythms but with distinct melodies is called **isorhythm.** Isorhythm represents the height of late medieval ingenuity and artifice in music, and it takes much practice to learn to hear such purely rhythmic repetitions. On our CD, indexing marks the beginning of the isorhythmic sections of this motet.

There are fast echoes between the soprano's two words in line 7 of her poem and the tenor's two words in line 2 of his, thus: "doubter—espoir—celer—d'avoir." This amusing device is called **hocket** (compare our word *hiccup*). Isorhythmic repetitions are easiest to hear at hocket points.

TEXT: **Machaut, "Quant en moy"**

The soprano's poem and tenor's poem start together, and are sung simultaneously.

SOPRANO

Quant en moy vint premièrement	When I was first visited by
Amours, si tres doucettement	Love, he so very sweetly
Me vost mon cuer enamourer	Enamored my heart;
Que d'un regard me fist present	A glance is what he gave me as a gift,
Et tres amoureus sentiment	And along with amorous sentiments
Me donna avuec doulz penser	He presented me with this delightful idea:
Espoir d'avoir	To hope to have
Merci sans refuser.	Grace, and no rejections.
Mais onques en tout mon vivant	But never in my whole life
Hardement ne me vost donner.	Was boldness a gift he meant for me.

TENOR

Amour et biaute parfaite	Thanks to love and consummate beauty,
Doubter, celer	Fearing, feigning
Me font parfaitement.	Are what consume me entirely.

(three more stanzas, in both soprano and tenor)

Hocket

Es - poir   d'avoir

Doubter,   celer

Chapter 6

The Renaissance

Renaissance ("rebirth") is the name given to a complex current of thought that worked deep changes in Europe from the fourteenth to the sixteenth century. By rediscovering and imitating their ancient Greco-Roman civilization, Italians hoped they could bring about the rebirth of their glorious past. It was a somewhat confused dream, which came to nothing in political terms. Instead of becoming a new Roman empire, Italy at the end of the Renaissance consisted of the same pack of warring city-states that had been at each other's throats all through the Middle Ages.

However, the revival of Greek and Roman culture provided a powerful model for new values, which were coming to the fore in Italy and the rest of Europe. In the words of a famous nineteenth-century historian, the Renaissance involved "the discovery of the world and of man." This was the age of Columbus, Leonardo da Vinci, Copernicus, and Shakespeare. Medieval society was stable, conservative, authoritarian, oriented toward God. The Renaissance laid the groundwork for the dynamic world we know today, a world in which human beings and nature, rather than God, have become the measure in philosophy, science, art, and even religion.

Accordingly, Renaissance artists strove to make their work more relevant to people's needs and desires. They began to reinterpret the world around them—the architect's world of space and stone, the painter's world of images, the musician's world of sound—in new ways to meet these ambitions.

Church singers, by the Renaissance sculptor Luca della Robbia (1400–1482). No elderly monks are represented on these panels (compare page 66), but instead handsome boys who seem to be taking the same sensuous pleasure in their singing as Luca did in sculpting them.

1 New Attitudes

A good indication of the Renaissance mindset, in the early fifteenth century, was a new way of treating plainchant in polyphonic compositions. Medieval composers writing organum or isorhythmic motets seem to have felt that so long as they used a traditional plainchant, there was nothing wrong with distorting it. They lengthened its notes enormously to accommodate the added counterpoints. They recast the meterless chant into fixed, arbitrary rhythms.

Renaissance composers no longer felt obliged always to use plainchants; but when they did they tended to treat them as melodies to listen to, not as set foundations for polyphonic structures. They embellished chants with extra notes, set them in graceful rhythms, and smoothed out passages that struck them as awkward or antiquated. This procedure is known as **paraphrase**. The following example shows a fifteenth-century plainchant paraphrase; asterisks mark the notes taken directly from the chant (shown above the paraphrase):

Veni Cre - a - tor Spiri - tus, Mentes tuorum vi-si-ta: Im-ple su - per - na gratia, Quae tu cre - a-sti   pectora.

Qui Pa - ra - cli - tus di - ce - ris,   Do - num De - i Al - tis - si - mi,

The emphasis was on the sonorous, sensuous aspect of the chant rather than the authoritarian. Sonority means either tone color or, more loosely, rich tone color. A new sensitivity to sonority and melody was perhaps the first sign of Renaissance attitudes toward music.

Having transformed plainchants into "modern" melodies with a more attractive profile, fifteenth-century composers put them not at the bottom of the polyphony but on top, in the soprano, where they could be heard most clearly. And the soprano voice was probably already considered to be the most beautiful.

Early Homophony

The fifteenth century also saw the beginning of composed *homophony*—that is, music in a harmonic texture (see page 35). In the simpler plainchant paraphrases of the time, the melody is often highlighted by an accompaniment that does not really sound polyphonic. Though there are still several polyphonic voices, most of the time their independence vanishes because they move along together and form simple chords.

The result is a plainchant harmonization. Once again the emphasis is on sensuous effect, that of homophony, rather than on the more intellectual process of polyphony.

Guillaume Dufay (c. 1400–1474)

Guillaume Dufay was born and bred in the north of France near Flanders (modern Belgium), a region that supplied the whole of Europe with musicians for many generations. For over twenty-five years he worked in Italy, where he came to know artists and thinkers of the Renaissance and (equally important!) the princely patrons who supported them. His later years were spent in a glow of celebrity at the important French cathedral of Cambrai.

Although Dufay's fame was and is based on relatively long and elaborate pieces—he wrote some of the most important early polyphonic Masses, for example—plainchant harmonizations such as the following make up an appreciable proportion of his output.

GUILLAUME DUFAY
Harmonized hymn, "Veni Creator Spiritus"

This is a homophonic setting of a Gregorian **hymn,** one of the most tuneful categories of Gregorian chant. A Gregorian hymn consists of a short tune sung through many stanzas, followed by an Amen—much like a modern hymn, in fact. Indeed, "Veni Creator Spiritus" ("Come, Holy Spirit") is still found in some modern hymnbooks, with just a few changes from its ancient melody.

Sung on Pentecost (a feast honoring the Holy Spirit), "Veni Creator Spiritus" is in the G (Mixolydian) mode. It contains seven stanzas, but Dufay set only the even-numbered ones to his own music, leaving the others to be chanted Gregorian-style in alternation. This makes it fairly easy to hear how he embellished the plainchant.

His music for stanzas 2, 4, and 6 is the same each time—almost entirely homophonic and quite suave. The top voice presents the hymn tune in a paraphrased version, as shown in the example on the preceding page. The embellishment consists of a few extra notes and extensions, with the free rhythm of Gregorian chant channeled into a graceful triple meter.

"Maistre Guille duFay": the one known portrait of Dufay, from a manuscript of a poem in which he and other early Renaissance composers are praised for their new musical style. Dufay is shown with a small portative (or portable) organ.

TEXT: **Dufay, "Veni Creator Spiritus"**

(STANZA 1: Plainchant)

Veni Creator Spiritus	Come, Holy Spirit, our souls inspire
Mentes tuorum visita:	And lighten with celestial fire;
Imple superna gratia	Thou the anointing spirit art
Quae tu creasti pectora.	Who dost thy sevenfold gifts impart.

(STANZA 2: Dufay's paraphrase)

Qui Paraclitus diceris,	Thy blessed unction from above
Donum Dei Altissimi,	Is comfort, life, and fire of love;
Fons vivus, ignis, caritas,	Enable with perpetual light
Et spiritalis unctio.	The dullness of our blinded sight.

(five more stanzas, of which three are on the recordings)

The Mass

The new treatment of traditional plainchant, as in the technique of paraphrase, shows Renaissance composers taking a relaxed attitude toward medieval authority. The same can be said of their reaction to medieval intricacy, as represented by that most intellectual of musical devices, isorhythm. Fourteenth-century composers such as Machaut had used isorhythm even when writing love songs, but composers now cultivated a much simpler style for their polyphonic songs, or *chansons:* simpler, gentler, and more supple. The modest style of these new chansons was sometimes used for sacred texts, including portions of the Mass.

The rejection of isorhythm did not mean, however, that composers abandoned the technical development of their craft, which had taken such impressive strides from the early days of organum. Rather, such efforts were focused on large-scale musical construction. For the first time, compositions were written to last—and to make sense—over twenty or thirty minutes.

The problem of large-scale construction that fascinated fifteenth-century composers was how to write music that would in some sense unify the **Mass.** As the largest and most important of all Church services, the Mass included some twenty musical items, originally sung in plainchant. By around 1450, the polyphonic Mass had been standardized into a five-section form. Composers now settled on these five sections for their polyphonic settings:

Kyrie	a simple prayer: "Lord have mercy, Christ have mercy"
Gloria	a long hymn: "Glory to God in the highest"
Credo	a recital of the Christian's list of beliefs, beginning
	"I believe in one God, the Father almighty"
Sanctus	another hymn: "Holy, holy, holy, Lord God of hosts"
Agnus Dei	another prayer: "Lamb of God . . . have mercy upon us"

The Mass has retained this five-section form down to the present day, in settings by Palestrina, Bach, Haydn, Schubert, Stravinsky, and many others.

In the late Middle Ages and the early Renaissance, the Virgin Mary was the subject of intense veneration. Countless plainchants, paintings, and sculptures were made to honor her. Childlike, serene, lost in her own thoughts, the Virgin by the German painter Stefan Lochner (1400–1451) seems almost oblivious to Jesus and even to God—and also, no doubt, to the music played for her by the baby angels.

The five sections of the Mass are very different in the length of their texts, they serve different liturgical functions, and they come at widely separated times in the actual service. Various musical schemes were invented to unify the sections. Similar music could be used to signal the beginning of all five movements, for example, or all the movements could paraphrase the same Gregorian chant.

So large and complex a structure presented composers with a challenge, and they took this up in a spirit of inventiveness and ambition characteristic of the Renaissance. What the symphony was to nineteenth-century composers and their audiences, the Mass was to their fifteenth-century counterparts: a brilliant, monumental test of artistic prowess.

2 The "High Renaissance" Style

Around 1500 a new style emerged for Masses, motets, and chansons that was to hold sway for much of the sixteenth century. The chief characteristic of this "High Renaissance" musical style was a careful blend of two vocal techniques, *imitative counterpoint* and *homophony* (see pages 34 and 35).

Imitation

Most polyphony at the beginning of the fifteenth century was nonimitative; most polyphony at the end of the century was imitative. This remarkable change is due partly to the fact that imitative polyphony, or imitation, reflects the ideals of moderation and balance that also characterize the visual arts of the High Renaissance. In the Raphael Madonna on page 57, the calm, dignified repose expressed by the figures and faces is as striking as the beautiful balance among all the pictorial elements.

By its very nature, imitative texture depends on a calm, smooth balance among multiple voice parts. A first voice begins with a motive (see page 32) specifically fashioned for the text being set. Soon other voices enter, one by one, singing the same motive and words, but at different pitch levels; meanwhile the earlier voices continue with new melodies, contrived to fit in with the later voices without swamping them. Each voice has a genuinely melodic quality, and all the melodies are drawn from a single source. None is mere accompaniment or "filler," and none predominates for very long.

We can get an impression of the equilibrium of imitative polyphony from its look on the page, even without reading the music exactly. The following excerpt is from the score of Josquin Desprez's *Pange lingua* Mass:

Homophony

Almost all polyphony involves some chords, as a product of its simultaneously sounding melodies. But in the music of Machaut, for example, the chords are more of a by-product. Late medieval composers concentrated on the "horizontal" aspects of texture at the expense of "vertical" ones, delighting in the separateness of their different voice parts. Chordal sonority was a secondary consideration.

A major achievement of the High Renaissance style was to create a rich chordal quality out of polyphonic lines that still maintain a quiet sense of independence. Composers also used pure homophony—passages of "block chord" writing. Though this was still not too common around 1500, composers fully understood the value of homophony both as a contrast to imitative texture and as an expressive resource in its own right.

Other Characteristics

In tone color, the ideal at this time becomes *a cappella* performance—that is, performance by voices alone. Tempo and dynamics are relatively constant factors. The rhythm is fluid, devoid of sharp accents, and shifting unobtrusively all the time, so that the meter is often obscured. The melodies never go very high or very low in any one voice; the ups and downs are carefully balanced. This music rarely settles into the easy swing of a dance rhythm or into the clear patterns of an actual tune.

Music in the High Renaissance style can sometimes strike modern listeners as vague, but if we listen more closely—and always listen to the words

A Kyrie from a dazzling illuminated manuscript book of Mass music. Did singers actually sing from such precious books? The man who commissioned the production of this book is shown here praying with the help of an angel, who below seems to be giving a seal of approval to the family arms.

THOMAS WEELKES (c. 1575–1623)   6 Cassette 1A-11/6 CD 1-11
Madrigal, "As Vesta Was from Latmos Hill Descending" (1601)

Thomas Weelkes never rose beyond the position of provincial cathedral organist-choirmaster; in fact, he had trouble keeping even that post in later life, when the cathedral records assert that he became "noted and found for a common drunckard and notorious swearer and blasphemer." Although he is not a major figure, as are the other composers treated in this unit, he is one of the best composers of madrigals in English.

Written in better days, Weelkes's contribution to *The Triumphs of Oriana* is a fine example of a madrigal of the lighter kind. (Weelkes also wrote serious and melancholy madrigals.) After listening to the music of Josquin and Palestrina, our first impression of "Vesta" is of the sheer exuberant brightness of the musical style. Simple rhythms, clear harmonies, crisp melodic motives—all look forward to music of the Baroque era and beyond. This music has a modern feel about it.

The next thing likely to impress the listener is the elegance and liveliness with which the words are declaimed. We have already stressed the importance of declamation in the Renaissance composers' program of attention to verbal texts. Weelkes nearly always has his words sung in rhythms that would seem quite natural if the words were spoken, as shown at the right (where — stands for a long syllable, ◡ for a short one). The declamation is never less than accurate, and it is sometimes expressive: the rhythms make the words seem imposing in the second phrase shown, dainty in the third.

Leav-ing their God-dess all a-lone

Then sang the shep-herds and nymphs of Di-a-na

To whom Di-a-na's dar-lings

As for the word painting, that can be shown in a tabular form. It is very high spirited and often amusing:

HIGH NOTES		FAST DOWNWARD SCALE
	As Vesta was from Latmos hill descending	FAST UPWARD SCALES
	She spied a maiden Queen the same ascending,	
	Attended on by all the shepherds' swain;	FAST DOWNWARD SCALE AGAIN
TWO VOICES, THEN THREE VOICES	To whom Diana's darlings came running down amain	FULL CHOIR
MINOR MODE, SLOW (VESTA ABANDONED)	First two by two, then three by three together	ONE VOICE (SOPRANO) ALONE
	Leaving their Goddess all alone, hasted thither;	
	And mingling with the shepherds of her train,	
	With mirthful tunes her presence did entertain.	
LONGA IN THE BASS VOICE	Then sang the shepherds and nymphs of Diana:	EFFECT OF SPONTANEOUS, IRREGULAR CHEERING
	Long live fair Oriana!	

(The "maiden Queen" is Elizabeth, and "Diana's darlings" are the Vestal Virgins, priestesses of Vesta, the Roman goddess of hearth and home. The archaic word *amain* means "at full speed.")

This brilliant six-part madrigal uses two sopranos, alto, two tenors, and bass. Weelkes makes particularly good use of this group in his extended imitative setting of the poem's last line. Here we can easily imagine many more than six loyal voices endlessly cheering their Queen in a spontaneous, irregular way, one after another. Shakespeare and his contemporaries, Weelkes among them, were very fond of puns. Weelkes has the word "long" sung by the bass voice on a note four times the duration of a whole note—a note whose Latin name was *longa*.

Queen Elizabeth I playing the lute. Her personal enthusiasm for music was a crucial factor in the flowering of music during her reign.

5 Instrumental Music: Early Developments

The best sixteenth-century composers concentrated almost entirely on vocal genres, on music with words. Except for the English master William Byrd, none of them devoted much attention to music for instruments alone. We have spoken above of the Renaissance preoccupation with expression in music, expression through the association of music with words.

Nevertheless, instruments and music for instruments developed significantly during this period. The first violins and harpsichords date from the sixteenth century; also, the lute—a guitarlike instrument that was perhaps the most popular of all at the time—was perfected, as were many other instruments. Instrumental music was to become one of the great glories of the Baroque era, and the basis for this was laid in the late Renaissance.

Around 1500, hardly any compositions were written specifically for instruments. Instrumentalists sometimes played along with singers in vocal music, and sometimes they performed vocal genres, such as the chanson and the motet, by themselves. The principal vocal genre after 1550, however, the madrigal, would not have made much sense performed without its words. And by this time, new genres had been developed for instrumental performance.

Renaissance Dances

The most widespread of Renaissance instrumental genres was the dance, a reflection of the great popularity of dancing at the time.

Many dance types are described meticulously in sixteenth-century instruction books—the steps themselves, and also their order or sequence. (In this regard, old dances were closer to square dances than to some modern social dancing, where there is no fixed order for steps or movements.) One of the most popular was the **pavane** (pronounced pa-*van*), a solemn dance in duple meter, with the participants stepping and stopping formally. The pavane was usually paired with the triple-meter **galliard.** Simpler, less formal Renaissance dance types include the Italian saltarello, the English jig, and the French branle—whose name is related to our word *brawl*.

Conforming to the dance steps, dance music was written in easy-to-follow phrases, almost always four to eight bars long. Ending with especially clear cadences, the phrases were each played twice in succession to produce forms such as **A A B B** or **A A B B C C.**

6 Cassette 1A-12, 13/6 CD
1-12, 13

ANONYMOUS
Pavane, "Celeste giglio"

In 1600 a Roman dancing master named Fabritio Caroso published a book explaining dance steps and the like. He included a number of dances, including one that he called "Divine Lily." He probably did not compose the music, however; most dances of the time used stock materials, and no doubt Caroso simply transcribed or edited a tune that was common property.

"Divine Lily" is played by a small band consisting of viols and a lute. It is in duple meter. The stately, expressive melody in **A A B B C C** form is furnished with elegant decorations during the second **A, B,** and **C** phrases:

Although the improvised lute part provides a certain amount of polyphony, the meter is kept very clear, and the distinct quality of the cadences ending **A, B,** and **C** makes it easy for the dancers to remember their place in the dance-step sequence. It also makes for easy listening. On our recording, the music fades as this dance is about to run into another, faster one.

The risqué leaps of the volta, as depicted in a French painting of a court ball at the end of the sixteenth century

ANONYMOUS
"Kemp's Jig"

Nobody knows exactly what a jig was, or even whether it had any connection with the later gigue, an important dance of the Baroque era (see page 141). An intriguing suggestion is that the term *jig* was used loosely, as the term *jazz* is a few hundred years later, to designate any kind of fast dance music with a particular swing and lilt to it.

In any case, the piece called "Kemp's Jig" is an attractive and seemingly simple dance in duple time. The original band music has not survived, only an arrangement for lute. The melody is in **A A B B** form, with ornaments on the repeated phrases, once again (that is, on the second **A** and **B**). Our performer plays the whole piece through twice:

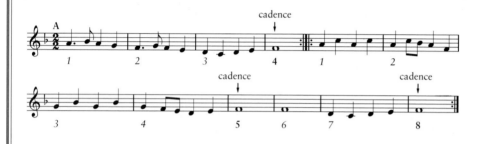

And who was Kemp? Will Kemp was an Elizabethan actor, comedian, and song-and-dance man, immortalized for having played comic roles in Shakespeare, such as Dogberry the Constable in *Much Ado About Nothing*. Kemp specialized in a type of popular dance number that was regularly presented in Elizabethan theaters after the main play. Perhaps "Kemp's Jig" was one of his favorite tunes for these dance entertainments.

Stylized Dance

There is more to say about this "simple" dance, "Kemp's Jig," however. Played on the lute, an instrument that sounds like a soft guitar, it could never have been used for actual dancing. This lute music must have come into existence because an amateur lutenist enjoyed playing popular dances, for his or her own enjoyment or else for playing for others.

An oddity of this particular dance is that in phrase **A**, the cadence—a stopping place (see page 32)—comes after four bars, whereas in phrase **B**, the cadence comes after five. A dancer might be confused, even thrown off by this. The listener, on the other hand, may well enjoy the piquant effect caused by the irregularity in the cadences. It's possible this detail was added by the lutenist, making an arrangement of a prototype jig that was regular in this regard, that was *truly* simple.

Indeed, "Kemp's Jig" illustrates a tendency that will assume more importance later: the tendency to make dance music more and more elaborate, more stylized and "artistic." Composers provided dance music with elements of a more strictly musical interest, such as irregular cadences, subtle phrase lengths, polyphony, and intricate harmonies. This was the first stage of a process that can be called the stylization of dance music.

Another sixteenth-century dance, the torch dance: an etching by the greatest German artist of the Renaissance, Albrecht Dürer (1471–1528). Three of the male dancers hold torches, while three others dance with the women in a circle; soon they will change roles.

Dance stylization was already well established by the end of the sixteenth century. For example, there is a keyboard pavan by William Byrd that includes a strict canon—that is, two polyphonic parts in exact imitation from beginning to end. Pieces of this kind are forerunners of the sophisticated stylized dances of Bach and the symphony minuets of Mozart. While vocal music experiences a sharp break between the Renaissance and Baroque eras, as we shall see, instrumental music was to undergo a steady development.

Chapter 7

The Early Baroque Period

At the end of the sixteenth century, music was undergoing rapid changes at the sophisticated courts and churches of northern Italy. Composers began to write motets, madrigals, and other pieces more directly for effect—with a new simplicity, in some respects, but also with the use of exciting new resources. A new style, the style of the early Baroque period, took hold rapidly all over Italy and in most of the rest of Europe.

1 From Renaissance to Baroque

As we have seen, the madrigal was the most "advanced" form in late Renaissance music. Toward the end of the sixteenth century, the thirst for expression led madrigal composers to increasingly esoteric extremes. All kinds of dissonances and rhythmic contrasts were explored in order to illustrate emotional texts in a more and more exaggerated fashion.

At the same time, a reaction set in *against* the madrigal. In Florence, an influential group of intellectuals attacked the madrigalists' favorite technique, word painting, as artificial and childish. And contrary to what the madrigalists thought, these critics insisted that the many voices of a madrigal ensemble could not focus human feeling or express it strongly. A choir singing counterpoint, they said, could only dilute strong emotions, not concentrate them.

True emotionality could be projected only by a single human agent, an individual, a great singer who would learn from great actors and orators how to move an audience to laughter, anger, or tears. The Florentines developed a new style, a style of solo singing that was half music, half recitation. This led inevitably to the stage: and as we shall see, *opera*, invented in Florence around 1600, became one of the most important and characteristic products of the Baroque imagination.

Music in Venice

Meanwhile, equally sensational developments were taking place in Venice. The "Serene Republic," as Venice called itself, cultivated especially brilliant styles in all the arts—matched, it seems, to the city's dazzling physical appearance. Wealthy and cosmopolitan, Venice produced architects whose flamboyant, varied buildings were constructed from multicolored materials, and painters—the Bellinis, Titian, Tintoretto—who specialized in warm, rich

Venice: a city as colorful as its music

hues. Perhaps, then, it is more than a play on words to describe Venetian music as "colorful."

From the time of Palestrina's *Pope Marcellus* Mass, sixteenth-century composers had often subdivided their choirs into low and high "semichoirs" of three or four voice parts each. The semichoirs would alternate and answer or echo each other. Expanding this technique, Venetian composers would now alternate two, three, or more whole choirs. Homophony crowded out polyphony as full choirs answered one another stereophonically, and seemed to compete throughout entire motets and Masses, coming together for climactic sections of glorious massed sound.

The resources of sonority were exploited even further when sometimes the "choirs" were designated for singers on some parts and instruments on others. Or else whole choirs would be made up of instruments. As the sonorous combinations of Venetian music grew more and more colorful, the stately decorum of the High Renaissance style was forgotten (or left to musical conservatives). Magnificence and extravagance became the new ideals, well suited to the pomp and ceremony that were particularly characteristic of Venice.

Extravagance and Control

Wherever they looked, knowledgeable travelers to Italy around 1600 would have seen that music was bursting out of its traditional forms, styles, and genres. Freedom was the order of the day. But they might have been puzzled to notice a tendency in the other direction as well. Musical form was becoming more rigorously controlled and systematic. As composers sought to make music more untrammeled in one respect, they found they had to organize it more strictly in another, so that listeners would not lose track of what was happening.

The control composers exercised over Baroque form, in other words, was an appropriate response to Baroque extravagance, exaggeration, and emotionality. We shall see rather similar forces and counterforces at other points in musical history later in this book.

GIOVANNI GABRIELI (c. 1555–1612)   6 Cassette 1B-1/6 CD 1-14
Motet, "O magnum mysterium" (published 1615)

The most important composers in Venice were two Gabrielis, Andrea (c. 1510–1586) and his nephew Giovanni. As organists of St. Mark's Cathedral, both of them exploited the special acoustics of that extraordinary building, which still amaze tourists today. By placing choirs of singers and instrumentalists in different choir lofts, they obtained brilliant echo effects that even modern audio equipment cannot recapture.

Giovanni's "O magnum mysterium," the second part of a longer motet, was written for the Christmas season. The text marvels that lowly animals—the ox and the ass—were the first to see the newborn Jesus.

And the music marvels along with the text. Quite in the manner of a madrigal, the exclamation "O" is repeated like a gasp of astonishment. Then incredibly lush chord progressions positively make the head spin, as the words *O magnum mysterium* are repeated to the same music, but pitched higher (that is to say, in sequence: see page 31). A momentary change in the meter—which slips from 4/4 into 6/4—provides a new feeling of majesty, as much as astonishment:

O,   o   ma-gnum my-ster-i - um,   O,   o   ma-gnum my-ster-i - um

As to the texture, what we are aware of at the start of the motet is brass instruments and voices mixed into a sumptuous blend. In fact, Gabrieli is using two large "choirs," each with four instrumental parts and three voice parts, plus organ, but we do not grasp this at first. We do hear solo voices emerge at *sacramentum.* First solo tenors, then boy sopranos echo one another during the line *iacentem in presipio,* where a new rapid figure bounces back and forth from tenors to sopranos to trumpets.

But it is only with the choral *alleluia* section that Gabrieli really unleashes his musical resources. The music moves in quick triple meter, matching the jubilation of repeated *alleluias,* and the two choirs echo back and forth across the sound space in a veritable stereophonic display:

	FAST—triple meter									SLOW—duple meter		
	1 2 3	1 2 3	1 2 3	1 2 3	1 2 3	1 2 3	1 2 3	1 2 3	1 2 3	1 2 3 4	1 2 3 4	1
CHOIR 1	Al--le-	lu--ia,	al-le-lu-	ia;			al-le-lu-	ia,	al-le-lu-	ia: Al- -le-	lu - - - - -	ia
CHOIR 2				Al--le-	lu--ia,	al-le-lu-	ia,	al-le-lu-	ia,	Al- -le-	lu - - - - -	ia

To make a grand conclusion, the choirs come together again. There is another wash of voice-and-brass sonority as the tempo changes to a slow duple meter for a climactic *alleluia*. For yet another *alleluia*, the music adds a solemn extra beat (the meter changes once again):

And for still more emphasis, Gabrieli repeats the entire *alleluia* section, comprising the fast triple-time alternations and the massive slow ending.

Notice the parallel between the beginning and the end of "O magnum mysterium." Similarities include the tempo and meter (slow, changing), the texture (massed choirs), and the musical technique used (sequence). In other words, Gabrieli has imposed organization and control behind the flamboyant chords and solo rhapsodies. Here is a simple example of the combination of extravagance and control in early Baroque music that we discussed above.

TEXT: Giovanni Gabrieli, "O magnum mysterium"

O magnum mysterium,	O, what a great mystery,
et admirabile sacramentum	and what a wonderful sacrament—
ut animalia viderunt Dominum natum	that animals should see the Lord new-born
iacentem in presipio:	lying in the manger
Alleluia, alleluia.	Hallelujah, hallelujah.

2 Style Features of Early Baroque Music

Music from the period of approximately 1600 to 1750 is usually referred to as "baroque," a term originally applied to large pearls of irregular shape. A number of broad stylistic features unify the music of this long period.

Rhythm and Meter

Rhythms become more definite and regular in Baroque music; a single rhythm or similar rhythms can be heard throughout a piece or a major segment of a piece. Compare the subtle, floating rhythms of Renaissance music, changing section by section as the motives change. (Renaissance dance music is an exception, and in the area of dance music there is a direct line from the Renaissance to the Baroque.)

Related to this new regularity of rhythm is a new acceptance of meter. One technical feature tells the story: bar lines begin to be used for the first time in music history. This means that music's meter is systematically in evidence, rather than being downplayed as it was in the Renaissance. The strong beats are emphasized by certain instruments, playing in a clear, decisive way. All this is conspicuous enough in Gabrieli's motet "O magnum mysterium."

Texture: Basso Continuo

Some early Baroque music is homophonic and some is polyphonic, but both textures are enriched by a feature unique to the period, the **basso continuo.**

As in a Renaissance score, in a Baroque score the bass line is performed by bass voices or low instruments such as cellos or bassoons. But the bass part in Baroque music is also played by an organ, harpsichord, or other chord instrument. This instrument not only reinforces the bass line, it also adds chords continuously (hence the term *continuo*) to go with it. The basso continuo—or just "continuo"—has the double effect of clarifying the harmony and of making the texture bind or jell.

One can see how this device reflects the growing reliance of Baroque music on harmony (already clear from Gabrieli's motet). In the early days, the continuo was simply the bass line of the polyphony reinforced by chords; but later the continuo with its chords was mapped out first, and the polyphony adjusted to it. Baroque polyphony, in other words, has systematic harmonic underpinnings.

This fact is dramatized by a characteristic Baroque form, the **ground bass.** This is music constructed literally from the bottom up. In ground bass form, the bass instruments play a single short figure many times, generating the same set of repeated harmonies (played by the continuo chord instruments). Above this ground bass, upper instruments or voices play (or improvise) different melodies or virtuoso passages, all adjusted to the harmonies determined by the bass.

Baroque ground bass compositions discussed in this book are "Dido's Lament" from the opera *Dido and Aeneas* by Henry Purcell (page 102) and Bach's great Passacaglia for organ (page 126). We shall also see a nineteenth-century reinterpretation of the form in the Fourth Symphony of Johannes Brahms (page 311).

A ground bass
(the Pachelbel Canon)

= repeated
many times

Functional Harmony

In view of these new techniques, it is not surprising that the art of harmony evolved rapidly at this time. Whereas Renaissance music had still used the medieval modes, although with important modifications, Baroque musicians developed the modern major/minor system. Chords became standardized, and the feeling of tonality in Baroque music—the feeling of centrality around a tonic or "home" pitch—grew much stronger than in music of the Renaissance.

Composers also developed a new way of handling the chords so that their interrelation was felt to be more logical, or at least more coherent. Each chord now assumed a special role, or function, in relation to the tonic chord (the chord on the "home" pitch). Thus when one chord follows another in Baroque music, it does so in a newly satisfactory, predictable, and purposeful way. "Functional" harmony, in this sense, could also be used as a way of organizing large-scale pieces of music, as we shall see later.

In a Baroque composition, compared with one from the sixteenth century, the chords seem to be going where we expect them to—and one feels that the chords determine the sense, the direction, or the purpose of the piece as a whole. Harmonies no longer seem to wander, detour, hesitate, or evaporate. With the introduction of the important resource of functional harmony, Baroque music brings us firmly to the familiar, to the threshold of modern music.

A torchlight concert in a German town square. The harpsichord continuo is at the center of the action. Notice the big music stands or racks, and the two timpani sunk in a panel, like a double sink.

3 Opera

Opera—drama presented in music, with the characters singing instead of speaking—is often called the most characteristic art form of the Baroque period. For Baroque opera combined many different arts: not only music, drama, and poetry, but also dancing and highly elaborate scene design. Set designers developed incredibly ingenious machines to portray gods descending to earth, shipwrecks, volcanos, and all kinds of natural and supernatural phenomena. Designers often received top billing, ahead of the composers.

The early Florentine operas were court entertainments put on to celebrate royal weddings and the like. But an important step was taken in 1637 with the opening of the first public opera theater. First in Venice and then in the whole of Italy, opera soon became the leading form of entertainment. By the end of the century, seven opera houses in Venice fulfilled much the same social function as movie theaters in a comparable modern city (around 145,000 people).

Opera was a perfect answer to the general desire in the early Baroque era for individual emotionalism. Opera provided a stage on which the single individual could step forward to express his or her feelings in the most direct and powerful fashion. Indeed, composers felt a need to relieve the constant emotional pressure exerted on their characters by the ever-changing dramatic action. They had to contrive moments of relaxation, and this led to a standard dualism that has been with opera ever since. This dualism between tension and repose reflects that other Baroque dualism, between freedom and strictness, extravagance and control.

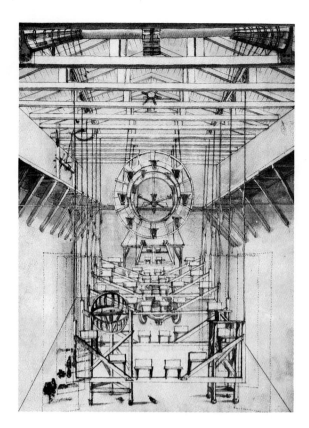

Stage designers of Baroque opera specialized in moving sets for their most dazzling effects. Shown here is the machinery for one such set and a drawing of the intended realization.

Recitative

Recitative (pronounced *re-sih-ta-téev*), from the Italian word for "recitation," is the technique of declaiming words musically in a heightened, theatrical manner. The singing voice closely follows the free rhythm of highly emotional speech; it mirrors and exaggerates the natural ups and down that occur as an actor raises his or her voice at a question, lowers it in an "aside," or cries out in distress. The accompaniment is usually kept to a minimum, so that the singer-actor can interpret the dialogue or the action as spontaneously as possible, and so that all the words can be heard clearly.

Recitative—the "free" side of the operatic dualism—is used for plot action, dialogue, and other situations in the drama where it is particularly important for the words to be brought out. On the other hand, where spoken drama would call for soliloquies or meditations, opera uses arias.

Aria

An **aria** is an extended piece for solo singer that has much more musical elaboration and coherence than a passage of recitative. The vocal part is more melodic, and typically the accompaniment includes the entire orchestra. Here the singer-actor mulls over his or her feelings at some leisure, instead of reacting moment by moment, as in recitative. Emotion is controlled and "frozen" into a tableau. Paradoxically, when the music gets more elaborate, the emotion stands still.

Louis XIV's palace of Versailles, with a procession of carriages arriving in the great courtyard. Note the formal gardens and canal.

mate stimulated by science had a significant effect on the art and the music we call Baroque.

Absolutism and science were just two of a number of vital currents that defined life in the seventeenth and early eighteenth centuries. The result was an interesting dualism that can be traced throughout Baroque art: a dualism of pomp and extravagance on the one hand, system and calculation on the other. The same dualism can be traced in Baroque music.

Art and Absolutism

Though Europe had long known royalty who practiced the arts of peace as well as the arts of war, patronage of the arts assumed new proportions in the Baroque era. The artistic glories of the Italian Renaissance had been supported by great magnates, such as the Medici family in Florence, who sought to add luster to the city-states they ruled. But never before the seventeenth century did any one state loom as large in the European firmament as did France under Louis XIV (1638–1715), the so-called Sun King.

Louis XIV, by the great Italian Baroque sculptor and architect Gianlorenzo Bernini (1598–1680)

All of French life orbited around the royal court, like planets, comets, and cosmic dust in the solar system. Pomp and ceremony were carried to extreme lengths: the king's *levée*—his getting-up-in-the-morning rite— involved dozens of functionaries and routines lasting two hours. Artists, architects, and musicians were supported lavishly, so long as their work symbolized the majesty of the state (and the state, in Louis's famous remark, "is me"—"l'état, c'est moi").

Baroque ceiling painting by
Giovanni Battista Tiepolo
(1696–1770)

The influence of this monarch and his image extended far beyond France, for other European rulers envied his absolute rule and did everything they could to match it. If they could not match his actual power, at least they sought to emulate his style. Especially in Germany—which was not a unified country, like France, but a patchwork of several hundred political units—dukes and princes vied with one another in patronizing artists who were to build, paint, and sing their glory. Artistic life in Europe was kept alive for many generations by the patronage of these nobles.

The splendor of much Baroque art stems from this sociological function. Art was to impress, even to stupefy. Thus Louis XIV built the most enormous palace in history, Versailles, outside of Paris. Versailles has over thirteen hundred rooms, including the eighty-yard-long Hall of Mirrors, and great formal gardens extending for miles. Many nobles and prelates built little imitation-Versailles palaces, among them the Archbishop of Würzburg, whose splendid residence was built during Bach's lifetime. The palace was decorated by the Venetian artist Giovanni Battista Tiepolo (1696–1770), a master of Baroque ceiling painting.

Looking up at the ceiling shown on this page, one is dazzled by figures in excited motion, caught up in great gusts of wind that propel them out of the architectural space.

The Music of Absolutism

Just as painting could glorify rulers through color and designs extending through space, music could glorify by sound extending through time. The nobility demanded squads of horn players for their ceremonial hunts, trumpeters for their battles, and orchestras for balls and entertainments. They required smaller groups of musicians for *Tafelmusik* ("table music") to accompany their lengthy banquets. And one musical genre was taken over as the specialty of absolutism: opera.

Opera today is an expensive entertainment in which a drama is presented with music and, usually, lavish stage spectacle. So it was in the Baroque era. The amazing stage set shown below was created by a member of the Bibiena family, foremost set designers of the time, for a German court opera. It conveys the majestic heights and distances of an ideal Baroque palace by means of perspective, though it was actually quite shallow. The figures gesture grandly, but they are dwarfed by pasteboard architecture that seems to whirl as dizzily as does the painted architecture on Tiepolo's ceiling.

One aspect of Baroque opera is unlike opera today: the dramatic subjects were generally allegorical tributes to the glory and virtue of those who paid for them. In one favorite Baroque opera story, for example, the Roman Emperor Titus survives a complicated plot on his life and then magnanimously forgives the plotters. This story was set to music by dozens of different court composers. It told courtiers that if they opposed their king, he might well excuse them out of the godlike goodness of his heart (for he claimed to rule by divine right). But it also reminded them that he was an absolute ruler—a modern Roman tyrant—who could do exactly the reverse if he pleased. Operas flattered princes while at the same time stressing their power and, not incidentally, their wealth.

Art and Theatricality

Opera was invented in Italy around the year 1600. Indeed, opera counts as Italy's great contribution to the seventeenth century's golden age of the theater. This century saw Shakespeare and his followers in England, Corneille and Racine in France, and Lope de Vega and Calderón in Spain.

Design for an opera stage set by G. G. Bibiena. This astonishing scene was intended for an opera at the Dresden court.

Madonna of the Pilgrims, by Michelangelo da Caravaggio (1565–1609), one of the earliest and most influential of Baroque painters

The very term *theatrical* suggests some of the extravagance and exaggeration we associate with the Baroque. But the theater is first and foremost a place where strong emotion is on display, and it was this that compelled the Baroque fascination with the theater. The emotionality that we generally sense in Baroque art has a theatrical quality; this is true even of much Baroque painting. Compare Raphael's calm Renaissance Madonna on page 57 with the early Baroque Madonna by Caravaggio. The pilgrim at the front is almost falling forward; the Virgin, deeply moved, cranes her neck in response to him. The whole dramatic scene is highlighted by sharply focused, stagey illumination.

Science and the Arts

All this may seem some distance away from the observatories of Galileo and Kepler, and the laboratories where Harvey discovered the circulation of the blood and Leeuwenhoek first viewed microorganisms through a microscope. And indeed, the scientific temper of the time had its most obvious effect on artists who were outside the realm of absolutism. The Dutch were citizens of free cities, not subjects of despotic kings. In Jan Vermeer's painting of his own city, Delft, the incredibly precise depiction of detail reflects the new interest in scientific observation. The painter's analysis of light is worthy of Huygens and Newton, fathers of the science of optics. There is something scientific, too, in the serene objectivity of this scene.

View of Delft, by Jan
Vermeer (1632–1675)

Man's control over nature is also symbolized by Baroque formal gardens.
Today, landscape architecture is not usually regarded as one of the major arts,
but it was very important in the age of the Baroque palace. Baroque gardens
regulate nature strictly according to geometrical plans. Bushes are clipped,
lawns tailored, streams channeled, and all is dominated by severe rows of
classical statuary. Such gardens spell out the new vision of nature brought to
heel by human reason and calculation.

Below the surface, furthermore, science is at work in even the most grandiose and stupefying of Baroque artistic efforts. The extraordinary perspective of Tiepolo's ceiling picture or Bibiena's stage set depends on the
application of very sophisticated geometrical knowledge. This dual influence
of extravagance and scientism, of the splendid and the schematic, can also be
traced in Baroque music.

Formal gardens in front of
the Nymphenburg Palace,
outside Munich—one of
the many Baroque palaces
inspired by Versailles

The Age of Absolutism and the Age of Science converge: Louis XIV pays a ceremonial visit to the Academy of Sciences, which he founded in 1666.

Science and Music

Various aspects of Baroque music reflect the new scientific attitudes that developed in the seventeenth century. Scales were tuned more precisely than ever before, so that for the first time all possible keys were available to composers. Their interest in exploring this resource is evident from collections of pieces in all the twenty-four major and minor keys, notably Bach's *Well-Tempered Clavier*. Harmony was systematized so that chords followed one another in a more logical and functional way.

Regularity became the ideal in rhythm, and in musical form—the distribution of sections of music in time—we find a tendency toward clearly ordered, even schematic plans. Whether consciously or not, composers seem to have viewed musical time in a quasi-scientific way, dividing it up and filling it systematically, almost in the spirit of the landscape architects who devised Baroque formal gardens.

In the important matter of musical expression, too, science was a powerful influence. Starting with the philosopher-mathematician René Descartes, thinkers applied the new rational methods to the analysis and classification of human emotions. It had always been felt that music has a special power to express and arouse emotions. Now it seemed that there was a basis for systematizing—and hence maximizing—this power.

Thus scientifically inclined music theorists compiled checklists of musical devices and techniques corresponding to each of the emotions. Grief, for example, was projected with a specific kind of melodic motive and a specific kind of rhythm—even with a specific key. By working steadily with these devices and saturating their pieces with them, composers believed they could achieve the maximum musical expressivity.

The emotions of Hope and Fear, as represented in a Baroque scientific treatise. Like composers of the time, the artist felt that feelings could be isolated and depicted in the abstract.

2 Musical Life in the Early Eighteenth Century

The eighteenth century was a great age for the crafts—the age of Chippendale in furniture making, Wedgwood in pottery, the Silbermanns in organ building, to name just a few. Though attitudes were changing, composing music was also regarded as a craft. The Romantic idea of the composer—the lonely genius working over each masterpiece as a long labor of love expressing an individual personality—was still far in the future. Baroque composers were more likely to think of themselves as servants with masters to satisfy. They were artisans with jobs, rather than artists with a calling, and they produced music on demand to fill a particular requirement.

This is why many Baroque pieces seem relatively anonymous, as it were. They are not so much unique masterpieces as entirely satisfactory examples of their style and genre, of which there are many other equally satisfactory examples.

There were three main institutions where composers could make a living by practicing their craft. In order of increasing glamour, these were the church, the court, and the opera house.

> *The church.* In the larger town churches, monasteries, and cathedrals of the Baroque era, the general assumption was that the organists or choirmasters would compose their own music, as well as play and conduct. Organists had to improvise or write out music to accompany solemn places in the ritual, and play long pieces to see the congregation out at the end of the service.

At the larger churches, both Catholic and Protestant, music for chorus and instruments was in demand for important occasions, such as special saints' days, and the ceremonial installation of new bishops. The musicians were also in charge of the education of the choirboys who sang in their choirs.

> *The court.* Under the patronage of kings or members of the lesser nobility, a musician was employed on the same terms as a court painter, a master of the hunt, or a head chef. Though musicians had to work entirely at the whim of their masters, they could nevertheless count on a fairly secure existence and a steady demand for their services.

Naturally, conditions varied from court to court, depending on the ruler's taste. For some, music was a good deal less interesting than hunting or banqueting. Others could not have enough of it. Frederick the Great of Prussia was an enthusiastic amateur flutist, so at his court concertos and sonatas for flute were composed at an especially healthy rate.

Court musicians kept in better touch with musical developments than church musicians, since they were required to travel with their employer. There were extended trips, sometimes, to major cities where diplomacy was eased along by the music they composed for the occasion.

> *The opera house.* Although many opera houses were attached to courts, others were maintained by entrepreneurs in major cities. (As a regular institution, the public opera house existed before the public concert hall, which in the Baroque era was still a thing of the future.) Audiences were alert to the most exciting new singers, and the composer's job was at least partly to keep the singers well supplied with music that showed off their talents. Composers traditionally conducted their own operas, sitting at the harpsichord.

The revival of an older opera—usually because a favorite singer liked his or her part in it—was nearly always the occasion for massive recomposition, because another singer might want *her* part redone too. If the opera's original

A Baroque opera performance (Turin, 1740). The stage set represents a great palace hall; the characters are striking various extravagant attitudes. Clearly visible are the orchestra, a boy selling oranges, and a security guard.

composer had moved to the next town, other musicians would have no hesitation about rewriting (or replacing) the music. It was an exciting, unpredictable life, promising great rewards as well as ignominious rejections.

The life stories of the two greatest composers of the late Baroque period show a good deal about the interaction between musicians, their patrons, and the institutions that required music. Johann Sebastian Bach labored as a church organist, a court musician, and then a major composer-administrator for the Lutheran Church. George Frideric Handel, who also had a court position, became a leading opera composer and opera promoter. Their biographies are given on pages 128 and 149.

3   The Style of Late Baroque Music

If any one characteristic can be singled out as central to the music of the late Baroque period, it would be its thorough, methodical quality. After listening to a Baroque piece carefully from beginning to end, we may be surprised to realize, first, how soon all the basic material is set forth, and second, how much of the music after that consists of inspired repetition and variation. It is as though the composers had set out with some enthusiasm to draw their material out to the maximum extent and wring it dry.

This does not mean that Baroque music is of merely technical interest and therefore unemotional or inexpressive. Quite the reverse: when applied to the depiction of feeling, Baroque thoroughness could lead to impressive emotional intensities, as we shall soon see. Indeed, the expressivity of Baroque music (as of any other kind of music) depends on its technical features: its rhythm, dynamics, melody, texture, tone color, and musical form.

Rhythm

Perhaps the chief attraction of late Baroque music is its rhythmic vitality. This vitality builds subtly on very methodical principles. A single rhythm or closely similar rhythms may be heard continuously throughout a whole piece or a major section of a piece. The meter nearly always stands out, emphasized by certain instruments playing in a clear, decisive way. Most characteristic of these "marking-time" instruments is the busy, crisp harpsichord.

Baroque music is brimming with energy, then, and the energy is channeled into a highly regular, determined sort of motion. Attentive listening will also reveal another aspect of regularity in the steady *harmonic rhythm*—that is, a Baroque piece tends to change chords at every measure, every beat, or at some other set interval. (This must not be taken absolutely literally, but it is a fair statement of the tendency.)

Dynamics

Another relatively steady feature of Baroque music is dynamics. Composers rarely used loud and soft indications (***f*** and ***p***) in their scores, and once a dynamic was chosen or set, it remained at about the same level for the whole section—sometimes even for the whole composition.

Neither in the Baroque period nor in any other, however, have performers played or sung music at an absolutely dead level of dynamics. Violinists and other instrumentalists made expressive changes in dynamics to bring out rhythmic accents, and singers certainly sang high notes louder than low ones. But composers did not go much beyond natural variations of these kinds. Gradual buildups from soft to loud, and the like, were not used.

Tone Color

Tone color in the Baroque period presents something of a contradiction. The early part of the period was marked by a new sensitivity to sonority; at the end of it, Handel laced his operas with highly inventive orchestration, Bach wrote music for the flute that revealed a special sensitivity to its sound, and a whole school of French composers developed the sonorous possibilities of the harpsichord remarkably. There are distinctive and attractive "Baroque sounds" that are not met with in other periods: the virtuoso recorder, the bright Baroque organ, the ever-present harpsichord, and the "festive" orchestra featuring high trumpets and drums.

Eighteenth-century instruments

On the other hand, a significant amount of music was written to allow for multiple or alternative performing forces. Thus it was a regular practice to designate music for harpsichord *or* organ, for violin *or* oboe *or* flute. Bach wrote a sonata for two flutes and continuo and rewrote it as a sonata for viola da gamba (a cello-like instrument) and harpsichord. Handel took solo arias and duets and rewrote them as choruses for his oratorio *Messiah*. In the last analysis, then, it seems the original tone color was often not critical.

For this very reason, incidentally, Baroque music has proved to be highly adaptable to various kinds of arrangements in later centuries. Bach has been arranged for synthesizer, jazz combo, symphony orchestra, and string quartet. Purists have a point when they complain that the original composers never dreamed of these tone colors, and would probably have wakened in a cold sweat if they had. Yet the fact that the process is possible at all, without destroying the music entirely, shows that tone color was secondary in the Baroque composer's scheme of things.

The Baroque Orchestra

The core of the Baroque orchestra was a group of instruments of the violin family. The orchestra maintained by Louis XIV in the late seventeenth century was called "The Twenty-Four Violins of the King"; it consisted of six

In the Baroque era, before there were concert halls, public music making often took place in taverns. The singers and small orchestra are grouped around the continuo harpsichord; a cello and a bassoon are playing the continuo bass line.

violins, twelve violas, and six cellos. A great deal of Baroque music in Louis's time and later was written for such an orchestra or a similar one—what would today be called a "string orchestra": violins, violas, cellos, and one or two bass viols.

To this was added a keyboard instrument—generally the harpsichord in secular music and the organ in church music.

Woodwinds and brass instruments were sometimes added to the string orchestra, too, but there was no fixed complement, as was to be the case later. For special occasions of a festive nature—Christmas music ordered by a great cathedral, for example, or a piece celebrating a military victory—composers would augment the "basic Baroque orchestra" with trumpets or French horns, timpani, and oboes and/or flutes. This "festive" Baroque orchestra has a particularly grand, open, and brilliant sound.

THE BASIC BAROQUE ORCHESTRA
as in Corelli's Concerto Grosso in D (page 105)

STRINGS	KEYBOARD
Violins (divided into two groups, called violins 1 and violins 2)	Harpsichord or organ
Violas	
Cellos	
Bass viol (playing the same music as the cellos, an octave lower)	

THE FESTIVE BAROQUE ORCHESTRA
as in Bach's Orchestral Suite in D (page 143)

STRINGS	WOODWINDS	BRASS	PERCUSSION	KEYBOARD
Violins 1	2 Oboes	3 Trumpets	2 Timpani (kettledrums)	Harpsichord
Violins 2				
Violas				
Cellos				
Bass viol				

Melody

Baroque melody tends toward complexity. Composers like to push melodies to the very limits of ornateness and luxurance. As a rule, the range of Baroque melodies is extended; they use many different rhythmic note values; they twist and turn intricately and elegantly as they reach high and low. It can be maintained that the art of melody reached a high point in the late Baroque era, a point that has never been equaled since.

These long, intricate melodies, with their wealth of "decorations" added to the main direction of the line, are not easy to sing, however. They hardly ever fall into any simple pattern resembling a tune. Even their appearance on the page seems to tell the story:

Not all melodies of the time are as ornate as this one, and some, such as the simpler Baroque dances, are exceptions to the rule. On the other hand, the most highly prized art of the elite musicians of the era, the opera singers, was improvising melodic decorations in the arias they sang night after night in the theater.

An easily recognized feature of Baroque melodies is their frequent use of sequence (see page 31; a sequence is shaded on the melody above). Baroque melodies repeatedly catch hold of a motive or some longer figure and repeat it at several pitch levels. Sequences provide Baroque music with one of its most effective means of forward motion.

Texture

The standard texture of Baroque music is polyphonic (or contrapuntal). Baroque polyphony is at its most impressive in large-scale pieces, which spin a web of contrapuntal lines filling every nook and cranny of musical space-time. While cellos, bass viols, bassoons, and organ pedals play the lowest line, the other string instruments stake out their places in the middle, with oboes and flutes above them and the trumpets piercing their way up into the very highest reaches of the sound universe. The density achieved in this way is doubly impressive because all the sounds feel alive—alive because they are in motion, because they are all parts of moving contrapuntal lines.

Again, some exceptions should be noted to the standard polyphonic texture of Baroque music. Such are the homophonic orchestra sections (called *ritornellos*) in the concerto grosso, and Bach's wonderfully expressive *chorales*, or hymn harmonizations (see page 155). But it is no accident that these textures appear *within pieces that feature polyphony elsewhere.* Typically, the concerto ritornello alternates with the polyphonic texture of the solo-instrument passages. Bach's chorale harmonizations come at the end of long church cantatas, where they have the effect of calming or settling the complex polyphony of the preceding music.

The Continuo

Yet all this polyphony is supported by a solid scaffold that is harmonic. The central importance of harmony in Baroque music appears in the universal practice of *basso continuo,* or just **continuo.**

The continuo is a bass part (the lowest part in polyphonic music) that is always linked to a series of chords. The term *continuo,* which indicates that the chords run continuously throughout the piece, may also be applied to the performer. Baroque compositions generally include in their scoring a harpsichord or an organ on which the continuo player plays simple chords while the other instruments are playing intricate melodies. The player's left hand doubles the bass part.

The *general* form of the chords is indicated by a numerical shorthand below the basso continuo notes. But the *specific* form of the chords is left to the player, who has to engage in a certain amount of improvisation in order to "realize" the continuo. Another name for continuo, the term **figured bass,** stems from this numerical shorthand.

Continuo chords provide the basic harmonic framework against which the contrapuntal lines of Baroque music trace their airy patterns. Under the influence of the continuo, Baroque texture may be described as "polarized" —a "polarity of voices" between a strong bass and a clear, high (soprano) range, the domain of the melody. Less clearly defined is a middle space containing the improvised chords. In Baroque works on the largest scale, this space is also filled in by polyphonic lines drawn from the median range of the orchestra and chorus, such as violas, tenors, and altos. In more modest works a characteristic texture is a spare, hollow one: one or two high instruments (violins, flutes) or voices, a bass instrument, and subsidiary chord improvisation in the middle.

Baroque music is usually easily identified by the presence of the continuo —by the continuous but discreet sound of the harpsichord or organ playing continuo chords in the background. Continuo texture is basic to Baroque musical thought; indeed, the Baroque era in music used to be called the "basso continuo era," not a bad appellation.

Continuo part

played:

HARPSICHORD

or

etc.

Musical Form

Musical forms are clearer and more regular in the Baroque period than in most other historical periods. Two factors that appear to have contributed to this, one of them social, the other intellectual, were mentioned earlier.

The social factor is the patronage system, whereby the court and the church demanded a large amount of music and expected it to be produced in a hurry, almost as soon as it was ordered. Therefore composers needed to rely on formulas that could be applied quickly and efficiently. What is amazing about the church cantatas that Bach wrote at Leipzig, one a week, is how imaginatively he varied the standard forms for the various components of a cantata. But it was very helpful—in fact, it was absolutely necessary—for him to have those standard forms there as a point of departure.

The other factor is the scientific temper of the age, which affected composers only indirectly, but affected them nonetheless. One can detect the composer's ambition to "map" the whole range of a piece of music, and to fill it in systematically, in an orderly, logical, quasi-scientific way. This ambition seems to have been based on the conviction that musical time could be encompassed and controlled at man's will, an attitude similar to that of scientists, philosophers, and craftsmen of the time.

Musical form involves contrasts, as well as repetitions. Just as Baroque composers tended to minimize sharp contrasts in rhythm and dynamics, they also preferred not to incorporate sharply contrasting themes in their pieces and play them off against one another. (To be sure, contrast is a relative matter—all music beyond a single unvarying pitch has *some* contrast—but music of this period employs less contrast than that of most others.) In extending music through time, Baroque composers preferred to work in a seamless, single-minded manner.

Where they did work to achieve contrast was *between* musical pieces, movements, or large sections of music, not so much *within* them. There are extreme contrasts in feeling (and in technique) between the successive movements of Bach's *Brandenburg* Concerto No. 5, for example, as we shall see in Chapter 9.

4 The Emotional World of Baroque Music

All music, it seems safe to say, is deeply involved with emotion. But in the music of different cultures, and also in the music of different historical eras within a single culture, the nature of that involvement can be very different. The emotional effect of Baroque music strikes the modern listener as very powerful and yet, in a curious way, also impersonal. Baroque composers believed firmly that music could and should mirror a wide range of human feelings, or "affects," such as had been analyzed and classified by the scientifically oriented psychology of the day. Composers did not believe, however, that it was their task to mirror feelings of their own. Rather, they tried to isolate and analyze emotions in general and then depict them as consistently as possible.

The exhaustiveness of their musical technique made for a similar exhaustiveness of emotional effect. As the rhythms and themes are repeated, the music intensifies and magnifies a single strong feeling. Sadness in Baroque music is presented as the deepest gloom, calmness as profound quiet, brightness as pomp and splendor, happiness as unbounded jubilation.

These are extreme sentiments; the people who can be imagined to experience them would have to be almost larger than life. All this fits perfectly into place with the Baroque fascination with the theater. The Baroque theater concentrated on grandiose gesture and high passion, on ideal emotions expressed by ideal human beings. Kings and queens were shown performing noble actions or vile ones, experiencing intense feelings, reciting thunderous tirades, and taking part in lavish stage displays. How these personages looked and postured can be seen in the picture on page 118.

Theatricality is a key to the emotional world of the Baroque, whether in music—it is no accident that opera was invented in this period—or the visual arts and poetry. Architectural interiors and formal gardens of the time look like stage sets. Or take a characteristically high-pitched passage from a poem of 1717 by Alexander Pope, retelling the medieval love story of Heloise and Abelard. Heloise awakes from a dream about her lover:

> Oh curst, dear horrors of all-conscious night!
> How glowing guilt exalts the keen delight!
> Provoking demons all restraints remove,
> And stir within me every source of love!
> I hear thee, view thee, gaze o'er all thy charms,
> And round thy phantom glue my clasping arms . . .
> I shriek, start up—the same sad prospect find,
> And wake to all the griefs I left behind.

The resonant words for the strong "affects," the grandiloquent phrases, and even the gestures suggested—gazing, clasping, starting up—all seem to come straight from the theater.

Theatrical emotion has the virtues of intensity, clarity, and focus; it has to have, if it is to reach its audience. Actors analyze the emotion they are required to depict, shape it and probably exaggerate it, and then methodically project it by means of their acting technique and craft. It is not their personal emotion, though for the moment they *make* it their own. We may come to feel that Baroque composers worked in much the same manner, not only in their operas—actual stage works set to music—but also in their oratorios and church cantatas, and even in their instrumental concertos and sonatas.

Chapter 9

Baroque Instrumental Music

In modern times, no one doubts that listening to instrumental music can be a serious aesthetic experience. The idea that beauty, profundity, and even spiritual uplift can be conveyed by instrumental music alone, without any words, is an article of faith with music lovers. We automatically think of symphonies as our most important musical compositions, symphony orchestras as our most prestigious musical organizations.

In most musical cultures, however, vocal genres, with their connection to words, have seemed the more natural and more relevant outlet for musical energies, and so it was in pre-Baroque European culture. When people thought of music, they thought of church music set to religious texts, and songs, both simple and complex, set to secular texts. To a large extent, this was still true in the Baroque era, as we shall see in Chapter 10.

But part of the importance of the Baroque era is that now, for the first time, listeners and musicians began to take instrumental music much more seriously. A momentous change was set in motion, and the reasons for it are not entirely clear. It can hardly be a coincidence, however, that the rise of instrumental music took place at the same time as a similar development in the technology of instrument making.

In any case, the rise of instrumental music meant that there had to be a basic understanding between composers and audiences about instrumental forms and genres. To pose the most basic question: when the music starts, how long should the composer keep going, and what should the listener expect? With vocal music, the answer was (roughly speaking) when the words end—when the sense of the sentence, paragraph, or total text is completed with a punctuation mark, a summing-up, or a concluding passage. For instrumental music, there was no such "sense." Conventional forms and genres had to supply it.

In this chapter we shall look at the most important instrumental forms and genres established, developed, and refined in the Baroque era. Baroque vocal music will be treated in Chapter 10.

1 Baroque Variation Forms

Variation forms are among the simplest and most characteristic of Baroque forms. Although they are not as common as other forms, they project the Baroque desire for systematic, thorough structures in the most direct way imaginable.

Variation form entails the successive, uninterrupted repetition of a clearly defined melodic unit, with changes that enlist the listener's interest without ever losing touch with the original unit. That unit may be an extended melody in the soprano range or a shorter pattern in the bass.

Given the emphasis in the Baroque era on the basso continuo, it is not surprising that Baroque variations usually work with bass patterns, rather than with soprano tunes. The variations differ mainly by having different polyphonic lines and different harmonies written (or improvised) above the bass. Sometimes the bass itself is slightly altered, or "decorated," rhythmically or melodically—though never to such an extent that its distinctive quality is hidden. Dynamics and tone color may be changed also, and (less often) the tempo, key, or mode.

There are a number of names for these pieces, which seem to have grown up independently all over Europe, first as improvisations and then as written-out compositions. An English term was *ground* or *ground bass*, a French (originally Spanish) term was *chaconne*, and Italian terms were *ciaccona*—translated from chaconne—and **passacaglia.**

As this child appears to be finding out, music lessons can often serve as a cover for lessons in something else—a fact which helps explain the popularity of "music lesson" pictures.

JOHANN SEBASTIAN BACH (1685–1750)
Passacaglia and Fugue in C minor for Organ (c. 1707)

This magnificent work is a tribute to the high level of organ technology, organ playing, and composition for the instrument in eighteenth-century Germany. As a young church organist, Bach first made his name as a brilliant virtuoso by playing compositions such as this after church services. He must have retained a liking for this passacaglia and fugue, for he touched them up later in life.

Passacaglia *(passacáhlia)* is one name for a Baroque set of variations on a bass figure. Bach's Passacaglia opens calmly and solemnly, as organ pedals play the theme for the variations to come without any accompaniment:

There follow no fewer than twenty variations on this theme, one directly after another. The theme appears in different guises or with different accompaniments. Often it appears exactly as shown in the example, the variations consisting simply of fresh contrapuntal lines above it. At other times the theme is somewhat obscured, though never so much that the listener loses it entirely. Through it all, Bach pours forth an inexhaustible supply of fascinating new musical ideas, which seem to spring up under the organist's fingers like an inspired improvisation.

We can develop a sort of "double listening" for music like this, listening simultaneously to the unchanging theme and to the ever-changing material presented along with that theme. (It is really no harder to do this than to admire a distant view while also inspecting someone in the foreground.) Our pleasure and interest in the piece depend on our double awareness of the fixed element—the regular, stately recurrence of the theme—and the versatile, changing additions to it.

Variations 1 through 10 consist of a steady buildup. It is interesting to note that in each group of five variations in the Passacaglia, there is one in which the theme is broken up into faster notes:

Then in Variations 11 through 15, the theme moves away from the bass and into the higher regions, with an effect of brightness and liberation. During most of these variations, the pedals do not play, so the music is automatically quieter; the organist will also *change registration,* that is, connect up a different set of organ pipes (sets of organ pipes are called *stops*). This changes the tone color. As a result, Variations 11 through 15 form a contrasting unit.

Variations 16 through 20 return to the powerful, majestic tone that was built up in the first group of variations. The Passacaglia reaches a grand climax. With the theme thundering away again in the organ pedals, each of the new accompaniments above it sounds more flamboyant and impressive than the last.

The music does not stop here, and if you feel an urge to keep listening, that is a good instinct—turn to page 133 for Listening Chart 4.

Pipe organ technology developed prodigiously in the Baroque era. Imposing instruments such as this one underpinned the church music of the time.

LISTENING CHART NUMBER 2[1]

Bach, Passacaglia in C minor for Organ

3 Cassette 1A-2/3 CD 1-2
6 Cassette 1B-8/6 CD 1-21

Variation form. 7 min., 35 sec.

0.01	**Theme**	In the organ pedals; unaccompanied	*5 variations:*
0.27	**Var. 1–2**	Theme accompanied by broken chords	*increasing complexity of texture*
1.13	**Var. 3–4**	More contrapuntal	
1.57	**Var. 5**	Theme in the pedals is broken up	
2.2 / 21.2 2.21	**Var. 6–8**	Scale figures of various kinds	*5 variations: scales and scale figures*
3.25	**Var. 9**	Theme in the pedals is broken up	
3.48	**Var. 10**	Theme, played detached, with chords above it	
2.3 / 21.3 4.08	**Var. 11–12**	Bass goes up into the high treble register	*5 variations: PEDALS DROP OUT (except in var. 12)*
4.49	**Var. 13**	Quieter: bass broken up	
5.10	**Var. 14–15**	Bass broken up into quiet arpeggios—var. 15 is quieter	
2.4 / 21.4 5.48	**Var. 16–17**	Theme back in the pedals: brilliant variations	*5 variations: PEDALS RETURN: Climax*
6.30	**Var. 18**	Theme in the pedals is broken up	
6.52	**Var. 19–20**	Two final variations, running directly into the Fugue	

[1] The figures at the left of the Listening Charts, within the double line, are index references. Use them if your CD player has the index function.

Johann Sebastian Bach

(1685–1750)

Chief Works: More than 200 sacred and secular cantatas; two Passions, according to St. Matthew and St. John; *Christmas Oratorio;* Mass in B Minor; *Magnificat;* motets

The Well-Tempered Clavier, consisting of 48 preludes and fugues in all major and minor keys for harpsichord or clavichord

Three sets of suites (six each) for harpsichord—the French and English Suites and the Partitas; *Goldberg* Variations

Organ works: many fugues (including the *St. Anne* Fugue) and chorale preludes

Brandenburg Concertos; concertos for harpsichord, violin, two violins; orchestral suites; sonatas

Late composite works: *A Musical Offering* and *The Art of Fugue*

Chorale (hymn) harmonizations

During the Baroque era, crafts were handed down in family clans, and in music the Bach clan was one of the most extensive, providing the region of Thuringia in central Germany with musicians for many generations. Most of the Bachs were lowly town musicians or Lutheran church organists; only a few of them gained court positions. Johann Sebastian, who was himself taught by several of his relatives, trained four sons who became leading composers of the next generation.

Bach's early career was like that of many German musicians at the time. Before he was twenty, he took his first position as a church organist in a little town called Arnstadt, then moved to a bigger town called Mühlhausen. Then he worked his way up to a court position with the Duke of Weimar. As a church organist, Bach had to compose organ music and sacred choral pieces, and at Weimar he was still required to write church music for the ducal chapel, as well as sonatas and concertos for performance in the palace.

The way his Weimar position terminated tells us something about the working conditions of court musicians. When Bach tried to leave Weimar for another court, Cöthen, the duke balked and threw him in jail for several weeks. At Cöthen, where the prince happened to be a keen amateur musician but was not in favor of elaborate church music, Bach concentrated on instrumental music.

In 1723 Bach was appointed Cantor of St. Thomas's Church in Leipzig, an important city in eastern Germany. He not only had to compose and perform, but also organize music for all four churches in town. Teaching in the choir school was another of his responsibilities. Almost every week, in his first years at Leipzig, Bach composed, had copied, rehearsed, and performed a new cantata—a religious work for soloists, choir, and orchestra containing several movements and lasting from fifteen to thirty minutes.

Bach chafed under bureaucratic restrictions and political decisions by town and church authorities. The truth is he was never appreciated in Leipzig. Furthermore, at the end of his life he was regarded as old-fashioned by modern musicians, and one critic pained Bach by saying so in print. Indeed, after his death Bach's music was neglected by the musical public at large, though it was admired by composers such as Mozart and Beethoven. The "rediscovery" of Bach was hastened by a performance of his *Passion According to St. Matthew* by the young Felix Mendelssohn in 1829.

Bach had twenty children—seven with his first wife, a cousin, and thirteen with his second, a singer, for whom he prepared a little home-music anthology, *The Note-Book of Anna Magdalena Bach.* The children were taught music as a matter of course, and also taught how to copy music; the performance parts of many of the weekly cantatas that Bach composed are written in their hands. From his musical response to the sacred words of these cantatas, and other works, it is clear that Bach thought deeply about religious matters. Works such as his Passions and his Mass in B Minor emanate a spirituality that many listeners find unmatched in any other composer.

Bach seldom traveled, except to consult on organ construction contracts (for which the customary fee was often a cord of wood or a barrel of wine). His last two years were spent in blindness, but he continued to compose by dictation. Before this time, he had already begun to assemble his compositions in orderly sets: organ chorale preludes, organ fugues, preludes and fugues for harpsichord. He also clearly set out to produce works that would

This painting is thought to depict Bach and three of his musician sons. The kindly, soberly dressed father is shown holding a cello—a basso continuo instrument—ready to support the treble lines of the boys, who are decked out in the frothy costumes of a later generation.

summarize his final thoughts about Baroque forms and genres; such works are the Mass in B Minor, the thirty-three *Goldberg* Variations for harpsichord, and *The Art of Fugue*, an exemplary collection of fugues all on the same subject, left unfinished at his death.

Bach was writing for himself, for his small devoted circle of students, perhaps for posterity. It is a concept that would have greatly surprised the craftsmen musicians who were his forebears.

2 Fugue

Fugue is one of the most important musical forms perfected in the Baroque period, and it counts as one of the greatest cultural products of the entire age. In broad general terms, fugue can be thought of as systematized imitative polyphony (see page 34). Renaissance composers invented imitative polyphony; Baroque composers, characteristically, systematized it.

A **fugue** is a polyphonic composition for a fixed number of voices or instruments, built on a single principal theme. This theme, called the **fugue subject,** appears at various times in each of the instruments or voices.

Exposition

A fugue begins with an **exposition,** in which all the voices present the subject in an orderly, standardized way. (Contrapuntal lines in fugues are referred to as "voices," even when the fugue is instrumental.) At the very start of a fugue, the subject is typically announced in the most prominent fashion possible—by appearing in a single voice without accompaniment. Then the subject

appears in a second voice, while the first continues with other musical material, called the **countersubject**—a distinctive contrapuntal line that regularly accompanies the principal subject. Countersubjects stand out from the subject because of their particular rhythmic or melodic profiles.

Then the subject appears in a third voice, and so on. This section of a fugue, the exposition, is over when all the voices have stated the subject.

VOICE 1   Subject—(Countersubject)———————————————————————————→

VOICE 2   Subject—(Countersubject)——— — — — — —   Subject ——— — — — →

VOICE 3   Subject—(Countersubject)——— — — — — — — — — — — — — →

VOICE 4   Subject—(Countersubject)——— — — — — — —   Subject — — →

Exposition	First episode	Later subject entries	Second episode

At intervals later in the fugue, the subject enters in one or another of the polyphonic voices. It may come at the top of the texture (the soprano), at the bottom (the bass), or else half hidden away in the middle. It may or may not be accompanied by the countersubject in one of the other voices.

Some of the later subject entries come in different keys. Although the modulations to these other keys are not very obvious—less so than in some later music we shall be hearing—without them a fugue would seem dull and stodgy.

Episodes

The later subject entries of a fugue are spaced off by short passages of other music, called **episodes**. In principle, the episodes provide a contrast to the subject entries—even though sometimes their musical material is derived from the subject or the countersubject. In such cases, the episodes sound less distinct and solid than the subject entries, and so stand apart from them.

After the exposition, the form of a fugue falls into an alternating pattern: episodes alternate with new subject entries in various keys. How long this goes on depends entirely on the skill of the composer:

| Exposition (subject enters in each voice) | First episode | Subject entry (or entries) | Second episode | Subject entry (or entries) | Third episode | Etc. |

Fugal Devices

Certain fugues feature some technical refinements in the treatment of the subject itself. The subject may be presented solemnly with all its note durations twice as long (called *augmentation*). It can be presented upside down (in *inversion*—that is, wherever the original subject goes up in pitch, the inversion goes down, and vice versa). A subject entry can overlap another entry in time, with the second coming in before the first is over (called *stretto*).

Often these devices are as academic and dry as they probably sound, but the Baroque masters of fugue drew unexpected expressive dividends from such technical procedures. Bach wrote fugues of many different kinds—long and short, somber and brilliant, learned and lighthearted—a magnificent testament to the expressive potentiality of this genre.

ARCANGELO CORELLI (1653–1713)
Fugue (Allegro) from Concerto Grosso in D, Op. 6, No. 1
(c. 1680; published 1714)

If you have worked through Unit II of this book, including Chapter 7 on the early Baroque period, you have already heard a little fugue for string orchestra that can fairly be described as effervescent. It was written by the Italian violinist-composer Arcangelo Corelli around 1680.

We need not turn back to the discussion on page 106; here is a minuscule Listening Chart for Corelli's fugue (page 132). The fugue subject is unusually short. We hear a cluster of subject entries at the beginning—the fugal exposition—and thereafter several more subject entries, spaced apart by episodes, and often prepared by strong cadences. There is also one brief solo passage—for just two violins and a cello—in which Corelli tries out several interesting altered versions of the fugue subject.

Fugue subject

Use the Listening Chart as a guide to your listening, not as a test of it. It's often tricky to hear subject entries in fugues, obscured as they are by rich counterpoint. In Corelli's fugue, in fact, the composer seems to be playing a game with his speedy entries, seeing how many of them he can sneak by the listener.

Arcangelo Corelli, Fugue (Allegro) from Concerto Grosso in D, Op. 6 No. 1

Fugue. 1 min., 35 sec.

0.00	**FUGAL EXPOSITION**	Four **Subject** entries:	*violin 1*		(soprano)
			violin 2	corresponding	(alto)
			viola (and cello)	to	(tenor)
			bass viol (and cello)		(bass)

0.13   **Subject entry:** *bass*

0.22   Several new **Subject entries**

0.37   Strong cadence, but there is no full stop: episode follows

0.51   Strong cadence; leads directly to

0.52   Solo passage—two violins and cello only.
New versions of the fugue subject are played by the solo instruments.

1.06   Strong cadence, in a minor key; leads directly to

1.07   **Subject entry:** *violin 1*

Long descending scale leads into

1.16   Final **Subject entry:** *bass*

1.26   Slowdown and final cadence

JOHANN SEBASTIAN BACH
Fugue, from the Passacaglia and Fugue in C minor for Organ (c. 1707)

We now return to Bach's Passacaglia and Fugue in C minor. After subjecting the Passacaglia theme to twenty variations, Bach had exhausted the possibilities of this kind of thematic treatment; but he had not exhausted the theme itself. In the second part of the Passacaglia and Fugue, he treats the theme in a new way. Fugue is sufficiently different from variation, he thinks, to lend fresh interest to what is by now a very old story.

The theme appears in a new, shortened form together with a countersubject:

(Most fugues begin with one voice alone, but Bach may have judged that in this case the subject by itself would sound too thin, coming right after the mighty cadence of the Passacaglia.) A higher voice comes in, then (after a few more measures) the pedals; then finally the original countersubject voice has the subject in the middle register. This concludes the four-voice fugal exposition.

From here on, we hear numerous subject entries in various keys and various registers—high, low, and middle. After the relentless minor-mode concentration of the Passacaglia, it is certainly good to hear the minor-mode theme come at last in several major keys.

In between the entries are episodes, an ever-changing flow of rich contrapuntal music. The word *flow* seems appropriate here because, compared with the Passacaglia, the music proceeds in flexible, irregular phrase lengths rather than monolithic, repeated eight-bar patterns. The motion never stops, but every once in a while a relatively strong cadence has the effect of focusing the flow, or articulating it.

In one section the organ pedals stop playing, which of course makes the music quieter. (We heard this happen in the Passacaglia, too.) And after the Fugue has gone on for some time, and we begin to think it may be coming to an end, a new upward scale figure begins an entirely new episode. As though renewed by this, the Fugue continues through several more episodes and subject entries.

By means of the repetitions of the theme in the Passacaglia, and of the subject in the Fugue, Bach has built up great cumulative momentum, as though the music were some gigantic flywheel. His final task is to apply the brake, which he does with the help of a flamboyant interruption of the music on a very unexpected chord. Then the piece plunges on into its final cadence. The organist must pull out all the stops here. This ending—more theatrical, no doubt, than churchly—caps an awesome Baroque structure with a superb sample of Baroque extravagance.

LISTENING CHART NUMBER 4

3 Cassette 1A-3/3 CD 1-3
6 Cassette 1B-9/6 CD 1-22

Bach, Fugue, from Passacaglia and Fugue in C minor for Organ

Fugue. 5 min., 13 sec.

0.00	Runs in directly from the Passacaglia (see Listening Chart 2, page 127)	
0.00	**FUGAL EXPO-SITION** Four **Subject entries** (with two countersubjects):	

high		(alto)
higher	corresponding to	(soprano)
pedals		(bass)
middle		(tenor)

0.55	Strong cadence, followed by another **Subject entry,** modulating to the major mode *(From now on, there are short episodes between all the subject entries.)*	
3.2 22.2 1.10	Strong cadence, in a major key, followed by Subject entry	*ORGAN PEDALS DROP OUT*
1.38	Subject entry, major mode	
3.3 22.3 2.08	Strong **Subject entry,** minor mode	*PEDALS RETURN*
2.39	**Subject entry,** minor mode—seems headed for a cadence	
3.4 22.4 2.52	Episode with unexpected new upward scale figure	
3.07	**Subject entry**	
3.25	Strong cadence, followed by **Subject entry** in the pedals: the lowest yet	
3.58	Strong cadence, scale figure, and expectant trill	
3.5 22.5 4.10	Climactic high **Subject entry**—the highest yet	
4.42	Dramatic stop, prior to a grandiose final cadence	

3 The Concerto Grosso

The concerto grosso (plural: concerti grossi) is the most important orchestral genre of the Baroque era. Basic to this genre is interplay between a group of soloists and the total orchestra. Indeed, the word *concerto* comes from the Latin *concertare,* "to contend"—an origin that accurately indicates a sort of contest between soloists and orchestra.

This contest pits the brilliance of the soloists, often involving or at least evoking improvisation, against the relative power and solidity of the orchestra. Thus the concerto grosso involves more contrast than do the genres we have just discussed. Composers needed such contrast if they wanted to develop viable large-scale forms; fugues and ground bass compositions can grow boring if they are extended very far. And composers wanted to develop large-scale forms because, then as now, an extended composition was more impressive to an audience than a short one.

At the same time, we should note that there is less contrast between the solo and orchestral forces in a Baroque concerto grosso than in the more familiar solo concertos of a later era, such as the piano concertos of Tchaikovsky and Rachmaninoff. The Romantic solo concerto makes a sharp separation between a single soloist and a large, varied orchestra. In the Baroque concerto grosso, the forces balance more evenly: there are more soloists and fewer orchestra players in the "basic" Baroque orchestra (page 120). Furthermore, those forces actually overlap. The soloists come from the ranks of the orchestra; they are simply the "first chair" or "first desk" players whose job it is to lead the other orchestra players when there is no special solo music. They separate off from them only when solo parts are called for.

Thus, constant interpenetration between the two "contesting" forces reduces the contrast in their relationship, and adds to its subtlety.

BAROQUE
CONCERTO GROSSO

Group of soloists (e.g., two violins, cello, continuo)	Small orchestra: strings, continuo

ROMANTIC
SOLO CONCERTO

Single soloist	Large orchestra: strings, woodwinds, brass, percussion

Movements

A **movement** is a self-contained section of music that is part of a larger total work. In Bach's Passacaglia and Fugue, for instance, the Passacaglia counts as the first movement, the Fugue as the second. Usually, there are three or four movements in a multimovement work, contrasting with one another in tempo, meter, key, or mood. For example, the second movement is nearly always in a new key, which will automatically sound fresh after the key of the first movement.

In the late Baroque period, the typical concerto grosso consisted of three movements. The *first* movement is generally an extroverted piece in fast tempo. After this, the *second* movement invariably strikes an obvious contrast: it is quieter, slower, more emotional. The *third* movement is fast again —if anything, faster and brisker than the first.

Ritornello Form

Many concerto grosso movements are in *ritornello form,* a Baroque form that is also used in other genres. **Ritornello** is the name for the orchestra material that typically starts the movement off. Contrast is basic to the concerto grosso, and ritornello form focuses contrast on two musical ideas, or groups of ideas—one belonging to the orchestra and the other to the soloists. The orchestral material (the ritornello) tends to be solid and forceful, the solo material faster and more brilliant.

Ritorno, the Italian word for "return," tells us that the function of the ritornello in ritornello form is to return many times as a stable element of the form. Usually it returns only in part, and usually it is played in different keys as the movement proceeds. As for the "musical ideas" referred to above, sometimes these are themes, sometimes larger sections including themes and other passages. To end the movement, the ritornello returns in the tonic key and, often, at full length.

Ritornello form can be diagrammed as follows, where RIT stands for the entire ritornello, [RIT] for any part of the ritornello, and Solo 1, 2, 3, . . . for the various elements comprising the group of solo ideas:

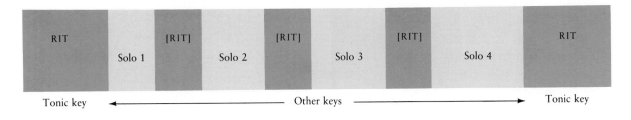

RIT		[RIT]		[RIT]		[RIT]		RIT
	Solo 1		Solo 2		Solo 3		Solo 4	

Tonic key ←——————————— Other keys ———————————→ Tonic key

We need not worry too much about the exact number of ritornello fragments, the keys, and other details shown in such form diagrams. More important is the general impression that the form gives: the sense of a sturdy, reliable underpinning in the orchestra for rapid and sometimes fantastic flights by the solo group. As a condition for the quasi-improvisational freedom of the solo instruments, the ritornello is always there, ready to bring them back down to earth and to remind the listener of the original point of departure.

Antonio Vivaldi

(1678–1741)

Chief Works: Concerti grossi (i.e., concertos for several solo instruments) for various instruments, including the very famous *Four Seasons*

Solo concertos for many different instruments

Sonatas; "La folia" Variations

21 extant operas; oratorios; cantatas

The son of a Venetian violinist, Antonio Vivaldi was destined to follow in his father's footsteps. He entered the priesthood—where his bright red hair earned him the nickname of the "Red Priest"—and in 1703 became a music teacher at the Seminario Musicale dell'Ospedale della Pietà, a Venetian orphanage for girls. The Ospedale was one of several such institutions in Venice that were famous for the attention they paid to the musical training of their students. A large portion of Vivaldi's works were composed for the school.

The Ospedale allowed him frequent leaves of absence, so Vivaldi traveled a good deal; for example, he spent some years at Mantua in the employ of the prince there. He was gone so much of the time, though, that the authorities of the school specified in the composer's contract that he should write two concertos a month for the pupils. If he happened to be in town at the time he would also rehearse those pieces. At the end of his life, Vivaldi left Venice permanently to settle in Vienna.

Internationally renowned as a virtuoso violinist, Vivaldi is remembered today chiefly for his brilliant concertos for solo or several instruments. He wrote more than four hundred of these, including concertos for harp, mandolin, bassoon, and all kinds of instrumental combinations. He also wrote operas, cantatas, and oratorios. Critics of the day complained that Vivaldi's

An "official" picture of a
bewigged Vivaldi, and a
caricature, dated 1723

music was thin and flashy, and that the composer was always playing for
cheap effects. But the young Bach, before writing his *Brandenburg* Concertos, carefully copied out many pages of Vivaldi, as a way of learning how
to write concertos himself.

Vivaldi's most popular works were published in sets provided with opus
numbers; *opus* (abbreviated Op.) is Latin for "work." Such numbers are
assigned by composers or publishers to compositions as a means of identifying them. Some of the concerto opuses have fanciful (and market-wise) titles:

> *L'estro armonico,* Op. 3 ("Harmonic Whims") Several of these concertos
were transcribed for keyboard instruments by Bach. Concerto No. 12 for
four violins and orchestra became a concerto for four harpsichords and
orchestra—an extraordinary sound.

> *La stravaganza,* Op. 4 ("Extravagances") As the name suggests, this set of
concertos includes some strange, daring harmonies and other bizarre effects
—a challenge to Vivaldi's critics.

> *Il cimento dell'harmonia,* Op. 8 ("Tests of Harmony") The first four
numbers in this set are *The Four Seasons,* concertos in which the music illustrates characteristic sounds associated with spring (birds singing, for example), summer (a nap in the sun), fall (a tipsy peasants' dance), and winter ("the
horrible wind"). Composed by Vivaldi with tongue in cheek, perhaps, these
concertos are now far and away his most famous. They have been recorded
well over a hundred times.

JOHANN SEBASTIAN BACH
Brandenburg Concerto No. 5, for Flute, Violin, Harpsichord,
and Orchestra (before 1721)

In 1721 Bach sent a group of six of his concertos to the Margrave of Brandenburg, a minor nobleman with a paper title: the Duchy of Brandenburg had recently been merged into the Kingdom of Prussia, Europe's fastest-growing state. It is not known what the purpose of the presentation was; probably Bach was angling for a job. The concertos themselves had been written over the previous ten years or more for Bach's employers, the dukes of Weimar and Cöthen.

As a demonstration of his virtuosity—and as a reflection of his encyclopedic turn of mind—Bach chose six concertos, each with a different combination of instruments, combinations that in some cases were never used before or after. Taken as a group, the *Brandenburg* Concertos present an unsurpassed anthology of dazzling tone colors and imaginative treatments of the Baroque concerto grosso contest between soloists and orchestra.

Brandenburg Concerto No. 5 features as its solo group a flute, violin, and harpsichord. The orchestra is the "basic" Baroque string orchestra (see page 120). The harpsichordist of the solo group doubles as the player of the orchestra's continuo chords, and the solo violin leads the orchestra during the ritornellos.

First Movement (Allegro)   In ritornello form, the first movement of *Brandenburg* No. 5 opens with a loud, bright, solid-sounding orchestral ritornello that is basically homophonic in texture. The melody is attractive and easily recognized but, like so many Baroque melodies, becomes more complicated as it proceeds:

(For simplicity's sake, this music example omits the note-repetitions on the eighth notes.) If asked to sing this melody, one could probably soon capture the first phrase **a,** but after that, things would become more difficult. There is no clear stop between phrases **b** and **c,** and the melody begins to wind around itself in an intricate, decorative manner. Yet it is undoubtedly just these features that give the melody its strength and its flair.

Once the ritornello ends with a solid cadence, the three solo instruments enter with rapid imitative counterpoint. They dominate the rest of the movement; they introduce new motives and new patterns of figuration, take over some motives from the ritornello, and toss all these musical ideas back and forth between them. Occasionally the orchestra breaks in again, with fragments of the ritornello in various different keys.

In the middle of the movement, there is a particularly striking central solo passage in the minor mode. The soloists abandon their motivic style and play Baroque mood music, with rich harmonies and intriguing special textures:

After this, part of the ritornello returns, and the solos thereafter are all closely related to solos heard before the minor-mode central section—all, that is, except the very last.

Here the harpsichord gradually outpaces the violin and the flute, until finally it seizes the stage and plays a lengthy virtuoso passage, while the other instruments wait silently. An improvised or improvisatory passage within a larger piece is called a **cadenza**. Cadenzas are especially common in the solo concerto, less common in the concerto grosso; in later concertos the biggest cadenza always comes near the end of the first movement, as it does in *Brandenburg* Concerto No. 5.

Bach himself, of course, would have played this cadenza (he seems to have lengthened it especially to impress the Margrave). With unexpected power, the harpsichord breaks out of the regular eighth-note rhythms that have dominated the movement. Its swirling patterns prepare inexorably for the final entrance of the orchestra. There is a real feeling of satisfaction, then, when the orchestra breaks in, like the releasing of a force that has been pent up for an intolerably long time. The whole ritornello is played, exactly as it was at the very beginning—a doubly satisfying conclusion, since at last we hear it as a complete and solid entity, not in fragments.

Second Movement (Affettuoso)   After the forceful first movement of a concerto grosso, there is a need for something quieter, slower, and more emotional. As is often the case, the second movement of the *Brandenburg* Concerto No. 5 is in a minor key, the first and last in a major key.

Baroque composers had a simple way of reducing volume: they could omit many or even all of the orchestra instruments. So here Bach employs only the three solo instruments—flute, violin, and harpsichord—plus the orchestra cello playing the continuo bass. The movement has two main motives:

These expressive motives are also played in *inversion*—that is, with all their melodic intervals reversed. Wherever the original motive goes up in pitch, the inversion goes down. Conceived in the abstract, inversion may seem like a merely mathematical device, but here it sounds perfectly elegant and natural.

Third Movement (Allegro)   The full orchestra returns in the last movement, which, however, begins with a lengthy passage for the three soloists. The lively compound meter with its triple component—one two three *four* five six—provides a welcome contrast to the duple meter that is so insistent in the two earlier movements.

LISTENING CHART NUMBER 5

3 Cassette 1A-8/3 CD 1-8
6 Cassette 2A-1/6 CD 2-1

Bach, *Brandenburg* Concerto No. 5, first movement

Ritornello form. 9 min., 45 sec.

	0.00	**Ritornello**	Complete ritornello is played by the orchestra, **forte**; bright and emphatic	
	0.20	**Solo**	Harpsichord, flute, and violin in a contrapuntal texture (often in trio style). Includes faster rhythms; the soloists play new themes and also play some of the motives from the ritornello	
8.2 1.2	0.45	**Ritornello (first phrase)**	Orchestra, *f*	
	0.50	**Solo**	Similar material to that of the first solo	
8.3 1.3	1.10	**Ritornello (middle phrase)**	Orchestra, *f*	
	1.16	**Solo**	Similar solo material	
8.4 1.4	1.37	**Ritornello (middle phrase)**	Orchestra, *f*; minor mode	
	1.43	**Solo**	Similar solo material at first, then fast harpsichord runs are introduced.	
8.5 1.5	2.24	**Ritornello (middle phrase)**	Orchestra, *f*	
	2.30	**Solo**	This solo leads directly into the central solo.	
8.6 1.6	2.55	Central solo	Quiet flute and violin dialogue (accompanied by the orchestra, *p*) is largely in the minor mode. The music is less motivic, and the harmonies change less rapidly than before.	
	3.20		Detached notes in cello, flute, and violin	
	4.03		Flute trills prepare for the return of the ritornello.	
8.7 1.7	4.08	**Ritornello (first phrase)**	Orchestra, *f*	
	4.12	**Solo**		
8.8 1.8	4.57	**Ritornello (first and second phrases)**	Orchestra, *f*; this ritornello section feels especially solid because it is longer than the others and in the tonic key.	
	5.08	**Solo**		
8.9 1.9	5.37	**Ritornello (middle phrase)**	Orchestra, *f*	
	5.43	**Solo**	Fast harpsichord runs lead into the cadenza.	
8.10 1.10	6.21	**Harpsichord cadenza**	*Section 1*: a lengthy passage developing motives from the solo sections	
	8.14		*Section 2*: very fast and brilliant	
	8.35		*Section 3*: long preparation for the anticipated return of the ritornello	
	9.18	**Ritornello**	Orchestra, *f*, plays the complete ritornello.	

Eighteenth-century Spanish
tiles (see also page 124)

The ways Bach finds of playing off the soloists against the orchestra are perhaps more varied and interesting in this movement than in the earlier ones. On the other hand, the two contending instrumental forces do not have distinct, contrasting material. The whole piece grows out of a single darting theme:

Allegro

SOLO VIOLIN   FLUTE

The theme is first played by the soloists as a fugue subject, in a regular fugal exposition; later it is developed more freely. It comes in an emphatic, homophonic version to provide the movement with a good-humored ending.

Baroque Chamber Music: Trio Sonata and Solo Sonata

Chamber music is a general term for music to be played (or, more rarely, sung) by small groups—in practice, from two to nine musicians. A string quartet or a woodwind quintet are familiar examples from later periods. The slow movement of Bach's *Brandenburg* Concerto No. 5, for flute, violin, and harpsichord, is in effect a chamber-music interlude within a larger, orchestral piece.

The most important chamber-music genre of the Baroque period was the sonata; there were two types, the *trio sonata* and the *solo sonata*. Originally the term *sonata* simply meant "sounded"—"a piece that is sounded," as distinct from *cantata*—"a piece that is sung." In the Baroque period, the sonata was a chamber-music piece for one to half a dozen instruments, consisting of several short movements in a variety of different forms. In later historical periods, the term *sonata* was used in a different sense, as we shall see.

Trio Sonata and Solo Sonata

The Baroque trio sonata was written for three main instruments, usually two equal-range treble instruments and a bass. And since all music of the time relies on the basso continuo, a trio sonata also includes a keyboard player, who performs the usual necessary but subsidiary function of filling in harmonies at the harpsichord or organ. The Baroque solo sonata, too, nearly always includes a bass part with continuo that is subsidiary to the single main solo instrument (though Bach provided some superb exceptions in his sonatas for violin alone and for cello alone).

The names of these sonatas can be deceptive, then. A Baroque trio sonata requires four players—three main players and one other, the continuo keyboard player—whereas a solo sonata usually requires three.

By far the most common trio-sonata combination was two violins plus cello. Other possibilities were two oboes plus bassoon, two flutes plus cello, or flute and violin plus cello (as in *Brandenburg* No. 5)—all plus harpsichord. Bach wrote trio sonatas for the organ: the organ-

ist's right hand and left hand play the two treble lines, and the organ pedals take care of the bass.

Baroque solo sonatas were composed for all the instruments that were popular at the time: violin, flute, recorder, oboe, bassoon, and cello.

Form in the Baroque Sonata

The same formal principles apply to the trio sonata and the solo sonata, though in the matter of form, too, simple definitions are hard to formulate. Once again, any formulation has to take history into consideration. Early in the Baroque period, the sonata was essentially improvisatory and amorphous in form. Later it was standardized into two distinct types, or prototypes:

> The **sonata di chiesa** (pronounced *kee-éh-sa*), church sonata: this contains a number of short slow movements which run right in—without a stop—to fast movements ("slow–fast"). The fast movements are often in a loose fugal style. A common plan for an entire sonata is slow–fast, slow–fast.

> The **sonata da camera,** chamber sonata, containing a series of distinct, unconnected movements in dance form. Essentially, this kind of sonata was simply a chamber-music suite (see page 141).

> By the time of Bach and Handel, however, the distinction had largely broken down. Most sonatas from the late Baroque period include elements from both of the two prototypes.

Recommended Listening Handel, Sonata in F for recorder and continuo, Op. 1 No. 11. A charming work in four short movements (slow–fast, slow–fast); the first fast movement is in dance form.

Georg Philipp Telemann (1681–1767): A famous contemporary of Bach and Handel, Telemann wrote great quantities of chamber music for various combinations. Any of his sonatas would make a good complement to the works covered in this book.

4 Baroque Dances: The Suite

Dance music was popular in the Baroque era, as has been true in every era, including of course our own. Dance music also inspired the greatest composers of the time to some of their best efforts.

The custom was to group a collection of miscellaneous dances together as a **dance suite**. Composers generally wrote "stylized" dances which were intended for listening rather than dancing, and which evoked well-liked, easily recognized dance norms. Compared with music written for the actual dance floor, such stylized dances naturally allowed for more musical elaboration and refinement.

Suites were written for orchestra, for chamber music combinations, or even for solo instruments such as the harpsichord or lute. Which dances occurred in a suite was not subject to any general rule, nor was there any specified order. All the dances in a suite were kept in the same key, and the last of them was always a fast number—frequently a gigue, a dance in compound meter that may have been derived from the Irish jig. Otherwise there was no overall "form" to a suite.

As for the dances themselves, what characterized them were features originally associated with the dance steps: a certain meter, a distinctive tempo, and some rhythmic attributes. For example, there are dances that always begin with an *upbeat,* a weak beat preceding the first strong beat (or *downbeat*) of a measure. A table lists these distinguishing features:

Dance	Usual Meter	Tempo	Some Rhythmic Characteristics
Allemande	4/4	Moderate	Upbeat sixteenth note; flowing motion
Courante	3/2	Moderate	Occasional substitution of 6/4 measures
Sarabande	3/4	Slow	Often a secondary accent on beat 2 (no upbeat)
Minuet	3/4	Moderate	Rather plain in rhythm (upbeat optional)
Gavotte	4/4	Moderate	Long upbeat of two quarter notes
Bourrée	2/2	Rather fast	Short upbeat
Siciliana	12/8	Moderate	Gently moving dotted rhythms; minor mode
Gigue	6/8	Fast	Short upbeat; dotted rhythms; lively movement

A German Baroque illustration of a country dance ("contredanse"). This is clearly a stylized dance, because the dancers are shown on a stage set.

Baroque Dance Form

Although the number, type, and arrangement of dances in a suite varied widely, the *form* of dances was firmly standardized. The same simple form was applied to all types, and it is an easily recognized feature of Baroque dance music.

A Baroque dance has two sections of roughly equal length, **a** and **b,** each of which ends with a complete stop and is then repeated immediately. Although the two sections usually include some similar motives, cadences, and other such musical details, there is usually no full-scale repetition of **a** after **b,** as we shall see happen in later dances.

Hence Baroque dance form is diagrammed

a a b b   *abbreviated as:* |: **a** :||: **b** :|

where the signs |: and :| indicate that everything between them is to be repeated. This form is also called *binary form*.

In addition, the shorter dances (such as the minuet and the gavotte) were sometimes grouped in pairs of the same type, with the first coming back again after the second. The result was a large-scale **A B A** form. The **B** dance in such a pair was called the <u>**trio,**</u> because in seventeenth-century orchestral music it had often been scored for only three instruments (and such scoring is sometimes still found in the eighteenth).

This made for a simple, agreeable contrast with the full orchestration of the **A** dance. Even when the trio is scored for full orchestra, the idea of contrast between the two dances was always kept; the second is quieter than the first, or it changes mode. (As for the term *trio,* that was still used in the waltzes of Johann Strauss and the marches of John Philip Sousa.)

Thus a Baroque minuet and trio, to choose this dance as an example, consists of one minuet followed by a second, quieter minuet, after which the first is heard again. This time, however, the repeats are omitted:

	Minuet	Trio	Minuet
	A	**B**	**A**
	a a b b	c c d d	a b
abbreviated as:	|: **a** :||: **b** :|	|: **c** :||: **d** :|	a b

The French Overture

A Baroque orchestral suite ordinarily begins not with the first dance but with a special preparatory number called a **French overture.** *Overture* is of course a general term for any substantial piece of music introducing a play, opera, or ballet. The French overture was a special type developed at the court of Louis XIV and widely used in the early eighteenth century.

The French overture consists of two sharply contrasted sections, a slow **A** section and a faster **B** section. They are arranged in a number of alternative ways, such as |: **A** :| **B** or |: **A** :||: **B** :| or |: **A** :||: **B A'** :|, where **A'** stands for a variant—often an abbreviated variant—of **A**.

The slow **A** section is the one that is distinctively "French." Dotted rhythms (see page 24), sweeping scales, heavy accents, and other such features give it a majestic, pompous gravity that is easily recognized (and was easily imitated). This section was typically labeled with the French word *Grave* (pronounced *grahv*), to indicate solemnity and gravity.

Early concerts were some-
times given in parks, where
music accompanied gossip,
flirting, and food.

The fast **B** section is in imitative polyphony. In some overtures this section amounts to a full-scale fugue.

BACH
Orchestral Suite No. 3 in D (c. 1730)

6 Cassette 2A, 2–4/6 CD 2,
2–4

It is thought that Bach wrote this suite for the Collegium Musicum of the
University of Leipzig, a student music organization that seems to have provided a congenial outlet for his later work. The Suite in D is scored for a
modified version of the "festive" Baroque orchestra diagrammed on page
120: strings, two oboes, three trumpets, two timpani, and harpsichord. Bach
carefully varied the style of orchestration from number to number.

Overture The French overture that starts the suite is scored for all the
instruments, and in fact it is the only movement in which the oboes have
(slightly) independent parts that do not always double the violins. What is
more, a solo violin emerges unexpectedly to dominate two passages during
the **B** part of the overture, which is a full-scale fugue.

The form of this overture is **A B A′**. Shown below is the beginning of the
A section, the "Grave," with its arresting drum roll and the obligatory
"French" dotted rhythms, and part of the fugal exposition in **B**:

The fugue proceeds with episodes and further entries, according to the general plan diagrammed on page 131.

GRAVE SECTION (A)	FUGUE SECTION (B)					GRAVE SECTION (A′)
	Exposition: orchestra (Entries of the subject in all voices, plus some extra entries)	First episode: solo violin (Orchestra plays some subject entries in the background)	Subject entries (orchestra)	Second episode: solo violin (Orchestra plays some subject entries in the background)	Subject entries (orchestra)	

The episodes in this fugue are played by the solo violin. Indeed, this **B** part of the movement can be understood in two ways: as a fugue with solo violin episodes, or as a Baroque solo concerto with a fugal ritornello.

Following the overture come four pieces in dance form. Three of them follow the Baroque pattern |: **a** :||: **b** :|. Notice the "full stop" effect after each playing of all the **a**'s and **b**'s. Only the gavotte, the second of the dances, has a trio and so falls into **A B A** form.

Air   Scored for strings alone, the Air that follows is perhaps Bach's most famous and beloved melody. An "air" is not a dance, of course—the title seems to evoke an opera aria—but since this music was to take its place in a suite, Bach cast it in dance form. The melody is played by the first violins, with a quiet, regular, downward-moving bass line in the cellos and bass viols. And there are subsidiary but highly expressive counterpoints in the second violins and violas.

On our recording, the Air is performed by a solo player, who adds expressive ornaments during the repeats of the **a** and **b** sections.

> The exquisite fluidity of this melody is a function of its unusual rhythmic variety. Most of the basic two-beat (half-measure) units in the melody have rhythms not duplicated elsewhere. Consequently, when measures 13–14 do repeat a rhythmic figure several times, they gain a special kind of climactic intensity. This intensity is underpinned by quiet *upward* motion in the bass, which had generally been moving downward, and by a newly prominent second violin part.

> Anticipated by some melodic figures in **a,** the figures in **b** keep reaching ever upward, in a wonderfully spontaneous way. This sense of aspiration is balanced by the graceful falling cadences ending **a** and **b**.

> To counteract all the rhythmic and melodic variety, Bach puts in several beautiful sequences, whose repetitive quality ensures a sense of organization: see measures 3–4, 13–14, and 15–16.

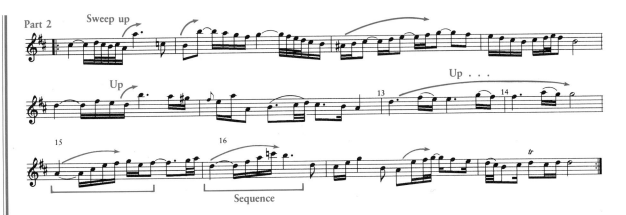

Gavotte   The wind instruments and timpani return in this number; the trumpets' military accent fits in well with the strong two-quarter-note upbeat of the gavotte (see page 141). Bach inverts the bold opening melody of **a** to obtain the opening of **b**. This inversion may *look* academic—a technical trick to be appreciated by the Collegium Musicum connoisseurs—but it *sounds* fresh and natural, another product of Bach's endlessly fertile melodic imagination:

The trio, with its unison fanfares at the beginning, strikes an even more explicitly military pose than does the first gavotte.

Bourrée   The lightest dance in this suite, a bourrée, is scored for full orchestra; the wind instruments and timpani are used mainly to underscore the sharp, exhilarating rhythms. With its regular phrase lengths (16 + 24 measures), this bourrée could easily be danced.

Gigue   Another drum roll (as in the French overture) launches this vigorous gigue, the most common dance for the last movement in a suite. The violins, doubled by the oboes, play almost continuous eighth notes in **6/8** time.

Chapter 10

Baroque Vocal Music

In today's music world, Bach's *Brandenburg* Concertos for instruments are performed much more often than his church cantatas for voices, and Handel's orchestral *Water Music* is heard more often than any of his operas or oratorios (with the single exception of the greatest of the oratorios, *Messiah*). When twentieth-century listeners think of Baroque music, we usually think first of instrumental music.

Nonetheless, vocal music—music for solo voices, choruses, or both—formed a major part of the output of virtually all Baroque composers. We have seen that composers were supported by three main institutions: the church, the opera house, and the court. Each of these demanded vocal music. Indeed, of the three, only the court was a major source of instrumental music—and every court had its chapel, for which the court composers were also required to provide vocal music. Courts had their own opera houses, too.

Words and Music

Theories of musical expression in the Baroque era were touched on in Chapter 8 (page 114). It was believed at the time that emotions could be isolated, categorized, and listed in a fairly simple way, and that music could enhance each emotion by means of certain musical devices applied consistently, even single-mindedly, throughout a piece. Theorists developed checklists of musical devices corresponding to each of the "affects," as they called emotions conceived in this way.

It was particularly in vocal music—where an actual text defines or suggests a specific emotion—that this musical "vocabulary of the emotions" was applied most consistently. If a text refers to "rejoicing," for example, a Baroque composer would almost inevitably match this with fast, lively runs; a mention of "victory" would probably require trumpets and drums to evoke battle music. More literally, when a text speaks of "high" or "low," a setting in high or low voices was likely, and so on.

1 Opera

principal genre of secular vocal music of the Baroque era was opera.
around the year 1600, opera flourished mightily all over Europe,
ame the most glamorous and in some ways the most adventur-
of the Baroque era.

In characterizing the emotional world of Baroque art (see page 121), we stressed its theatrical quality. The Baroque was fascinated by the theater, and especially by opera—the ultimate multimedia experience, combining poetry, drama, music, vocal virtuosity, scenic splendor, dance, and more. Spectacular singing was of the essence in Baroque opera, and not far behind it in importance was spectacular stage architecture, featuring amazing transformation scenes and the like. Systems of pulleys and counterweights could rapidly change the set from a palace to a magic garden, with gods and goddesses descending from the heavens in a fiery chariot. Opera offered a wealth of satisfactions—most obviously, no doubt, for the vocal connoisseurs of the day, the fans of great singers. They are said to have gossiped and played cards in the boxes while waiting for their favorite prima donnas to sing their special arias.

But opera's propensity for emotional expression was the real basis of its appeal. First and foremost, opera erected a stage on which individual singers could step forward to express feelings in the most direct and powerful fashion. The basic convention of opera—having dramatic characters sing instead of speak—may always have seemed artificial, even unnatural; but since the singers *were* dramatic characters, they were repeatedly thrown into situations which made it natural for them to experience (and vent) intense emotions. Such emotions were further intensified, of course, by music.

Emotion could be intensified by great vocal virtuosity, too. The most obvious kind of vocal virtuosity is *coloratura* singing—fast brilliant runs, scales, high notes, vocal cadenzas, and so on, stressing technique for its own sake. But the legendary singers of old moved their audiences not only by singing faster than anyone else, but by singing more beautifully, more delicately, and more emotionally.

Italian Opera Seria

The principal type of Italian Baroque opera was **opera seria,** or serious opera. The plots—mostly derived from ancient history, with all kinds of alterations

A German opera house of the Baroque era. Notice that the best seats were actually on the stage.

and additions—were designed to stir up powerful emotions, such as passion, rage, grief, and triumph. This gave the singers many opportunities to excel in one kind of expression or another. The most important of these singers were sopranos and altos; tenors and basses took the second place. Opera seria consists almost exclusively of solo singing, with few duets or choruses.

The text of an opera is called the *libretto* ("little book"), and the poet who wrote it is the *librettist*. Librettists were required to build up their total story from texts for *recitatives* and *arias*.

Recitative

Recitative (pronounced *re-si-ta-téev*), from the Italian word for "recite," is a technique of declaiming words musically in a heightened, theatrical manner. There is always an instrumental accompaniment. The singing voice closely follows the free rhythm of emotional speech; it mirrors and indeed exaggerates the natural ups and downs that occur as an actor raises his or her voice at a question, lowers it in "asides," or cries out in distress. The composer makes no effort to "organize" these speechlike utterances into real melodies.

Recitative was used for plot action, dialogue, and other places in the drama where it is particularly important for the words to be brought out. Text phrases and individual words are not ordinarily repeated, of course, any more than they would be in speech.

Most of the time, recitative accompaniment was kept to a minimum—basso continuo (cello and harpsichord) alone—so that the singer could interpret the dialogue or the action as spontaneously as possible. A name for recitative with continuo accompaniment is **secco recitative,** from the Italian word *secco*, meaning "dry" (think of the sound of the harpsichord). In every opera, however, one or two of the most excited recitatives were provided with orchestral accompaniment of one kind or another. This type is called **accompanied recitative.**

Aria

An **aria** is a set piece for solo singer that has much more musical elaboration and coherence than a passage of recitative. The vocal part is more melodic, and typically the accompaniment includes the orchestra, not just the continuo. Here the singer-actor is mulling over his or her emotions at some leisure, "getting his feelings out," instead of reacting moment by moment, as in recitative. Consequently in arias the repetition of poetic phrases or words is common and, in principle, appropriate.

The standard form for the Baroque Italian opera aria is **da capo form, A B A** (less usual is free da capo form, **A B A′**). Both the words and music of **A** are repeated after **B**; *da capo* ("from the head") is a direction on scores meaning repeat from the beginning. The composer wrote the music for **A** and **B** only, leaving the performers to do the rest. Indeed, the singer would do more than just repeat **A.** He or she would also ornament the music with improvised runs, cadenzas, and so on, so as to create an exciting enhanced effect the second time around.

For connoisseurs of the day, a great deal depended on the **A** repeats, since it was there that the singers really dazzled their audiences. Many modern singers have relearned the lost improvisational art of the Baroque era, and we can recapture some of the original excitement on records.

A much more informal picture of a Baroque opera performance—evidently during a recitative, to judge from the close engagement of the characters on stage and the inattention of the audience. (The painting is perhaps by Antonio Longhi, 1702–1785.)

George Frideric Handel

(1685–1759)

Chief Works: 40 Italian operas, including *Giulio Cesare* (*Julius Caesar*), *Rodelinda*, and *Tamerlano*

Near-operatic works in English: *Semele, Hercules,* and *Acis and Galatea*

Oratorios, including *Messiah, Israel in Egypt, Samson,* and *Saul*

Concerti grossi and organ concertos

Water Music, written for an aquatic fete on the River Thames, and *Fireworks Music,* celebrating the end of the War of the Austrian Succession, in 1747

Sonatas for various instruments; variations ("The Harmonious Blacksmith") for harpsichord

Georg Friedrich Händel—he anglicized his name to George Frideric Handel after settling in England—was one of the few composers of early days who did not come from a family of musicians. His father, who was sixty-three when Handel was born, was a barber-surgeon and a valet at a court near Leipzig. He disapproved of music, and the boy is said to have studied music secretly at night, by candlelight. In deference to his father's wishes, Handel studied law for a year at Halle, one of Germany's major universities, before finally joining the orchestra at Hamburg, Germany's leading center of opera.

From then on, it was an exciting, glamorous life. Still in his teens, Handel fought a duel (about who was to get top billing) with another Hamburg musician. In 1706 he journeyed to the homeland of opera and scored successes at Venice, Florence, and Rome. Though he became a court musician for the Elector of Hanover, in northern Germany, he kept requesting (and extending) leaves to pursue his career in London, a city that was then beginning to rival Paris as the world capital.

Here Handel continued to produce Italian operas, again with great success. He also wrote a flattering birthday ode for Queen Anne and some big pieces to celebrate a major peace treaty; for this he was awarded a substantial annuity. In 1717, after the Elector of Hanover had become George I of England, Handel got back into his good graces by composing music to be played on boats in a royal aquatic fete on the River Thames—the famous *Water Music* (two suites for "festive" orchestra).

A portrait of Handel, in late years, with the score of his most famous composition, *Messiah*

Handel's pompous funerary statue at Westminster Abbey, by the Baroque sculptor Louis Roubillac

As an opera composer, Handel had learned to gauge the taste of the public and also how to flatter singers, writing music for them that showed off their voices to the best advantage. He now also became an opera impresario —today we would call him a *promoter*—recruiting singers and negotiating their contracts, planning whole seasons of opera and all the while composing the main attractions himself: an opera every year, on average, between 1721 and 1743. He also had to deal with backers—English aristocrats and wealthy merchants who supported his opera companies, and persuaded their friends to take out subscriptions for boxes.

Handel made and lost several fortunes, but he always landed on his feet, even when Italian opera went out of style in Britain, for he never lost a feel for his audience. After opera had failed, he popularized oratorios—retellings of Bible stories (mostly from the Old Testament) in a semioperatic, semi-choral form. Opera audiences, who had been ready to identify opera's virtuous Roman emperors with local princes, were now delighted to identify oratorio's virtuous People of Israel with the British nation.

Handel was a big, vigorous man, hot tempered but quick to forget, humorous and resourceful. When a particularly temperamental prima donna threw a scene, he calmed her down by threatening to throw her out the window. At the end of his life he became blind—the same surgeon operated (unsuccessfully) on both him and on Bach—but he continued to play the organ brilliantly and composed by dictating to a secretary.

GEORGE FRIDERIC HANDEL   6 Cassette 2A-5/6 CD 2-5
Rodelinda (1725)

As a young man, Handel wrote a few German operas for the Hamburg opera company (most of the music is lost) and a few Italian operas for theaters in

Florence and Venice; in his maturity he wrote as many as forty Italian operas for London. *Rodelinda* is one of a trio of Handel masterpieces written in the years 1724–25, the others being *Tamerlano* and *Giulio Cesare (Julius Caesar).*

Background Most opera plots of the late Baroque era deal with subjects from Roman antiquity (like Handel's *Julius Caesar*). The subject of *Rodelinda*, however, is very remotely derived from the history of the medieval Lombards, in north Italy.

Queen Rodelinda of Lombardy mourns her husband, who is presumed dead in battle. Both she and her sister have to fend off a pair of villains called Grimoaldo and Garibaldo (though Grimoaldo, it turns out, has a good side to him). When Grimoaldo seeks Rodelinda's hand and kingdom, she puts him off with elaborate schemes and oblique promises. Then it turns out that her husband, Bertarido, had not perished after all. He returns in disguise, and is very upset when he misunderstands his wife's machinations.

After many more turns to this tangled tale, Bertarido saves Grimoaldo from the sword of the murderous Garibaldo, and Grimoaldo is grateful enough to obey his better instincts and return the throne to the reunited couple.

The plot is certainly farfetched, but it does have one virtue: it lands the characters in situations that call for strong emotions, which they can then express in some of Handel's finest music. Thus Rodelinda laments her lost husband, and cries out in indignation at Grimoaldo's harshness. Bertarido longs for his wife in one of the opera's greatest hits. Grimoaldo struggles musically with the conflict between his passions and his conscience.

Aria, "Tirannia" And Garibaldo can express the deepest-dyed villainy. Our short recitative and aria show the type of alternation characteristic of opera seria—the recitative accompanied by harpsichord, the aria by orchestra. Unulfo, a minor character, is shocked to hear Garibaldo encouraging Grimoaldo to kill Rodelinda's little son Flavio. But Garibaldo insists; once Grimoaldo has taken the bloody path to power, he says, there can be no stopping now.

When Garibaldo belts out the word *tirannia* on a highly emphatic repeated note, four times in all, we sense that while he may be talking about Grimoaldo's rise to power, "tyranny" is something he craves for himself. Arrogance, power, sheer evil: Handel makes the bass voice project all of these. "Tirannia" is in strict **A B A** form, with the orchestral ritornello before **A** coming back after **A** in an abbreviated form. Since the brief **B** section contains some of the same material as **A,** there is no strong sense of contrast.

People often laugh at the amount of word repetition in Italian operas. The eight words in this aria's **A** section are strung out in four stretches:

Tirannia gli diede il regno, gliel conservi crudeltà, *gliel conservi crudeltà, gliel conservi crudeltà;*
Tirannia gli diede il regno, gliel conservi crudeltà, *gliel conservi crudeltà;*
Tirannia gli diede il regno, gliel conservi crudeltà, *crudeltà, gliel conservi crudeltà;*
Tirannia gli diede il regno, gliel conservi crudeltà.

But the most important effect of all these repetitions is to keep bringing Garibaldo back to the word *crudeltà* with strong—sometimes very strong—cadences. It is as though we are watching an obsessive, sadistic individual gloat about his cruelty. And in the second **A** section, the singer's improvised decorations and his violent, exciting cadenza make Garibaldo sound more malevolent than ever.

Samuel Ramey—the Garibaldo on our recording—singing another, equally villainous Handel bass role (Argante, in *Rinaldo*)

Ti - ran - nia...

TEXT: Handel, *Rodelinda,* "Tirannia," Recitative and Aria

RECITATIVE (SECCO)

Unulfo: Massime così indegne
consigli così rei tu porgi, o duca,
a chi sostien la maestà real?
Garibaldo: Lascia che chi è tiranno opra da tale.
Unulfo: Vorrai?
Garibaldo: Sì, che spergiuro
tradisca la sua fè.
Unulfo: Vorrai?
Garibaldo: Che impuro insidi l'onestà.
Unulfo: Vorrai?
Garibaldo: Che crudo con massime
spietate, ingiuste ed empie . . .
Unulfo: . . . sparga il sangue reale?
Garibaldo: Così d'usurpatore il nome adempie.

Such shameful notions—
can you give such evil counsel, O duke,
to the upholder of royal majesty?
Let him who is the ruler act like one.
You want . . .
      Yes, I want that perjurer
to betray his word!
You want . . .
. . . that villain to subvert her virtue!
Can you really want . . .
. . . that oaf, with his instincts
for villainy, injustice, and evil . . .
. . . to spill royal blood?
That's how to earn the name of usurper!

ARIA

Garibaldo: A   Tirannia gli diede il regno;
gliel conservi crudeltà.

Tyranny brought him the kingdom;
he will retain it only by cruelty.

B   Del regnar base e sostegno
è il rigor, non la pietà.

Power's base and support
is severity, not pity!

A   Tirannia . . . *etc.*

Tyranny . . . *etc.*

For a note on Italian pronunciation, see page 101: "Tirannia li dyehd'il rehnyo."

2 Sacred Vocal Music

Sacred, or religious, vocal music of the Baroque era exhibits considerable diversity in style and form. Most (but not all) of it was written directly for church services, and so its style and form depend first of all on whether those services were of the Catholic, Lutheran, or Anglican rite. Every service has places where music is appropriate, if not actually specified by the liturgy. In principle, each place gives rise to a different musical genre.

There are, however, two important general facts—one traditional in origin, the other specific to the Baroque era—that hold, by and large, for all Baroque sacred-music genres, including Mass and motet, cantata, passion, and oratorio.

> The traditional fact is the participation of the choir. Choral music has had a functional place in the religious music of virtually all rites and of virtually all ages. For when one person utters a religious text, he or she speaks as an individual, but when a choir does so, it speaks as a united community. A church choir, by extension, can be said to speak for the whole church, even for the whole of Christianity.

> The other important fact about Baroque sacred vocal music is its strong tendency to borrow from secular vocal music—which is to say, from opera. Arias inspired by Italian opera seria appear even in the Catholic Mass. Solo singers could display their vocal prowess at the same time as they were presenting parts of the divine service.

In the Lutheran service, an important musical genre derived from opera was the **church cantata,** which was actually constructed like a little opera scene, though of course it was not staged. Characters such as Christ and the Sinner, Hope and Fear, or (more often) various anonymous commentators discuss Christian issues in both arias and recitatives.

And the most operatic of all religious genres was the oratorio, which existed in Catholic and Protestant countries alike.

The Oratorio

An **oratorio** is basically an opera on a religious subject, such as an Old Testament story or the life of a saint. The Baroque Mass and the cantata incorporate such operatic features as recitatives and arias; in addition, the oratorio has a narrative plot in several acts, real characters, and implied action—even though oratorios were not staged, but presented in concert form, that is, without a set, costumes, or gestures. And like other religious genres, the oratorio makes much use of the chorus—a major difference from Italian opera of the time.

Unlike most other religious genres, the oratorio was not actually part of a church service. Indeed, in opera-crazed Italy, the oratorio was prized as an entertainment substituting for opera during Lent, a season of abstinence from opera as well as other worldly diversions.

In England, the oratorio was also a substitute for opera, though in a different sense. Thanks largely to Handel, Italian opera became very popular in London for a quarter of a century, but finally audiences tired of it. At that point, Handel, already in his mid-fifties, turned to oratorios, and these turned out to be even more popular yet, the pinnacle of his long career.

GEORGE FRIDERIC HANDEL
Messiah (1742)

3 Cassette 1A-9, 1B-1/3 CD 1, 9-10
6 Cassette 2A, 6-7/6 CD 2, 6–7

Handel's *Messiah*, his most famous work, is also one of the most famous in the whole of Western music. It is perhaps the only composition from the Baroque era that has been performed continuously—and frequently—since its first appearance. Today it is sung at Christmas and Easter in hundreds of churches around the world, as well as at symphony concerts, and there is a recent custom of "*Messiah* sings," where people get together just to sing along with the Hallelujah Chorus and the other well-known choral numbers, and listen to the well-loved arias.

Unlike most oratorios, *Messiah* does not have actual characters acting out a biblical story in recitatives and arias, although its text is taken from the Bible. In a more typical Handel oratorio, such as *Samson,* for example, Samson sings an aria about his blindness and argues with Delilah in recitative, while choruses represent the People of Israel and the Philistines. Instead, *Messiah* works with a group of narrators, relating episodes from the life of Jesus in recitative. The narration is interrupted by anonymous commentators who react to each of the episodes by singing recitatives and arias.

All this is similar in many ways to opera in concert form (that is, not staged); but in addition, the chorus has a large and varied role to play. On one occasion, they speak for a group of angels that is actually quoted in the Bible. Sometimes they comment on the story, like the soloists. And often they raise their voices to praise the Lord in Handel's uniquely magnificent, enthusiastic manner.

We shall first examine the numbers in *Messiah* covering the favorite Christmas story about the announcement of Christ's birth to the shepherds in the fields. Included is a recitative in four sections and a chorus.

***Recitative** Part 1 (secco)*   Sung by a soprano narrator accompanied by continuo (cello and organ), this recitative has the natural, "proselike" flow typical of all recitatives. Words that would be naturally stressed in ordinary speech are brought out by rhythms, higher pitches, and pauses: "*shep*herds," "*field*," "*flock*," and "*night*." No words are repeated.

Part 2 (accompanied)   The slowly pulsing high-string background, a sort of musical halo for the angel, is also a signal for more vigorous declamation —the words *lo, Lord,* and *glory* are brought out with increasing emphasis. The end of this little accompanied recitative is heavily punctuated by a standard cadence formula, played by the continuo. This formula is an easily recognized feature of recitatives.

Part 3 (secco)   Notice that the angel speaks in a more urgent style than the narrator. And in part 4 (accompanied), the excited, faster pulsations in the high strings depict the beating wings, perhaps, of the great crowd of angels. When Handel gets to what they will be "saying," he brings the music to a triumphant high point, once again over the standard recitative cadence.

TEXT: **Handel, *Messiah*, "There were shepherds,"** Recitative

Part 1 (secco)	**Part 2 (accompanied)**	**Part 3 (secco)**	**Part 4 (accompanied)**
There were **shep**herds abiding in the **field**, keeping watch over their **flock** by **night**.	And **lo**! the angel of the **Lord** came upon them; and the **glory** of the Lord shone round about them; **and they were sore afraid.** (STANDARD CADENCE)	And the angel said unto **them**: "Fear not, for be**hold**, I bring you good **tidings** of great **joy** which shall **be to all people.** (STANDARD CADENCE) For unto **you** is born this **day**, in the city of David, a **Sa**viour, which is **Christ**, the **Lord**. (STANDARD CADENCE)	And **sudd**enly there was with the **angel** a **multitude** of the heav'nly host: praising **God, and saying:** (STANDARD CADENCE)

(**Bold type** *indicates accents.*)

Chorus, "Glory to God"   "Glory to God! glory to God in the *highest*!" sing the angels—the *high* voices of the choir, in an enthusiastic marchlike rhythm, accompanied by the orchestra, with the trumpets prominent. The *low* voices alone add "and peace on *earth*," much more slowly. Fast string runs following "Glory to God," and slower reiterated chords following "and peace on earth," recall the fast and slow string passages in the two preceding accompanied recitatives.

After these phrases are sung and played again, leading to another key, the full chorus sings the phrase "good will toward men" in a fugal style. The important words are *good will*, and their two-note motive is happily sung (in imitation) again and again by all the voices of the angel choir. At its last appearance, the "good will" motive is isolated out in a triumphant ascending sequence.

good will to-ward men

The whole chorus is quite concise, even dramatic; the angels do not stay long. At the very end, the orchestra gets quieter and quieter—a rare effect in Baroque music, here indicating the disappearance of the shepherds' vision.

Massed choirs performing Handel's *Messiah* in London's Westminster Abbey, 1784

Hallelujah Chorus This famous chorus brings Part II of *Messiah* to a resounding close. In some ways, it resembles the chorus "Glory to God," for Handel wrote brilliant homophony for the opening words, "Hallelujah! Hallelujah!" and a grand fugal passage for the phrase "And he shall reign for ever and ever":

Hallelujah,   Hallelujah, Hallelujah, Hallelujah, Halle - lujah.

and he shall reign for ever and ev - er

But of the two choruses, the Hallelujah Chorus is more leisurely and splendid. One magnificent passage has the sopranos solemnly intoning the words "King of Kings, and Lord of Lords"—answered by "for ever, Hallelujah!" in the other voices—on higher and higher notes, all accompanied by the trumpets.

George II of England, attending the first London performance of *Messiah*, was so moved by this chorus that he stood up—in tribute to the King of Kings, perhaps, or to Handel who had praised him so superbly. The whole audience rose too, of course. It is still customary for audiences to stand for the Hallelujah Chorus.

TEXT: **Handel,** *Messiah,* **Hallelujah Chorus**

(Italics indicate phrases of text that are repeated.)

Hallelujah, *Hallelujah!* . . .
For the Lord God omnipotent reigneth. *Hallelujah!* . . .
For the Lord God . . .
The Kingdom of this world is become the kingdom
   of our Lord and *of his Christ.*
And He shall reign for ever and ever, *and he shall reign* . . .
KING OF KINGS *for ever and ever, Hallelujah!* . . .
AND LORD OF LORDS *for ever and ever* . . .

The Lutheran Chorale

There are several genres of Lutheran church music, remembered today mainly for magnificent examples of them written by Bach: the church cantata, the passion, the oratorio, and the motet. All share one feature that was special to the Lutheran Church, and that is their use of traditional congregational hymns. Lutheran hymns are called **chorales,** from the German word for hymn *(Choral).*

Martin Luther, the father of the Protestant Reformation, had made a special point of hymn singing in his directions for setting up services. Two hundred years later, in Bach's time, a large body of chorales served as the foundation for Lutheran worship, both in church services and also at informal pious devotions in the home. Certain chorales were prescribed for specific days such as Easter and Christmas; everybody knew the words and music of these chorales, which they had learned in their childhood. Consequently when composers introduced chorale tunes into church music genres —such as the church cantata and the oratorio—they were drawing on a rich source of association.

A Leipzig church cantata performance

JOHANN SEBASTIAN BACH (1685–1750)
Christmas Oratorio (1734–35)

The way chorale tunes were used can be seen from a comparison of two oratorios—one Lutheran, one not—that both include the episode of the angel's announcement to the shepherds. One is Handel's *Messiah*, the other Bach's *Christmas Oratorio*. The table on page 157 lines up the two works; the words in color indicate additional commentaries on the basic Bible story. It is interesting to see how much Baroque audiences seem to have enjoyed additions of this kind. Meditative interpolations, they found, made the Bible story more vivid and moving.

Just as Handel's librettist for *Messiah* inserted an aria ("Rejoice greatly") commenting on the angel's announcement, Bach's librettist inserted recitatives and arias, too—many of them. In addition, he added two textually relevant chorale stanzas that Bach's congregation would have recognized at once. Indeed, they would have just been singing these same chorales at Christmas services themselves.

Notice that, as in *Messiah,* on one occasion Bach's chorus sings the words of the angels, "Glory to God in the highest." However, when they sing chorales, the chorus changes its role—from telling part of the story to commenting on it, commenting on behalf of the congregation.

Chorale: "Wie soll ich dich empfangen"   There are very many chorales scattered through Bach's *Christmas Oratorio.* For the first and last chorale positions in this long piece, Bach's librettist specified two different stanzas of the same chorale tune, doubtless as a way of providing a unifying thread. The composer set these two stanzas in different ways.

The chorale in question is often called the Passion Chorale, since one of its best-known stanzas, "O Haupt voll Blut und Wunden" ("O head crowned with blood and wounds"), refers to Jesus's crucifixion, and because Bach sets this stanza to music with special pathos in the *St. Matthew Passion,* one of his greatest masterpieces. But other parts of the chorale convey quite different messages. Hence at the beginning of the Christmas story, when Jesus is born, the librettist could appropriately pick a stanza that says:

Wie soll ich dich empfangen,	How should I receive Thee,
Und wie begeg'n ich dir?	And how am I to encounter Thee?
O aller Welt Verlangen,	O, you the desire of all the world,
O meine Seelen Zier!	O, you my soul's adornment!
O Jesu, Jesu! setze	O Jesu, Jesu, shine
Mir selbst die Fackel bei	Upon me Thy light,
Damit, was dich ergötze	So that whatever pleases Thee
Mir kund und wissend sei.	May be shown and known to me.

Bach set this to music simply and meditatively, the tune sung in a straightforward way by the sopranos backed by wonderfully rich harmonies from the rest of the choir. The orchestra part is restricted to doubling the choral parts:

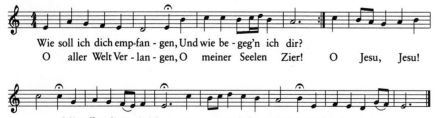

The Angel's Announcement to the Shepherds, As Presented—with Additions
—in Two Baroque Oratorios, Handel's *Messiah* and Bach's *Christmas Oratorio*

Handel, from *Messiah*

3 Cassette 1A-9/3 CD 1-9; 6 Cassette 2A-6/6 CD 2-6
(Additions to the Bible narrative are shown in color.)

RECITATIVE, part I (soprano) (Luke 2:8): There were shepherds abiding in the field, keeping watch over their flocks by night.

RECITATIVE, part II (soprano) (Luke 2:9): And lo, the angel of the Lord came upon them, and the glory of the Lord shone round about them: and they were sore afraid.

RECITATIVE, part III (soprano) (Luke 2:10–11): And the angel said unto them, Fear not: for, behold, I bring you good tidings of great joy, which shall be to all people. For unto you is born this day in the city of David a Saviour, which is Christ the Lord.

RECITATIVE, part IV (soprano) (Luke 2:13): And suddenly there was with the angel a multitude of the heavenly host, praising God, and saying:

CHORUS (Luke 2:14): Glory to God in the highest, and peace on earth, good will toward men.

ARIA (soprano) (Zechariah 9:9–10): Rejoice greatly, O daughter of Zion; shout, O daughter of Jerusalem: behold, thy King cometh unto thee. He is the righteous Saviour, and he shall speak peace unto the heathen.

Bach, from *Christmas Oratorio*, Part II

(not on the record set)

RECITATIVE (tenor) (Luke 2:8–9): There were shepherds . . . and they were sore afraid.

CHORALE: Break through, oh lovely light of morn,
And let the heavens dawn!
You shepherd folk, be not afeared,
Because the angel tells you
That this weak babe
Shall be our comfort and joy . . .

RECITATIVE (tenor and soprano) (Luke 2:10–11): And the angel said unto them: Fear not; behold, I bring you good tidings of great joy, which shall be to all people. For unto you today the Saviour is born, which is Christ, the Lord, in the City of David.

RECITATIVE (bass): The shepherds have been privileged to see God . . .

ARIA (tenor): Hasten, you glad shepherds, and do not wait too long to see the beloved child! . . .

RECITATIVE (tenor) (Luke 2:12): And this shall be a sign: ye shall find the babe wrapped in swaddling clothes, lying in a manger.

CHORALE: Behold, there in the gloomy stable lies
He whose sovereignty encompasses all;
Where the oxen used to look for food
There rests now the Virgin's child.

RECITATIVE (bass): Go, shepherds, behold the wonder, and sing to Him . . .

ARIA (contralto): Sleep, my darling, in peace; awake for the good of mankind . . .

RECITATIVE (tenor) (Luke 2:13): And suddenly there was with the angel a multitude of the heavenly host, praising God, and saying:

CHORUS (Luke 2:14): Glory to God in the highest, and peace on earth, good will toward men.

Eighteenth-century French plaques

An oratorio performance, caught by the satirical pen of Handel's contemporary William Hogarth (1697–1764)

Chorale: "Nun seid Ihr wohl gerochen"   The very end of the *Christmas Oratorio* provided a fine place for another stanza of the same chorale tune. The words of this other stanza are appropriate to the listener's exultant feelings on contemplating the completed Christmas story and all that it means. The birth of Christ frees mankind of its greatest terrors, death and evil:

Nun seid ihr wohl gerochen	Now indeed you are avenged
An eurer Feinde Schar,	On the multitude of your enemies,
Denn Christus hat zerbrochen	For Christ has shattered
Was euch zuwider war.	All that opposed you.
Tod, Teufel, Sünd, und Hölle	Death, the devil, sin, and hell
Sind ganz und gar geschwächt,	Are all disarmed utterly;
Bei Gott hat seine Stelle	Close by to God shall mankind
Das menschliche Geschlecht.	Henceforth have its place.

Bach viewed this as the victory of Christ over the enemies of mankind. An independent orchestral part, featuring trumpets and drums, sounds positively military. The orchestra plays a brilliant opening passage before the choir sings the first line of the chorale, loudly and triumphantly. Snatches of similar orchestral music are heard during gaps between each of the later lines.

A chorale setting of this kind may be called a "gapped" chorale. By punctuating the chorale and delaying the lines, the orchestra gives each one of them special emphasis.

This expanded, gapped chorale setting—expanded so as to provide a strong, satisfying conclusion to the whole *Christmas Oratorio*—ends with the same orchestral passage as at the beginning. The musical form is a little like a miniature concerto grosso, with an orchestral ritornello and with the chorale lines taking the place of the solos.

The Chorale Prelude

The **chorale prelude** or *organ chorale* is an organ composition incorporating a hymn (chorale) tune. Such works were sometimes played by the church organist as a prelude to congregational singing of the chorale in question.

Is it paradoxical to end a chapter entitled "Baroque Vocal Music" with an *organ* chorale—a piece for organ alone? Yes and no. For even though words and voices to sing them are not actually heard in a chorale prelude, they are implicitly present. For as we have already noted, Lutherans knew their hymns by heart; hence the tune played on the organ would immediately bring to mind the hymn text.

BACH   6 Cassette 2A-10/6 CD 2-10
Chorale Prelude: "Herzlich tut mich Verlangen" (c. 1710)

German composers wrote both continuous and gapped organ chorales, analogous to the two types of vocal chorales we have seen in the *Christmas Oratorio,* and other kinds, too. Bach's organ chorale "Herzlich tut mich Verlangen," which is based on the same tune he used at the beginning and end of that oratorio, follows through the tune without gaps. The melody is played by an organ stop (set of pipes) that imitates the sound of an oboe; occasionally it breaks into ornamental patterns that enrich the cadences. The rich, expressive harmony is played (with the organist's left hand, and with the feet on the pedal board) by another, quieter combination of stops.

Bach sets the tune slowly, in a sober, meditative mood appropriate to the text of the designated stanza, "Lord, hear my deepest longing."

St. Thomas Church, where Bach worked; an engraving from the nineteenth century, before the Leipzig church was remodeled

Chapter 11

The Viennese Classical Style

In the second part of the eighteenth century, a new musical style emerged in Europe. Called the Classical style, it had important pioneers in Italy and northern Germany, one of the most influential of whom was Carl Philipp Emanuel Bach, a son of Johann Sebastian. But the Classical style was developed particularly by several great composers active in Vienna, capital of Austria. Here conditions seem to have been ideal for music. Geographically, Austria stands at the crossroads of four other musical nations—Germany, Czechoslovakia, Hungary, and Italy—and Vienna was also central in political terms. As the capital of the powerful Hapsburg empire, Vienna was plunged into every European conflict of the time and exposed to every new cultural and intellectual current.

Vienna's greatest years were from 1780 to 1790, during the reign of Emperor Joseph II, the most enlightened of the illustrious line of Hapsburg monarchs. Joseph emancipated the peasantry, furthered education, and reduced the power of the clergy; he patronized music and literature and encouraged a free press. In a city of only 150,000 people, there were three hundred newspapers and journals during Joseph's reign, representing every shade of opinion.

In this liberal atmosphere, Franz Joseph Haydn of nearby Eisenstadt became recognized as the principal composer of Europe; his symphonies were commissioned from far-off Paris and London. The young Wolfgang Amadeus Mozart was drawn to the capital in 1781 from Salzburg, a hundred miles to the west, to spend his brilliant last decade there. And in 1792 a young musician from the other end of Germany, who had composed a big cantata mourning Emperor Joseph's death, decided to come to this great musical center to launch his career. His name was Ludwig van Beethoven.

Emperor Joseph II

1 The Enlightenment and Music

To describe Joseph II as an "enlightened" ruler is both to commend him and also to locate him in European intellectual history. Like a number of other rulers of the time, Joseph II derived his principles of governance from an important intellectual movement of the eighteenth century known as the Enlightenment, a movement that also helped to define the music that flourished under his reign.

The Vienna of Mozart and Haydn; in the center is the Court Theater (Burgtheater), where operas by both composers were performed.

Centered in France, the Enlightenment had strong roots in English philosophy and strong offshoots in Germany and Austria. Back of the Enlightenment was the faith in reason that had led to the great scientific discoveries of the Baroque period. Now, however, the emphasis veered away from the purely intellectual and scientific toward the social sphere. People were less intent on controlling natural forces by science than on turning these forces to universal benefit. People also began to apply the same intelligence that solved scientific problems to problems of public morality, education, and politics.

Social injustice came under especially strong fire in the eighteenth century. So did established religion; for the first time in European history, religion ceased to be an overriding force in most people's minds. There were currents of agnosticism and even outright atheism—to the outrage of the poet and mystic William Blake:

> Mock on, mock on, Voltaire, Rousseau:
> Mock on, mock on, 'tis all in vain!
> You throw the sand against the wind,
> And the wind blows it back again.

The two French philosophers named by Blake are always mentioned in connection with the Enlightenment: François Marie Arouet, whose pen name was Voltaire (1694–1778), tireless satirist and campaigner for justice and reason, and the younger, more radical, more disturbing Jean Jacques Rousseau (1712–1778). Rousseau is one of the few major figures of European philosophy who had a direct effect on the history of music, as we shall see.

Voltaire, by Jean-Antoine Houdon (1740–1828), master sculptor of the neo-Roman busts that were much favored at the time. All the other portrait busts in this chapter are also by Houdon.

"The Pursuit of Happiness"

The Enlightenment was also the occasion for the first great contribution to Western civilization from America. In colonial days, the austere Puritan spirit was hardly in step with the growing secularization of European society, but the Declaration of Independence and the Federalist Papers proved to be the finest flowers of Enlightenment idealism. The notion that a new state could be founded on rational principles, set down on a piece of paper, and agreed to by men of good will and intelligence—this could only have emerged under the influence of the political and philosophical writings of the eighteenth century.

"Life, liberty, and the pursuit of happiness": the last of these three famous rights, too, was very much of its time. One can imagine the medieval barons who forced King John to accept the Magna Carta insisting on life and liberty, of a sort, but it would never have occurred to them to demand happiness as a self-evident right for all. Voltaire and Rousseau fought passionately for social justice so that people might live good lives according to their own convictions.

The eighteenth century was an age of good living, then, an age that valued intelligence, wit, and sensitivity. The age cultivated elegant conversation, the social arts, and hedonism. One of its inventions was the salon—half party, half seminar: a regular gathering in a fashionable lady's home where notables would discuss books, music, art, and ideas. Other innovations of the time were the coffee house and the public concert.

Jefferson

Art and Entertainment

Entertainment, for most people, contributes to the good life—though certainly Thomas Jefferson was thinking of more than entertainment when he wrote of "the pursuit of happiness." However, the pursuit of entertainment was not something that the eighteenth century looked down on at all. The arts were expected to *please* rather than to instruct, impress, or even express, as had been the case in the Baroque era. The result of this attitude is evident in the style of all the arts in the eighteenth century.

For a time at midcentury a light and often frothy style known as *Rococo* was fashionable in painting, decoration, furniture and jewelery design, and so on. Our illustration—a ceramic plaque—catches the spirit of this entertainment art with special charm. Wreathed in leaves that fit in with the border

A French Rococo ceramic plaque

two impeccably dressed court gentlemen seem to be playing the role of peasants; one plays the flute while the other dances. The subject, the feathery designs on the frame, even the pretty rim itself, are all characteristic of the light art of the Rococo.

Music at midcentury, just before the formation of the Viennese Classical style, was also very light—and often frivolous. A genre that was typical of the time was the **divertimento,** a piece designed to divert, amuse, and entertain. Elaborately decorated musical boxes, playing little tunes, were extremely popular. Major composers of the day—among them another of Bach's sons, Johann Christian—wrote simple, light music which at its best can be charming; much of the time, however, it sounds empty.

A superb portrait of Johann Christian Bach (1735–1782) by Thomas Gainsborough (1727–1788). The youngest son of Johann Sebastian, the "English Bach" was a highly successful Rococo composer who met Mozart and won both his admiration and affection.

The Viennese Classical music of Haydn and Mozart is far from this, yet these composers never put pen to paper without every expectation that their audiences were going to be "pleased." Every historical era, of course, has had its entertainment music. But only in the Classical era was great music of the highest quality put forth quite frankly and plainly as entertainment.

Jean Jacques Rousseau and Opera

Rousseau is remembered today as Europe's first "alienated" intellectual. Whatever his subject, he always came around to blasting the social institutions of his day as stifling to the individual. Passionately devoted to nature and to personal feeling, he disseminated the very influential idea of "natural man," who is born good but corrupted by civilization.

To the great French *Encyclopédie* of 1751–1765, which was the bible of Enlightenment thought, Rousseau contributed the articles on two subjects: politics and music. Interestingly, Rousseau was also a self-taught composer, who made his living for years as a professional music copyist.

Rousseau

Both by means of his fiery writings and by actual example, Rousseau launched a devastating attack on the aristocratic opera of the late Baroque era. And to attack opera—the most important, extended, and glamorous musical genre of the time—was to throw Baroque music itself into question. For Rousseau, the complicated plots of Baroque operas were as impossibly artificial as their complicated music. He demanded a kind of opera that would portray real people in actual life. What he and his contemporaries meant by this was simple people, close to nature, singing "natural" music.

Thus Rousseau acclaimed a famous Italian comic opera of the time, which played in Paris, Giovanni Battista Pergolesi's *La serva padrona* ("The Maid as Mistress," 1733). The music is lively and catchy, with no elaborate coloratura singing, rich harmonies, or exaggerated emotional tirades, and the story could scarcely be more direct or uncomplicated: a servant girl uses a simple ruse to trick a rich old bachelor into marriage. Rousseau himself wrote a highly successful little opera, *Le Devin du village* ("The Village Soothsayer," 1753), in which some guileless peasants work out their love affairs almost entirely in folklike ditties.

Thanks to Pergolesi and Rousseau—and to Mozart—comic opera became the most progressive operatic form of the later part of the century. It dealt not with Roman emperors and their idealized noble sentiments, but with contemporary middle- and lower-class figures expressing everyday feelings in a relatively vivid and natural way. *Opera buffa*, as Italian comic opera was called, will be discussed on page 204.

Rousseau's opera of simple country life, *The Village Soothsayer* (1752)

The Novel

In its ideals, this new kind of opera was comparable to the most important new literary genre that grew up at the same time. This was the novel, which —together with the symphony—counts as the Enlightenment's greatest artistic legacy to the nineteenth and twentieth centuries.

Precursors of the novel go back to ancient Rome, but the genre did not really capture the European imagination until around 1750. The earliest novelists of the eighteenth century were English, but the novel spread rapidly to France and Germany. Among the best-known early novels are Henry Fielding's *Tom Jones*, the tale of a rather ordinary young man and his adventures in town and country, and Samuel Richardson's *Pamela*, a domestic drama that manages to be explicit, sentimental, and moralistic all at the same time. Just before the end of the century, Jane Austen began her subtle explorations of the social forces at work on the hearts of her very sensitive (and sensible) characters in novels such as *Pride and Prejudice*.

Sharp, sympathetic observation of contemporary life, and sensitive depiction of feeling—these are the ideals shared by late eighteenth-century opera and the novel. It is no accident that within a few years of their publication, both *Tom Jones* and *Pamela* were turned into major operas. Nor is it an accident that the composer of *Le Devin du village*, Rousseau, also wrote two of the most widely read novels of the time, *La nouvelle Héloïse* and *Émile*.

In Mozart, opera buffa found a master comparable to Jane Austen in his sensitive response to feeling and action. In his opera *Don Giovanni*, for example, the three women romantically involved with the hero—the coquettish country girl, Zerlina, the steely aristocrat, Donna Anna, and the sentimental Donna Elvira—are depicted in music with the greatest psychological penetration and human sympathy. One can come to feel that the same qualities are reflected in Mozart's symphonies and concertos.

Neoclassicism

It is from the standpoint of "the natural," that great rallying cry of the Enlightenment, that we should understand Neoclassicism, the movement in the visual arts at this time. The Greek and Roman classics have meant many things to many eras; to the eighteenth century, they meant a return to simple, natural values. They meant a rejection of the complex solemnities of the Baroque on the one hand, and of the pleasant frivolities of the Rococo on the other. The designs of Wedgwood pottery, the impressive portrait busts (modeled on Roman busts) by Jean-Antoine Houdon, and the scenes from ancient history painted by Jacques-Louis David are just a few examples of eighteenth-century Neoclassical art.

A late-eighteenth-century court musician surrounded by the tools of his trade. However, he is depicted not in a palace of the era, but in a sober imitation classical temple—amusing testimony to the Neoclassical enthusiasms and aspirations of the time.

Austere classical subjects were made into powerful operas by Christoph Willibald von Gluck (1714–1787), an important composer active in both Vienna and Paris. His most famous opera is *Orfeo ed Euridice* (1762), based on the Greek myth of Orpheus. When his *Alceste* (derived from a classical Greek drama) was produced in Paris, it was greatly admired by the aging Rousseau.

Apart from the operas of Gluck, however, Neoclassical art has no direct connection with music in what is traditionally called the Classical style. One can perhaps see that a taste inclined toward moderation, simplicity, and balance would also appreciate the order and clarity of late eighteenth-century music, but the traditional label is not a very happy one. It was the nineteenth century that coined the label "Classicism" to distinguish the music of Haydn and Mozart from the "Romanticism" that was then actively being developed.

Gluck

Today, the waters are muddied by yet another sense of the word *classical*. Mozart's music from the Classical period is called "classical" (as is Bach's music from the Baroque period or Brahms's from the Romantic period) simply as a label to distinguish it from "popular" music.

2 The Rise of Concerts

A far-reaching development in the sociology and economics of music was the rise of public concerts. Sporadic concerts had been put on before, in taverns, private homes, palaces, and theaters, but it was only in the middle of the eighteenth century that they became a significant force in musical life. Series of concerts, with financing from subscriptions, were put on by entrepreneurs, and concerts for the benefit of charities were set up on a regular basis as major society events.

In 1748 Europe's first hall designed especially for concerts was built in a university town, Oxford. Still in use, the Holywell Music Room holds about 150 people.

Music of all kinds was presented at these new public concerts; one major series, the Parisian *Concert spirituel* founded in 1725, originally concentrated on sacred vocal music. But orchestral music was the staple. The importance of concerts lay mainly in the impetus they gave to the composition of orchestral music—symphonies and concertos. For there were, after all, other public forums for church music (churches) and opera (commercial opera houses, which had existed alongside court theaters from the mid-seventeenth century on). Now purely orchestral music, too, moved into the public domain, and its importance and prestige grew rapidly.

Though ultimately the concert hall became the focal point of musical life —the main center of interest for listeners and the main source of support for composers—the late eighteenth century was still a period of transition. The basic economic facts of music remained as they had been earlier: court pat-

A late-eighteenth-century concert in Venice. The hall looks like a splendid room in a palace, except for the special gallery for the musicians—who are the orphan girls of the Ospedale where Vivaldi had worked (see page 133).

ronage, the opera house, and the church were still the chief sources of a composer's livelihood (though in an increasingly secular age, the church was becoming less important). As we shall see, concerts were a factor in the lives of both the great masters of Classical music already mentioned: Haydn's last symphonies, the *London* symphonies, were commissioned for highly successful concerts arranged for the composer's London tours, and most of Mozart's piano concertos—among his greatest works—were written for yearly benefit concerts that he put on in Vienna. All the same, concerts were a resource that Haydn did not draw on in a major way until he was already well established; and they were not an adequate resource, alas, to sustain Mozart.

3 Style Features of Classical Music

In discussing the musical style of the late Baroque period, we started with a single guiding concept. There is a thorough, systematic, even rigorous quality in the ways early eighteenth-century composers treated almost all aspects of music, and this quality seems to underpin the expressive gestures of grandeur and overstatement that are characteristic of the Baroque. Classical music cannot be discussed quite so simply as this. We have to keep two concepts in mind for its understanding, concepts that were constantly on the lips of men and women of the time. One was "the natural," and the other was "pleasing variety."

In the late eighteenth century, it was taken for granted that these two artistic ideals went hand in hand, and provided mutual support. Today we can see that sometimes they pulled in opposite directions. For although "variety" was invoked as a guard against boredom, it was also an invitation to complexity, and complexity would seem to run counter to "natural" simplicity and clarity.

In any case, in Classical music one or the other—and sometimes both—of these qualities can be discerned in all the elements of musical technique: in rhythm, dynamics, tone color, melody, texture, and form. A new expressive quality developed in this music as a result of its new technique.

Rhythm

Perhaps the most striking change in music between the Baroque and the Classical periods came in rhythm. In this area the artistic ideal of "pleasing variety" reigned supreme. The unvarying rhythms of Baroque music were regarded as dreary, obvious, and boring.

Classical music is highly flexible in rhythm. Throughout a single movement, the tempo and meter remain constant, but the rhythms of the various themes tend to differ in both obvious and subtle ways. In the first movement of Mozart's Symphony in G Minor, for example, the first theme moves almost entirely in eighth notes and quarters, whereas the second theme is marked by longer notes and shorter ones—dotted half notes and sixteenths. And the rhythm of the background accompaniment is completely different in each case.

Audiences wanted variety in music; composers responded by refining the rhythmic differences between themes and other musical sections, so that the differences sound like more than differences—they sound like real contrasts.

Domestic music making in the eighteenth century: George, 3rd earl of Cowper, with the family of Charles Gore, by Johann Zoffany (1733–1810), one of the main fashionable painters in Britain (and British India).

They also cultivated contrast *within* themes. Rhythmic surprises are frequent (in late Baroque music, they are very infrequent). The music may gradually increase or decrease its rhythmic energy, stop suddenly, press forward by fits and starts, or glide by with a carefully calculated smoothness. All this gives the sense that Classical music is moving in a less predictable, more interesting, and often more exciting way than Baroque music does.

Dynamics

Variety and flexibility were also introduced into dynamics. Passages were now conceived more specifically than before as loud, soft, very loud, and so on, and marked **f, p, ff, mf** by composers accordingly. Again, concern for variety went along with a new sensitivity to contrast. By insisting on the contrast between loud and soft, soft and very soft, composers made variety in dynamics clearly perceptible and, we must suppose, "pleasing."

Furthermore, instead of using the steady dynamics of the previous period, composers now worked extensively with gradations of volume. The words for growing louder *(crescendo)* and growing softer *(diminuendo)* first came into general use in the Classical period. Orchestras of the mid-eighteenth century were the first to practice long crescendos, which, we are told, caused audiences to rise up from their seats in excitement. Doubtless these passages were subtly managed in terms of rhythm also.

The clearest sign of the new flexibility in dynamics was the rise in popularity of the piano, at the expense of the omnipresent harpsichord of the Baroque era. The older instrument could manage only one sound level, or at best a few sound levels, thanks to its two or three separate sets of strings. The new pianoforte (meaning "soft-loud") could produce a continuous range of dynamics from soft to loud. It attracted composers because they wished their keyboard instruments to have the same flexibility in dynamics that they were teaching to their orchestras.

Tone Color: The Orchestra

The Classical composers also devoted increasing attention to tone color. The clearest sign of this was the emergence of the Classical orchestra. The orchestra standardized in this period formed the basis of the symphony orchestra of later times.

The foundation of the Classical orchestra was still (as in the Baroque orchestra) a group of stringed instruments: violins, divided into two groups, first violins and second violins; violas; and cellos, with a few basses playing the same music as the cellos an octave lower. As we saw on page 118, there was a "basic" Baroque orchestra consisting of just these instruments, plus the continuo, and various other possibilities, including the "festive" Baroque orchestra:

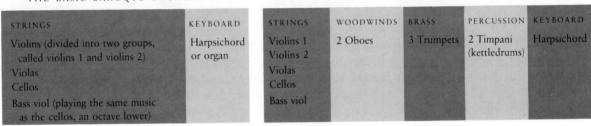

THE BASIC BAROQUE ORCHESTRA

STRINGS	KEYBOARD
Violins (divided into two groups, called violins 1 and violins 2)	Harpsichord or organ
Violas	
Cellos	
Bass viol (playing the same music as the cellos, an octave lower)	

THE FESTIVE BAROQUE ORCHESTRA

STRINGS	WOODWINDS	BRASS	PERCUSSION	KEYBOARD
Violins 1	2 Oboes	3 Trumpets	2 Timpani (kettledrums)	Harpsichord
Violins 2				
Violas				
Cellos				
Bass viol				

In the Classical orchestra, however, the woodwind and brass instruments were given clearly defined regular roles. With the strings as a framework, woodwind instruments were added: in the high range, pairs of flutes, oboes, and clarinets; in the low, bassoons. These instruments provided "pleasing variety" by playing certain melodies and other passages; each of the woodwinds contributed its characteristic tone color and participated in carefully calculated combinations of tone colors. They also strengthened the strings in loud sections.

Brass instruments were added in the middle range. The function of French horns and trumpets was mainly to provide solid support for the main harmonies, especially at points such as cadences when the harmonies needed to be made particularly clear. The only regular percussion instruments used were two timpani, which generally played along with the brass.

The great advance in the orchestra from the Baroque to the Classical era was in flexibility—flexibility in tone color and also in rhythm and dynamics. The orchestra now became the most subtle and versatile musical resource that composers could employ, as well as the grandest.

THE CLASSICAL ORCHESTRA

STRINGS	WOODWINDS	BRASS	PERCUSSION
First violins	2 Flutes	2 French horns	2 Timpani
Second violins	2 Oboes	2 Trumpets*	
Violas	2 Clarinets*		
Cellos	2 Bassoons		
Bass viols		*Optional	

Melody: Tunes

The Enlightenment ideal of "pleasing variety" was a secondary issue with Classical melody. Rather the demand was for simplicity and clarity, for relief from the complex, richly ornamented lines of the Baroque period. When people at the time demanded "natural" melodies, what they meant were tunes: simple, singable melodies with clear phrases (and not too many of them), melodies with easily grasped parallelisms and balances.

Confronted with a Baroque work such as Bach's Suite No. 3 in D (see page 141), a late eighteenth-century audience might have tolerated the fairly straightforward Gavotte, but would have been unmoved by the beautiful Air (the so-called Air on the G String). Its elegant winding lines and the mere fact of its great length would have struck them as completely "unnatural":

Hence composers of the Classical period moved much closer to folk and popular music than their Baroque predecessors. There is an unmistakable popular lilt in Haydn's music that people have traced to the Croatian folk melodies he may have heard in childhood. Short tunes—or, more often, attractive little phrases that sound as though they might easily grow into tunes—are heard again and again in Classical symphonies, quartets, and other pieces. Tunes are not the only melodic material to be heard in these works, as we shall see in a moment. Nonetheless, by comparison with a Baroque concerto grosso, a Classical symphony leaves listeners with a good deal more to hum or whistle as they leave the concert.

Often entire tunes were worked into larger compositions. For example, the theme and variations form grew popular both for separate pieces improvised by virtuosos and as movements in multimovement genres. Haydn wrote variations on the Austrian national anthem (he also wrote the tune), and Mozart wrote variations on "Twinkle, Twinkle, Little Star" or "Baa Baa Black Sheep," which he knew in its original French version:

Occasionally, popular songs were even introduced into symphonies. There is a contemporary opera ditty in Mozart's *Jupiter* Symphony, the last he composed.

Texture: Harmony

The predominant texture of Classical music is homophonic. In Classical compositions, melodies are regularly heard with a straightforward harmonic accompaniment in chords, without counterpoint and without even a melodic-sounding bass line. Again, this was thought (not unreasonably) to be a more "natural," clearer way of presenting a melody than polyphony.

All this made, and still makes, for easy listening. The opening of Mozart's famous Symphony in G Minor proclaims the new sonorous world of the late eighteenth century:

Molto allegro

STRINGS

etc.

A single quiet chord regrouped and repeated by the violas; the simplest possible bass support below; and above them all a plaintive melody in the violins —this simple, sharply polarized texture becomes typical.

Homophony or melody with harmony was not, however, merely a negative reaction to what people of the time saw as the heavy, pedantic complexities of Baroque counterpoint. It was also a positive move in the direction of sensitivity. When composers found that they were not always occupied in fitting other contrapuntal parts to their melodies, they also discovered that they could handle other elements of music with more "pleasing variety." In particular, a new sensitivity was developed to harmony for its own sake.

Porcelain musicians, c. 1770

One aspect of this was a desire to specify harmonies more precisely than in the Baroque era. The first thing to go was the continuo, which had spread its unrelenting and unspecified (because improvised) chord patterns over nearly all Baroque music. Classical composers, newly alert to the sonorous quality of a particular chord, wanted it "spaced" and distributed among various instruments in just one way. They were not prepared to allow a continuo player to obscure the chord with unpredictable extra notes and rhythms.

It may seem paradoxical, then, but the thrust toward simplicity in texture led through the back door to subtlety in other areas, notably in rhythm and in harmony.

Classical Counterpoint

The rise of homophony in the Classical period represents a major turnaround in musical technique. For although Baroque composers did write some homophonic pieces, as we have seen, the predominant texture of music at that time was polyphonic. This turning point was, in fact, one of the most decisive in all of musical history, for polyphony had monopolized music since the Middle Ages.

Yet it is not the way of history to abandon important resources of the past completely, even when the past is completely discredited. Classical composers rejected Baroque music, but they cautiously retained the basic principle of counterpoint. They were able to do this by refining it into a more delicate, unobtrusive kind of counterpoint than that practiced in the Baroque era. And there was a sharper awareness now of counterpoint's expressive possibilities. In a texture that was predominantly "natural" and homophonic, counterpoint attracted special attention; this texture could be used to create the impression of tension, of one line rubbing against another. The more intense, "artificial" texture of polyphony stood out against "natural" homophonic texture.

Hence, as we shall see in the next chapter, the section in Classical sonata form called the development section, whose basic function is to build up tension, typically involves contrapuntal textures. Sonata form was the most important musical form of the time, and so counterpoint was often heard.

4 Form in Classical Music

How can a piece of music be extended through a considerable span of time, when listeners expect everything to be "natural," simple, and easily understood? This was the problem of musical form that faced composers of the Viennese Classical era. They arrived at a solution of considerable elegance and power, involving several elements.

Repetitions and Cadences

First, themes in Classical music tend to be *repeated* immediately after their first appearance, so that listeners can easily get to know them. (In earlier music, this happened only in dance music, as a general rule.) Later in the piece, those same themes will be repeated again.

Second, themes are *led into* in a very distinctive manner. The music features prominent transitional passages that do not have much melodic profile, only a sense of urgency about arriving someplace—the place where the real theme will be presented (and probably presented twice).

Third, after themes have been played, they are typically *closed off* just as distinctively. There are often quite long passages consisting of cadences repeated two, three, or more times, as though to make it clear that one musical idea is over and another, presumably, is coming up. Composers would devise little cadential phrases, often with minimal melodic interest, that could be repeated and thus allow for such multiple cadences.

Multiple cadences are a characteristic and easily recognizable feature of Classical music, particularly, of course, at the very ends of movements. Many illustrations can be found in Mozart's G-minor Symphony:

> *Second movement* (Andante): A brief phrase in the strings is heard three times. Each time, though the phrase is a little different, it comes to a cadence and a real stop, with little interpolations by the wind instruments:

> *Third movement* (Minuet and Trio): The trio ends with a small phrase played twice, producing a double cadence. The end of the first playing of the cadence phrase coincides, or overlaps, with the beginning of the second playing (so there is only one full stop, not two):

Classical Forms

A third feature designed to cope with the problem of musical form in Classical music is perhaps the most far reaching. Composers and their audiences came to rely on a limited number of "forms," or standard formal patterns, the most important of which are minuet form, sonata form, theme and variations, and rondo.

There was thus a commonly understood frame of reference for composing music and appreciating it. Broadly speaking, after listening for just a short time to some new piece, an eighteenth-century music lover could always tell what sort of themes and keys it would include, when they would be returned to, and about how long the piece would last. This frame of reference is not so obvious today, so Chapter 12 will devote itself to the four Classical forms just mentioned.

The repetitions, self-conscious transitions, and emphatic cadences that are so characteristic of the Classical style all help clarify the forms. And the forms themselves were a special necessity at a time when composers were filling their compositions with contrasts of all kinds. It is a mark of the aesthetic success of Classical music that the contrasts don't always sound too drastic, because the forms control and, as it were, tame them. The seemingly inexhaustible emotional range of Classical music is in direct proportion to the extent of those contrasts, on the one hand, and, on the other, the elegance of their control by musical form.

Houdon's most unclassical portrait bust—of his wife

Chapter 12

Classical Forms

It is not by chance that the one chapter in this book devoted specifically to musical form should be the one dealing with the forms of Viennese Classicism. For of all the periods of music history, the Classical period nurtured its forms the most and developed them to the highest state of sophistication.

In the later, Romantic period—an age that was very conscious of its "freedom"—Classical forms were sometimes criticized as stereotyped and constraining. But the great Viennese composers were not constrained by Classical forms. They found them an inspiration for all kinds of explorations and refinements. The "givens" of a musical form allowed them to explore audacities that could never have occurred to them in a completely uncontrolled environment.

Haydn and Mozart (also Beethoven and Schubert in the early nineteenth century) worked *within* Classical forms, molding them imaginatively to their unique artistic visions. We shall not get very far with their music simply by identifying its form and counting up the requisite **A**'s and **B**'s, cadences, repeats, and so on, even though this is the necessary preliminary to understanding the composer's approach to the form. In the following discussions of individual works we try to highlight each composer's special treatment of minuet form, sonata form, and the rest. We shall try to see, in other words, how composers personalized Classical forms for their own expressive purposes.

1 Minuet Form (Classical Dance Form)

We shall start our discussion of Classical music with its minuet movements. Since minuets are the shortest of all classical movements, their form is relatively simple and easy to discern. Furthermore, this form bears a clear logical relation to one that has already been studied. The form of the minuet is simply dance form—the dance form of the Baroque era, modified to accommodate some of the concerns of the Classical era.

The Minuet

Stylized dances—music of considerable elaboration in the style and form of dances, but intended for listening rather than dancing—reached a state of

Above and facing page, top: the minuet, the favorite dance of eighteenth-century high society

high development in the Baroque era. As we saw in Chapter 8, dances or dancelike movements occur in dance suites and also in many sonatas, concerti grossi, and works in other genres.

The sole dance type from the Baroque suite to survive in the multimovement genres of the Classical period was the **minuet.** One reason for this was simply that the dance itself, originally popularized at the court of Louis XIV in the seventeenth century, continued as one of the major fashionable social dances during the eighteenth. Another reason was more technical. As a moderately paced piece in triple meter, the minuet makes an excellent contrast to the duple meter that was virtually standard in the fast movements of Classical symphonies, quartets, and the like.

Every four-movement genre of the Classical period—every symphony, string quartet, and four-movement sonata—has a place for a minuet, usually as a light contrast after the slow movement. Mozart even managed to fit minuets into several of his greatest piano concertos, though traditionally the concerto, a three-movement genre, did not leave room for a minuet.

Baroque and Classical Dance Form

A Baroque minuet (like every other Baroque dance) consists of two sections; each comes to a complete stop and is immediately repeated (|: **a** :||: **b** :|). Minuets tend to come in pairs, alternating in an **A B A** pattern. The second dance, **B**, is called the **trio,** because in early days it was played by three instruments.

A Baroque minuet movement can be diagrammed as follows. (Remember that |: :| means repeat, and that in the second **A** the parts are not repeated.)

Minuet	Trio	Minuet
A	B	A
|: a :||: b :|	|: c :||: d :|	a b

Classical composers generally extended the internal form of their minuets and trios by bringing back the music of the first section, **a** or **c**, at the end of the second section, **b** or **d**. In other words, their minuets and trios developed internal **a b a** structures. Classical dance form is sometimes called *ternary form.*

Most Classical minuets fall into one of the following schemes:

Minuet	Trio	Minuet
A	B	A
|: a :||: b a :|	|: c :||: d c :|	a b a

or (more often)

Minuet	Trio	Minuet
A	B	A
|: a :||: b a′ :|	|: c :||: d c′ :|	a b a′

Eighteenth-century social dancing—a satirical view

Prime marks (**a′** and **c′**) indicate significant extension or alterations of the original **a** and **c** sections. And indeed, a great deal of the art of Classical stylization was focused on changes of this kind.

Franz Joseph Haydn

(1732–1809)

Chief Works: Over 100 symphonies, notable among them the set of twelve composed for London in 1791–1795, including the *Surprise, Clock, Drum Roll,* and *London* symphonies

A cello concerto and a delightful trumpet concerto

Over 80 string quartets; piano trios and piano sonatas

Choral music of his late years, including fine Masses and the famous oratorios *The Creation* (1798) and *The Seasons* (1801)

The most famous of all Haydn's compositions is a popular one—a simple Austrian patriotic song later taken over as the German national anthem, *Deutschland über Alles,* and as the Anglican hymn "Glorious Things of Thee Are Spoken." He included it with variations in his *Emperor* Quartet, Op. 76 No. 3 (1797).

Joseph Haydn was born in Rohrau in Lower Austria, the son of a village wheelwright who was a keen amateur musician. Another of his sons, Michael, also became a composer. As a boy Joseph had a beautiful voice, and at the age of eight was sent to Vienna to be a choirboy in St. Stephen's Cathedral. After his voice broke, he spent a number of difficult years as a free-lance musician in Vienna before obtaining the position of Kapellmeister with Prince Paul Anton Esterházy, one of the most lavish patrons of music at the time.

After this, Haydn's career exemplifies the situation in the later eighteenth century, when the old system of court patronage coexisted with an early form of the modern concert system. Indeed, there is no finer tribute to the system of court patronage than Haydn's thirty-year career with the Esterházys. The post of Kapellmeister involved managing and writing music not only for the prince's chapel (the *Kapell*), but also for palace chamber music and orchestral performances, for his private opera house, and for his marionette theater. Haydn had a good head for administration. Hiring his own musicians, he was able over many years to experiment with the symphony and other genres and develop his style under ideal conditions.

The Esterházys had a splendid estate some miles outside of Vienna, but Haydn's extensive duties there did not prevent him from spending a good deal of time in the capital. His string quartets, published from 1771 on, made a particularly strong impression in the metropolis. In the 1780s he befriended Mozart, and the two actually played together in an amateur string quartet.

Haydn's output was staggering. He composed dozens of symphonies, divertimentos, string quartets, trios, and sonatas, and over twenty operas and marionette operas. He also had to write a great deal of music for baryton—a bizarre archaic instrument fancied by the next Esterházy prince, Nikolaus, which was something like a cello with extra strings that could be plucked, like guitar strings.

The spread of Haydn's international fame in the 1770s was accelerated by the growth of public concerts, the major sociological development of late

Haydn at the height of his career in the 1790s: a formal portrait (right) and an unassuming pencil drawing (left). The latter was Haydn's choice—not the choice of a vain man!—as the best likeness of himself he had seen.

eighteenth-century music. At first his symphonies were picked up by French concert organizers (who paid Haydn nothing). Then in the 1780s his six *Paris* symphonies were expressly commissioned for concerts in that city. Perhaps Haydn's greatest works are the twelve *London* symphonies of 1791–1795, commissioned for two enormously successful tours arranged for the composer—by then retired and pensioned—by an enterprising London impresario.

Toward the end of his life Haydn turned to choral music, and wrote impressive masses and two oratorios in German, inspired by Handel. *The Creation* and *The Seasons* were seen by both the composer and his admirers as the climax of a long, distinguished career.

Haydn had an unhappy marriage (the couple separated), but if he had other affairs of the heart, they were handled with discretion. An autumnal flirtation with a German lady living in London is memorialized in the dedication of a late piano sonata.

One of the most attractive personalities in the gallery of the great composers, Haydn was shrewd but generous minded, humorous, always honorable, and though fully aware of his own worth, quite ready to praise his young, "difficult" colleague, Mozart. "Friends often flatter me that I have some genius," he once said—without contradicting them—"but he stood far above me."

Haydn's music combines good-humored simplicity of melody with a very sophisticated delight in the manipulations of musical form and technique. In his reasonableness, his wit, and his conviction that his art should serve humanity, a conviction he both expressed and acted upon, Haydn is the true musical representative of the Enlightenment.

Baryton

An Eighteenth-Century Ballroom Minuet

It may be interesting to consider briefly a minuet of the time that was intended for actual dancing. Here is a characteristic piece by an able, if unexceptional composer, Antonio Salieri (1750–1825), one of many eigtheenth-century Italians who made a musical career in Vienna. Posterity remembers Salieri mainly for the absurd rumor that he poisoned Mozart, but in his day he was esteemed for his operas and church music, in particular. Both Beethoven and Schubert took lessons from him.

(In the movie *Amadeus,* he kills Mozart in a slightly more plausible way—by scaring him half to death and then goading him to work when he is sick and exhausted; none of this really happened. After the movie came out, Salieri's music enjoyed a considerable vogue.)

Salieri's "unstylized" minuet exemplifies both the subvarieties of Classical minuet form diagrammed on page 175, one with the exact repetition of the opening element (c), and the other with a free repetition (a′).

Phrases of four, eight, or twelve measures were standard for the minuet dance steps, and Salieri followed these norms strictly.

The minuet is as usual both vigorous and rather stately, with a graceful **b** section played by a solo violin. The Trio is in a different key and features French horns at the beginning; this makes a simple but effective contrast. The second **c** is the same as the first, but the players add a little ornament at the cadence.

Attractive, unassuming, and instantly forgettable, this functional dance music stays well below the artistic level developed by Haydn and Mozart for minuet movements in their symphonies and quartets. It appears on 6 Cassette 2B-1 and 6 CD 2-11.

Recommended Listening Mozart, 6 German Dances, K. 509; Beethoven, 12 Contredanses. Like the minuet, the contredanse was a popular dance of the time, but livelier and in duple meter. The young Beethoven, after coming to Vienna, wrote this set of ballroom dances in the Viennese Classical style.

	Minuet		Trio		Minuet
	|: **a** :||: **b a′** :|	|: **c** :||: **d c** :|	**a b a′**
measures:	8	8 8	12	8 12	8 8 8

FRANZ JOSEPH HAYDN
String Quartet in D, Op. 64 No. 5 (The *Lark*) (1790), third movement: Menuetto

For a full discussion of Haydn's *Lark* Quartet, see page 214.

In his many symphonies and string quartets, composed over a long, productive lifetime, Haydn fashioned the minuet into a light but superbly elegant small-scale form, a form that constitutes a microcosm of the art of Classical music. Like many others, the present minuet has one foot in the ballroom, but its heart is clearly with those musical connoisseurs who enjoyed the more sophisticated music of the time, and played this themselves.

Minuet (Allegretto)   The **a** section is a simple phrase of the standard, danceable length (8 measures):

The section contains two main motives: a strongly metrical rocking figure at the start, and a forceful upward-running scale at the end. As is always the case in stylized dances, section **a** ends with a definite stop, and is then repeated exactly.

The rocking figure is also used for the **b** section, which touches on the minor mode. After another stop, **a** returns, modified into **a'**—for the scale figure is presented in inversion (running down instead of up).

This phrase, too, comes to a stop. Haydn has completed the form and produced a nicely balanced piece; this is all he would have written if this minuet had been ordered for the ballroom. Instead, he added an extra passage, one that shows his Classical sensitivity to fine points of musical form. The extra passage introduces new rhythmic variety and then restores the original upward scale motive (twice—in high and then low instruments). This makes the cadence to the second section, **b a'**, much more interesting. A potentially routine little minuet has been turned into a stylized dance of considerable verve.

It is only after the repeat of **b a'**, perhaps, that the listener fully appreciates this. The repeats have a real aesthetic function, then, over and above that of providing the composer with an easy way to extend his music.

Trio   The scale motive from the minuet also dominates the trio. (It is *not* usual for a trio to take over motives from its minuet: Haydn treats this unusual procedure as a paradox—another witty feature.) But if using the same motive seems to *minimize* the traditional contrast between minuet and trio, other features *maximize* contrast: the trio is quieter and more contrapuntal than the minuet, and it comes in the minor mode.

The return of **c** (**c'**) is rather tricky; nearly hidden in the cello, it comes after only four measures of **d** and hurries to the trio's final cadence.

Minuet   The minuet returns verbatim, though this time without repeats. This second **A**, with its expansive, forceful final section, makes a perfect response to the feeling of unfinished business that was left over from the hurried end of the trio.

3 Cassette 1B-2/3 CD 1-11
6 Cassette 2B-2/6 CD 2-12

LISTENING CHART NUMBER 6

Haydn, Quartet in D (The *Lark*), third movement

Minuet form. 3 min., 10 sec.

MINUET (A)

0.00	**a**	First phrase: scale motive goes up.	
		Stop.	
0.08	**a**	Repeat	
		Stop.	
11.2 12.2 0.17	**b**	Next phrase: goes through the minor mode	
		Less firm stop.	

11.3 12.3 0.26 **a'** {
First phrase returns, but the ending is different: the scale goes down (inversion).

Less firm stop.

Extension phrase: ends with scale going up, low instruments.
}

Stop.

11.4 12.4 0.54	**b**	Repeat	
1.02	**a'**	Repeat	
		Stop.	

TRIO (B)

11.5 12.5 1.31	**c**	First trio phrase: contrapuntal; second violin leads.	
		Stop.	
1.46	**c**	Repeat	
		Stop.	
11.6 12.6 2.00	**d**	Second trio phrase (short) runs into return of **c'**.	
11.7 12.7 2.04	**c'**	The cello leads.	
		Stop.	
2.10	**d**	Repeat	
2.15	**c'**	Repeat	
		Stop.	

MINUET (A)

2.21	**a**	First phrase: scale motive goes up.	
		Stop.	
2.30	**b**	Next phrase: goes through the minor mode	
		Less firm stop.	

First phrase returns, but the ending is different (inversion).

2.39	**a'**	Less firm stop.	

Extension phrase: ends with scale going up, low instruments.

Stop.

2 Sonata Form

Sonata form was the most important form developed by the Viennese Classical composers, and it was still a major force in the Romantic music of the mid- and late-nineteenth century, the music of Schumann, Berlioz, Brahms, and Mahler. Classical composers found sonata form particularly flexible in expressive application—something they could use for forceful, brilliant, pathetic, or tragic opening movements, meditative or dreamy slow movements, and lively, often humorous last movements.

The first movement of virtually every Classical multimovement composition is in sonata form, and it nearly always counts as the intellectual and emotional center of these works. Many symphonies and sonatas have two, even three movements in sonata form. The importance of this form goes even further, for its underlying principles spread to other eighteenth-century forms, such as rondos, opera numbers, sections of the Mass, and even minuets.

Eighteenth-century women often chose to show off their musical accomplishments when sitting for portraits. This was as true of the French princess portrayed by the fashionable court painter Marie-Louise Elizabeth Vigée-Lebrun (1755–1842) as of the unknown American girl painted by Mather Brown (1761–1831).

Sonata Form and Minuet Form

The sonata-form movement that starts a symphony or a sonata is never as simple as the minuet movement, yet for all their difference in scope, these two forms are basically similar in plan.

The similarity appears on the largest level: both sonata form and minuet (dance) form consist of two main portions which—in principle—come to complete stops and are then marked for repetition.[1] Furthermore, both forms have the same important feature, a free return of the opening material:

---

[1] These repetitions were marked less and less frequently in the later history of sonata form, and today it is regarded as the performer's option whether or not to actually carry them out.

The main ballroom in the Vienna of Mozart and Haydn's time, called the Redoutensaal

| MINUET | is comparable to | SONATA FORM | (the repeats in sonata form are optional) |

|: **a** :||: **b a′** :| |: **A** :||: **B A′** :|

Exposition ┘ └ Recapitulation
Development

Whereas the **a**, **b**, and **a′** sections of a minuet may be as short as eight-measure phrases, the **A**, **B**, and **A′** sections of a sonata-form movement (called the *exposition, development,* and *recapitulation,* respectively) are rich aggregates of contrasting themes, transitional passages, cadence formulas, and much more. With this difference clearly in mind, however, it can be useful to think of sonata form as a vastly blown-up type of minuet form.

Another difference, a difference in style, is more fundamental than that of dimensions. The guiding force behind the minuet is dance rhythm. The guiding force behind sonata form is contrast. Indeed, sonata form is the form that most exploited what was perhaps the overriding interest of Classical composers, their interest in musical contrasts of every kind—in particular, contrast of thematic material and contrast of key, or tonality.

Exposition (A)

A movement in sonata form begins with a large section of music called the **exposition**—so called because its basic material is presented or "exposed" here. This material consists of a number of different elements.

➤ To begin, a main theme is presented in the first key, the tonic key (see page 37; this key is the key of the piece as a whole—in Mozart's Symphony in G Minor, the tonic is G minor). This **first theme** may be a tune, a group of small phrases that sound as though they are about to grow into a tune, or simply a motive or two (see page 33) with a memorable rhythmic character.

➤ After the first theme is firmly established, perhaps with the help of a free repetition, there is a change in key, or *modulation*. The subsection of the exposition that accomplishes this is called the **bridge,** or the *transition*.

➤ The modulation in the bridge is an essential feature (even *the* essential feature) that gives sonata form its sense of dynamic forward movement. With a little experience, it is not hard to hear the contrast of key and sense the dynamism, for the idea is not to make the crucial modulation sound too smooth. There has to be a sense of tension in the way the new themes, now to be introduced, "set" in the new key.

➤ The group of themes in the new key is called the **second group.** Composers generally make these new themes contrast with the first in melody, rhythm, dynamics, and so on, as well as in key. There is nearly always one that stands out by its melodious quality; this is called the **second theme.**

The last theme in the second group, the **cadence theme,** or *closing theme,* is constructed so as to make a solid ending prior to the full stop and the big repeat. The very end of the exposition is marked by a loud series of repeated cadences, as though the composer wanted listeners to know exactly where they are in the form. This **A** (exposition) section was almost always repeated.

Development (B)

The following section, the **development,** heightens the tonal-thematic tension set up by the contrasting keys and themes of the exposition. The themes are "developed"—by being broken up, recombined, reorchestrated, extended, and in general shown in unexpected and often exciting new contexts.

Eighteenth-century American spinet

Most development sections use counterpoint to create a sense of break-up and turmoil. In tonality, this section moves around restlessly; there are frequent modulations, which are easily heard.

After considerable tension has been built up in this way, the last modulation of the development section returns to the first key. The passage that accomplishes this, sometimes referred to as the **retransition,** has the function of discharging the tension and preparing for the recapitulation to come. Classical composers were amazingly inventive of ways to make this crucial juncture of the form seem both fresh and inevitable.

Recapitulation (A′)

With a real sense of relief or resolution, we hear the first theme again; then all the other themes and other elements of the exposition come back in their original order (or something close to their original order). Hence the name for this third section—the **recapitulation** (meaning a step-by-step review).

But there is an important difference: everything now remains in the same key: the tonic key. Stability of key is especially welcome after the instability of the development section—and what is more, the old material now has a slightly new look. Thus the strong feeling of balance between the exposition and the recapitulation (**A B A′**) is a weighted balance, because **A′** has achieved a new solidity.

If, after the big repeat of **B A′**, even more solidity seems to be needed, another section is added at the end, as though to deliver concluding remarks on the material at hand. This optional section is called the *coda* (the term used for such a concluding section in any musical form).

In the following schematic diagram for sonata form, changes of key are represented by different vertical levels of a continuous line or band:

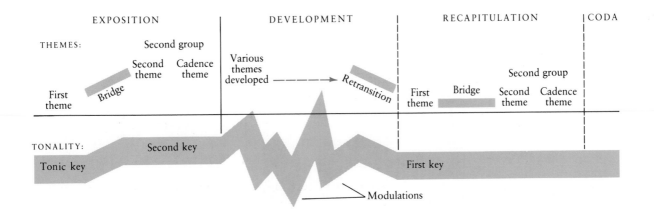

Notice that sonata-form terminology—exposition, development, recapitulation—resembles the terminology employed in discussions of drama. Sonata form has a "dramatic" quality compared with the more "architectural" quality of Baroque music such as a fugue. In a Classical sonata, the themes seem almost like individuals to whom things are happening. They seem to change, go through various vicissitudes, and react to other themes and musical processes.

Wolfgang Amadeus Mozart

(1756–1791)

Chief Works: The great comic operas *The Marriage of Figaro, Don Giovanni, Così fan tutte* (That's What They All Do), and *The Magic Flute*

Idomeneo, an *opera seria*

Church music—many masses, and a requiem (Mass for the dead) left unfinished at his death

Symphonies, including the *Prague,* the G minor, and the *Jupiter*

String quartets and four superb string quintets; a quintet for clarinet and strings; a quartet for oboe and strings.

Concertos: seventeen particularly fine concertos for piano; four amusing ones for French horn; also concertos for violin and one for clarinet

Piano sonatas; violin sonatas

Lighter pieces (such as divertimentos, etc.), including the famous *Eine kleine Nachtmusik*

Mozart was born in Salzburg, a charming town in central Austria, which today is famous for its music festivals. His father, Leopold, was a court musician and composer who had also written a fascinating book on violin playing. Mozart showed extraordinary talent at a very early age. He and his older sister, Nannerl, were trotted all over Europe as infant prodigies; between the ages of six and seventeen, Wolfgang never spent more than ten months together at home. His first symphony was played (at a London concert) when he was only eight years old.

But mostly Wolfgang was displayed at courts and salons, and in a somewhat depressing way, this whole period of his career symbolizes the frivolous love of entertainment that reigned at mid-century. The future Queen Marie Antoinette of France was one of those for whose amusement the six-year-old prodigy would guess the keys of compositions played to him, and sight-read music at the piano with a cloth over his hands.

It was much harder for Mozart to make his way as a young adult musician. As usual in those days, he followed in his father's footsteps as a musician at the Archbishop's court at Salzburg (one of their colleagues, incidentally, was Haydn's brother Michael). But unlike Haydn's patrons, the Esterházy princes, the Archbishop of Salzburg was overbearing and philistine, and Mozart hated working for him. In 1781 Mozart extricated himself from his court position, not without a humiliating scene, and set himself up as a free-lance musician in Vienna.

It seems clear that another reason for Mozart's move was to get away from his father, who had masterminded the boy's career and now seemed to grow more and more possessive as the young man sought his independence. Leopold disapproved of Wolfgang's marriage around this time to Constanze Weber, a singer. (Mozart had been in love with her older sister, Aloysia—a more famous singer—but she had rejected him.)

To the left, a still from the 1984 Oscar-winning film *Amadeus:* Mozart is shown as a good-looking and irrepressible antiestablishment type. To the right, an unfinished (and probably somewhat idealized) portrait by Mozart's brother-in-law. He saw the composer as passive, pensive, and ultimately enigmatic.

Mozart wrote his greatest operas in Vienna, but only the last of them, *The Magic Flute,* had the success it deserved. Everyone sensed that he was a genius, but his music seemed too difficult—and he was a somewhat "difficult" personality, too. He relied for his living on teaching and on the relatively new institution of concerts. Every year he would set up a concert at which he introduced one of his piano concertos. In addition, the program might contain arias, a solo improvisation, and an overture by somebody else.

The Mozart family: Nannerl, Wolfgang, and Leopold (with violin; Leopold's book on violin playing was famous). Mozart's mother, who had died when this picture was painted, is represented by a portrait.

But as happens with popular musicians today, Mozart seems (for some unknown reason) to have suddenly dropped out of fashion. After 1787, his life was a struggle, though he did receive a minor court appointment and the promise of a church position, and finally scored a hit with *The Magic Flute.* When it seemed that financially he was finally getting out of the woods, he died suddenly at the age of thirty-five.

Mozart's death occurred under poignant, even dramatic conditions. His last commission was a macabre one: a mysterious anonymous patron ordered a requiem, or Mass for the dead, and Mozart began to think he was writing for his own demise. When he died, it was whispered about that he had been poisoned by Antonio Salieri (see page 177). Myths have continued to grow up around Mozart ever since.

Like Haydn, Mozart was a master of the Classical style; unlike Haydn, he sometimes allowed a note of disquiet, even passion, to emerge in his compositions that the Romantics correctly perceived as a forecast of their own work. Once we recognize this, it is hard not to sense something enigmatic beneath the intelligence, sharp humor, and sheer beauty of all Mozart's music.

WOLFGANG AMADEUS MOZART
Overture to *Don Giovanni* (1786), K. 527[2]

For further discussion of
Don Giovanni, see page 206.

Opera overtures in the Classical period were written in sonata form; the overture to Mozart's opera *Don Giovanni* also includes an introductory slow (Adagio) section. Such slow introductions often launch symphony first movements, too; they are not considered part of sonata form, though they are certainly an essential part of the total musical experience.

The highly impressive slow music in the minor mode—by turns solemn, weird, and tragic in feeling—finds an explanation in the opera's plot (outlined on page 206), as does the helter-skelter, hilarious, major-mode Molto allegro (very fast) sonata-form section that follows. Even without reference to the plot, what is striking is the way Mozart joins the two sections together in a single piece. This overture is an excellent example of the Classical composers' incorporation of contrast into their music.

Exposition   The *first theme* itself makes a vivid introduction to the liveliness and high contrast that mark the Classical style. This theme comprises two tiny portions that are strictly homophonic, as is the rule in Classical music, but otherwise they contrast utterly: soft and loud, strings and winds, tricky rhythms and an obvious one, a sinuous melody and a brassy fanfare:

One can almost hear a pair of characters mocking each other.

To make much of an impression, a theme usually needs to be repeated. This one shoots off in a new direction when it is repeated, makes a crescendo, and comes to a sudden stop.

Here the *bridge* commences with a new busy rhythm, and with many more sudden changes of dynamics—unsettling features that forecast its role in making the modulation. A little fragment of tune is heard as this bridge rushes by:

Another stop, and the *second theme* makes its sharp contrast to everything that has gone before. The melody is very different, the key is new. This theme, too, bristles with internal contrast: a stern, heavily accented fragment in the full orchestra, **f**, alternates with a light, fluttering fragment in the strings, **p**. Once again, the effect is of speedy repartee.

After a brief dialogue between flute and oboe (there is a passing modulation here) comes the loud *cadence theme,* the ending part of the second group. It sounds very conclusive, indeed it leads to the firmest stop of all.[3]

---

[2] Mozart's works are known by K numbers, after the catalog prepared by Ludwig von Köchel. K numbers are especially useful in distinguishing Mozart's many works in the same genre and key —for example, his thirteen symphonies in D major.

[3] At this point, as we have seen, sonata form normally demands a repetition of the entire exposition section. But in opera overtures, perhaps because everyone was anxious to get on with the actual show, the rule was to omit such repeats.

Development   Here Mozart works with both main themes, beginning with the second. Already at the second playing of this theme, there is a melodic change—a "development":

Development of another sort is manifested by a vigorous contrapuntal treatment of the stern part of the second theme, which is made to modulate repeatedly. Underneath this part of the theme in the winds, we may be able to hear the theme's other part fluttering away in the strings simultaneously:

Theme 2, part 1, developed: four contrapuntal entries

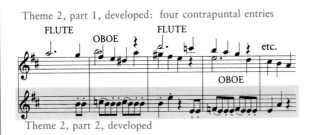

Theme 2, part 2, developed

As in most development sections, counterpoint is used in contrast to the prevailing homophonic texture to give an impression of heightened tension.

The modulations lead to an uncertain, tentative-sounding key; and here Mozart briefly develops the first theme. First heard in its original form, complete with fanfares, when repeated it wanders off and comes to a stop—but a less affirmative stop than before, more questioning. The answer is provided by the second theme. A series of powerful modulating sequences adds an unexpectedly serious note—a real "development" in mood, one might say. Minor keys are prominent for the first time since the slow introduction.

After all this melodic and tonal shaking up, a *retransition* high in the strings leads the listener with a sense of relief back to the original key, and back to the first theme in its original form, at the recapitulation.

Recapitulation   The recapitulation follows the exposition closely: first theme, bridge, second group (comprising second theme, woodwind dialogue, and cadence theme). The sense that everything has been stabilized in the tonic key is as clear as possible.

Perhaps for the first time, the listener has the leisure to appreciate the orchestral tone colors. They glitter constantly, whether in loud passages or soft. Better yet, tone color is used in an integral way to bring out the character of the musical material. The fanfare in theme 1 would sound pale without its trumpets. The contrapuntal treatments of theme 2 would lack bite if the imitations were not staggered between strings and winds.

In his concert version of this overture, heard here, Mozart added a short emphatic coda after the recapitulation so as to bring the composition to a close. What happens at this point in the actual opera is something much more surprising—the music modulates mysteriously and runs directly into the first sung number of the opera. But that is another story.

Mozart, Overture to *Don Giovanni*

Sonata form. 6 min., 26 sec.

3 Cassette 1B-4/3 CD 1-13
6 Cassette 2B-3/6 CD 2-13

SLOW INTRODUCTION

	0.00		Solemn music in the minor mode. Rich orchestration; notice the low trumpets. Mysterious harmonies, heavy cadences. Leads into theme 1

EXPOSITION

13.2 / 13.2	2.11	**Theme 1** (main theme)	In the major mode, *p;* throbbing accompaniment in the strings; brief wind and brass fanfare, *f*
	2.20		Theme 1 repeated. Crescendo, brass instruments help make a strong cadence.
			Stop.
13.3 / 13.3	2.35	**Bridge**	Bridge theme, *f,* modulates to new key; includes brief, quieter, more melodic section in the woodwinds.
			Stop.

Second Group

13.4 / 13.4	2.55	**Theme 2**	Theme 2 alternates between stern *f* fragment and faster, quieter answer. Contrapuntal treatment of theme 2 in the woodwinds
13.5 / 13.5	3.16	**Cadence theme**	Cadence theme, *f,* and repeated cadences
			Stop.

DEVELOPMENT

13.6 / 13.6	3.37	**Theme 2** developed	Modulations: the two parts of theme 2 are alternated, then developed simultaneously in the woodwinds and strings.
	3.56	**Theme 1**	Strings, *p,* in an unsettled-sounding key (including the wind-instrument fanfares)
			A tentative stop.
	4.12	**Theme 2** developed	Solemn feeling recalls the slow introduction; further modulations, to minor keys.
	4.34	**Retransition**	Crescendo prepares for return of theme 1.

RECAPITULATION

13.7 / 13.7	4.46	**Theme 1**	Theme 1 played twice, exactly as before
			Stop.
	5.08	**Bridge**	Bridge is in the tonic key, otherwise much as before.
			Stop.

Second Group

	5.28	**Theme 2**	In the tonic key; otherwise much as before
	5.49	**Cadence theme**	In the tonic key, much as before, but leading without a stop to the brief coda

CODA

	6.05		Brief, emphatic coda makes the final cadence.
			Stop.

3 Theme and Variations

The next two Classical forms to be discussed are theme and variations and rondo. We have seen an example of Baroque variations in Bach's Passacaglia in C minor (page 128).

   Neither theme and variations nor rondo form are absolute fixtures in symphonies and sonatas, as is the case with sonata form and the minuet. The popularity of these forms lay elsewhere. Both were the stock in trade of instrumental virtuosos, who excelled in improvising variations and rondos based on favorite tunes of the day. Then they wrote out special versions for circulation and publication.

   The theme and variations was basically a popular form, then, and in some ways a simple one. It was calculated to entertain audiences by repeating and varying tunes that they already knew and liked. When the form is found in a symphony or a concerto, it usually casts a popular light on the proceedings.

Variations in the visual arts: three monotype paintings (from a total of seventeen) by the contemporary American artist Jasper Johns. While the "variations" all differ from the original "theme"—an actual coffee can with paint brushes, all bronzed—they never lose it entirely.

Classical Variation Form

A Classical theme and variations usually begins with a tune (the "theme"), which is nearly always in |: **a** :||: **b** :| or |: **a** :||: **b a** :| or |: **a** :||: **b a′** :| form. (In the Baroque period, variations were typically based on bass patterns; see page 126.) Then the basic outline of the tune is played over and over again, with various changes: in rhythm, tone color, meter, tempo, and so on.

The point is to obtain many contrasting moods out of the same theme, which is transformed but always somehow discernible. Nothing much distracts attention from this process, at least until the end, where there is often a coda. In principle there are no transitions, cadence sections, or developmental passages, as there are in sonata-form movements (and even in some complicated minuets).

Variation form can be diagrammed as follows. Notice the possibility shown under Variation **n**:

Theme	Variation 1	Variation 2	Variation n	Coda
|: **a** :||: **b** :|	|: **a¹** :||: **b¹** :|	|: **a²** :||: **b²** :|	a^n $a^{n'}$ b^n $b^{n'}$	(free)

Whereas virtuosos writing for their own use often piled up variations for maximum effect—twelve in a set was a common number—composers writing theme and variation movements in symphonies, concertos, and the like had to balance these movements with all the others. Such movements therefore tend to contain only up to five or six variations, sometimes even fewer.

Indeed, composers often employed the variation *principle* selectively, rather than the theme and variation *form;* thus they might write a quartet slow movement in **A B A′** form in which **A′** is a single variation of **A**. Such a movement is contained in Haydn's *Lark* Quartet (page 214).

MOZART
Piano Concerto No. 17 in G, K. 453, third movement (1784)

For a full discussion of Mozart's Piano Concerto in G, see page 211.

The concerto was one of the main genres for the virtuoso, and the theme and variations was a favorite virtuoso form; naturally, then, many concertos include theme and variation movements. This is the case with Mozart's Piano Concerto in G. Some such movements have popular tunes or opera ditties as their themes. Although Mozart wrote an original theme for this concerto movement, that theme has the lilt of a popular song.

Theme   The orchestra without the piano soloist plays the theme, a bouncing little tune in |: **a** :||: **b** :| form. Each half of the theme is the same length, and the ends of the sections are clearly demarcated with stops. Yet in spite of its popular tone, this tune includes a contrapuntal detail in the **b** section that is preserved in delightful ways through most of the variations:

In the next example, the theme's **a** section is lined up with the corresponding sections of Mozart's five variations, which may be labeled a^1, a^2, a^3, a^4, and a^5. Color shading shows parallel melody notes, but a glance at this example shows how much else is different—that is, how much has been "varied":

Variation 1 The solo begins, and seems almost to silence the orchestra by showing how to make the theme so much more expressive and personal. Its method is to provide the theme with fluid melodic decorations and some harmonic enrichment. Each half of this variation (a^1 and b^1) is repeated verbatim.

Variation 2 In this variation, where the piano shows off its agility and brilliance, the repeats of each half are varied differently. In a^2 and b^2, the soloist has fast *right-hand* runs while the orchestra plays the theme; in $a^{2\prime}$ and $b^{2\prime}$, the soloist has *left-hand* runs.

Variation 3 The next variation is a songlike dialogue between the woodwind instruments—oboe, flute, bassoon in a^3, then flute, bassoon, oboe in b^3. After each half, in sections $a^{3\prime}$ and later $b^{3\prime}$, the piano makes varied repeats by picking up the woodwinds' material and decorating it flexibly.

Variation 4 Woodwinds are replaced by strings, the mode changes to the minor, and the dynamic drops to a mysterious *pp.* This fascinating variation, with its syncopated melody and its almost ominous-sounding counterpoint, departs farthest from the actual theme, but the original dimensions and cadence structure are easily recognized.

In the repeats ($a^{4\prime}$ and $b^{4\prime}$), the piano works over this mysterious material more quickly and even more expressively.

The variations have gradually been getting more and more profound; only a great composer could have written this fourth variation. But the deepening serious mood of the piece is about to be shattered.

3 Cassette 1B-5/3 CD 1-14
6 Cassette 2B-4/6 CD 2-14

LISTENING CHART NUMBER 8

Mozart, Piano Concerto No. 17 in G, third movement

Variation form. 8 min., 8 sec.

	Theme	Orchestra alone. Note the woodwind and horn figure at the cadences of **a** and **b**.	
	0.00	|: **a** :|	
	0.23	|: **b** :|	
14.2 14.2	**Variation 1**	Mainly piano, *p;* orchestral part is subsidiary.	
	0.47	|: **a**^{1} :|	Piano enters; plays theme with melodic decorations.
	1.11	|: **b**^{1} :|	
14.3 14.3	**Variation 2**	Mainly piano, more brilliant; woodwinds	
	1.34	**a**^{2}	Fast right-hand runs
	1.45	**a**$^{2\prime}$	Fast left-hand runs
	1.57	**b**^{2}	Right-hand runs
	2.08	**b**$^{2\prime}$	Left-hand runs
14.4 14.4	**Variation 3**	Woodwinds alternating with piano	
	2.20	**a**^{3}	Songlike dialogue in woodwinds
	2.33	**a**$^{3\prime}$	Piano answers with its own version of the woodwind dialogue.
	2.47	**b**^{3}	Woodwinds
	3.00	**b**$^{3\prime}$	Piano
14.5 14.5	**Variation 4**	Minor mode; strings alternating with piano, *p*	
	3.13	**a**^{4}	Strings play mysterious, syncopated counterpoint.
	3.27	**a**$^{4\prime}$	Strings answered by piano version; more expressive
	3.42	**b**^{4}	Orchestra
	3.56	**b**$^{4\prime}$	Piano
14.6 14.6	**Variation 5**	Major mode; full orchestra alternating with piano, *f*	
	4.11	**a**^{5}	Strongly metrical march played by the orchestra
	4.24	**a**$^{5\prime}$	Piano counters with original **theme.**
	4.36	**b**^{5}	March continues in orchestra.
	4.49	**b**$^{5\prime}$	Piano
	5.03		Short transition and slowdown
	5.24	**Cadenza**	
14.7 14.7	**Coda**	Faster; orchestra in free, often rapid dialogue with the piano	
	5.39		Orchestra plays new theme and insistent cadential passage.
	5.57		Piano and orchestra play the new theme with new continuations.
	6.42		New version of the original theme (only |: **a**$''$:| and cadential passages)
	7.50		Ends with theme fragments echoed.

Variation 5 Suddenly a rather comical, loud march variation of the theme is presented by the orchestra, which has not been heard in full force since the opening of the movement. The solo cannot match anything as emphatic as this. So instead of a varied repeat, it takes an entirely new tack: it catches fresh interest by reintroducing the long-lost theme. The theme is certainly welcome back, after all the beautiful mystifications it has endured.

Section **b⁵′** is extended; there is a slowdown, and a place that Mozart marked for the soloist to improvise a short cadenza (see page 138).

Coda The riotous conclusion to this piece reminds us that for piano virtuosos of the Classical period, the theme and variations was meant to entertain and to dazzle. This unusual coda almost sounds as though it is starting up a new movement; but in fact most codas are unusual in one way or another—this is an element of the form for which it is impossible to draw up rules.

One common feature of theme and variation codas is represented here: the return of the original theme in something very much like (but not exactly like) its original form.

4 The Rondo

The rondo, like the theme and variations, is a relatively light and simple form with popular leanings. In multimovement genres, it was used mainly for the last movements, which tend to be relatively light. But in his later symphonies, Mozart always used the more "serious" sonata form, even for last movements. And though Haydn preferred rondo form, he complicated his rondos with elements derived from sonata form.

The fact that the rondo and the theme and variations had popular connotations does not mean, of course, that Classical composers did not sometimes write serious, even tragic compositions in these forms. When they did, there is always a special surprise, even a special pathos, in the effort to convey serious sentiments by means of lighter forms.

Rondo Form

The basic principle of rondo form is simply repetition—not varied repetition, as in variation form, but "spaced" repetition. A main tune (**A**) comes back again and again after episodes that serve as spacers between its appearances. If the **A** tune falls into the favorite |: **a** :‖: **ba′** :| pattern of the time, the repeats may present only **a b a′** or **a b**, but there is always enough for listeners to recognize.

The episodes **B, C, D,** and so on, which space out the appearances of **A,** may be other tunes (in simpler rondos), or passages including transitions to new themes, cadence formulas, and even development (in more complex rondos). Rondos come in a variety of schemes, such as: **A B A C A, A B A C A D A,** or **A B A C A B A.** And they often end with codas.[4]

---

[4] In some ways, rondo form resembles ritornello form (see page 134), but the differences are worth noting. Ritornello form usually brings back its ritornello in fragments and in different keys; rondo form usually brings back its theme complete and in the same key. Therefore rondos are typically simpler and lighter than ritornello movements.

Nineteenth-century illustration of a Turkish military band

MOZART
Rondo "alla Turca," from Piano Sonata in A, K. 331 (1783)

For a full discussion of Mozart's Sonata in A, see page 217.

This delightful and deliberately simple rondo is a parody of Turkish military band music. The Viennese were often at war with Turkey in the eighteenth century, and they seem to have found their enemy's "ethnomusic" (as we might call it today) naïve and comical.

Mozart reflects the naïveté by making all the rondo episodes little tunes without any transitions whatsoever. The form—a little unusual in that the first tune comes only twice—is as follows:

A	B	C	B	A	B′	Coda
Minor key	Major key	Another minor key	Original major key	Original minor key	Variation, major key	Major key
|: a :||: b a′ :|	|: c :|	|: d :||: e d′ :|	|: c :|	|: a :||: b a′ :|	|: c′ :|	|: f :|

HAYDN
Symphony No. 88 in G, fourth movement (1789)

For a full discussion of Haydn's Symphony No. 88, see page 198.

The last movement of a symphony is likely to be more elaborate than that of a piano sonata. The rondo at the end of Haydn's Symphony No. 88 is certainly lighthearted, like Mozart's Turkish rondo. But the humor is less broad. It is predicated on the idea that since a rondo brings its tune back many times, those returns should be made especially interesting—and maybe a little tricky.

The theme, **A**, is a cheerful, busy tune in \|: **a** :\|\|: **b a′** :\| form. The end of **b**, which abruptly changes in dynamics from **f** to **p,** features a "witty" detail, a detail that Haydn will return to later in the rondo. One could almost miss the return of **a** in the theme (**a′**), since it begins with two upbeat Ds, and the end of **b** runs right into them with two other Ds:

The form outline of this piece is **A B A′ C A Coda.** The rondo episodes here are not simple tunes, as in the Mozart, but passages of a more dynamic nature. (They show, in fact, the influence of sonata form.) Section **B** begins *f* with a vigorous transitional passage, continues with a quiet new melodic unit (it is hardly a new theme) derived from the tune's opening motive:

and ends with a forceful cadential passage, running into upward leaps that seem like rough questions concerning the note D.

A mild answer is provided by the rondo tune, with its upbeat Ds:

This first return, **A′,** consists of **a b** only, with some reorchestration and changes of dynamics. Just when the listener is expecting **a′,** Haydn runs off into a modulating contrapuntal passage—the second episode, **C.** This ends up harping quietly on those same upbeat Ds, in such a way that the listener never quite knows when the theme is going to return:

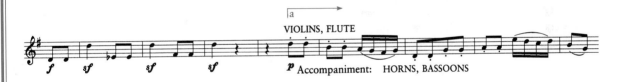

In the second return, **A″,** the entire theme is heard (**a b a′**). This goes directly into the coda. There is a sudden (and welcome!) break in the rhythm, and another vigorous running passage brings the rondo to a close—after some more references to the opening motive, accompanied by loud trumpet fanfares.

Haydn, Symphony No. 88 in G, fourth movement

3 Cassette 1B-6/3 CD 1-15
6 Cassette 2B-5/6 CD 2-15

Rondo. 4 min., 4 sec.

0.00	**A (Tune)**	The entire tune is presented by the strings with bassoon and then flute, starting *p*.	
0.00	a		
0.07	a		
0.15	b		
0.29	a′		
0.37	b		
0.52	a′		
		Leads into episode 1	
15.2 / 15.2 0.59	**B (Episode 1)**	Transitional passage, *f;* modulation	
1.18		A new melodic unit, *p,* derived from the tune's first motive; strings. Repeated in the minor mode	
1.30		Cadential passage, *f*	
1.44		Upward leaps—still *f*—emphasizing the note D in preparation for the return of the tune, which starts on D	
15.3 / 15.3 1.48	**A′ (Tune)**	Part of the tune (**a b**) is presented, starting *p;* French horns accompany **a.** Leads into episode 2	
2.10	**C (Episode 2)**	A developmental episode, *f;* contrapuntal, modulating	
2.41		Another preparation passage, this time *p,* harping on two Ds. Strings alternate with French horns.	
15.4 / 15.4 2.57	**A″ (Tune)**	The entire tune is presented, but without repeats (**a b a′**).	
3.26	**Coda**	A brief break in the rhythm, *f,* followed by exuberant runs	
3.47		Final cadence, including echoes of the tune's opening motive. Trumpet fanfares	

Esterháza, the castle of the Esterházy princes where Haydn spent most of his life

Chapter 13

Classical Genres

The genres of music that arose in the Classical period, replacing those of the Baroque, continued to hold their own in the nineteenth century. Indeed, some of them are still in use today. The continuity this suggests can be a little deceptive, however, for the number of movements and the forms employed differ widely between a symphony written today and one dating from the eighteenth century.

Classical instrumental music used a general plan for the arrangement and types of movements that was adapted in one way or another for all the specific genres—symphonies, concertos, string quartets, sonatas, and so on. This standard movement plan can be laid out as follows:

1 A fast or moderately paced movement. Written in sonata form, this first movement is usually the most elaborate in form and the most impressive of the four. It sets the tone for the whole work.
The first movement is sometimes preceded by, and prepared by, a relatively short passage of slow music, the *slow introduction.*

2 A slow movement. Serving as a point of relaxation between the more vigorous movements around it, this second movement is generally songlike and relatively quiet in dynamics. It is likely to contain the composition's most beautiful and moving music.

3 Minuet and trio. This third movement offers relaxation of another kind —the simple, satisfying swing of dance music.

4 Another fast movement, often the fastest of the four. The last movement also tends to be lighter and more brilliant than the others. It almost always brings the piece to an upbeat, exhilarating close.

1 The Symphony

The symphony—a large, impressive concert piece for orchestra—is the major genre developed by the Classical composers.

The rise of the symphony went hand in hand with a major development in the sociology of music that was discussed in Chapter 11, the growing popularity of public concerts. As concerts became more and more frequent, the need was felt for some genre that would make an effective concert centerpiece. The symphony filled that need; and symphonies, in turn, required more variety and flexibility of sound than any of the ensembles of the Baroque era could provide. So the symphony spurred a major technical development within music, the evolution of the Classical symphony orchestra.

Following the standard movement plan for Classical genres given on the previous page, the general plan for a symphony is as follows:

1 Fast or moderately paced movement in sonata form. A *slow introduction* prior to the sonata-form movement is fairly common.

2 Slower, lyric movement.

3 Minuet and trio. In a symphony, the stylized minuet is often closer to its dance prototype than in other Classical genres.

4 Faster and somewhat lighter movement: usually written in sonata form or in extended rondo form.

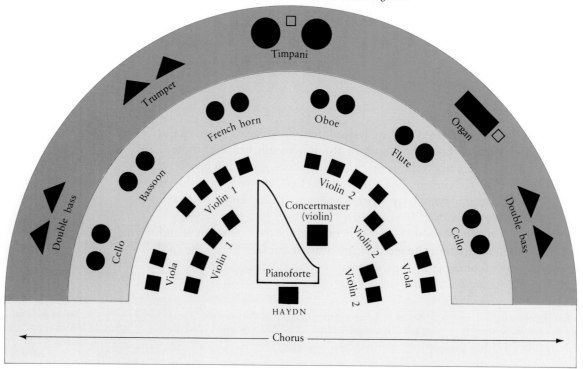

Reconstruction of the amphitheater arrangement of the orchestra introduced to London by Haydn for his concerts in the 1790s.

FRANZ JOSEPH HAYDN (1732–1809)
Symphony No. 88 in G (1787)

During the last twenty years of his active career, from around 1780 to 1800, Joseph Haydn averaged better than one symphony a year, nearly all of them masterpieces. Like most Haydn symphonies, No. 88 is a cheerful piece; concert audiences wanted entertainment—high-level entertainment—and Haydn was always happy to oblige. Listeners of the time also wanted simple, "natural" melodies, and Haydn responded with the melody of the slow second movement, one of the most beautiful he ever composed. Symphony No. 88 is scored for a rather small orchestra, without clarinets (compare the Classical orchestra chart, page 169)—and what is more, the trumpets and timpani do not play at all during the forceful first movement.

First Movement (Adagio—Allegro)   Haydn treats sonata form differently than Mozart does, for example, in the Overture to *Don Giovanni* (see page 186). Mozart's themes are clearly separated and sharply differentiated in character. Haydn runs themes and sections into one another, and he treads the fine line between providing just enough contrast to keep the interest up and making the themes similar enough in rhythm to create confusion and fun.

The ingenuity Haydn shows in finding new ways of making this rhythm sparkle—there is even a new version of it in the very last measures—seems unlimited. It is qualities of this kind that make people speak of "wit" in Viennese Classical music.

Slow Introduction This section, in triple meter, is short and rather routine —at least by comparison with that of the *Don Giovanni* Overture. Its function is simply to prepare us for the fast music to come.

Exposition On the other hand, the fast sonata-form section is trickier in structure than Mozart's. The first theme is a lively miniature tune with a folk-like swing:

When the second playing of this tune runs into a blustery bridge passage, it soon dawns on the listener that Haydn is not going to wait till the official development section to start developing his themes. The rhythm of motive *r* in the theme, ♩♪ | ♪♪, is heard repeatedly in this bridge. The same rhythm also delivers the four heavy accents on E (marked *sf*), which end the bridge and drive home the modulation to the second key:

After a strong cadence (though there is only a very brief stop), the dynamics drop to a hush for the tiny second theme, which also includes the rhythm of motive *r*. Still another version of this rhythmic motive is present in the cadence theme, which is initially played only by the wind instruments:

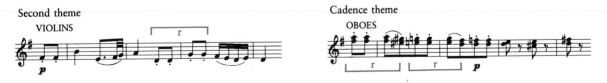

The exposition comes to an expectant halt, and is repeated. (Repeats of sonata-form expositions do not include the slow introductions.)

Development The development section begins with fragments of the main theme modulating quietly through many keys. These keys sound very tentative—an effect enhanced by Haydn's use of halting rhythms. A sudden forte launches a new phase of development. This second phase is highly contrapuntal, a riot of confusion in which the bridge, second theme, and cadence theme are all heard modulating around the reigning rhythm of motive *r*.

Each of these themes now assumes a very different quality. The second theme is no longer quiet, the bridge no longer points in any clear direction, and the cadence theme no longer makes a firm cadence.

Recapitulation and Coda   Following another expectant stop, the tension built up in the development section is relieved when the first theme returns, safe and sound in the original key. But Haydn provides the theme with a charming new feature—a cool counterpoint added high above it by the flute. Then comes the bridge, completely rewritten from its exposition version, and an abbreviated second group.

A short coda, after the cadence theme, provides yet another new twist on the first theme. The French horns blare out a new echo version of motive *r,* as though to prove that the theme was really intended for them all along.

Second Movement (Largo)   We have already stressed the importance of tunes in the formation of the Viennese Classical style. Tunes satisfied the general desire for music that would be "natural" and pleasing. Haydn's own affection for tunes is certainly evident from the slow movement of Symphony No. 88, for this Largo contains scarcely any music besides repetitions of the main melody:

Haydn provides the tune with fresh interest by putting it into new keys and by adding different accompaniment figures, but he seemingly couldn't bear to have them disturb this lovely melody too much. Brief, solemn interludes between its many appearances feature the trumpets and timpani, for the first time in the symphony. This warm, somewhat hymnlike melody shows another side of Haydn, one that is just as typical as the wit in the first (and also the last) movement.

Third Movement (Menuetto: Allegretto)   Like many Haydn minuets, this one has a rollicking country-dance feeling about it. It is set up in the customary **A B A** form. The trio, **B** (|: **c** :||: **d   c′** :|), contrasts with the minuet by its quiet dynamics, but it also has a rustic quality: low drone notes held by the violas and bassoons seem to evoke bagpipes, or some other peasant instrument. Still, this "popular" tone did not prevent Haydn from putting in many ingenious details, such as making the return of **c** (that is, **c′**) a disguised return.

Fourth Movement (Allegro con spirito)   This rondo was discussed on page 194. If we hear it at the end of the symphony, rather than out of context, we realize that Haydn deliberately made it sound rather like the first movement.

The rhythm heard so frequently in this fourth movement, ♪│♩♩♫♫│♪ , is an extension of the obsessive rhythmic motive in the first, ♩♪│♩♩♪│♩.

So this "spirited" rondo—Haydn's term for it—does more than end the symphony in a good-natured, even humorous mood. It also serves to unify the work by thematic means. Haydn has gone to some effort to shape the symphony into an artistic whole. Later symphonies, as we shall see, carry this idea of artistic cohesion much further.

WOLFGANG AMADEUS MOZART
Symphony No. 40 in G Minor, K. 550 (1788)

Written a year later than Haydn's Symphony No. 88, Mozart's Symphony in G Minor is one of his most famous works. It is a deeper, darker work than the Haydn. It is also a simpler one in its treatment of sonata form—which Mozart uses for each of the four movements except the minuet. There is a sharper contrast between themes, and in general a clearer distinction between sections and subsections.

Some kind of struggle against inevitable restraints seems to be at the heart of the unusual mood of this composition. Mozart's themes alone would not have created this effect; expressive as they are in themselves, they only attain their full pathos as a result of their context. Mozart needed sonata form to contain these highly expressive themes—in a sense, to give them something to struggle against.

First Movement (Molto allegro) This symphony has no slow introduction. The first theme is presented with a strictly homophonic accompaniment, which starts up quietly one measure ahead of the melody (given on page 171). The unique nervous energy of this theme, a blend of utter refinement and subdued agitation, stamps the first movement unforgettably.

Exposition The first theme is played twice; the second playing already begins the modulation to the exposition's second key. A forceful bridge completes this process, and the music comes to an abrupt stop. Such stops will become characteristic of this movement.

The second theme, in the major mode, is divided up, measure by measure or phrase by phrase, between the strings and the woodwinds:

Then it is repeated with the role of the instruments reversed, the strings taking the notes originally played by the winds, and vice versa. The instrumental alterations contribute something absolutely essential to the character of the theme, and show Mozart's fine ear for tone color.

Development The development section begins quietly, with the first theme accompanied as before. But with a sudden jarring effect, the central part of the section embarks upon furious contrapuntal treatments of that tender, nervous melody. Smaller and smaller portions of it are used, as the music modulates continuously. The portions can be recognized by their rhythms alone: first ♫ | ♩ ♫♩ ♫ | ♩ ♩ 𝄾 ♫ | ♩ ♫♩ ♫ | ♩ ♩ , then ♫ | ♩ ♫♩ ♫ | ♩ ♩ , then ♫♩ ♩ ♫ | ♩ ♩ , and finally ♫ | ♩ . The theme has been *fragmented* down to just its opening three-note rhythmic motive.

In the retransition (the passage leading from the development to the recapitulation), Mozart hammers away at this fragment-motive with echoes between various orchestral groups, like a summons for the entire first theme to reappear.

Recapitulation   After its rough treatment in the development section, the first theme is somehow invested with new pathos when it is now played exactly in its original form. Overall, the sense that everything is in the same key—with the result that the recapitulation feels more stable than the exposition—is particularly clear because the second group is now in the minor mode, like the first. At the same time, this mode change makes the second theme sound much more emotional than before, and the cadence theme more desperate.

Near the end, there is a poignant final reference to the first theme.

Second Movement (Andante)   The second movement, which is in a major key, serves as a slow interlude between the intense minor-mode movements on either side. But it is not an entirely peaceful interlude; the lovely, flowing first theme is countered later by sterner material:

In this sonata-form movement, the retransition gives a wonderful sense of quiet inevitability to the return of the first theme in the tonic key. The piece ends with the graceful repeated cadences shown on page 173.

Third Movement (Menuetto: Allegretto)   Back in the minor mode, this minuet has been transformed in spirit from the usual easygoing dance. It is as though the mood of the first movement has been made more gloomy and relentless:

Besides using the minor mode, Mozart writes most of the minuet in contrapuntal style, and with many unusually intense syncopations. As we have said, polyphony generally means tension to a Classical composer, whereas a Baroque composer takes it as a normal and neutral stylistic element.

The minuet and the contrasting trio (in the major mode) follow the usual **A B A** form.

Fourth Movement (Allegro assai)   A serious symphony requires a serious, dramatic last movement. For this reason Mozart did not choose rondo form, which tends to emphasize good-natured tunes and witty returns, rather than dramatic contrast; instead he chose sonata form once again. The taut, explosive first theme is a long one, by sonata-form standards, and one that incorporates sharp internal contrasts of the kind we saw in the themes of Mozart's *Don Giovanni* Overture.

LISTENING CHART NUMBER 10   3 Cassette 1B-7/3 CD 1-16
6 Cassette 2B-6/6 CD 2-16

Mozart, Symphony No. 40 in G Minor, first movement

Sonata Form. 8 min., 9 sec.

EXPOSITION

0.01	**Theme 1** (main theme)	Theme 1, *p*, minor key (G minor); cadence is *f*.
0.24		Theme 1 repeats and begins the modulation to a new key.
16.2 / 16.2 0.32	**Bridge**	Bridge theme, *f*, confirms the modulation.
		Abrupt stop.

Second Group

16.3 / 16.3 0.52	**Theme 2**	Theme 2, *p*, in major key; phrases divided between woodwinds and strings
1.03		Theme 2, again; division of phrases is reversed; new ending. Crescendo to *f*
1.20		Other shorter themes, *f* and *p*; echoes of theme 1 motive
16.4 / 16.4 1.47	**Cadence theme**	Cadence theme, *f*, downward scales followed by a vigorous concluding figure
		Abrupt stop.
2.02	**Exposition**	Exposition repeats.

DEVELOPMENT

16.5 / 16.5 4.10	**Theme 1 developed**	Theme 1, *p*, with its original accompaniment—modulating
4.23	**Central development passage**	Sudden *f;* contrapuntal treatment of fragments of theme 1
16.6 / 16.6 4.50	**Fragmentation**	Sudden *p;* beginning of theme 1 echoes between strings and woodwinds; theme fragmented from ♪♪♩ | ♩ ♪♪♩ | ♪♪♩ | ♩ ♩ to ♪♪♩ | ♪♪♩ | ♩ ♩ and finally to ♪♪♩ | ♩
5.07		Retransition *f* (full orchestra), *p* (woodwinds), which leads into the recapitulation

RECAPITULATION

16.7 / 16.7 5.21	**Theme 1**	Theme 1, *p*, G minor, as before
5.44		Theme 1, again, but modulates differently than before.
5.52	**Bridge**	Bridge, *f*, considerably longer than before, with more elaborate counterpoint (from the scale part of the cadence theme)
		Abrupt stop.

Second Group

6.35	**Theme 2**	Theme 2, *p*, this time in the minor mode (G minor) All the other second-group themes are in the tonic key (minor mode), otherwise much the same as before.
7.35	**Cadence theme**	Scale part of the cadence theme, *f*
16.8 / 16.8 7.47		New imitative passage, *p*, strings; based on theme 1 motive
7.56		Vigorous concluding figure of the cadence theme, *f*
		Stop, this time "confirmed" by three solid chords.

The *exposition* continues with a long bridge built out of a motive from the first theme; a contrasting major-mode second theme; and—after more references to the first theme—an abrupt cadence theme.

The first theme in an extraordinary, angry transformation opens the *development section,* which then goes on to give that theme an exhaustive workout in many different keys. It sets up a mood of conflict that the *recapitulation* brings under control only with difficulty. The second theme gains special pathos when it is recapitulated in the minor mode (compare this with the first movement).

There is no coda. The brusque conclusion leaves the listener considerably shaken, disturbed as well as moved by Mozart's unaccustomed display of passion.

2   Opera Buffa

In the late eighteenth century, comic opera grew to equal in importance the serious opera that had monopolized the grandiose theaters of the Baroque era. The new flexibility of the Classical style was perfectly suited to the casual, swift, lifelike effects that are the essence of comedy. As much as its humor, it was this "natural," lifelike quality of comedy that appealed to audiences of the Enlightenment.

Italian comic opera was the most important, though there were also notable parallel developments in Germany, France, and England. Serious Italian opera was called *opera seria;* comic Italian opera was called **opera buffa.** Just as Italian opera seria was very popular in London in Handel's time, so Italian opera buffa was in Vienna at the time of Haydn and Mozart. Thus Haydn, whose court duties with the Esterházys included running their opera house, wrote twelve comic operas—all in Italian. Mozart in his mature years wrote six comic operas, three each in German and Italian.

The eighteenth-century theater at Drottningholm, Sweden, presents opera buffa in its original staging, using scenery actually preserved from the time.

The Ensemble

Baroque opera seria, as we have seen, consists of two elements in alternation: recitatives for the dialogue and the action, and numbers that are fully musical —almost exclusively solo arias—for static meditation and "tableaus" of emotional expression. Classical opera buffa works with the same basic scheme, except that the fully musical numbers include *ensembles* as well as arias.

An **ensemble** is a number sung by two or (often) more people. And given the Classical composers' skill in incorporating contrast into their music, they were able to make their ensembles depict the different sentiments of the participating characters simultaneously. This meant that sentiments could be presented much more swiftly and vividly: swiftly, because we don't have to wait for the characters to sing whole arias to find out what they are feeling, and vividly, because the sentiments stand out in sharp relief one against the other.

The music also depicts these sentiments in flux. For in the course of an ensemble, the action proceeds and the situation changes. This is usually projected by means of new sections with different tempos, keys, and themes. A Classical opera ensemble, then, is a sectional number for several characters in which the later sections represent new plot action and the characters' new reactions to it.

In short, whereas the aria was essentially a static number, the ensemble was a dynamic one. At the end of a Baroque da capo aria, the return of the opening music tells us that the dramatic situation is just where it was when the aria started. But at the end of a Classical ensemble, the drama has moved ahead by one notch or more, and the music, too, has moved on to something different. The ensemble was the ingenious tool that transformed opera into a much more dramatic genre than had been possible within the Baroque aesthetic.

In a Haydn opera buffa ensemble, a whole lot of characters register different feelings both visually and musically—by their grimaces, their gestures, and the contrasting melodies they sing.

6 Cassette 3A, 1–2/6 CD 3, 1–2

MOZART
Don Giovanni (1787)

Mozart wrote *Don Giovanni* in 1787 for Prague, the second largest city of the Austrian empire, where his music was enjoying a temporary spurt in popularity. While technically it counts as an opera buffa, *Don Giovanni* is neither a wholly comic drama nor wholly tragic. A somewhat enigmatic mixture of both—what might be called today a "dark comedy"—it seems to convey Mozart's feeling that events have both comical and serious dimensions, and that life's experiences cannot be pigeonholed. Earlier we encountered this ambivalence in the opera's overture, with its strange, somber, slow introduction and its manic, fast, sonata-form section (see pages 186–87).

Background Don Giovanni is the Italian name for Don Juan, the semi-legendary Spanish libertine. The tale of his endless escapades and conquests is meant to stir up incredulous laughter, usually with a bawdy undertone. Certainly a subject of this kind belongs to opera buffa.

But in his compulsive, completely selfish pursuit of women, Don Giovanni ignores the rules of society, morality, and God. Hence the serious undertone of the story. He commits crimes and mortal sins—and not only against the women he seduces. He kills the father of one of his victims, the Commandant, who surprises Giovanni struggling with his daughter.

This action finally brings Don Giovanni down. Once, when he is hiding from his pursuers in a graveyard—and joking blasphemously—he is reproached by the marble statue that has been erected over the Commandant's tomb. He arrogantly invites the statue home for dinner. The statue comes, and in return drags Giovanni off to *his* home, which is hell. The somber music associated with the statue was planted ahead of time by Mozart in the overture's slow introduction.

Thanks to Mozart's music, our righteous satisfaction at Don Giovanni's end is mixed with a good deal of sympathy for his verve and high spirits, his bravery, and his determination to lead a life of high comedy, ruled only by his own desires. The other characters in the opera, too, awaken ambivalent feelings: they amuse us and move us at the same time.

Act I, scene iii The opera's third scene begins with a chorus of peasants, celebrating the betrothal of Masetto and Zerlina. Don Giovanni enters with his manservant Leporello and immediately takes a fancy to Zerlina. He promises Masetto various favors, and then tells him to leave—and tells Leporello to take him away by force if necessary.

Aria, "Ho capito" This opera buffa aria, sung by Masetto, shows how vividly (and rapidly!) Mozart could define character in music. Singing almost entirely in very short phrases, Masetto almost insolently tells Don Giovanni that he will leave only because he has to, because great lords can always bully peasants. Then he rails at Zerlina in furious, fast asides; she has always been his ruin (an Italian peasant's honor is shattered when his woman is unfaithful). He sings a very sarcastic little tune when he promises her that Don Giovanni is going to make her into a fine lady:

Fac-cia il nostro ca-va-lie-re Ca - va - lie-ra ancora te, ca-va-liera ancora te!

Toward the end of the aria he forgets all about Don Giovanni and the opening music that he employed to address him, and thinks only of Zerlina, repeating his furious words to her as well as his sarcastic tune. He gets more and more worked up as he sings repeated cadences, so characteristic of the Classical style. A variation of the tune, played by the orchestra, ends this tiny aria in an angry rush.

The total effect is of a simple man (judging from the music he sings) who nonetheless feels deeply and is ready to express his anger. There is also a clear undercurrent of class conflict: Masetto the peasant versus Don Giovanni the aristocrat. Mozart was no political radical, but he had indeed rebelled against court authority; and the previous opera he had written, *The Marriage of Figaro,* was based on a famous French play whose anti-aristocratic sentiments caused it to be banned in its nonoperatic version. Two years after *Don Giovanni* was composed, the French Revolution broke out in Paris.

Recitative In an amusing secco recitative, sung with just continuo accompaniment, as in Baroque opera, Giovanni invites Zerlina up to his villa, promising to marry her and make her into a fine lady, just as Masetto had ironically predicted.

Duet, "Là ci darem la mano" Operas depend on memorable tunes, as well as on musical drama. The best opera composers are able to write melodies that are not only beautiful in themselves, but also further the drama at the same time. Such a one is the most famous tune in *Don Giovanni,* the main tune in the following duet (an ensemble for two singers) between Don Giovanni and Zerlina.

Section 1 (Andante) Don Giovanni sings his first stanza to a simple, unforgettable tune that combines seductiveness with a delicate sense of banter:

When Zerlina sings the same tune to *her* first stanza, we know she is playing along, even though she hesitates (notice her tiny rhythmic changes, and her reluctance to finish the tune in eight measures—she delays for two more).

In stanza 3, as Don Giovanni presses more and more ardently, yet always gently, Zerlina keeps drawing back. Her reiterated "non son più forte" ("I'm weakening") makes her sound very sorry for herself, but also coy. When the main tune comes back—section 1 of the ensemble falls into an **A A′ B A″ coda** form—Giovanni grows more insistent, Zerlina more coquettish. The words they sing (from stanzas 1–3) are closer together than before, and even simultaneous. Taking a cue from the music, the stage director will place them physically closer together, too.

Section 2 (Allegro) Zerlina falls happily into Don Giovanni's arms, echoing his "*andiam*" ("let us go"). The "innocent love" they now mean to celebrate is depicted by a little rustic melody (Zerlina is a peasant girl, remember) in a faster tempo. But a not-so-innocent sensuous note is added by the orchestra after the singers' first phrase in this section.

How neatly and charmingly an ensemble can project dramatic action; the whole duet leads us step by step through Don Giovanni's successful "technique." By portraying these people through characteristic action or behavior —Don Giovanni winning another woman, Zerlina playing her own coy game—Mozart exposes their personalities as convincingly as any novelist or playwright.

TEXT: Mozart, *Don Giovanni:* from Act I, scene iii

ARIA: "Ho capito"

Masetto:	Ho capito, *signor, sì!*	I understand you, yes *sir!*
(to Don Giovanni)	Chino il capo, e me ne vò	I touch my cap and off I go;
	Ghiacche piace a voi così	Since that's what you want
	Altre repliche *non fò. . . .*	I have nothing else to say.
	Cavalier voi siete già,	After all, you're a lord,
	Dubitar non posso affè,	And I couldn't suspect you, oh no!
	Me lo dice la bontà,	You've told me of the favors
	Che volete *aver per me.*	You mean to do for me!
(aside, to Zerlina)	Briconaccia! malandrina!	You wretch! you witch!
	Fosti ognor la mia ruina!	You have always been my ruin!
(to Leporello)	Vengo, vengo!	Yes, I'm coming—
(to Zerlina)	Resta, resta!	Stay, why don't you?
	È una cosa molto onesta;	A very innocent affair!
	Faccia il nostro cavaliere	No doubt this fine lord
	cavaliera ancora te.	Will make you his lady, too!

(*last seven lines repeated*)

Don Giovanni and Zerlina, in an early engraving and in a modern production.

RECITATIVE (with continuo only)

Giovanni: Alfin siam liberati,	At last we're free,
Zerlinetta gentile, da quel scoccone.	My darling Zerlinetta, of that clown.
Che ne dite, mio ben, so far pulito?	Tell me, my dear, don't I manage things well?
Zerlina: Ma signore, io gli diede	But sir, I gave him
Parola di sposarlo.	My word that we would be married.
Giovanni: Tal parola	That word
Non vale un zero! voi non siete fata	Is worth nothing! You were not made
Per esser paesana. Un'altra sorte	To be a peasant girl. A different fate
Vi procuran quegli occhi bricconcelli,	Is called for by those roguish eyes,
Quei labretti sì belli,	Those beautiful little lips,
Quelle dituccia candide e odorose,	These slender white, perfumed fingers,
Parmi toccar giuncata, e fiutar rose.	So soft to the touch, scented with roses.
Zerlina: Ah, non vorrei—	Ah, I don't want to—
Giovanni: Che non voresti?	What don't you want?
Zerlina: Alfine	To end up
Ingannata restar! Io so che raro	Deceived! I know it's not often
Colle donne voi alti cavalieri	That with women you great gentlemen
siete onesti e sinceri.	Are honest and sincere.
Giovanni: É un' impostura	A slander
Della gente plebea! La nobiltà	Of the lower classes! The nobility
Ha dipinta negli occhi l'onestà.	Is honest to the tips of its toes.
Orsù non perdiam tempo; in quest'instante	Let's lose no time; this very instant
Io vi voglio sposar.	I wish to marry you.
Zerlina: Voi?	You?
Giovanni: Certo io.	Certainly, me;
Quel casinetto è mio, soli saremo;	There's my little place; we'll be alone—
E là, gioella mio, ci sposeremo.	And there, my precious, we'll be married.

DUET "Là ci darem la mano"

Section 1 Andante, **2/4** meter

Giovanni:	**A**	Là ci darem la mano	There *[in the villa]* you'll give me your hand,
		Là mi dirai di si!	There you'll tell me yes!
		Vedi, non è lontano;	You see, it isn't far—
		Partiam, ben mio, da qui!	Let's go there, my dear!
Zerlina:	**A'**	Vorrei, e non vorrei;	I want to, yet I don't want to;
		Mi tremo un poco il cor.	My heart is trembling a little;
		Felice, è ver, sarei,	It's true, I would be happy,
		Ma può burlami ancor.	But he could be joking with me.
Giovanni:	**B**	Vieni, mio bel diletto!	Come, my darling!
Zerlina:		Mi fa pietà Masetto . . .	I'm sorry for Masetto . . .
Giovanni:		Io cangierò tua sorte!	I shall change your lot!
Zerlina:		Presto *non son più forte* . . .	All of a sudden I'm weakening . . .

(repetition of phrases [both verbal and musical] from stanzas 1–3)

Giovanni:	**A''**	Vieni, vieni! Là ci darem la mano
Zerlina:		Vorrei, e non vorrei . . .
Giovanni:		Là mi dirai di si!
Zerlina:		Mi trema un poco il cor.
Giovanni:		Partiam, ben mio, da qui!
Zerlina:		Ma può burlami ancor.
Giovanni:	coda	Vieni, mio bel diletto!
Zerlina:		Mi fa pietà Masetto . . .
Giovanni:		Io cangierò tua sorte!
Zerlina:		Presto *non son più forte* . . .
Both:		Andiam!

Section 2 Allegro, **6/8** meter

Both:	Andiam, andiam, mio bene,	Let us go, my dear,
	A ristorar le pene	And relieve the pangs
	D'un innocente amor.	Of an innocent love.

(words and music repeated)

3 The Classical Concerto

On page 134 we discussed the Baroque concerto grosso at the time of Bach and Vivaldi in terms of the basic concerto idea—the contest between a group of soloists and an orchestra. This basic idea was refined and sharpened as the eighteenth century progressed.

The norm now became the **solo concerto,** with a single soloist, who was therefore much freer than the concerto grosso's solo group, and could be treated as a formidable virtuoso. Virtuosity was especially appreciated by the new audience for music, the audience of the concert hall. At the same time, the orchestra was growing. With its well-coordinated string, woodwind, and brass groups, the Classical orchestra was much more flexible and powerful than the Baroque concerto orchestra had ever been.

So the balance between the two contesting forces presented a real problem—but it was the sort of problem that brought out the best in the great Viennese composers. Mozart worked it out in a series of seventeen superb piano concertos written during his years in Vienna, mostly for his own concert use. He pitted the soloist's greater agility, brilliance, and expressive capability against the orchestra's increased power and variety of tone color. The contestants are perfectly matched; neither one can ever emerge definitely as the winner.

Double-Exposition Form

For the first movements of concertos, Mozart developed a special form in order to capitalize on the contest that is basic to the genre, **double-exposition form.** Though the diagram for this form may look rather cluttered, it is in fact simply an extended variant of sonata form. Compare the sonata-form diagram, page 183:

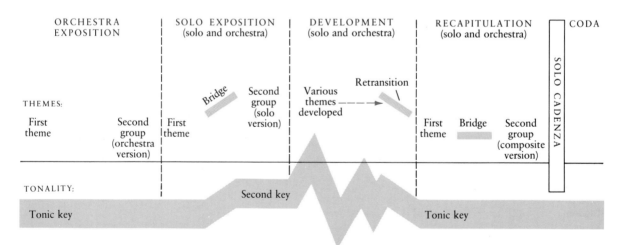

In place of the repeated exposition of sonata form, here each of the competing forces presents the exposition in its own somewhat different version. Note that unlike the exposition in a symphony, in a concerto the **orchestra exposition** does not modulate—an important difference. The point is to save the change of key that counts for so much in all sonata-form compositions until the **solo exposition.** Modulation is a resource that demonstrates the soloist's superior range and mobility.

The recapitulation in double-exposition form amounts to a composite of the orchestral and solo versions of the exposition. And shortly before the end, there is a big, formal pause for the soloist's **cadenza** (see page 138). The soloist was supposed to improvise at this point—to show his or her skill and flair by working out new thematic developments on the spot, and also by carrying off brilliant feats of virtuosity.

Referring to the standard movement plan for Classical genres at the beginning of this chapter, we can summarize the plan for the Classical concerto as follows. Note that there is no minuet movement.

1 Fast or moderately paced movement in double-exposition sonata form. There is a cadenza near the end.	2 Slower, lyric movement; occasionally in double-exposition form, more often a rondo or theme and variations.	3 Faster and somewhat lighter movement; almost always in rondo or variation form.

MOZART
Piano Concerto No. 17 in G, K. 453 (1784)

Mozart wrote the Piano Concerto in G for one of his favorite students, Barbara Ployer, then nineteen years old. It is a more delicate, intimate work than most of the concertos he wrote to play himself at his own money-making concerts. The eighteenth century would have called it more "feminine."

Characteristically, the first movement simply overflows with musical material—themes and motives of almost every possible kind. The second movement calls up an indescribable mood, a blend of melancholy and tranquility shaken more than once by displays of deeper emotion. And the last movement exists strictly for fun.

First Movement (Allegro)   The first theme, presented quietly at the start of the *orchestra exposition,* is elegance itself. The more expressive second theme makes a sharp contrast; a jaunty cadence figure carried forward by the bassoon and the flute introduces this second theme, and assumes considerable prominence as the work proceeds. The true cadence theme comes later.

In the *solo exposition,* the piano plays a more ornamental version of the first theme. Then it adds a new, brighter theme of its own, before taking up —and taking over—the orchestra's expressive second theme. On the other hand, most of the loud music from the orchestral exposition is now subtracted. The solo winds up a brilliant virtuoso passage with a trill and a big cadence. The orchestra plays part of the cadence theme (from the orchestra exposition).

The *development* consists largely of rapid piano passages, modulating repeatedly to remote keys; behind them, the wind instruments develop one of the exposition themes. In the *recapitulation,* the dialogue between solo and orchestra becomes closer and more spirited. The composite second group assembles all the material—elegant and bright, loud and soft—from both expositions.

As for the cadenza, Mozart actually wrote out two alternatives as a sort of lesson for Ployer. Most pianists today use one or the other, though Mozart himself would surely have improvised something flashier.

Second Movement (Andante)   Here double-exposition form is used more simply, and for a more profound expressive effect, than in the first movement. Mozart probably never used the form more beautifully.

Orchestra Exposition   The first theme is unusual, consisting of a single quiet phrase leading to a fermata, as though silently posing a question:

An answering theme is played by the woodwinds in transparent, imitative counterpoint. This leads to a loud-soft theme, then to a lovely cadence theme featuring minor-mode harmonies:

Solo Exposition   The piano enters and questions with theme 1—and provides its own new answer, an uneasy, emotional one that modulates to the new key before introducing the woodwind dialogue. This the piano takes under control and extends, and it does the same with the cadence theme. The solo exposition ends with a piano trill and a cadence.

Development   Now it is the woodwinds that ask the question. The piano answers with new expressive material; in the background, the woodwinds develop a short motive from the cadence theme. Finally—as a retransition—the orchestra wrenches the music back to the original tonic key.

Recapitulation   All the themes are heard in the "composite" recapitulation. But one feature of musical form is unique to this movement—a feature that grows out of the unique first theme. After the cadenza, the woodwinds play this theme once again, with its questioning suddenly shadowed by anxious minor-mode harmonies.

Although the piano answers have been growing more and more emotional throughout the movement, this last one—a cadential answer—is simple and serene, like a gentle reproof. At last the movement can come to rest, with an exquisite new piano commentary on the cadence theme.

Third Movement (Allegretto, leading to Presto)   We examined this lighthearted theme and variations in Chapter 12 on page 190. If we hear it in context, we may enjoy its third variation, with its woodwind dialogue, all the more for the echoes of similar dialogues in both earlier movements.

From Mozart's score of one of his concertos

String quartets, then and now (below and next page). Nineteenth-century quartets were often led by celebrated violin soloists; shown here is a group led by violinist-composer Henry Vieuxtemps (1820–1881), at the left.

4   The String Quartet

The **string quartet**—a composition for two violins, viola, and cello—is the most important genre of Classical chamber music. It emerged as a particular kind of expansion of the Baroque trio sonata. In a similar way, the Classical sonata, to be discussed shortly, can be thought of as a contraction of the Baroque solo sonata.

Both the expansion and the contraction were mandated by the elimination of the continuo. The trio sonata, like the later string quartet, included two treble instruments and a cello—top and bottom—but it was weak in the middle range, where the fourth instrument, the continuo harpsichord or organ, improvised chords in a relatively indiscriminate way that Classical composers were no longer willing to tolerate. In the quartet, the middle-

The Juilliard Quartet, perhaps the leading American quartet, was formed at the Juilliard School in New York in 1946 and is still active. They play Béla Bartók's Quartet No. 2 on our recording set (see page 354).

The Kronos Quartet, based in San Francisco, plays almost exclusively contemporary music, including jazz arrangements and other "crossover" items.

range string instrument, the viola, received a part of equal importance, in principle, to those of the violins and the cello. The cello, too, was given more to do than just providing bass support, which was its main function in Baroque music.

In Haydn's hands, the four instruments grow more and more similar in their actual musical material, and more and more interdependent. There is a subtle interplay as they each respond to musical gestures made by the others. This interplay has been aptly compared to the art of cultivated conversation —witty, sensitive, always ready with a perfectly turned phrase—that was especially prized in eighteenth-century salons.

Referring to the standard movement plan for Classical instrumental genres at the beginning of this chapter, we can summarize the plan for the string quartet as follows:

| 1 Fast or moderately paced movement in sonata form (nearly always; there are some exceptions). | 2 Slower, lyric movement. Occasionally the slow movement comes in third position, after the minuet. | 3 Minuet and trio. Occasionally the minuet movement comes in second position, before the slow movement. | 4 Faster and somewhat lighter movement in rondo or sonata form. |

HAYDN
String Quartet in D, Op. 64 No. 5 (The *Lark*) (1790)

Haydn wrote sixty-seven string quartets, and left a sixty-eighth unfinished at the end of his life. The lark in the nickname of the present quartet refers to the soaring main melody of the first movement.

3 Cassette 1B, 2–3/3 CD 1, 11–12
6 Cassette 2B-2, 7/6 CD 2-12, 17

It was the custom to publish chamber music in sets of three or six works. The set of six issued as Opus 64 was composed for Johann Tost, a violinist and wheeler-dealer who had been one of Haydn's colleagues in the service of Prince Esterházy. They are sometimes called the Tost Quartets.

First Movement (Allegro moderato) Though the first violin always plays the "lark" melody, the second violin leads off with a significant little tune which then becomes a steady counterpoint below that melody. The whole movement affords an excellent example of the sharing of material among the four quartet members. Their dialogue is always easy, always alert.

This sonata-form movement has a sort of double recapitulation, two sections in the tonic key both starting with the lark melody. The development section includes all the exposition themes—the lark melody, the syncopated second theme, and the fast, scalewise cadence theme.

Second Movement (Adagio cantabile) A beautiful slow melody (**A**) in a a′ b a″ form grows richer in rhythm and harmony as it proceeds:

The movement as a whole is in **A B A′** form, with a **B** section derived from **a′** in different keys. The return of **A** is a variation, consisting of exquisite little decorations of the first violin's melody, in an improvisational spirit. Perhaps Haydn knew that Tost would add melodic ornamentations to any slow melody like this one on his own initiative, if the composer didn't get there first.

Third Movement (Menuetto: Allegretto) After the extended reverie of the slow movement, the earthy dance rhythms of the minuet are especially welcome. As is always the case with Haydn, this minuet is full of fine points: see page 178.

Fourth Movement (Vivace) *Vivace* meaning "vivaciously," the minuscule last movement is usually played at breakneck speed, *presto* or *prestissimo*. Haydn's special idea is to keep very fast, even notes going without any letup whatsoever until just before the end—and so the faster it goes the better the fun, like a roller coaster. This is an early instance of a type of piece called a *perpetuum mobile* (perpetual motion; well-known later ones are Chopin's "Minute Waltz" and Rimsky-Korsakov's "The Flight of the Bumble Bee"):

Most of the perpetual moving is done by the first violin, but in the fugal **B** section of this **A B A′** form, all the other instruments join in too. The movement is a brilliant demonstration not of personal virtuosity, but—as befits this eminently democratic genre—that of the entire quartet.

Mozart composing at his billiard table: a still from the 1984 film *Amadeus*. Mozart is known to have liked billiards; perhaps the cool, smooth, elegant aspects of the game reminded him of his music.

5   The Sonata

The term *sonata* has multiple meanings, as we have already noted. We know its adjectival use in the term "sonata form," the scheme employed in the first movements of Classical overtures, symphonies, quartets, and also (as it happens) sonatas. As a noun *sonata* refers to a piece for a small number of instruments or a single one. And whereas in the Baroque period there were trio sonatas and solo sonatas—solo plus continuo, usually—in the Classical period the term was restricted to compositions for one or two instruments only.

Sonatas were composed for violin and piano, for example, in which the piano is not a mere accompaniment, as in a Baroque solo sonata with continuo, but an equal partner with the violin. But the most important Classical sonatas were solo pieces for the favorite new instrument of the time, the piano—so much so that the term *sonata* by itself has come to mean a piano sonata, unless another instrument is mentioned.

The number and order of movements in a sonata is less standardized than in the other main Classical genres. A common arrangement is analogous to that of the concerto: sonata-form movement, slow movement, and a final fast movement in rondo or sonata form. But though statistically it may be true that most sonatas follow this three-movement pattern, there are many exceptions.

MOZART
Piano Sonata in A, K. 331 (1783)

A conspicuous exception to the arrangement just mentioned is Mozart's
Piano Sonata in A, one of the best-known of all his works for piano. Scholars
have recently discovered that he wrote it in 1783, not in 1778 as was formerly
believed—important information, since five years in one's twenties covers a
world of experience, and since in this case that experience included leaving a
dull court position in Salzburg and setting up as a free-lance composer at
music's greatest center, Vienna. In Vienna, where Mozart's livelihood
depended on students, this sonata was probably very useful to him for teaching—as it has been for piano teachers ever since.

First Movement (Andante graziozo)   The sonata begins not with a sonata-
form movement, but with a set of variations on this "graceful" theme:

This is Mozart at his most rococo. The first four variations are in the same
gently moving tempo as the theme; variation 5 moves slower, and variation 6
faster. Variation 3 changes to the minor mode.

Second Movement (Menuetto)   Perhaps because there was no opening
sonata-form movement, Mozart makes the minuet in this sonata longer and
much more intricate than usual. The trio is especially interesting, with its
sleepy echoes in the **c** section and its strange contrasts in the **d** section.

Third Movement (Alla turca: Allegretto)   This rondo was discussed in
Chapter 12.
    What is striking about the Sonata in A, considered as a whole, is the way
the mood gradually gets tougher as the unusual sequence of movements proceeds. The first movement may have struck Mozart's students from Viennese
high society as elegant and pretty enough. The second movement is surprisingly intellectual, though, and the last movement is a wicked parody.

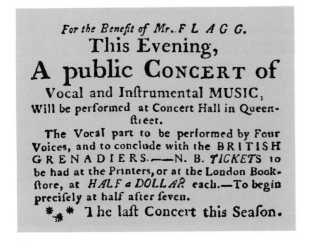

Advertisement from the
Boston Chronicle of 1769.
With only around 15,000
inhabitants, Boston already
had a concert hall and a
concert producer (Flagg).

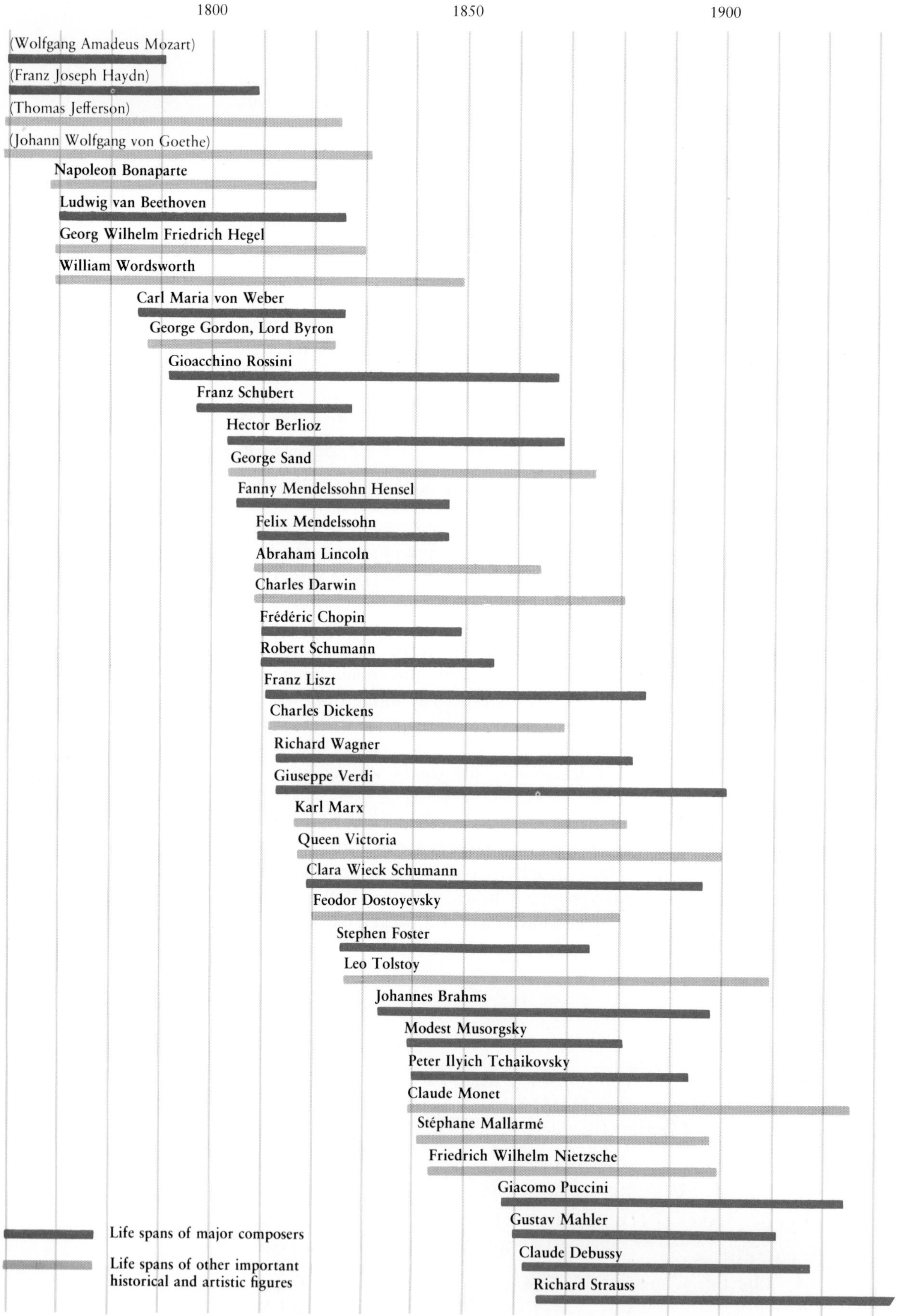

1800   1850   1900

(Wolfgang Amadeus Mozart)

(Franz Joseph Haydn)

(Thomas Jefferson)

(Johann Wolfgang von Goethe)

Napoleon Bonaparte

Ludwig van Beethoven

Georg Wilhelm Friedrich Hegel

William Wordsworth

Carl Maria von Weber

George Gordon, Lord Byron

Gioacchino Rossini

Franz Schubert

Hector Berlioz

George Sand

Fanny Mendelssohn Hensel

Felix Mendelssohn

Abraham Lincoln

Charles Darwin

Frédéric Chopin

Robert Schumann

Franz Liszt

Charles Dickens

Richard Wagner

Giuseppe Verdi

Karl Marx

Queen Victoria

Clara Wieck Schumann

Feodor Dostoyevsky

Stephen Foster

Leo Tolstoy

Johannes Brahms

Modest Musorgsky

Peter Ilyich Tchaikovsky

Claude Monet

Stéphane Mallarmé

Friedrich Wilhelm Nietzsche

Giacomo Puccini

Gustav Mahler

Claude Debussy

Richard Strauss

Life spans of major composers

Life spans of other important
historical and artistic figures

Unit IV

The Nineteenth Century

In Unit IV we take up music of the nineteenth century. Starting with the towering figure of Beethoven in the first quarter of the century, famous names now crowd the history of music: Schubert, Schumann, Chopin, Mendelssohn, Berlioz, Wagner, Liszt, Verdi, Brahms, Tchaikovsky, Musorgsky, and others. Nearly everyone, whether conscious of it or not, knows a fair amount of music by these masters, or at least some of their timeless tunes. The latter have proved their resilience by surviving Muzak, Mantovani, and mutilation into pop tunes and advertising jingles.

Indeed, Romantic music—the music of the nineteenth century—is such a strong presence in today's musical life that for some time people have been troubled about musical progress, as if music were some kind of car spinning its wheels in a rut. We need only observe that the appeal of this music in the symphony hall, the opera house, and the teaching studio today seems to rest on much the same grounds as those governing its great success a hundred years ago and more. It is important to realize, first of all, that nineteenth-century music was a great success story. For the first time in history, music was taken entirely seriously as an art on the highest level. Composers were accorded a new, exalted role, to which they responded magnificently, writing music that sounds important and impressive; and listeners ever since have been thoroughly impressed.

Music and Individual Emotion

Music's prestige, in the Romantic scheme of things, derived first and foremost from its unique power to convey individual feeling. Again, composers rose to the challenge. Nineteenth-century music is more direct and unrestrained in emotional quality than the music of any earlier time. And for most audiences, full-blooded emotion in music—even exaggerated emotion—seems never to lose its powerful attraction.

The individuality of all artists, including composers, was accorded special value in the nineteenth century. Composers produced music with much more pronounced personal attributes than in the late Baroque period or the Classical period (when many pieces by Haydn and Mozart, for example, sounded rather similar in character). It is therefore a natural tendency to think of the history of nineteenth-century music in terms of great names, such as those in the list given above. The prospect of getting to know all these distinct, unusual, and probably fascinating characters—meeting them, as it were, under the emotional conditions of Romantic music—surely contributes to the appeal of this particular body of music.

Like eighteenth-century music, music of the nineteenth century is not stylistically homogeneous, yet it can still be regarded as a larger historical unit. We shall take up the Romantic style—usually dated from the 1820s—after discussing the music of Beethoven, who was born in 1770 and who traveled twice to Vienna, the city of Classicism, in his youth—first to meet Mozart and then to study with Haydn.

But while in technique Beethoven was clearly a child of the eighteenth century, in his emotionalism, his artistic ambition, and his insistence on individuality he was a true inhabitant of the nineteenth. Beethoven was, indeed, the immediate or the remote model for almost every great nineteenth-century composer who came after him. Understanding Beethoven is the key to an understanding of Romantic music.

Chapter 14

Beethoven

If any single composer deserves a special chapter in the history of music, that composer is Ludwig van Beethoven (1770–1827). Probably no other figure in the arts meets with such a strong universal response. People may pity Van Gogh, respect Michelangelo and Shakespeare, and admire Leonardo da Vinci, but Beethoven instantly summons up a powerful, positive image: that of the tough, ugly, angry genius delivering himself of one deeply expressive masterpiece after another in the teeth of adversity. Beethoven's music has enjoyed broad-based, uninterrupted popularity from his own day to the present. Today its place is equally secure with unsophisticated listeners and with the most learned musicians.

There is a sense, furthermore, in which music may be said to have come of age with Beethoven. For despite the great music that came before him—that of Bach, Mozart, and many other composers we know—the art of music was never taken so seriously until his symphonies and sonatas struck listeners of his time as a revelation. They were almost equally impressed by the facts of his life, in particular his deafness, the affliction that caused him to retire from a career as a performing musician and become solely a composer.

A new concept of artistic genius was evolving at the time, and Beethoven crystallized this concept powerfully for his own age. He still exemplifies it today. No longer a mere craftsman, the artist suffers and creates; endowed not just with greater talent but with a greater soul than ordinary mortals, the artist suffers and creates for humanity. Music is no longer merely a function of bodily parts like the ear or the fingers. It exists in the highest reaches of the artist's spirit.

Beethoven, 1814

1 Between Classicism and Romanticism

Beethoven is special in another sense, in the unique position he occupies between the Viennese Classical style and the Romanticism of the last three-quarters of the nineteenth century. Beethoven's roots were firmly Classical. Haydn was at the height of his fame when Beethoven came to Vienna to study with him in 1792, just after Mozart's great final decade there. From Haydn he learned the secrets of the Viennese Classical style, and as a young man he wrote a great deal of excellent music adhering to that style. Indeed, Beethoven remained committed to the principles of the Classical style until the end of his life.

Committed to the *principles* of Classicism—but not to every one of its manifestations, and certainly not to the mood behind it. There is almost always a sense of excitement, urgency, and striving in Beethoven's music that makes it instantly distinguishable from that of Haydn and Mozart. These qualities emerged in response to Romantic stirrings of a kind that we shall consider more carefully in the next chapter.

The French Revolution

Romanticism, as we shall see, was originally a literary movement. Though well under way by the beginning of the nineteenth century, it was not yet influential in Vienna; and, in any case, Beethoven did not have a very literary sensibility. At the root of Romanticism, however, there lay one great political event that made a profound impact on the composer's generation. This was the French Revolution. Beethoven was one of many artists who felt compelled to proclaim their sympathy with the ideal of freedom symbolized by that cataclysmic event.

When the Parisian crowd stormed the Bastille in 1789, Beethoven was a highly impressionable eighteen-year-old, already grounded in liberal and humanistic ideals. More than a decade later, Beethoven's admiration for Napoleon as hero of the revolution led him to an extravagant and unprecedented gesture—writing a descriptive symphony called *Bonaparte*. Retitled the *Eroica* (Heroic) Symphony, this was the decisive "breakthrough" work of Beethoven's maturity. It was the first work to show his full individual freedom as an artist.

Storming the Bastille, a contemporary engraving of the most famous event of the French Revolution

Before Beethoven could send the symphony to Paris, Napoleon crowned himself Emperor of France. Liberal Europe saw this as a betrayal of the revolution, and Beethoven scratched out the title in fury. But idealism dies hard.

Napoleon's coronation as Emperor of France in 1803, as portrayed by Jacques-Louis David (1748–1825), the greatest practitioner of Neoclassical art (see page 165). Today this huge (20 by 30 feet) picture turns off some viewers as much as the actual event it depicts enraged Beethoven.

To Beethoven, and to very many of his contemporaries, the French Revolution still stood for an ideal of perfectibility—not so much of human society (as Beethoven himself acknowledged by deleting Napoleon's name) as of human aspiration. That ideal, too, is what Beethoven realized by his own triumph over his deafness. The point was not lost on those of his contemporaries who were swept away by his music.

And that is what listeners have responded to ever since. Listening to the *Eroica* Symphony, we sense that it has less to do with Napoleon than with the composer's own self-image. The quality of heroic striving and inner triumph is what emerges so magnificently in Beethoven's most famous compositions.

(1770–1827)

Ludwig van Beethoven

Chief Works: Nine symphonies, the most famous being the Third *(Eroica),* Fifth, Sixth *(Pastoral),* Seventh, and Ninth *(Choral)*

The opera *Fidelio* (originally called *Leonore),* for which he wrote four different overtures; overtures to *Egmont* and *Coriolanus*

Violin Concerto and five piano concertos, including the *Emperor* (No. 5)

It must have been a miserable childhood. Beethoven's father, a minor musician at the court of Bonn in the west of Germany, tried unsuccessfully to promote him as an infant prodigy like Mozart. A trip to Vienna to make contacts (with Mozart, among others) was cut short by the death of his mother. When he was still in his teens, Beethoven had to take charge of his family because of his father's drinking.

Nonetheless, Bonn was an "enlightened" court, ruled by the brother of the liberal Emperor Joseph II of Austria. The talented young musician had an opportunity to mix with aristocrats and intellectuals. The idealism that is so evident in Beethoven's later works—such as his Ninth Symphony, ending with a choral hymn to universal brotherhood—can be traced to this early environment.

16 string quartets

32 piano sonatas, including the *Pathétique, Waldstein, Appassionata,* and the late-period *Hammerklavier* Sonata

Mass in D *(Missa solemnis)*

Unlike Mozart, Beethoven was a slow developer, but by the age of twenty-two he had made enough of an impression to receive a sort of fellowship to study with Haydn in Vienna, then the musical capital of the world. He was soon acclaimed as a magnificent and powerful virtuoso pianist, playing his own compositions at the palaces of the music-loving aristocracy of that city. He remained in Vienna until his death.

After the age of thirty, he became progressively deaf—a devastating fate for a musician, which kept him from making a living in the traditional manner, by performing. The crisis that this caused in Beethoven's life is reflected by a strange, moving document called the "Heiligenstadt Testament," after the town where it was written, in 1802. A letter to his brothers that was never sent, the testament is half proclamation of artistic ideals, half suicide note. But Beethoven overcame his depression and in 1803 wrote the first of his truly powerful and individual symphonies, the Third *(Eroica).*

Beethoven all but demanded support from members of the nobility in Vienna, who were awed by his extraordinarily forceful and original music as well as by his uncompromising character. An alarmingly brusque and strong-willed person, he suffered deeply and seemed to live for his art alone. His domestic life was chaotic; one anecdote has him standing in the middle of the floor and pouring water over himself to cool off in summer and being asked by his landlord to leave. (He changed lodgings on an average of once a year.) At the end of his life he was well known on the streets of Vienna as an eccentric.

Beethoven's method of composing was to sketch themes, passages, and even whole movements again and again. As if sensing that this creative process was an essential part of his being, Beethoven never discarded sketches—such as these for the Fifth Symphony.

Beethoven striding through Vienna: a caricature by one of his contemporaries

Probably the first musician to make a career solely from composing, Beethoven was regarded as a genius even in his lifetime. He had an immense need to receive and to give affection, yet he never married, despite various love affairs. After he died, passionate letters to a woman identified only as his "Immortal Beloved" were found; she has only recently been identified as Antonie Brentano, the wife of one of Beethoven's friends. In his later years Beethoven adopted his own orphan nephew, but his attitude was so overprotective and his love so smothering that the boy could not stand it and actually attempted suicide.

Beethoven had always lived with ill health, and the shock of this new family crisis hastened his death. Twenty thousand attended his funeral; his eulogy was written, and delivered at the funeral, by Vienna's leading poet.

Taste in many matters has changed many times since Beethoven's lifetime, but his music has always reigned supreme with audiences and critics. The originality and expressive power of his work seem never to fade.

A modern impression of Beethoven in his later years. The artist has captured both the famous scowl of defiance, and also the chaotic state of Beethoven's household—the broken piano strings, the sheets of musical sketches all over the place, and the useless ear trumpets.

2 Beethoven and the Symphony

Beethoven is especially associated with the symphony, a Classical genre that he completely transformed after the turning point of the *Eroica*. We can summarize Beethoven's main innovations by reference to another symphony, the Fifth, a work that more than any other seems to sum up and typify the genre as a whole.

Three main features have impressed generations of listeners to Beethoven's Fifth Symphony: its rhythmic drive, its motivic unity, and the sense it gives of a definite psychological progression. The first feature is apprehended at once, after only a few measures; the second by the end of the opening movement; and the third only after one has experienced the entire four-movement symphony.

➤ *Rhythmic drive* Apparent immediately is the almost hectic drive and blunt power of Beethoven's rhythmic style. He was never a "pretty" composer, even in his early pieces, which recall the style of Haydn and Mozart. In later works, such as the Fifth Symphony, the sheer rhythmic force seems a far cry from the elegance and wit of the Viennese Classical style. Beethoven's surging rhythm has probably contributed more to his appeal than any other technical feature.

➤ *Motivic consistency* During the first movement of the Fifth Symphony, a single rhythmic motive, ♪♪♪ ♩, is heard almost constantly, in many different forms. They are not random forms; the motive becomes more and more vivid and significant as the movement progresses. People have marveled at the "organic" quality of such music, which seems to them to grow like a plant's leaves out of a basic seed.

> *Psychological progression*   Over the course of the Fifth Symphony's four movements, Beethoven creates an impression that was quite novel in the instrumental music of his or any earlier time. The four movements seem to trace a coherent and dramatic psychological progression in several stages. "There Fate knocks at the door!" Beethoven is supposed to have said about the symphony's first movement—but after two eventful middle stages, Fate is completely defeated in the last movement, trampled under by a military march.

In Beethoven's hands, the multimovement symphony seems to trace an inspirational life process, a process so basic and universal that it leaves few listeners unmoved. This was, perhaps, the greatest of all his forward-looking innovations.

A bizarre nineteenth-century impression of Beethoven's Fifth Symphony. The artist imagined all kinds of fateful (indeed, demonic) fancies behind the bland exterior of the orchestra players.

The Scherzo

Another of Beethoven's technical innovations should also be mentioned. On the whole, Beethoven continued to use Classical forms for the movements of his symphonies and other multimovement works. As early as his Second Symphony, however, he substituted another kind of movement for the traditional minuet.

This was the **scherzo** (which he had already experimented with in sonatas and quartets). The scherzo is a fast, rushing movement in triple meter—inherited from the minuet—and in the basic minuet-and-trio form, **A B A**. With their fast tempo, Beethoven's scherzos sometimes need more repetitions to make their point, and so he sometimes extended the **A B A** form to **A B A B A**.

The word *scherzo* means "joke" in Italian. Beethoven's brand of humor is very different from, say, Haydn's: broad, brusque, jocular, even violent. Clearly for Beethoven the mood of the Classical minuet was too closely associated with eighteenth-century formality and elegance. The scherzo became an ideal vehicle for Beethoven's characteristic rhythmic drive.

LUDWIG VAN BEETHOVEN
Symphony No. 5 in C Minor, Op. 67 (1808)

Beethoven composed his Fifth Symphony together with his Sixth *(Pastoral)* for one of the rare concerts in which he showcased his own works. This concert, in December 1808, was a huge success, even though it lasted for five hours and the heating in the hall failed.

First Movement (Allegro con brio)   As we have already said, motivic consistency is a special feature of Beethoven's work. The first movement of the Fifth Symphony is dominated by a single rhythmic motive, ♪♪♪𝅗𝅥 . This famous motive forms the first theme in the exposition, initiates the bridge, appears as a subdued background to the lyrical, contrasting second theme, and emerges again in the cadence material:

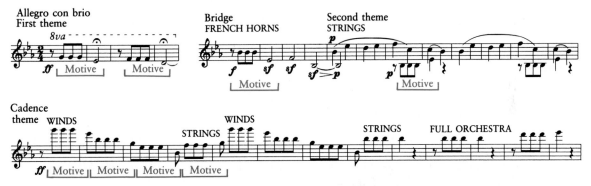

The motive then expands further in the development section and continues growing in the long coda.

How is this different from Classical motivic technique? In such works as Mozart's Symphony in G Minor and Haydn's Symphony No. 88, a single motive is likewise carried through an entire movement with consistency and a sense of growth. But the way Beethoven manages all this gives the Fifth Symphony its particular gripping urgency. The difference is not in basic technique but in the way it is being used—in the expressive intensity it is made to serve. Beethoven is using a Classical device here for non-Classical ends.

Exposition   The movement begins with an arresting presentation of the first theme, in the key of C minor (shown above). What is initially striking about the theme is its minor-mode gloom and its stark, gestural feeling. The meter is disrupted by fermatas, which give the music an improvisational, primal quality, like a great shout. Even after the theme rushes on and seems to be picking up momentum, it is halted by a new fermata, making three fermatas in all.

The horn-call bridge (see above) performs the usual function of a bridge in an unusually dramatic way. That function is to firmly cement the new key —a major key—and prepare the way for the second theme with power and authority.

The second theme introduces a new gentle mood, despite the main motive rumbling away below it. But this mood soon fades—Beethoven seems to brush it aside impatiently. The main motive bursts out again in a stormy cadence passage. After a complete stop, the exposition is repeated.

Development   The development section starts explosively with the first theme making an immediate modulation, a modulation back to the minor mode. It sounds like the crack of doom.

For a time the first theme (or rather its continuation) is developed, leading to a climax when the ♪♪♩ rhythm multiplies itself furiously, as shown to the right. Next comes the bridge theme, modulating through one key after another. Suddenly the *two middle pitches* of the bridge theme are extracted and echoed between high wind instruments and lower strings. This process is called **fragmentation** (for an example from Mozart, see page 201). Then the two-note echoing figure breaks apart, and echoes start up on just one note:

Beethoven is famous for the tension he builds up in the retransition section of sonata form to prepare for recapitulations. In the Fifth Symphony, the hush at this point becomes almost unbearable. Finally the whole orchestra seems to grab and shake the listener by the lapels, shouting the main motive again and again until the first theme settles out in the original tonic key.

Actually, this is the same technique used by Haydn in preparing humorous thematic returns (see, for example, the rondo of Symphony No. 88, page 195). The opening motive of a theme is played over and over again until it serves as the kickoff for the theme itself. But in place of Haydn's wit, Beethoven gives a sense of tremendous, heroic achievement.

Recapitulation The exposition version of the main theme was jolted by three striking fermatas. Now, in the recapitulation, the third fermata is filled by a slow expressive cadenza for solo oboe. This extraordinary moment provides a brief rest from the incessant rhythmic drive. Otherwise the recapitulation stays very close to the exposition—a clear testimony to Beethoven's Classical allegiance.

Coda On the other hand, the action-packed coda that follows is an equally clear testimony to Beethoven's freedom from Classical formulas.

In the exposition, we recall, the stormy cadence passage had been defused by an affirmative "Classical" cadence and a complete stop. At the end of the recapitulation, the parallel passage seems to reject any such easy solution. Instead, after a violent climax reminiscent of the development section, a powerful contrapuntal idea appears:

STRINGS, FRENCH HORNS

Compare the bottom contrapuntal line of this with the example on page 227. Here the main-theme *pitches* (G E♭ F D) are played in the bridge *rhythm* (♪♪♩ ♩♩♩), so that GGGE♭ FFFD becomes GGGE♭ F D. Then the two middle notes E♭ and F—the common ground between the themes—are emphasized by a long downward sequence.

The sequence evolves into a sort of grim minor-mode march—a moment of respite from the endless thematic evolutions of the main motive. A final appearance of the original theme leads this time to continuations that are unexpectedly poignant. But the very end of the movement consists of affirmative, defiant-sounding cadences, built once again out of the main motive.

LISTENING CHART NUMBER 11

Beethoven, Symphony No. 5 in C Minor, first movement

Sonata form. 7 min., 3 sec.

3 Cassette 2A-1/3 CD 2-1
6 Cassette 3A-3/6 CD 3-3

EXPOSITION

0.02	**Theme 1**	Main theme with two fermatas, followed by the *first continuation* (based on ♩♩♩𝅗𝅥); another fermata 
0.20		Main motive (♩♩♩𝅗𝅥), **ff,** is followed by a *second continuation:* timpani, crescendo.
0.42	**Bridge theme**	French horn, *f*

Second Group

0.45	**Theme 2**	Major mode, *p*, strings and woodwinds (♩♩♩𝅗𝅥 in background) 
1.13	**Cadence theme**	Based on ♩♩♩𝅗𝅥 motive
1.21		Stop.
1.22	**Exposition Repeated**	The entire exposition is repeated.

DEVELOPMENT

2.45		First modulation, using ♩♩♩𝅗𝅥 motive; French horns, **ff;** minor mode
2.50		Development of *first continuation* of theme 1
3.15		Climactic passage of powerful reiterations: ♩♩♩ | ♩♩♩♩ | ♩♩♩♩ | 𝅗𝅥
3.19		Development of bridge theme
3.29		Fragmentation of bridge theme to two notes, alternating between strings and winds 
3.38		Fragmentation of bridge theme to one note, alternating between strings and winds, *p*
3.57	**Retransition**	Based on ♩♩♩𝅗𝅥 , **ff,** runs directly into the recapitulation.

RECAPITULATION

4.02	**Theme 1**	Harmonized; two fermatas. *First continuation* of theme; woodwind background
		Slow oboe cadenza in place of the fermata 
4.35		*Second continuation* of theme 1
4.55	**Bridge theme**	Bassoons, *f*

Second Group

4.58	**Theme 2**	Strings and winds, *p* (♩♩♩𝅗𝅥 in timpani); major mode
5.31	**Cadence theme**	This time it does not stop.

CODA

5.38		Another climax of reiterations (as in the development)
5.52		New expanded version of bridge theme, in counterpoint with new scale figure; minor mode 
6.07		New marchlike theme, brass; winds and strings build up. 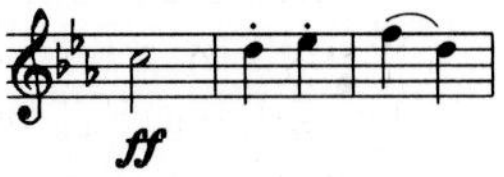
6.39		Theme 1: climactic presentation in brass. Last fermata
6.47		*First continuation* of theme 1, with a pathetic coloration; oboe and bassoon figures
6.52		Strong conclusion on ♩♩♩𝅗𝅥

The Later Movements   The defiant-sounding final cadence of the first movement feels like a standoff at the end of a heroic struggle. Beethoven now builds on this to give the impression of a dramatic psychological progression: another characteristic feature of his symphonic writing.

The later movements of the Fifth Symphony feel like responses to—and, ultimately, a resolution of—all the tension Beethoven had summoned up in the first movement. We are never allowed to forget the first movement and its mood, not until the very end of the symphony. The main reason for this is that a form of the first movement's rhythmic *motive,* ♪♪♪ ♩ , is heard in each of the later movements. This motive always stirs uneasy recollections. Furthermore, the later movements all refer to the *key* of the first movement. Whenever this key returns in its original minor mode (C minor), it inevitably recalls the struggle that Beethoven associated with "Fate knocking at the door." When it returns in the major mode (C major), it signifies (or foretells) the ultimate resolution of all that tension—the triumph over Fate.

You need not worry about recognizing C major or distinguishing it from any other major-mode key. Almost any time you hear a very loud, triumphant theme in the later movements, it is in the key of C major. As important as the melody of those themes and their orchestration (often with brass) is the fact that they come in C major, thus negating the first movement's struggle.

A special abbreviated Listening Chart outline for the entire symphony is provided on page 231. All the C-major sections are indicated.

A New Year's card from Beethoven to Baroness Ertman, one of many women with whom his name has been romantically linked

Second Movement (Andante con moto)   The first hint of Beethoven's master plan comes early in the slow movement, after the cellos have begun with a graceful theme, which is rounded off by repeated cadences. A second placid theme commences, but it soon gets derailed by a grinding modulation—to C major, where it is started again by the trumpets, ***ff.***

This enormously solemn fanfare fades almost immediately into a mysterious passage where the ♪♪♪ ♩ rhythm of the first movement sounds quietly. Beethoven is not ready to "resolve" the C-minor turmoil of the first movement just yet. Variations of the first theme follow (one is in the minor mode), but there is something aimless about them. What stays in the memory from this movement are two more of those impressive fanfares in C major.

Third Movement (Allegro)   This movement, in **3/4** time, is one of Beethoven's greatest scherzos (though the composer did not label it as such, probably because its form is so free). There are two features of the smooth, quiet opening theme (**a**) that immediately recall the mood of the first movement—but in a more muted, apprehensive form. One is the key, C minor. The other is the interruption of the meter by fermatas.

Then a forceful second theme (**b**), played by the French horns, recalls in its turn the first movement's rhythmic motive. The two themes alternate and modulate restlessly, until the second makes a final-sounding cadence.

When now a bustling and somewhat humorous fugal section starts in the major mode—in C major—we may recognize a vestige of the old minuet and trio form, **A B A** (though the **A** section, with its two sharply contrasted themes **a** and **b,** has nothing in common with a minuet beyond its triple meter). **B,** the major-mode "trio," is in the traditional |: c :|: d c′ :| form, but with an important modification. The second **d c′** is reorchestrated, becoming quieter and quieter.

First movement:

Third movement:

LISTENING CHART NUMBER 12

Beethoven, Symphony No. 5 in C Minor, complete work

31 min., 2 sec.

3 Cassette 2A, 1–4/3 CD 2, 1–4

6 Cassette 3A, 3–6/6 CD 3, 3–6

FIRST MOVEMENT (Allegro con brio, 2/4; sonata form)		C minor, *ff*	
See first movement, Listening Chart Number 11.			

SECOND MOVEMENT (Andante, 3/8; variations)			A♭ major, *p*	
0.00	**Theme 1**	Ends with repeated cadences		
0.54	**Theme 2**	Played by clarinets and bassoons		
1.15		Trumpets enter.	(goes to C major, *ff*)	
2.01	**Theme 1**	Variation 1, played by strings		
2.52	**Theme 2**	Clarinets and bassoons		
3.14		Trumpets enter.	(goes to C major, *ff*)	
3.59	**Theme 1**	Variations 2–4, ending *f*; then a quiet transition: woodwinds		
5.56	**Theme 2**	Trumpets	C major, *ff*	
6.42	**Theme 1**	Variations 5 (minor; woodwinds) and 6 (full orchestra); cadences		
8.11	**Coda**		A♭ major	

THIRD MOVEMENT (Scherzo, 3/4; A B A′)		C minor, *pp*	
Scherzo (A)			
0.00	**a b**		
0.38	**a′ b′**		
1.16	**a″ b″**	Ends with a loud cadence built from **b**	
Trio (B)		C major, *ff*	
1.47	ǀ: c :ǀ	Fugal	
2.17	d c′		
2.44	d c′	Reorchestrated, *p*; runs into scherzo	(goes to C minor, *pp*)
Scherzo (A′)			
3.14		Scherzo repeated, shorter and reorchestrated, *pp*	
4.26	**Transition**	Timpani; leads directly in to the fourth movement	(goes to C major, *ff*)

FOURTH MOVEMENT (Allegro, 2/2; sonata form)			
Exposition			
0.00	Theme 1	March theme	
0.37	Bridge theme	Low horns and bassoons	
1.05	Theme 2		
1.34	Cadence theme		
Development			
2.06		Development begins; modulation	
2.12		Theme 2 developed	
3.43	**Retransition**	Recall of the scherzo (**A′**, 3/4 meter)	(recall of C minor, *pp*)
Recapitulation		C major, *ff*	
4.18	Theme 1		
4.54	Bridge theme		
5.26	Theme 2		
5.54	Cadence theme		
Coda			
6.25		Lengthy coda, in several sections, uses elements of the bridge, cadence theme, and theme 1. Accelerates!	C major, *ff*

Beethoven's last piano. It looks rather like a modern instrument, but since pianos did not then have metal frames, the string tension was much less and the tone much quieter.

Ensuing from this, the return of the opening minor-mode music, **A′**, is transformed in tone color. Hushed *pizzicato* (plucked) strings for **a** and a brittle-sounding oboe for **b** replace the smooth and forceful sounds heard before. Everything now breathes a quite unexpected mood, approximating mystery, numbness, even terror.

Fourth Movement (Allegro)   The point of this reorchestration appears when the section does not reach a cadence but runs into a marvelous ghostly transition passage, with timpani tapping out the rhythm of **b** over a strange harmony. The music gets louder and louder and clearer and clearer until a forceful military march erupts—in the key, needless to say, of C major.

Minor cedes to major, *pp* to *ff,* mystery to clarity; the arrival of this symphony's last movement has the literal effect of triumph over some sort of adversity. This last movement even brings in three trombones, for the first time in the symphony. (They must have really waked up the freezing listeners at that original 1808 concert.)

The march turns out to be the first theme of a sonata-form movement; the second theme includes a speeded-up version of the ♪♪♪ ♩ rhythm. The end of the development section offers another example of Beethoven's inspired manipulation of musical form. The second theme (**b**) of the previous movement, the scherzo, returns quietly, a complete surprise in these surroundings (there is even a change from the **4/4** of the march back to **3/4**). This theme now sounds neither forceful nor ghostly, but rather like a dim memory. Perhaps it has come back to remind us that the battle has been won.

All that remains is a great C-major celebration, in the recapitulation and then later in a huge accelerating coda. "There Fate knocks at the door"—but fate and terror alike have yielded to Beethoven's optimistic major-mode vision.

A portrait gallery of stellar nineteenth-century figures deeply immersed in music: Dumas, Hugo, Sand, Paganini, Rossini, and Liszt. Shown in a portrait bust is Beethoven, the hero of musical Romanticism.

For us, the word *romantic* refers to love; this usage dates from the nineteenth century and derives from the literary movement. But the glorification of love was only one of the many themes of Romantic literature, themes that were also central to the music of the nineteenth century.

The Cult of Individual Feeling

The true forefather of Romanticism was Jean Jacques Rousseau—the same Enlightenment philosopher and novelist who had spoken up in the mid-eighteenth century for "natural" human feelings, as opposed to the artificial constraints imposed by society. He also spoke up for simple, "natural" music, particularly in comic opera. Rousseau was hailed as the ideological father of the French Revolution; his music was played at revolutionary ceremonies. His call for individual human fulfillment met an even deeper, more universal response.

Striving for a better, higher, ideal state of being was at the heart of the Romantic movement. Everyday life, to the Romantics, seemed dull and meaningless, repressed and overrational. Only through the free exercise and expression of individual will and feeling could such an existence be transcended. Freedom of feeling, unconstrained by convention, religion, or social taboo (or anyone else's feelings, often enough)—this became the highest good, and its expression became the highest artistic goal. The Romantics proclaimed romantic love, wore odd clothes, and led highly irregular lives that were frowned upon at the time as "Bohemian." All of this is familiar enough today in the outdated, but tenacious, stereotype of the artist.

Romanticism and Revolt

But social convention opposed individual freedom, and so the Romantics were inevitably cast in the role of rebels against the established order. By the end of the eighteenth century, an entire generation of writers and artists was striving actively for freedoms of every kind.

Revolution was the central fact in the politics of the age, beginning with our own American Revolution. The French Revolution of 1789 traumatized Europe as deeply as did the Russian Revolution in our century. It was followed by a whole set of aftershocks up to 1848, a year of major upheavals in France, Germany, Austria, and Italy.

Many composers associated themselves with libertarian politics, starting with Beethoven, who wrote a symphony named *Bonaparte* (which he renamed the *Eroica*). In a later generation, Liszt briefly espoused a strange half-communistic, half-religious movement founded by Father François Lammenais. Giuseppe Verdi's name became an acronym for the Italian liberation movement, and the composer himself was made an honorary deputy of the first Italian parliament. More dramatically, Richard Wagner was thrown out of Germany in 1849 for inflammatory speeches he made from the revolutionary barricades in the town of Dresden.

Along with political revolution went social revolution. The barriers of hereditary nobility were breached, and the lower and middle classes assumed more social mobility. Thus Franz Liszt, who was the son of an estate foreman, could conduct glamorous liaisons—one stormy, the other stable—with a French countess and a Russian princess. The importance of this was not lost on Liszt's contemporaries; the countess is another of the celebrities included in the picture of Liszt at the piano (though the artist tactfully hid her face).

Visible on Paris's most prominent monument, the Arc de Triomphe, is this 1836 representation of *La Marseillaise,* the great rallying song of the French revolution.

Romanticism and the Macabre

The dark side to the cult of individual feeling was also nurtured. In their pursuit of emotional sensation of all kinds, the Romantics did not neglect cruelty and violence, fantasy and nightmare. In *Nightmare,* a weird picture by the early Romantic painter Henry Fuseli, the combination of horror, irrationality, and sexuality is a forecast of many such effusions to come.

The supernatural loomed large in the Romantic firmament. The Grimms' fairy tales—with their frequently ominous undertone—were as characteristic of the era as Johann Wolfgang von Goethe's great dramatic poem about Faust pledging his soul to the Devil for a single moment of transcendent happiness. Mary Shelley wrote the nightmarish story *Frankenstein* in 1818. The American writer most admired in early nineteenth-century Europe was that specialist in the macabre, Edgar Allan Poe. An opera about vampires was composed a little later—*Der Vampyr,* by the German composer Heinrich Marschner.

Composers cultivated strange harmonies and sinister orchestral sounds as their contribution to this aspect of Romanticism; such sounds became clichés in early movie music and can still be heard on some television soundtracks today. A famous scene of devilish conjuration in a deep forest, the Wolf's Glen scene in Carl Maria von Weber's opera *Der Freischütz* ("The Magic Bullet," 1821), was the first impressive monument to Romanticism in music. Verdi wrote spooky music for the witches in his Shakespeare opera *Macbeth,* and Wagner did the same for the ghost ship and its spectral crew in *The Flying Dutchman.* And in the *Fantastic* Symphony, Hector Berlioz wrote a movement called "Dream of a Witches' Sabbath" that bears comparison with Fuseli's *Nightmare.*

Nightmare, by Henry Fuseli, an eighteenth-century pre-Romantic painter, poet, and revolutionary who emigrated from Switzerland to England for political reasons

Romantic Nostalgia

Romanticism's dissatisfaction with the real world pointed on the one hand to revolution, and on the other to fascination with the past. Indeed, the term *romantic* comes originally from "romance," meaning a type of long medieval narrative poem or story. Both music and the visual arts followed literature in this nostalgia for the mysterious Middle Ages.

The Fall of an Avalanche in the Grisons, by J. M. W. Turner (1775–1851)

In literature, taste in fiction moved away from contemporary subjects, such as *Tom Jones* and *Pride and Prejudice*, to tales of historical adventure, such as *Ivanhoe* and *The Hunchback of Notre Dame*. Poems were often set in times of yore—Scott's "Lochinvar," Keats's "La Belle Dame sans Merci," and Tennyson's *Idylls of the King*, a lengthy work in "romance" style about King Arthur and the Knights of the Round Table. Longfellow's *Song of Hiawatha* is an American example of the same sort of work as the *Idylls*—a grandiose blend of Romanticism, nostalgia, and national pride.

But the best example of all is Richard Wagner's four-evening opera *The Ring of the Nibelung*, based on the main early medieval Nordic cycle of myths. One of the towering art works of the century, the *Ring* tells how the world ruled by Wotan, king of the gods, is corrupted by gold and then redeemed by the love of Wotan's daughter Brünnhilde and the hero Siegfried. Wagner himself wrote the words, a cloudy but powerful tract with political, ethical, and nationalistic overtones.

Some composers experimented with real or simulated old music to give their work an antique flavor. We shall see Berlioz import a Gregorian chant (the *Dies irae*) into his *Fantastic* Symphony. There was something of a cult at this time for the famous Renaissance composer Giovanni Pierluigi da Palestrina (see page 85). Though Palestrina lived in the sixteenth century, long after the Middle Ages, he was about the earliest composer whose music was known in the early nineteenth century. The modal harmony and spiritual style of Palestrina's church music were much admired and imitated.

An American Romantic painting of a newer myth: *Daniel Boone and His Cabin on the Great Osage Lake,* by Thomas Cole (1801–1848)

Chapter 15   Music after Beethoven: Romanticism

Two Romantic depictions of nature: *Mountainous Landscape* by Caspar David Friedrich (left) and *The Bard* by John Martin (right). The paintings suggest both the menacing and inspirational aspects of nature.

Artistic Barriers

The Romantic artists' restless search for higher experience and higher expression made them spurn all restraints of artistic form and genre. Thus they often tried to break down the barriers between the arts. Poetry was made more "musical"; paintings and musical compositions received more and more "poetic" titles. Wagner's operas, once again, represent a climax of this tendency, for the composer combined his own poetry, drama, philosophy, music, and stagecraft in a unique "total art work," or *Gesamtkunstwerk*.

Within any single art, artists resisted all rules and regulations, any abstract notions of "beauty" or "decorum" that they felt might hamper their spontaneity. Eighteenth-century drama, for example, was hemmed in by such rules until the Romantics overturned them, citing the works of Shakespeare. Locations change dizzily from scene to scene in Shakespeare's plays, as tragedy clashes with farce, rich poetry with bawdy prose, and noble characters with clowns. The lifelike turbulence and the loose, casual form of these plays made Shakespeare enormously popular in the nineteenth century. The list of composers who wrote music associated with them is practically endless, from Mendelssohn and Berlioz to Tchaikovsky, Wagner, and Verdi.

In music itself, composers worked to break down barriers of harmony and form. All the Romantic composers experimented with chords, or chord progressions, that had previously been forbidden by the textbooks. From the time of Schubert on, their music was immeasurably enriched by imaginative new harmonies. And sonata form, the hallmark of Classicism, was treated so freely in Robert Schumann's piano sonatas, written in the 1830s, that he finally labeled the last (and greatest) of them "Fantasy"—a proclamation of his spontaneity on the one hand, and insurance against accusations of "breaking the rules" on the other.

The Music Party, one of relatively few interiors painted by J. M. W. Turner

Music and the Other Arts

"Shakespearean," discursive, open-ended, sometimes fragmentary, and above all contemptuous of formal barriers—these are the characteristics of Romantic art. Resistance to barriers sometimes extended to a rejection of sharp distinctions. Blurred effects were cultivated—verbal meanings, color blends, and musical sounds that are imprecise but rich and evocative.

No one went further in this respect than the English landscape painter J. M. W. Turner, with his swashes of nearly "abstract" color. Whereas Rousseau in the eighteenth century had admired nature for its simplicity, Turner in the nineteenth captured what was called at the time its "sublime" quality: the majesty and mystery of nature, its boundlessness, even its menace. The human figures in a Turner painting (if there are any) are dwarfed by the vastness and vibrancy of nature. The great Romantic artists stared unblinkingly at the infinite, and tried to set it down in their art.

It was exactly the boundless quality of music that gave it its enormous prestige and status. Music, people felt, could express inner experience more deeply than the other arts because the musician's imagination is not tied down to the meaning of words (like the poet's) or to the representation of things (like the painter's). Music's age-old power to stir the emotions was now seen as nothing less than a revelation of life's deepest meaning. This explains the solemn, rapturous expression on all the eminent faces in the Liszt picture.

The special place of music in the Romantic scheme of things was forcefully expounded by Arthur Schopenhauer, a much-read German philosopher of the time. Wagner's opera *Tristan und Isolde* practically spells out Schopenhauer's philosophy, as we shall see. "All art aspires to the condition of music," wrote a famous Victorian critic, Walter Pater, meaning that all Romantic art tried to capture music's depth and freedom of emotional expression, and its continuous, "infinite" quality.

2 Concert Life in the Nineteenth Century

First introduced in the Baroque era, during the age of aristocratic patronage of the arts, public concerts rapidly grew more important in the days of Haydn, Mozart, and Beethoven. As the nineteenth century progressed, the concert hall came to dominate the presentation of music. Every town of any size had its symphony association, organized by merchants, bankers, government officials, lawyers, and other members of the middle class. The concert halls built to accommodate symphony concerts were also expressions of civic pride. In May of 1891 the New York Symphony, that city's second orchestra (the New York Philharmonic was founded in 1842) proudly presented a five-concert music festival led by Tchaikovsky in brand-new Carnegie Hall.

Ground-breaking ceremony for Carnegie Hall in New York (visible is the famous railroad and steel baron Andrew Carnegie, the donor) and the program of the first music festival there

By the end of the century, even intimate musical genres, designed for the drawing room or the studio, were presented on the concert stage. Concerts of *Lieder* (songs) and quartet concerts became established, though they were not as important as orchestral and solo instrumental concerts. Concerts made more and more music available to more and more people. Improved transportation brought musicians on tour to remote areas, such as the American west.

However, the institutionalization of musical life in concerts also had its negative aspect, in that audiences gradually became more conservative in their musical tastes. The old aristocratic system had actually been more neutral in this respect. While many aristocratic patrons cared less about music than display, and some exercised the most whimsical of tastes, others actually encouraged composers to pursue new paths, or at least left them alone to do so. On the other hand, the concert public tended to conservatism. The mainly middle-class buyers of concert tickets and subscriptions naturally wanted "value," as with anything else they bought. What counted as value was something already established as a "masterpiece," something that they already knew and liked.

The Artist and the Public

For the reasons above, composers with an interest in innovation—and that includes every composer discussed in this unit—felt at one time or another that their work was being neglected by the concert world. A paradoxical situation developed. The composer's dependence on the public was tinged with resentment, and the public's admiration for composers was tinged with distrust, even hostility. A similar situation developed in all the other arts, and artists in general began to feel more and more alienated from their audiences.

Thus the composer Robert Schumann started an important magazine to campaign for Romantic music, in the face of public indifference to serious art and preference for what he regarded as flashy trivia. Editor Schumann invented a "League of David" to slay the "Goliath" of the concert audience (Goliath was the champion of the Philistines; it was around this time that the adjective "philistine" came to mean "uncultured"). Later, the music of Liszt and Wagner was attacked by hostile critics as formless, dissonant, and overheated. Later still, the symphonies of Gustav Mahler were repeatedly rejected in Vienna, in spite of Mahler's important position as head of the Opera there.

The gap between innovative music and a conservative concert public, which opened up in the nineteenth century, widened in the twentieth, as we shall see. Here as elsewhere, the nineteenth century set the tone for twentieth-century musical life.

3 The Style of Romantic Music

Since the main artistic value in the Romantic era was the integrity of personal feeling, every genuine artist was expected to have a personal style. Many artists cultivated styles that were highly personal and even eccentric. Furthermore, Romanticism's constant striving after ever-new states of consciousness put a premium on innovation; this could be seen as an exciting breaking down of artistic barriers on the one hand, and as a heroic personal breakthrough on the other. Consequently it is harder to define the Romantic style in general than to spot innovations, novelties, and individual peculiarities.

To be sure, nineteenth-century composers were united by some common interests, which will be discussed below: technical interests concerning melody, harmony, tone color, and perhaps especially musical form. But it is important to remember that one such common interest was to sound different from everybody else.

Rhythm: Rubato

The general Romantic tendency to blur all sharp edges found its musical counterpart in the rhythmic practice of *tempo rubato,* or just **rubato**. Rubato means that in musical performance the rhythm is handled flexibly; the meter itself may waver, or else the beat is maintained strictly in the accompaniment while the melody is played or sung slightly out of phase with it. (Literally *tempo rubato* means "robbed time"—that is, some time has been "stolen" from the beat—but the beat is likely to be slowed and the time "given back" a moment later.)

Rubato was practiced in the service of greater individual expressivity. Though seldom indicated in a score—indeed, musical notation has never developed an accurate way to indicate rubato—its practice is documented by old recordings, made around 1900 by musicians who were close to the Romantic composers (or even by the composers themselves). Improvisation, in the sense of adding notes to a score, gradually died out during the nine-

From a French horn instruction book, 1835

teenth century. But performers from the time of Chopin and Liszt improvised rhythmically, in that they applied rubato freely to almost every score they played.

Considered a sign of bad taste in Baroque or Classical music, at least when applied vehemently, rubato is an essential expressive resource in the playing, singing, and conducting of Romantic music. A musician's sensitivity and "feeling" depends to a great extent on his or her artistic use of rubato.

Romantic Melody

No doubt the most instantly recognizable feature of Romantic music is its melodic style. Melody in the Romantic era is more emotional, effusive, and demonstrative than before. Often the melodic lines range more widely than the orderly, restrained melodies of the Classical era; often, too, they build up to more sustained climaxes. Melodies became more irregular in rhythm and phraseology, so as to make them sound more spontaneous.

A fine example is the so-called "love" theme of Tchaikovsky's Overture-Fantasy *Romeo and Juliet* (page 301). It begins with a great outburst—a climax, at the very start—and then sinks down an octave and more, in melodic curves whose yearning quality grows more and more sensuous. Especially striking is the second part of the melody, the **b** section in an **a b a'** form. Here a rhythmic figure surges up and up, seven times in all, before exploding into a return of the opening **a** melody, this time made doubly intense:

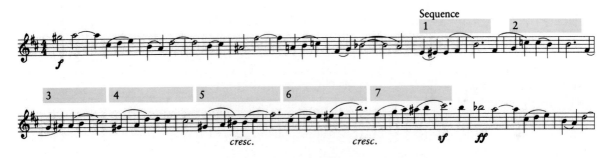

When one thinks of Romantic melody, what comes first to mind is the grand, exaggerated emotionality of Tchaikovsky, perhaps, or Mahler. Some Romantic melodies are more intimate, however—and they are no less emotional for sparing the handkerchief, as it were. Each in an individual way, Romantic composers learned to make their melodies dreamy, sensitive, passionate, ecstatic, or whatever shade of feeling they chose to express.

Romantic Harmony

Harmony was one of the areas in which Romantic music made the greatest technical advances. On the one hand, composers learned to use harmony to underpin melody in such a way as to bring out its emotionality. Romantic melody is, in fact, inseparable from harmony. In the *Romeo and Juliet* love theme, for example, a rich new chord goes hand in glove with the warm upward scoop of the melodic line in measure 5.

On the other hand, harmony was savored for its own sake, and composers experimented freely with new chord forms and new juxtapositions of chords. These, it was found, could contribute potently to those mysterious, sinister, rapturous, ethereal, or sultry moods that Romantic composers sought to evoke. There are even some themes and motives in Romantic music that gain their memorable quality from harmony, rather than from melody and rhythm, as in earlier music (see page 289).

<u>Chromaticism</u> is a term for a style that employs all twelve notes of the chromatic scale (see page 15) liberally. Baroque and Classical style is not "chromatic" in this sense, but all Romantic composers pursued chromaticism to some extent, in order to expand the expressive range of both their melodies and their harmony. If you look at the *Romeo and Juliet* theme, you will find all twelve notes of the chromatic scale included—something that seldom if ever happens in earlier music. Chromaticism was carried furthest in the nineteenth century by Richard Wagner, and further yet by the early twentieth-century modernists.

The Expansion of Tone Color

While tone color had been treated with considerable subtlety by the Viennese Classical composers, the Romantics seized on this aspect of music with particular enthusiasm. For the first time in Western music, the sheer sensuous quality of sound assumed major artistic importance on a level with rhythm, melody, and musical form.

All instruments went through major technical developments during the nineteenth century—the piano not least. As orchestral instruments reached their present-day forms, the orchestra was expanded, soon reaching its present standard make-up. The chart below for a typical Romantic orchestra, when compared with the Classical orchestra chart on page 169, shows how the ranks of the brass, woodwind, and percussion sections were filled out:

A TYPICAL ROMANTIC ORCHESTRA

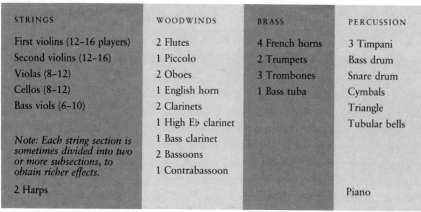

STRINGS	WOODWINDS	BRASS	PERCUSSION
First violins (12–16 players)	2 Flutes	4 French horns	3 Timpani
Second violins (12–16)	1 Piccolo	2 Trumpets	Bass drum
Violas (8–12)	2 Oboes	3 Trombones	Snare drum
Cellos (8–12)	1 English horn	1 Bass tuba	Cymbals
Bass viols (6–10)	2 Clarinets		Triangle
	1 High E♭ clarinet		Tubular bells
	1 Bass clarinet		
Note: Each string section is sometimes divided into two or more subsections, to obtain richer effects.	2 Bassoons		
	1 Contrabassoon		
2 Harps			Piano

What such charts cannot show, however, are the ingenious and fascinating new *combinations* of instruments that were now investigated. Composers learned to mix instrumental colors with something of the same freedom and virtuosity with which painters mix actual colors on a palette. The clear, sharply defined sonorities of the Classical era were replaced by iridescent shades of blended orchestral sound.

Romantic composers and audiences alike were fascinated by the symphony orchestra, and for the first time conductors came to the fore. In earlier times, orchestras had simply followed the first violin or the continuo player, but now the need arose for experts to control and balance out those special blended effects. The orchestra also became increasingly important in nineteenth-century opera; major opera composers, such as Weber, Meyerbeer,

An early picture of a conductor using a baton—or, rather, a tight scroll of paper. He is the German opera composer Carl Maria von Weber (see page 277).

and Wagner, specialized in orchestral effects that sometimes even threatened to put the voices in the shade. If today the symphony orchestra comes to mind almost automatically when one thinks of "classical music," that is a holdover from the Romantic nineteenth century.

4 The Problem of Form in Romantic Music

Individual spontaneity was an important goal of the Romantic movement. And if there was any area in which composers wanted to seem particularly free and spontaneous, it was the area of musical form. The music should bubble out moment by moment, irrepressible and untrammeled, like churning emotion itself. The problem that composers faced was how to channel and control that spontaneity. They had to provide their music with enough sense of coherence so that listeners could follow it.

In their use of standard forms or form types, nineteenth-century composers broke with Classical norms. To return to the distinction we noted on page 58, the Romantics wanted each work of art to express its own individual "inner form"; "outer forms" they distrusted as dry and conventional. Even when they did use such forms as sonata form and rondo, they tended to follow them so loosely and freely that it becomes a matter of opinion whether they were doing so at all. Themes blend into one another, and there is less of the neat, clear cadencing of Classical music. Beethoven, incidentally, never moved his music very far in this direction. He still held, by and large, to the clear forms and clear demarcations of Classicism.

Some Romantic compositions actually work to break down the boundary between music and nonmusical silence. Beginning quietly, as though in the middle of a transition, the composer may give the impression that the composition has already been going on for some time, and it is the listener who has just begun to attend to it. Instead of ending decisively, the music may fade away or stop on a questioning dissonance. Schumann's song "Im wunderschönen Monat Mai" (page 259) provides a wonderful example of both these effects. The vague, atmospheric quality on the one hand, and the suggestion of "infinity" on the other—again, these are typically Romantic.

Yet the music had to avoid real formlessness if it was to hold the attention of an audience. Once again, for Romantic composers the problem was how to create the impression of spontaneity while at the same time providing enough formal structure to give the listener some means of following the music. They developed a number of interesting and characteristic solutions.

"Miniature" Compositions

While many nineteenth-century compositions are about the same length as works from the eighteenth century, special classes of music arose with quite different dimensions.

First of all, composers cultivated what we shall call "miniatures," pieces lasting only a few minutes. Mostly songs and short piano pieces, these were designed to convey a particularly pointed emotion, momentary and undeveloped. In this way the composer could commune with the listener memorably, intensely, intimately, as though giving him or her a single short, meaningful glance.

Though short pieces were also written in earlier times—the minuet movements in Classical symphonies, for example—usually they were elements within larger units where their effect was balanced by other, longer movements. In the Romantic era, miniatures came singly, standing out as individuals in their own right. Piano miniatures were sometimes given general titles, such as Schubert's Impromptus, Chopin's Preludes, and Brahms's Intermezzos, and sometimes they masqueraded as dances, like Chopin's Mazurkas. Often they were given more poetic titles: Mendelssohn's *Songs without Words,* Chopin's Ballades, the *Woodland Sketches* by the late Romantic American composer Edward MacDowell. (Admittedly, Chopin's Ballades are not all that "miniature"—one of them lasts for eleven minutes; still, they are much more contained than symphonies or sonatas.) Schumann was particularly imaginative with the names of his miniatures: "The Poet Speaks," "Confession," "The Bird as Prophet," "Why?"

The man has put down his violin to sit with the woman at the piano; we can imagine the four-hand music they are playing, perhaps, but we cannot see their faces. This picture catches both the intimacy and privacy of the Romantic "miniature" and also its characteristic milieu, the middle-class living room.

FRANZ SCHUBERT
"Der Jüngling an der Quelle" ("The Youth at the Spring") (c. 1817)

6 Cassette 1B-10/6 CD 1-23

The earliest and (for most musicians) the greatest master of the lied is Franz Schubert. There are many unsuspected treasures among the more than six hundred songs he wrote; let us begin with a very short, lesser-known one. The speaker of the song's rather faint poem has been communing with nature in an effort to forget his unkind beloved, but he hears her name echoing in the trees and the rippling water of a spring.

The piano begins with a delicate, crystalline evocation of the spring. The water is just barely flowing, it seems; the lovesick boy himself is half asleep, and can hardly rouse himself to sing a full-fledged melody. The harmonies are extremely simple—up to the repetition of the word *seufzen* (sigh), the poem's most emotive word. This word is underpinned by one rich, quiet, romantic harmony, like a fleeting evocation of some amorous encounter. The trickling, tinkling spring lulls the boy back into a delicious dream.

The song lasts for less than two minutes. A perfect Romantic miniature, it conveys an unforgetable whiff of intimate emotion. With Schubert and the best lieder composers who followed him, a quiet Romantic song with piano accompaniment can be as moving as a great symphony or an opera.

Leise, rieselnder Quell,	Gentle, rippling spring
Ihr wallenden, flispernden Pappeln:	With your tossing, whispering poplars:
Euer Schlummergeräusch	Your lullaby stirrings
Wecket die Liebe nur auf.	Speak of nothing but love.
Linderung sucht ich bei euch	Comfort I sought with you,
Und sie zu vergessen, die Spröde;	And to forget her, that coy one;
Ach, und Blätter und Bach	Ah, both the leaves and the brook
Seufzen, Luise, dir nach.	Are sighing, Louise, for you.

SCHUBERT
"Erlkönig" ("The Elfking") (1815)

6 Cassette 3B-2/6 CD 3-8

"The Elfking," probably Schubert's best-known lied, is a musical setting of a poem by Johann Wolfgang von Goethe. The greatest literary figure of the day, Goethe was by turns a Romantic and a Neoclassical poet, playwright, novelist, scientist, philosopher, and inspiration for several generations of lieder composers. Cast in the old ballad form, which enjoyed a vogue in the Romantic era, and dealing with death and the supernatural, the poem is famous in its own right.

Though the poem consists of eight parallel stanzas, Schubert did not set them to the same music. He wrote different or modified music for the later stanzas; such a song is said to be **through-composed** (in contrast to a **strophic** song, which uses the same music for each of its poetic stanzas: see page 259). In mood, Goethe's poem changes so dramatically as it proceeds that it almost demands this kind of musical setting. It tells of a father riding furiously through the night with a feverish child who thinks he sees and hears the demon Elfking beckoning him. The Elfking first invites the child to join him, then cajoles him, then threatens and assaults him. The father, uncomprehending, tries to quiet his child, but by the time they reach home the boy is dead.

The piano introduction sets the mood of dark, tense excitement. The right hand hammers away at repeated notes, suggesting the horse's hooves, while the left hand has an agitated motive:

Fast

Schubert wrote different music for each of the poem's three characters (and also for the narrator). Each "voice" characterizes the speaker and differentiates him from the others. The father is low, stiff, and gruff; the Elfking sings ominously graceful tunes; and the boy sounds frantic.

Two things help hold this long song together as an artistic unity. First, there are some dramatic musical repetitions: the agitated bass motive associated with the riding (stanzas 1 and 8), and the frantic melodic phrase sung higher and higher by the boy (stanzas 4, 6, and 7). Second, the piano's repeated notes continue ceaselessly, until just before the end, when the ride is over. During the Elfking's first and second speeches, when the child is hearing him in a feverish half-sleep, the horse's hooves are muted *(p)*. But during the third speech they pound away distinctly; as Schubert saw it, when the Elfking claims the child, he is wide awake in terror.

A contemporary illustration of "The Elfking"

TEXT: Schubert, "Erlkönig"

Wer reitet so spät, durch Nacht und Wind?
Es ist der Vater mit seinem Kind;
Er hat den Knaben wohl in dem Arm,
Er fasst ihn sicher, er hält ihn warm.

"Mein sohn, was birgst du so bang dein Gesicht?"
"Siehst, Vater, du den Erlkönig nicht?
Den Erlenkönig mit Kron' und Schweif?"
"Mein Sohn, est ist ein Nebelstreif."

"Du liebes Kind, komm, geh mit mir!
Gar schöne Spiele spiel' ich mit dir;
Manch bunte Blumen sind an dem Strand;
Meine Mutter hat manch' gülden Gewand."

Who rides so late through the night and wind?
It is the father with his child.
He holds the youngster tight in his arm,
Grasps him securely, keeps him warm.

"Son, what makes you afraid to look?"
"Don't you see, father, the Elfking there?
The King of the elves with his crown and train?"
"Son, it's only a streak of mist."

"Darling child, come away with me!
I will play the finest of games with you;
Many gay flowers grow by the shore;
My mother has many golden robes."

"Mein Vater, mein Vater, und hörest du nicht Was Erlkönig mir leise verspricht?" "Sei ruhig, beibe ruhig, mein Kind: In dürren Blättern säuselt der Wind."	"Father, father, do you not hear What the Elfking is softly promising me?" "Calm yourself, be calm, my son: The dry leaves are rustling in the wind."
"Willst, feiner Knabe, du mit mir gehn? Meine Töchter sollen dich warten schön; Meine Töchter führen den nächtlichen Reihn Und wiegen und tanzen und singen dich ein.	*"Well, you fine boy, won't you come with me?* *My daughters will wait upon you.* *My daughters lead the nightly round,* *They will rock you, dance for you, sing you to sleep!"*
"Mein Vater, mein Vater, und siehst du nich dort Erlkönigs Töchter am düstern Ort?" "Mein Sohn, mein sohn, ich seh es genau: Es scheinen die alten Weiden so grau."	"Father, father, do you not see The Elfking's daughters there in the dark?" "Son, my son, I see only too well: It is the grey gleam in the old willow trees."
"Ich liebe dich, mich reizt deine schöne Gestalt, Und bist du nicht willig, so brauch' ich Gewalt." "Mein Vater, mein Vater, jetzt fasst er mich an! Erlkönig hat mir ein Leids getan!"	*"I love you, your beauty allures me,* *And if you're not willing, then I shall use force."* "Father, father, now he is seizing me! The Elfking is hurting me!"
Dem Vater grauset's, er reitet geschwind, Er hält in Armen das ächzende Kind, Erreicht den Hof mit Müh und Not; In seinen Armen das Kind war tot.	Fear grips the father, he rides like the wind, He holds in his arms the moaning child; With effort and toil he reaches the house; The child in his arms was dead.

The Song Cycle

A **song cycle** is a group of songs with a common poetic theme or an actual story connecting all the poems. Composers would either find whole coherent groups of poems to set, or else make their own selections from a larger collection of a poet's work. Schubert, who wrote two great song cycles relatively late in his career, was able to use ready-made groups of poems published by a minor Romantic poet named Wilhelm Müller: *Die schöne Müllerin* ("The Fair Maid of the Mill") and *Winterreise* ("Winter Journey").

The advantage of the song cycle was that it extended the rather fragile expression of the lied into a larger, more comprehensive, and hence more impressive unit. It was, in a sense, an effort to get beyond "miniaturism." The "unity" of such larger units, however, is always loose, even when the songs are related by melodic or rhythmic means, as occasionally happens. The individual songs can often be sung separately, as well as in sequence with the rest of the cycle.

Robert Schumann
Clara Wieck Schumann

(1810–1856)

(1819–1896)

Chief Works—Robert Schumann: Sets of "miniatures" for piano, among them *Scenes of Childhood, Album for the Young, Arabesque, Papillons* ("Butterflies"), and *Carnaval*

Robert Schumann's father, a bookseller and writer, encouraged the boy's musical talent and started him studying the piano at the age of six. When his father died, his mother wanted him to go into law; he attended the University of Leipzig, but finally persuaded her to let him pursue the career of a piano virtuoso. He had to give this up, however, after an injury sustained when he tried to strengthen his fingers with a mechanical device.

Besides his musical talent, Schumann had a great flair for literature, no doubt inherited from his father. When he was twenty-three, Schumann

Songs and song cycles: *Woman's Life and Love, A Poet's Love*

Piano Fantasy (a sort of free sonata); Piano Concerto; four symphonies

Chamber music: a quintet and a quartet for piano and strings

An opera, *Genoveva;* incidental music to Byron's *Manfred* and Goethe's *Faust;* choral works

Chief works—Clara Schumann: Miniatures for piano, with names such as *Romances* and *Soirées musicales* ("Musical Evenings"); songs

A piano concerto and a trio for piano, violin, and cello

Piano Variations on a Theme by Robert Schumann (Brahms wrote a set of variations on the same theme)

founded a magazine to campaign for a higher level of music, *Die Neue Zeitschrift für Musik* ("The New Music Journal"—it is still being published). For several years he wrote regular music criticism, often couched in a fanciful romantic prose style. For example, he signed some of his reviews with the names "Florestan" or "Eusebius," representing the opposite (but both thoroughly romantic) sides of his character—the impetuous side and the tender, dreamy side. He encouraged fledgling composers such as Chopin and (later) Brahms.

Schumann fell in love with Clara Wieck, the daughter of his music teacher, Friedrich Wieck. Wieck had his own piano method and was determined to make his first child, Clara, a great pianist; at sixteen, she was already launched on a stellar concert career. Thanks to her father's fanatical opposition, the couple had to wait until she was twenty-one (minus one day) before getting married, in 1840. A charming outcome of the marriage was that Robert, whose early compositions were almost entirely for the piano, suddenly started to write love songs for Clara. Nearly 150 songs were composed in this "song year."

A little later, he also turned to the composition of larger works, such as concertos and symphonies. Thereafter he assumed some important musical positions, but his withdrawn personality made him less than successful. Robert had had breakdowns in his youth, and now he began to develop tragic signs of insanity. Clara continued her career as best she could; more and more, she had to take charge of the family. During the 1848 revolution in Leipzig, for example, it was up to her to get the five Schumann children out of town (three more were born later).

In 1854, tormented by voices, hallucinations, and loss of memory, Robert tried to drown himself in the Rhine and was committed to an asylum. He died two years later. It was a very difficult time for Clara. At the age of thirty-seven, having just lost the husband whom she revered and loved, she found herself more than half in love with his twenty-two-year-old protegé, the composer Johannes Brahms (see page 310). Perhaps Clara withdrew from the relationship, or perhaps Brahms did. They remained fast friends; Brahms was a lifelong bachelor and Clara did not remarry.

Robert and Clara Schumann

For the last forty years of her life, Clara continued to teach and concertize. She was also a distinguished composer, but unhappily this talent had been allowed to atrophy—as a result, it seems clear, of a tacit understanding between her and Robert. With music of the past, we naturally appreciate composers (whose compositions we can experience) more than performers (whose performances we cannot); we may feel differently about music of the present. Who contributes more to musical life today, Luciano Pavarotti the performer or his compatriot Luciano Berio the composer (see page 370)? Clara Schumann, one of the greatest pianists and pedagogues of her time, was a major figure in nineteenth-century music.

ROBERT SCHUMANN (1810–1856)
Dichterliebe ("A Poet's Love") (1840)

6 Cassette 3B, 3-4/6 CD 3, 9–10

"Schubert died. Cried all night," wrote the sixteen-year-old Robert Schumann in his diary under a date in 1828. Yet living in Zwickau, Germany, far from Schubert's Vienna, Schumann did not know many of the older composer's best-known works, his lieder. He loved Schubert's piano music, and indeed, for the first ten years of his own career as a composer, Schumann wrote only piano music.

Then in 1840, the year of his marriage, he suddenly started pouring out lieder. Given this history, it is not surprising that in Schumann's songs the piano is given a more complex role than in Schubert's. This is particularly true of his most famous song cycle, *Dichterliebe,* the first and last songs of which (nos. 1 and 16) we shall examine here. *Dichterliebe* has no real story; its series of love poems traces a psychological progression from cautious optimism to disillusionment and despair. They are the work of another great German poet, Heinrich Heine, a man who reacted with bitter irony against Romanticism, while acknowledging his own hopeless commitment to its ideals.

"Im wunderschönen Monat Mai" ("In the wonderfully lovely month of May")   The song begins with a piano introduction, halting and ruminative in quality—which seems at first to be a curious response to the "wonderfully lovely" month of May. The piano part winds its way in and out of the vocal line, ebbing and flowing rhythmically and sometimes dwelling on quiet but piercing dissonant harmonies.

What Schumann noticed was the hint of unrequited longing in Heine's very last line, and he ended the song with the piano part hanging in midair, without a true cadence, as though in a state of reaching or yearning: a truly Romantic effect. Technically, the last sound is a dissonance that requires resolution into a consonance but does not get it (until the next song).

In this song, both stanzas of the poem are set to identical music. As mentioned earlier, such a song is called *strophic;* strophic setting is of course familiar from folk songs, hymns, popular songs, and many other kinds of music. For Schumann, this kind of setting had the advantage of underlining the similarity in the text of the song's two stanzas, both in meaning and in actual words. Certainly his music deepens the tentative, sensitive, hope-against-hope quality of Heine's understated confession of love.

Im wunderschönen Monat Mai,	In the wonderfully lovely month of May,
Als alle Knospen sprangen,	When all the buds were bursting,
Da ist in meinem Herzen	Then it was that in my heart
Die Liebe aufgegangen.	Love broke through.

Im wunderschönen Monat Mai	In the wonderfully lovely month of May,
Als alle Vögel sangen,	When all the birds were singing,
Da hab' ich ihr gestanden	Then it was I confessed to her
Mein Sehnen und Verlangen.	My longing and desire.

"Die alten, bösen Lieder" ("The bad old songs")   After many heart-wrenching episodes, the final song in the *Dichterliebe* cycle begins strongly. The very insistent rhythm in the piano part sounds a little hectic and forced, like the black humor of Heine's poem. Although basically this is a through-composed song, there are musical parallels between many of the stanzas, and the music of stanza 1 comes back even more forcefully in stanza 5.

But there is a sudden reversal of mood in stanza 5, as the poet suddenly offers to tell us what this morbid action is about. In the music, first the accompaniment disintegrates and then the rhythm. All the poet's self-dramatization vanishes when he speaks of his grief in recitativelike accents; the end of the song would be a whimper if Schumann at the piano did not take over quietly and firmly. In a lovely meditative piano solo, the composer comments on and comforts the frantic poet.

Not only does the composer interpret the poet's words with great art, both in the hectic early stanzas and the self-pitying final one, but he adds something entirely his own. The sixteen vignettes by Heine and Schumann in *A Poet's Love* add up to a memorable anthology of the various fervid states of love celebrated by the Romantics.

TEXT: Schumann, "Die alten, bösen Lieder"

Die alten, bösen Lieder,	The bad old songs,	Und holt mir auch zwölf Riesen,	And fetch me, too, twelve giants
Die Träume bös' und arg,	The dreams that are bad and gross,	Die mussen noch stärker sein	Who must be stronger
Die lasst uns jetzt begraben:	Let's now have them buried;	Als wie der starke Christoph	Than strong St. Christopher
Holt einen grossen Sarg.	Fetch up a great coffin.	Im Dom zu Köln am Rhein.	In the Cathedral at Cologne on the Rhine.

Hinein leg' ich gar Manches,	I've a lot to put in it—	Die sollen den Sarg forttragen	They must carry the coffin away
Doch sag' ich noch nicht, was.	Just what, I won't yet say;	Und senken in's Meer hinab,	And sink it in the sea,
Der Sarg muss sein noch grösser	The coffin must be even bigger	Denn solchem grossen Sarge	For a great coffin like that
Wie's Heidelberger Fass.	Than the Great Cask of Heidelberg.	Gebührt ein grosses Grab.	Deserves a great grave.

Und holt eine Todtenbahre	And fetch a bier,	Wisst ihr, warum der Sarg wohl	Do you know why the coffin, then,
Und Bretter fest und dick,	Boards that are strong and thick;	So gross und schwer mag sein?	Should be so large and heavy?
Auch muss sie sein noch länger	They too must be longer	Ich senkt' auch meine Liebe	I sank my love, yes,
Als wie zu Mainz die Brück'.	Than the river bridge at Mainz.	Und meinen Schmerz hinein.	And my grief in it.

An amazing nineteenth-century score of a lied by Schumann, "Moon-night." The poem (by the Romantic poet J. Eichendorff) is given in ornate calligraphy and illustrated in a rich, evocative Romantic style.

2 The "Character Piece" for Piano

Besides the lied, the other chief type of Romantic miniature composition was the short piano piece. Such pieces were written in great profusion in the nineteenth century, and they appeared under many names. Frédéric Chopin preferred simple genre titles such as Nocturne, Waltz, Scherzo, or Etude (study). Schumann preferred descriptive titles. Piano miniatures were composed at all levels of difficulty, ranging from virtuoso tours de force, which hardly anyone but their composers could negotiate, to unassuming pieces playable (and enjoyable) by beginning students.

A good general name for these short Romantic piano pieces (one sometimes used by the Romantics themselves) is **character pieces,** for the essential point about them is that each portrays some definite mood or character. In principle, at least, this is as true of the brilliant virtuoso works as of the simple ones. Each conveys an intense, distinct emotion—an emotion often hinted at by an imaginative title supplied by the composer.

This explains why the Romantic character piece can be thought of as analogous to the Romantic song, or lied, though without its poem. Indeed, six books of such piano pieces by Felix Mendelssohn—pieces that enjoyed a great vogue in Victorian times—are entitled *Songs without Words.* Some of them have subtitles that stress still further their similarity to lieder: "Spinning Song," "Venetian Boat Song," and the famous "Spring Song."

ROBERT SCHUMANN
Carnaval (1833–35)

6 Cassette 3B, 5–8/6 CD 3, 11–14

Schumann's style of piano writing has a warmth and privacy that set it somewhat apart from the elegance and glitter of other pianist-composers of his day, such as Chopin and Liszt. A favorite marking on his scores is the German word *innig,* meaning "inward," "intimate," or "heartfelt." Schumann typically assembled his piano pieces into collections with some general title and, often, some interesting musical means of connection among them. If the Romantic character piece for the piano is analogous to the Romantic lied, these collections are analogous to song cycles.

Such a collection is *Carnaval,* a set of twenty very short character pieces that really *are* characters—musical portraits of masked guests at a Mardi Gras ball. After the band strikes up in an introduction, the sad clown Pierrot arrives, followed by the pantomime figures Harlequin and Columbine, Schumann himself, two of his girlfriends masquerading under the names Estrella and Chiarina, a Coquette, the composers Paganini and Chopin, and many others. This diverse gallery provided Schumann with an outlet for his whimsy and humor, as well as all his Romantic melancholy and passion.

"Eusebius"   "Eusebius" was Schumann's pen name for his tender, dreamy self, and this little piece presents him at his most introspective. In the passage below, the yearning effect of the high notes (G, G, F, and C) is compounded by the vague, languorous rhythm. The right-hand triplets and quintuplets blur with the left-hand eighth notes, especially when played with Romantic rubato:

"Florestan"   After "Eusebius" ends very tentatively, Schumann's impetuous other self makes his entrance. "Florestan" is built almost entirely out of a single explosive motive; the piece moves in fits and starts. The end gets faster and faster, and is on the point of self-destructing when it is suddenly confronted by the next character, Coquette.

"Coquette"   Both the rhythm and the form of this number seem capricious and teasing. The piano style enhances the feeling—the crisp chords at the beginning and end, and the **ff** octave emphasis of the melodic climaxes throughout.

"Replique"   In this tiny number (whose title means "reply"), Florestan changes back into Eusebius and wistfully rejects Coquette, fending off her music.

Frédéric Chopin

(1810–1849)

Chief Works: Character pieces for piano: Preludes (including the "Raindrop" prelude), Nocturnes, Etudes, Ballades, Waltzes (including the "Minute" waltz) and Polish Mazurkas and Polonaises

Three piano sonatas, including one with a famous funeral march as the slow movement

Two piano concertos

A cello sonata; a few Polish songs

Chopin was born near Warsaw, where his father, a Frenchman who had emigrated to Poland and married a Polish lady, ran a private school for young gentlemen. In this atmosphere Fryderyk—later he adopted the French form Frédéric—acquired his lifelong taste for life in high society. Provided with the best teachers available, he became an extraordinary pianist. There are many reports of the exquisite delicacy of his playing, and his miraculous ability, as it seemed at the time, to draw romantic sounds out of the piano.

Furthermore, his Variations on Mozart's "Là ci darem la mano" (see page 207), written when he was seventeen, was already a sufficiently impressive composition to earn a rave review from Robert Schumann.

At the age of twenty, Chopin settled in Paris, where he found ready acceptance from society people and from other artists and intellectuals, such as the novelist Honoré de Balzac and the painter Eugène Delacroix, who produced a famous portrait of the composer. Chopin made his way as a highly fashionable piano teacher and by selling his music to publishers. The facts that he was Polish, and that Poland was being overrun by Russia at that time, seem to have made him even more glamorous to the French. Among Chopin's piano miniatures are over fifty Mazurkas and sixteen Polonaises, which are stylized Polish dances.

Chopin and George Sand, by their friend Eugène Delacroix, the French Romantic painter. His *Chopin* is alive with the inner fire and agony of genius—one of the greatest of all composer portraits.

Chopin was a frail and fastidious personality. Though he sometimes played in public, he truly disliked the hurly-burly of concert life and preferred to perform for select audiences in great houses. More than any other of the great composers, he restricted his work to music for *his* instrument, the piano. Even his works for piano and orchestra—two concertos and a few other works—were all from his pre-Paris days.

The major event of his personal life was his ten-year romance with Madame Aurore Dudevant, an early feminist and a famous novelist under the pen name George Sand. (They were introduced by Liszt, who wrote an admiring book about Chopin after his death.) The relationship was a rocky one; Sand sketched some unkind scenes from their life together in one of her novels. After the affair broke up in 1847, Chopin's health declined with his spirits. He toured England and Scotland unhappily in 1848, and died the next year, at the age of thirty-nine, of tuberculosis, a major killer in the nineteenth century.

FRÉDÉRIC CHOPIN
Etude in C Minor, Op. 10, No. 12 ("Revolutionary" Etude) (?1830)

6 Cassette 3B-9/6 CD 3-15

More than any other composer, Chopin transformed the piano into an ideal medium for Romanticism, rather than the rather matter-of-fact instrument it had been in earlier times. He created entire new sound worlds of pianistic melancholy, languor, and delicacy; technically, he developed a range of power and brilliance that far outshone the efforts of the barnstorming virtuoso pianists of his day. Besides his sensitivity to piano tone color, Chopin had a fantastic ear for harmony and a great instinct for rhythm. There is always a rhythmic sparkle to his music, in addition to the exquisite piano sound.

Chopin's Etudes ("studies"), which are still unequaled for perfecting keyboard technique, have as distinct a "character" as any other Romantic miniature. The Etude in C Minor begins in the middle of things (like many Romantic works), with a sort of furious summons answered by a rush of left-hand scales. After this, the etude consists of two playings of a melody that catches the Romantic spirit at its most hectic and magnificent. Just when the piece seems to have settled down to an ominous hush, it explodes into a dramatic loud conclusion.

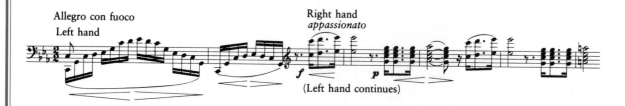

Nicknamed (*not* by Chopin) the "Revolutionary" Etude, this piece was said to express his anguish after the Russian capture of Warsaw in 1831.

6 Cassette 3B-10/6 CD 3-16

FRÉDÉRIC CHOPIN
Nocturne in F-sharp, Op. 15 No. 2 (1831)

Chopin's twenty-one Nocturnes, meaning "night pieces," written throughout his career, are as different as twenty-one different nights. But each features a particularly striking tune—a languid serenade, for example, or a dark secret lament. Something else is usually heard or overheard in the night, too, such as a distant procession, a passionate encounter, or even a fragment of a dance or a folk song.

The opening tune in Chopin's Nocturne in F-sharp has an elegance unique to the composer—an elegance that stems partly from the wonderfully graceful rhythm, partly from the Romantic turns of harmony, and partly from the pianistic decorations of the melodic line. We have seen decorated melodies before, but Chopin's have an almost liquid quality, caused partly by chromaticism—by the free use of all the notes of the chromatic scale, as in this fragment:

Romantic form contributes to the Romantic effect. Chopin avoids sharp demarcations and literal returns; the music seems to grow spontaneously, in an almost improvisational way. The main tune does not really end; it is interrupted by plaintive sounds emerging out of nowhere, which surge up to a moment of real passion. Then the return of the tune is fragmentary, though in a way more intense, and the whole is capped by an unexpected little coda: delicious right-hand arpeggios over a bolero rhythm in the left. Free rhythm in the performance (rubato) mirrors the freedom of form.

Was this striking painting, by a minor late nineteenth-century artist, done with Chopin's nocturnes in mind? Called *Notturno*, its cool elegance, faint sensuality, and vaguely apprehensive quality might suggest so.

Franz Liszt

(1811–1886)

Chief Works: *Les Préludes* and twelve other symphonic poems; *Faust* and *Dante* symphonies (program symphonies, both with chorus)

Two piano concertos and the *Totentanz* ("Dance of Death"), a sort of program concerto; the popular "Rákóczy March" and Hungarian Rhapsodies

For piano solo: Sonata in B Minor; Transcendental Etudes; other miniatures, including the famous *Liebestraum* ("Dream of Love")

Piano versions of Schubert songs and opera medleys

Songs (a neglected portion of his enormous output)

Masses and oratorios

Liszt learned music on the estate of the princes Esterházy near Vienna, where Haydn had once served, and where Liszt's father worked as an estate manager. By the time he was eleven, the young Hungarian was giving his first concert in Vienna. He was introduced to Beethoven, and published his first music, in 1823.

His dashing looks and personality, his radical opinions, and his liaisons with noblewomen dazzled Europe as much as his incredible piano technique. He attracted crowds like a modern rock star, and cultivated the flamboyant manner, on stage and off, that seems necessary to sustain such fame. Among his most popular concert numbers were brilliant piano transcriptions of Schubert songs and of opera highlights from Mozart, Wagner, and Verdi.

In 1833, when he was twenty-two, he met the Countess Marie d'Agoult, who wrote novels under the name Daniel Stern, and went with her to Geneva. She left her elderly husband and bore Liszt three children, one of whom, Cosima, became notorious in her turn when she abandoned *her* husband for Richard Wagner, some twenty years later. Liszt's relationship with Marie had a strong intellectual component; she had an influence on many piano compositions he wrote in those years. After this relationship came to a stormy end, Liszt spent a few years touring Europe, giving triumphant concerts from Portugal to Turkey and Russia.

Finally, Liszt tired of concert life and settled at Weimar, in Germany, where there was still a court that supported the arts in the eighteenth-century manner. He became a conductor and the director of the theater there. In his composing, he pioneered a highly influential new Romantic musical genre, the symphonic poem. From this period also date his two program symphonies, entitled *Dante* and *Faust*.

At Weimar he took up with another formidable woman, Princess Carolyne Sayn-Wittgenstein. Under the princess's influence, Liszt turned to religion and became an *abbé,* an unordained priest. This vocation would have allowed him to marry, if only the princess had been able to secure a divorce. He spent most of his last years in Rome, and composed a number of "grandiose" Masses and other compositions for the Catholic church.

Like so many other Romantic composers, Liszt was a writer as well as a musician, though some of his comments on the musical scene may have been written in collaboration with d'Agoult and Sayn-Wittgenstein. He was a powerful advocate of Wagner's music; at Weimar in 1850, he produced Wagner's opera *Lohengrin* for the first time, at a time when Wagner was in exile from Germany. The two men learned a good deal from each other's music. Friend and foe alike linked Liszt's symphonic poems with Wagner's "music dramas" as "Music of the Future" (see page 286).

As a personality, however, Liszt was as generous and magnanimous as his son-in-law was self-centered and devious. Admittedly, there was something theatrical about his stance as a "grand seigneur," but his generous efforts on behalf of other musicians, great and small, continued unabated all through his life. The grand old man died in 1886 at Bayreuth, where Wagner had built a theater for his operas, during the Wagner Festival there.

6 Cassette 3B-11/6 CD 3-17

FRANZ LISZT
Transcendental Etude No. 10 in F Minor (1851)

Liszt was, in his younger days, the greatest of the nineteenth-century piano virtuosos. The very title of his celebrated *Etudes of Transcendental Execution* defied any mere earthbound pianist to play them. In its dazzling cascade of piano sounds, Etude No. 10 catches both the intense agitation and the super-charged melodic style that thrilled Liszt's devotees.

As in a highly compressed sonata-form movement, an opening piano fig-ure (theme 1) soon leads to a long melody (theme 2). This reaches up and up with now ethereal, now lamenting, now passionate accents:

The melody is cut off by brusque, brilliant cadences, and there is a solemn descending cadence theme in the left hand. After a short developmentlike passage, the opening figure returns, again leading to the melody. This time the melody develops even more intensely, with richer and richer Romantic har-monies. The cadence theme is followed by a brilliant coda.

Sometimes Liszt actually did break, if not pianos, piano strings. This helped to ruin one prominent Viennese piano maker (Graf).

Fanny Mendelssohn Hensel
Felix Mendelssohn

(1805–1847)

(1809–1847)

Chief Works—Felix Mendelssohn: Overtures, including *The Hebrides (Fingal's Cave);* overture and incidental music to *A Midsummer Night's Dream*

Five symphonies, including the *Italian, Scottish,* and *Reformation;* other orchestral works

Concertos, including the famous Violin Concerto

Oratorios: *St. Paul, Elijah;* other choral works

Songs; chamber music; piano pieces, including several volumes of very popular miniatures called *Songs without Words*

Chief Works—Fanny Mendelssohn Hensel: Piano miniatures, including some *Songs without Words,* modeled after those by Felix

Songs, including some that Felix published under his own name(!)

Cantatas, oratorios—a total of about 400 works, most of them still not published

Fanny and her younger brother Felix were the children of a Hamburg banker, the son of a distinguished Enlightenment philosopher named Moses Mendelssohn. When Napoleon's troops occupied Hamburg in 1811, the family transferred to Berlin; it was at that time that they converted to Christianity from Judaism.

It was a happy, cultivated home, and Fanny and Felix were particularly close. They took music lessons—Fanny was the better pianist—and read Shakespeare together. One of their favorite plays was *A Midsummer Night's Dream,* and at the age of seventeen Felix wrote a marvelous Overture to this play, which is still regarded as one of his finest works.

Felix went on to a brilliant career both as a composer and, touring extensively, as a pianist and conductor. He visited England ten times in his short life and was warmly received at Buckingham Palace by Queen Victoria. His oratorios *St. Paul* and *Elijah* were very popular in England, and made a great impression in the United States, too. Mendelssohn conducted the Leipzig Gewandhaus Orchestra—one of Europe's first great orchestras, thanks to his efforts—and organized (and taught at) the Leipzig Conservatory. Robert Schumann also taught there; the two composers became fast friends.

And Fanny? She was as gifted a composer as her brother; not surprisingly, their musical styles were similar. Her father made it clear, however, that an upper-class lady could not become a professional musician. Fanny married, but kept up her music; she took charge of the lavish family concerts given weekly in the Mendelssohns' Berlin home. She once broached the question of publishing her compositions. Although her husband, a painter, approved, Felix did not—and Fanny listened to Felix. It was only much later, and then not without an internal struggle, that she took the plunge and sent some of her music to the printer. Most of it still remains unpublished and unknown.

Alert as we are today to discrimination against women, in the arts as in other aspects of life, it is impossible not to cringe at the behavior of the Mendelssohn men. Fanny, it is true, became an accomplished composer, and she remained very close to her brother; no one can read their letters without marveling at the deep admiration, love, and professional fellowship that existed between them. Yet how much richer her musical career might have been if she had been granted the opportunities enjoyed by Felix!

And if she had, would we now regard her as one of the great composers? Possibly, if she had developed rather differently than her brother. For the truth is that with a few notable exceptions, Felix's music has faded with time, much more so than that of the other early Romantic luminaries Schumann, Chopin, Liszt, and Berlioz.

Felix means "happy" in Latin, but the Mendelssohn story does not have a happy ending. In May 1847, Fanny died tragically of a stroke during a rehearsal for one of the family concerts. Felix was shattered; although his health was failing, due to his punishing work and travel schedule, he wrote a string quartet in Fanny's memory and journeyed to visit her grave. This experience unnerved him, and hastened his own death, less than six months after the death of his sister. His body was taken to Berlin and buried near Fanny.

Felix and Fanny Mendelssohn

3 Early Romantic Program Music

The lied and the character piece for piano—the two main forms of early Romantic miniature compositions—were intimately tied up with nonmusical, usually poetic, ideas. Furthermore, in a work such as Schumann's *Carnaval*, the various piano portraits are juxtaposed in such a way as to hint at their interaction—hint, that is, at some kind of shadowy story line. Poems, stories, and nonmusical ideas in general were also associated with large-scale instrumental pieces.

Program music is a term used for instrumental compositions associated with poems, stories, and the like. Program music grew up naturally in opera overtures, for even in the eighteenth century it was seen that an overture might gain special interest if it referred to moods or ideas in the opera to come by citing its themes. Mozart's *Don Giovanni* Overture begins with solemn, ominous music that will be sung by the Commandant two hours later. This idea was carried much further in Romantic works such as the Prelude (Overture) to Richard Wagner's opera *Tristan und Isolde*, discussed in Chapter 17.

A further step, conceptually, was the **concert overture**, an overture never intended to be followed by an opera or a stage play—never intended, indeed, for the theater. An example is Felix Mendelssohn's well-known Overture to *A Midsummer Night's Dream* of 1826; only much later was it used in theatrical productions of the Shakespeare play. A work in sonata form, following classical models, this overture nonetheless includes some representational features. Music illustrates the delicate, fluttering fairies in the service of King Oberon and Queen Titania, the sleep induced by Puck's magic flower, and even the braying of Bottom the Weaver when he is turned into a donkey.

Another example by Mendelssohn is the *Hebrides* Overture, an evocative depiction of lonely Scottish islands rich in romantic associations. This is evidently program music, but what makes it an overture? Nothing more than the fact that it follows the standard scheme for overtures at the time—namely, a single movement in sonata form.

HECTOR BERLIOZ
Fantastic Symphony: Episodes in the Life of an Artist (1830)

> PROGRAM OF THE SYMPHONY: A young musician of morbidly sensitive temperament and passionate imagination poisons himself with opium in a fit of lovesick despair. The dose of the narcotic, too weak to kill him, plunges him into a heavy sleep accompanied by the strangest visions, during which his sensations, his emotions, and his memories are transformed in his diseased mind into musical thoughts and images. Even the woman he loves becomes a melody to him, an *idée fixe* [fixed idea], as it were, that he encounters and hears everywhere. . . .

This was the beginning of a long pamphlet distributed to an astonished Paris audience at the first performance of a new symphony in 1830. The young composer, Hector Berlioz, was certainly taking a more radical approach to program music than Mendelssohn had taken with his concert overtures. Berlioz, too, had written a concert overture, to Sir Walter Scott's novel *Waverley,* but he now felt the need for a broader canvas. In his **program symphonies**— entire symphonies with programs—Berlioz set the tone for the "grandiose" compositions that were to become as characteristic of Romanticism as its musical miniatures.

The first of these symphonies is a most unusual work—indeed, one of the most sensational works in the whole history of music. The composer himself called it "Fantastic." Clearly Berlioz had a gift for public relations, for the program was not a well-known play or novel but an intimate autobiographical essay of his own, as the above excerpt shows.

Here was music which encouraged listeners to think that it had been written under the influence of opium, the drug that attracted many of the Romantics and that shocked society at large. What is more, half of Paris knew that Berlioz was madly in love (from afar) with an Irish actress, Harriet Smithson, who had taken the city by storm with her Shakespearean roles.

Audiences have never been quite sure how seriously to take it all, but they continue to be bowled over by Berlioz's effects of tone color. He demanded an orchestra of unprecedented size, which he used in incredibly original and imaginative ways. Also highly original was the notion of having a single theme recur in all the movements as a representation of the musician's beloved—his *idée fixe.* Here is the *idée fixe* theme as it first appears:

This tune shows many typical features of Romantic melody. The whole of line 2 seems like a passionate struggle to inch higher and higher up the scale. Measure 19, just before the final cadence, provides a positive shudder of emotion. Notice, too, the profusion of dynamic, rubato, and other marks added by the composer to ensure just the right expressive quality.[1]

---

[1] The music example has been simplified to facilitate reading. *Canto espressivo* = expressive song; *dolce* = sweetly; *poco* = somewhat; *poco a poco* = bit by bit; *animato* = animated; *ritenuto* = slowed down (ritardando); *a tempo* = back to the original tempo.

(1803–1869)

Hector Berlioz

Chief Works: Program symphonies: *Fantastic* Symphony, *Harold in Italy*, *Romeo and Juliet*

Concert overtures, among them the *Roman Carnival* Overture

Operas: *Benvenuto Cellini, The Trojans* (after Virgil's *Aeneid*)

Oratorios: *The Damnation of Faust, The Childhood of Christ;* a Requiem Mass for orchestra, chorus, and four brass bands, and a *Te Deum*

If the deaf Beethoven was the first great composer who made his living actually as a composer, rather than a performer or conductor, Berlioz was the first who was not an instrumentalist at all. His father, a country doctor, sent him to medical school in Paris. But, as Berlioz told it, he was so horrified when he entered the dissecting room, where the rats were nibbling at the scraps, that he leaped out the window and went to the Paris Conservatory of Music instead.

The anecdote is typical of his emotional and utterly Romantic personality. More than any other composer of his generation, except Wagner, Berlioz "thought the unthinkable" in music; his "grandiose" program symphonies had simply no precedent and were not matched in ambition until the time of Gustav Mahler. The only instrument he played well was the guitar, but his imagination for orchestral tone color was extraordinary. Like almost all the Romantic composers, he was inspired by literary models, including especially Shakespeare—his bizarre *Lélio* is a meditation on *Hamlet,* and his opera *Béatrice et Bénédict* is taken from *Much Ado about Nothing*—and Virgil. *The Trojans* (1858), his long two-part opera derived from Virgil's *Aeneid,* was seldom performed until modern times, but it is now regarded as his masterpiece.

Berlioz had two unhappy marriages, the first to the Irish Shakespearean actress Harriet Smithson, who is immortalized as the *idée fixe* in the *Fantastic* Symphony. In spite of suffering from constant gibes on the one hand, and wretched health on the other, it was a triumph of his impetuous personality that Berlioz ultimately managed to get most of his enormous compositions performed and to gain a good measure of recognition in musically conservative Paris.

He was obliged throughout his life to support himself with musical journalism, at which he was a master; his *Memoirs* is one of the most delightful books ever written about music. He also wrote important treatises on orchestration and conducting. One of the first great conductors, Berlioz toured extensively as a conductor of his own music, especially in Germany, where he was welcomed in modernist circles.

His last years were spent in physical pain and depression. After 1862 he listened to little music and composed none. Berlioz died in Paris in 1869.

To illustrate his drastic mood swings, Berlioz subjects the *idée fixe* to thematic transformation (see page 250) for all its other appearances in the dream. The last movement, for example, has a grotesque parody of the theme:

The new jerky rhythm and the squeaky orchestration (using the small E-flat clarinet) both thoroughly undermine the original Romantic mood.

First Movement (Largo—Allegro agitato e appassionato assai)

> REVERIES, PASSIONS: First he remembers the soulsickness, the aimless passions, the baseless depressions and elations which he felt before seeing her whom he loves. Then—the volcanic love that she instantly inspired in him; his jealous furies; his returns to tenderness; his religious consolations.

We first hear a short, quiet run-in—a typically Romantic touch suggesting that the music has grown up imperceptibly out of silence. Then the "soulsickness" mentioned in the program is depicted by a halting, passionate melody. This early part of the movement hardly sounds like a preface to something else, as would a Classical symphony's slow introduction; rather, it sounds like a moderate-sized slow movement in its own right.

A faster section begins with the *idée fixe*, and the music picks up energy (the "volcanic love" of the program). This fast section follows sonata form, but only very loosely indeed. The *idée fixe* is the main theme, and a second theme which appears in the exposition's unusually short second group is simply a derivative of the first theme.

There is no clear stop after the "exposition." Some of the finest strokes in this movement run counter to Classical principles—for example, the arresting up-and-down harmonized chromatic scale that crops up in the development section without any logical connection to anything else. The recapitulation, too, is extended in a very un-Classical fashion; it actually includes a whole new melody for the oboe.

Near the end, beginning an outsized coda, the *idée fixe* returns noisily at a faster tempo—the first of its many transformations. At the very end, slower music depicts the program's "religious consolations."

Second Movement (Allegro non troppo)

> A BALL: He meets his beloved at a ball, in the midst of a noisy, brilliant fete.

A symphony needs the simplicity and easy swing of a dance movement, and this ballroom episode of the opium dream conveniently provided one. The dance in question is not a minuet or a scherzo, but a waltz, the most popular ballroom dance of the nineteenth century. Its introduction to the waltz tune features four fast-moving, resonant harps.

Berlioz takes over the **A B A** form of Classical dance (minuet) form (but without the traditional internal phrase structure, |: **a** :||: **b a′** :|). The *idée fixe*, transformed into a lilting triple meter, first appears in the position of the trio (**B**) and then returns hauntingly in the coda. The return of the main waltz (**A′**) is an intensified, reorchestrated version of **A.**

Third Movement (Adagio)

> SCENE IN THE COUNTRY: On a summer evening in the country, he hears two shepherds piping in dialogue. The pastoral duet, the location, the light rustling of trees stirred by the wind, a few recently conceived grounds for hope—all this gives him a feeling of unaccustomed calm, and a brighter color to his thoughts. But she appears again, his heart misses a beat—what if she is deceiving him again? . . . One of the shepherds resumes his simple lay; the other does not answer. The sun sets. Distant thunder. Solitude. Silence.

Invoking nature to reflect human emotions was a favorite Romantic procedure. The "pastoral duet" introducing this long country scene is played by an English horn (evidently the boy shepherd) and an off-stage oboe (the girl). Then at the end of the movement, the English horn returns to the accompaniment of distant thunder sounds, played on four differently tuned timpani. Significantly, the oboe is no longer to be heard.

In between these evocative pipings, the movement is built on another rich melody. The *idée fixe* returns in a new, strangely agitated transformation. It is interrupted by angry sounds swelling to a forceful climax, indicative of the anxieties chronicled in the program.

3 Cassette 2A-5, 2B-1/
3 CD 2, 5–6
6 Cassette 3B-12, 4A-1/
6 CD 3-18, 4-1

Fourth Movement (Allegretto non troppo)

> MARCH TO THE SCAFFOLD: He dreams he has killed his loved one, that he is condemned to death and led to execution. A march accompanies the procession, now gloomy and wild, now brilliant and grand, during which the dull sound of heavy footsteps follows abruptly on the noisiest outbursts. Finally the *idée fixe* appears for a moment, to be cut off by the fall of the axe.

The final fall of the axe is illustrated vividly by the sound of a guillotine chop and a snare-drum roll, right after two bars of the *idée fixe*.

Up to this grisly or ludicrous effect (depending on how you look at it), the fourth movement is fairly traditional in form, though the orchestration and mood are certainly *not* traditional. The two main themes are a simple theme consisting of a long downward scale ("gloomy and wild") and a blaring, ominous military march ("brilliant and grand"). Later the scale theme appears divided up in its orchestration between plucked and bowed strings, woodwinds, brass, and percussion—a memorable instance of Berlioz's novel imagination for tone color. Finally the scale theme appears in a truly shattering inverted form (that is, moving upward).

Fifth Movement (Larghetto—Allegro)

> DREAM OF A WITCHES' SABBATH: He finds himself at a Witches' Sabbath, in the midst of a frightful crowd of ghosts, sorcerers, and all kinds of monsters come to bury him. Unearthly sounds, groans, shrieks of laughter, distant cries echoed by others. The melody of his beloved is heard, but it has lost its character of nobleness and timidity. It is *she* who comes to the Sabbath! A roar of joy at her arrival. She joins in the devilish orgies. The funeral knell; burlesque of the *Dies irae*.

Now the element of parody is added to the astonishing orchestral effects pioneered earlier in the symphony. But first, an introduction depicts the unearthly sounds of the nighttime locale of the witches' orgy. Their swishing broomsticks are heard, and some kind of distant horn calls that are summoning them. Mutes are used in the brass instruments—perhaps their first "poetic" use ever.

As Berlioz remarks, the "noble and timid" *idée fixe* sounds thoroughly vulgar in its last transformation, played in a fast jig rhythm by the shrill E-flat clarinet. The treatment of the *idée fixe* here is strictly "programmatic": when the theme first arrives, only two phrases are played before the orchestra breaks in, with a "roar of joy" welcoming Harriet Smithson to the orgy. Then all join her in a raucous dance.

As the merriment is brought to an end by a dramatic funeral bell, Berlioz prepares his most sensational stroke of all—a burlesque of one of the most solemn and famous of Gregorian chants, the *Dies irae* (Day of Wrath):

Original Gregorian chant:

Di - es i - rae di - es il - la Sol - vet sae - clum in fa - vil - la
Day of wrath, that dreadful day,   When heaven and earth shall pass away

Allegro
TUBAS and BASSOONS

f 8va - - - - - - - - - - - - -

FRENCH HORNS and TRUMPETS

E♭ CLARINET, PICCOLO, STRINGS pizzicato, etc.

This Gregorian chant is the centerpiece of Masses for the dead, or Requiem Masses; in Catholic France, any audience would have recognized the *Dies irae* instantly. Its presentation in distorted rhythms and in grotesque orchestral sounds painted a blasphemous, shocking picture of the witches' black mass. The early Romantics enjoyed flirting with the macabre and the diabolical, as we have seen.

The final section of the movement is a "Witches' Round Dance." Berlioz wrote a free fugue—a traditional form in a nontraditional context; he uses counterpoint to give a feeling of tumult. The subject is an excited one:

The climax of the fugue (and of the symphony) comes when the Round Dance theme is heard together with the *Dies irae,* played by the trumpets. Berlioz wanted to drive home the point that it is the witches, represented by the theme of their round dance, who are parodying the church melody, which is heard simultaneously. The *idée fixe* seems at last to be forgotten. But in real life Berlioz did not forget; he married Smithson and both of them lived to regret it.

LISTENING CHART NUMBER 13

3 Cassette 2B-1/3 CD 2-6
6 Cassette 4A-1/6 CD 4-1

Berlioz, *Fantastic* Symphony, fifth movement

10 min., 22 sec.

	INTRODUCTION		
	00.00		Mysterious orchestral effects
	0.27	*Fanfare*	Like a distant trumpet or horn summons; woodwinds. Echoed by muted French horn
	1.19	*Fanfare*	Again.
	IDÉE FIXE		
	1.38		Prefatory statement: two phrases (only) of the *idée fixe*; riotous orchestral response, *ff*
6.2 / 1.2	1.56	*Idée fixe*	Entire tune presented in a grotesque transformation, in 6/8 meter, played by "squeaky" E-flat clarinets
	2.27	*Crescendo*	
	2.47	**Upward motive**	A short, expectant motive (later this motive initiates the fugue subject of the "Round Dance")
	2.51	*Transition*	Quiet descending passage
	3.09	**Funeral bells**	Three sets of three bells (the third set is muted); the upward motive also appears
	DIES IRAE		
6.3 / 1.3	3.34	**Phrase 1**	Phrase 1 of the plainchant is played in three versions:
			(1) tubas and bassoons—slow
	3.55		(2) horns and trombones—faster
	4.06		(3) woodwinds—faster still (the rhythm here recalls that of the *idée fixe*)
	4.12	**Phrase 2**	Phrase 2 of the plainchant, in the same three versions
	4.36	**Phrase 3**	Phrase 3 of the plainchant, in the same three versions
			(Meanwhile the funeral bells and the upward motive are occasionally heard)
	5.12	*Transition*	The upward motive is developed; crescendo
	WITCHES' ROUND DANCE (free fugue)		
6.4 / 1.4	5.32	**Exposition**	Four entries of the fugue subject
	6.00	*Episode 1*	
6.5 / 1.5	6.23	**Subject entries**	Three more entries, in stretto
	6.37	*Episode 2*	A passage starting with a loud rhythmic motive, derived from the subject, comes four times.
	7.02		The music dies down.
	7.21		Fragments of the *Dies irae*
	7.38		Long transition; big crescendo over a drum roll
	8.19	**Subject entry**	The original subject returns.
6.6 / 1.6	8.28	**Subject plus** *Dies irae*	The two themes together in a polyphonic combination. This is a climax; trumpets play the *Dies irae* for the first time.
6.7 / 1.7	9.01	**Subject entry**	Final appearance of subject: over strings *col legno* (played with the wood, that is, the back of the bow)
6.8 / 1.8	9.37	*Dies irae*	Phrase 1 hastily recollected in the same three versions as at its first appearance; big drum strokes
	9.45	**Conclusion**	Final passage of cadences: very loud

Chapter 17

Romantic Opera

An important theme of Romanticism was the transcendence of artistic barriers. The idea of combining music with poetry and other forms of literature, and even with philosophy, made perfect sense to Romantic composers and their audiences. The age that produced the lied—a German song with an important poetic dimension—was also fascinated by the union of music and drama. The nineteenth century was a golden age of opera, which flourished all over Europe from Germany, France, and Italy to Czechoslovakia (Bohemia) and Russia.

Opera in the nineteenth century was affected by another important Romantic theme: the celebration of music as the most profound of all the arts. Opera composers and librettists began thinking seriously about the meaning and "message" of their work; they came to view opera as a type of serious drama in music, not just a vehicle for song, spectacle, and entertainment, as had often been the case before. Richard Wagner is famous for embracing, publicizing, and even co-opting this notion. Indeed, he pursued it much further than anyone else in his "music dramas"—works that fascinated the nineteenth century. Nonetheless, Wagner was building on new attitudes toward opera that were developing all over Europe even when he was still an unknown provincial conductor.

The Wolf's Glen Scene from Weber's *Der Freischütz*, most famous of early German Romantic operas (see opposite)

Early Romantic Opera

Romantic opera made its serious start in the 1820s, after the end of the Viennese Classical period. It did not, however, start or flourish in the heartland of Classical music which was Vienna. In that city, both Beethoven and Schubert felt threatened by the popular rage for the operas of Gioacchino Rossini, a young Italian whose meteoric career left a mark on the whole of Europe.

Gioacchino Rossini (1792–1868)

Rossini is most famous today for crisp, elegant opera buffas in a style that is not all that far from Mozart—the immortal *Barber of Seville* among them. And the ever popular overtures of these operas are even written in sonata form, the true trademark of Classicism in music.

But in his own day Rossini was admired equally for his serious operas, which established the style and form of Italian Romantic opera. This is called *bel canto* opera because of its glorification of beautiful singing (*bel canto* means just that—"beautiful song"). Rossini's operas provided models of Romantic emotional melodic expression, such as Desdemona's "Willow Song" from his Shakespeare opera *Otello*. The same operas are also well stocked with coloratura arias, showcases for the legendary virtuoso singers of that era.

Gaetano Donizetti (1797–1848)

Donizetti, who dominated Italian *bel canto* opera after Rossini's sudden retirement in 1830, moved decisively in the direction of simple, sentimental arias and blood-and-thunder "action" music. Enormously prolific, he wrote more than sixty operas in his relatively short lifetime.

The most famous are *Lucia di Lammermoor,* based on the historical novel by Scott mentioned on page 278, and *Don Pasquale,* a very late example of opera buffa. In the 1970s, the American soprano Beverly Sills starred in a Donizetti trilogy featuring famous queens of English history: *Anna Bolena* (Anne Boleyn, the ill-fated second wife of Henry VIII), *Maria Stuarda* (Mary Stuart—Mary,

Queen of Scots), and *Roberto Devereux* (about Queen Elizabeth I and Robert Devereux, Earl of Essex).

Vincenzo Bellini (1801–1835)

Vincenzo Bellini strikes listeners today as the most refined among the three early *bel canto* composers. He wrote many fewer operas than the others, and his most beautiful arias have a unique Romantic sheen. The title role in *Norma,* his finest work, is the final testing ground for sopranos, for it demands highly expressive singing, coloratura fireworks, and great acting, all in unusual quantities.

Verdi often expressed his admiration for the supremely melodious Bellini. All the same, he learned more from the more robust and dramatic Donizetti.

Carl Maria von Weber (1786–1826)

Weber was the founder of German Romantic opera. His most important work, *Der Freischütz* (The Magic Bullet), has the quality of a German folk tale or ballad put to music. Max, a somewhat driven young huntsman, sells his soul to the devil for seven magic bullets, but is redeemed by the sacrifice of his pure, blond fiancée, Agatha.

Two spiritual arias sung by Agatha in this opera represent Romantic melody at its best; there are also German choruses in a folk-song style. A famous scene of devilish conjuration in the Wolf's Glen depends for its effect on sensational orchestral writing of a kind previously unknown to opera.

The supernatural subject matter, with its strongly moral overtone—very different from the historical subjects chosen by Donizetti, for example—and the emphasis on the orchestra became characteristic of German Romantic opera. These features can still be clearly discerned in the mature "music dramas" of Richard Wagner, who started his career in the 1830s as an opera composer in Weber's mold. Otherwise, however, Wagner's music dramas leave early Romantic opera far behind.

Legendary singers of the *bel canto* era: Pauline Viardot (1821–1910), Maria Malibran (1808–1836), and Giulia Grisi (1811–1869), along with a playbill for one of their favorite showcases, the opera *Norma* by Vincenzo Bellini

Thus many operas took their subjects from highly regarded Romantic novels, among them *Ivanhoe, The Lady of the Lake,* and *The Bride of Lammermoor,* to mention only a few by Sir Walter Scott. Since poets and playwrights were turning with new enthusiasm to Shakespeare's plays, opera composers, too, drew on them widely. Giuseppe Verdi set versions of Shakespeare's tragedies *Macbeth* and *Othello* as well as the comedy *The Merry Wives of Windsor.* Over his long career, Verdi developed his own form of musical drama, which bears comparison with that of Wagner or anyone else for seriousness and power.

Giuseppe Verdi

(1813–1901)

Chief Works: Twenty-four operas, including *Nabucco, Macbeth, Rigoletto, Il trovatore, La traviata, Don Carlo, The Force of Destiny, Aida*

Two great Shakespeare operas composed after his retirement, *Otello* and *Falstaff*

A Requiem Mass, and a few other choral works; a string quartet

The son of a storekeeper in a tiny village in northern Italy, Verdi had a spotty education. He played church organ and conducted the band of the neighboring little town. A local merchant, Antonio Barezzi, who became a patron and almost a second father to the young man, sent him to Milan to study music.

In those days, the center of musical life in Italy was Milan's famous opera house, La Scala. After several discouraging years in that city, Verdi scored a huge success with his biblical opera *Nabucco* (Nebuchadnezzar) when he was twenty-nine years old. For the next ten years—Verdi called them his *anni di galera,* his years as a galley slave—he composed operas at a furious rate for opera houses in Italy, Paris, and London. After three particularly famous operas in the early 1850s, *Rigoletto, Il trovatore,* and *La traviata,* Verdi's success was assured worldwide. Henceforth he took more time with his operas, and his later works became more and more innovative.

Verdi was an ardent supporter of the Risorgimento, or Italian liberation movement, and many of his early operas had patriotic themes. The most beloved number in *Nabucco* was a nostalgic hymn of the Hebrew slaves in Babylon—a clear reference to the Italians under the heel of the Austrian Empire. In the year of revolution, 1848, Verdi wrote the rousing *Battle of Legnano.* "Verdi" actually became a patriotic acronym for the popular choice for king—Vittorio Emmanuele, *Re d'Italia*—and after independence was achieved, the composer was made an honorary deputy in the first Italian parliament.

Verdi was devoted to Italian traditions in opera, naturally enough, and suspicious of any others. Rossini was his idol. He kept his peace about Wagner's music dramas, but he reacted very bitterly when his own later works were criticized as Wagnerian (mainly because of their increasingly rich and sophisticated orchestral style).

A dour character and a tough businessman, Verdi drove hard bargains with opera impresarios, bullied his librettists, and insisted on supervising the production of his new operas. When he had accumulated enough money, he retired to a fine country estate near his birthplace and spent his later years hunting and raising livestock. After fifteen years of this life, he was coaxed out of retirement by his canny publisher and by an eminent librettist, Arrigo Boito. In his seventies, Verdi wrote his two greatest operas with Boito, both to Shakespearean subjects: the tragedy *Otello* and the comedy *Falstaff.*

Verdi's first marriage, to the daughter of his early patron Barezzi, ended in tragedy when his young wife and two babies all died within two years. The composer bore the emotional scars of this all his life, and it may be that the

A popular graffito of the Italian revolution: "Viva VERDI" (meaning "Long live Victor Emmanuel, King of Italy")

many moving scenes between fathers and daughters in Verdi's operas served to channel his feelings about fatherhood. He later married a remarkable woman, Giuseppina Strepponi, a singer who had assisted him in his early career and starred in his first success, *Nabucco*. She had been Verdi's mistress for many years. The marriage was a long and devoted one, but the couple had no children.

By the time he died, at the age of eighty-eight, Verdi was a national institution, and he was mourned throughout Italy. Schools closed. Eulogies were delivered in a special session of the senate in Rome. Nearly 300,000 people saw the old man to his grave. His operas remain the most popular of all in the international repertory.

1 Verdi and Italian Opera

Giuseppe Verdi, the greatest of Italian opera composers, was the dominant figure in nineteenth-century opera houses. For while Wagner's "music dramas" and his theories of opera attracted much excited attention, Verdi's operas got many more performances. Then as now, people were inevitably drawn to compare and contrast these two masters.

The heart of the contrast lies in Verdi's unswerving commitment to the human voice. In this, he was a faithful follower of the *bel canto* principles of Rossini, Donizetti, and Bellini. Verdi never allowed the voice to be overshadowed by the orchestra, and over the course of his long career he learned to write more and more beautiful melodies. Opera was a singing art to Verdi, and generations of Italians before, during, and after his lifetime have enthusiastically agreed with him.

But while audiences have always loved Verdi's melodies, what he himself cared most about was the dramatic quality of his operas. First and foremost, Verdi was interested in people, people placed in situations in which strong exciting actions bring out equally strong emotions. He sought out dramatic subjects full of stirring action, and he had a genius for finding just the right vocal melody to enhance a dramatic situation.

Recitative and Aria: The Orchestra

As an opera composer, Verdi never wavered in his commitment to the human voice. Once this basic point has been made, however, it must also be said that the orchestra plays a much richer role in Verdi's operas than in those of any of his Italian predecessors. This was all but inevitable in the orchestra-intoxicated nineteenth century.

The role of the orchestra was especially expanded in passages of recitative or near-recitative—the relic or descendant of the recitatives of Baroque opera seria and Classical opera buffa. Italian opera still held roughly to the old division of declamation (recitative) for the "action" and dialogue portions of an opera and melody (arias) for reflective, emotional expression. (Ensembles encompassed both.) But plot action and dialogue were now always accompanied by the full orchestra. The orchestra is usually not restricted to the simple chords that were usual in earlier recitative styles; it plays more active, motivic, and excited music that points up the words and urges the singers on.

"Recitative" is no longer a satisfactory name—though no other name exists—for this "action" music in Verdi's operas. Highly melodramatic, it is always on the point of merging into a full-fledged melodic style. What distinguishes this music from actual arias is that arias are formally complete and distinct. Unlike passages of Verdian "recitative," Verdian arias can be (and often are) extracted and sung separately, as concert numbers.

In arias and duets, the orchestra's role is smaller; here, however, Verdi makes use of another Romantic resource, that of rich harmonies underpinning melodic high points and climaxes. Many—though by no means all—of Verdi's arias might be described as simple strophic songs in his own exuberant style of Romantic melody. Some of his most famous music consists of timeless tunes such as the tenor aria *"La donna è mobile"* from *Rigoletto,* the choral hymn *"Va pensiero"* from *Nabucco,* and the duet *"O terra, addio"* from *Aida,* which we will examine next.

GIUSEPPE VERDI
Aida (1871)

6 Cassette 4A, 2–4/6 CD 4, 2–4

Aida is one of the most frequently performed of all operas. It includes gorgeous arias—including a tenor favorite, *"Celeste Aida"*—and grandiose stage display, including elephants. Africa is the locale; this work was written to celebrate a milestone in the history of nineteenth-century imperialism, the opening of the Suez Canal in Egypt in 1869. In view of his commission, Verdi chose an Egyptian subject and wrote some exotic Egyptian-sounding music.

In other hands, perhaps, all this might have been merely pretentious. But Verdi's arias, display, and exoticism are coupled with an absorbing drama, a drama of credible human beings destroyed by powerful political forces and equally powerful emotions.

Background   The plot of *Aida* is thoroughly romantic (in the sense of amorous). A tragic love triangle is projected against a war between ancient Egypt, controlled by a sinister priesthood, and Ethiopia.

Acts I and II introduce a young Egyptian general, Radames, and a captive Ethiopian slave girl, Aida, who are secretly in love. (The Egyptians don't know that Aida is the daughter of Amonasro, King of Ethiopia.) Unfortunately, Radames has also attracted Amneris, a passionate and jealous Egyptian princess.

Amneris

In Act III, by a turn of the plot that we need not follow here, Radames is tricked into revealing his country's battle plans to Aida. Amneris has eavesdropped on their tryst, and she turns Radames over to the all-powerful priests for judgment as a traitor. Aida escapes in the confusion.

In Act IV Amneris offers to save Radames if he will return her love. To her dismay, he says he would rather die than live without Aida; Amneris realizes too late that she has assured the doom of the man she loves. His trial by the priests, in Act IV, scene i, which she witnesses, is one of the most dramatic in the entire opera. Radames makes no defense and is condemned to be buried alive in a tomb under the temple, sealed up by a huge stone.

Aïda

The final scene of *Aida:* from a contemporary illustrated newspaper

Tomb Scene (Act IV, scene ii)   Radames has just been entombed. Verdi called for a very striking stage set, divided horizontally: below, a cramped cell containing Radames; above, the Temple of Vulcan, complete with altar, colossal statue of Osiris, and other grandiose Egyptian paraphernalia. Although the impact of Verdi's music seldom fails, outside of the theater a special effort is required to envisage the stage and the action, so as to appreciate the full range of Verdi's dramatic art.

Recitative   The scene opens with quiet, ominous music in the strings—already, in its understated way, a forecast of doom. The first singing consists of three short passages of recitative. Each follows the same general plan. In each recitative passage, simple declamatory singing (with very light orchestral accompaniment) leads to an intense moment of genuine melody, with rich harmonic and orchestral support.

Thus Radames begins singing on a lengthy monotone, but works up some emotion when he thinks of Aida and hopes she will be spared knowledge of his fate. Then his more excited second speech is still fragmentary, up to the point when he discovers that Aida has hidden in his tomb to see him once again and die with him. He cries out "You, in this tomb!" on a high note, picking up from an anguished downward scale in the orchestra.

The third recitative passage, Aida's reply, begins simply, over a knell-like orchestral accompaniment. It melts into a beautiful and sensuously harmonized melodic phrase when she tells him she wants to die in his arms.

Amonasro

Ariosos   There follow two concise tunelike sections, or *ariosos* (see page 100). In the first of them, sung by Radames, notice the subdued, subservient role of the orchestra. The next arioso is more tuneful yet, with Aida's phrases falling into an almost Classical **a a′ b a′ c** pattern. The harmony is fully Romantic, however, especially in phrase **b**.

Duet (with Chorus)   Then Verdi mounts his impressive final scene. At the top level of the stage, priests and priestesses move slowly as they sing a funeral hymn with an exotic, Near Eastern flavor. They are invoking the great god Ptah. At the bottom level, Aida and Radames begin their final duet, a farewell to the sorrows of earth and a welcome to eternity. It is a famous instance of Verdi's simple and yet highly expansive melodic style:

Andante

AIDA, then RADAMES

O terra ad - dio addi - o, val - le di pianti,   Sogno di gaudio che in do-lor sva - nì   A noi si
Farewell to earth, farewell, vale of tears,   *Dream of happiness, which vanishes in grief;*   *The*

schiude, si schiude il ciel, si schiude il ciel e l'alme erran - ti   Volano al raggio dell'eter - no di.
heavens open and our fleeing souls   *Escape to the rays of eternal day.*

There is an exquisite Romantic harmony at the climax of the melody, in **c** of the **a a′ b a′ c** form—and that climax, on just about the highest note in the tenor's range, has to be sung very softly. This gives the melody a uniquely ethereal effect, as befits a couple who are about to die from lack of oxygen.

Other features reinforce this effect: the melodic line that focuses on just a few notes (high and low G♭ and D♭), and the high accompanying haze of string instruments that later swell up ecstatically. We sense that Aida and Radames are already far out of this world, perfectly attuned to each other (they sing the same tune in octaves) in a love that transcends death itself.

Conclusion   Before the final curtain, a figure in mourning enters the temple above the tomb to pray. Drained of all the emotion that she poured out in earlier scenes, Amneris can only whisper on a monotone, "Peace, I pray for peace" *(Pace t'imploro)*. The different psychic states of the characters are made more vivid by simultaneous contrast, a principle we saw at work in Mozart's opera buffa ensembles (see page 205). Amneris's grief is set directly against the ecstatic, otherworldly togetherness of Radames and Aida.

High violins take over the duet melody; one can almost visualize the souls of Aida and Radames ascending to "eternal day." And by giving the last words to the priests—the judges of Radames and the proponents of Egypt's wars—Verdi hands them the ultimate responsibility for the threefold tragedy.

CHORUS OF PRIESTS (with harp accompaniment)

Im - menso, immenso Ftha, del mon - do spirito ani - ma-tor
Great Phtha, the world's creative spirit

TEXT: Verdi, *Aida,* Tomb Scene, Act IV, scene ii

RECITATIVE: Radames alone, then Aida

Part 1: Radames reflects *Quiet orchestral introduction (strings) sets the mournful mood. Radames sings his first three lines on a monotone. Accompaniment: slow and halting.*

Radames: La fatal pietra sovra me si chiuse;	The fatal stone closes over me;
Ecco la tomba mia.	This is my tomb.
Del dì la luce più non vedro . . .	The light of day I'll never see again.
Non rivedrò più Aida.	I'll never see Aida.
Aida, ove sei tu? possa tu almeno	Aida, where are you?
Viver felice, e la mia sorte orrenda	Live happily, and never know
Sempre ignorar!	Of my terrible death.

Part 2: Radames hears a sound *Accompaniment: the rhythm picks up*

Radames: Qual gemito—una larva—un vision . . .	What sound was that? a ghost? a vision?
No! forma umana è questa . . . Ciel, Aida!	No, a human form . . . Aida!
Aida: Son io . . .	Yes . . .
Radames: Tu, in questa tomba!	You, in this tomb!

Part 3: Aida explains *Accompaniment: mournful low notes*

Aida: Presago il core della tua condanna,	A presentiment of my heart foretold your sentence;
In questa tomba che per te s'appriva	This tomb awaited you—
Io penetrai furtiva,	I hid secretly in it,
E qui lontana da ogni umano sguardo	And here, far from any human gaze,
Nelle tue braccia desiai morire	I wanted to die in your arms.

ARIOSO I

3.1 **Radames reacts in despair** *"Con passione"—passionately*

Radames: Morir! si pura e bella!	Dying, so innocent and beautiful,
Morir per me d'amore,	Dying, for love of me!
Degli anni tuoi nel fiore,	So young,
degli anni tuoi nel fiore fuggir la vita!	so young to give up life!
T'avea in cielo per l'amor creata,	You were made in heaven for love
Ed io t'uccido per averti amata!	And I have killed you by loving you!
No, non morrai, troppo t'amai, troppo	You cannot die! you are too beautiful, I
sei bella!	love you too much!

ARIOSO II

Aida, "almost in a trance" *Ethereal high strings*

Aida: Vedi? di morte l'angelo	See, the angel of death
Radiante a noi s'appressa,	Approaches us in radiance,
Ne adduce a eterni gaudii	Leading to eternal joys
Sovra i suoi vanni d'or.	On his golden wings.
Già veggo il ciel dischiudersi;	I see the heavens open;
Ivi ogni affano cessa,	Here pain ceases,
Ivi *commincia l'estasi*	Here begins the ecstasy
D'un immortal amor.	Of immortal love.

CHORUS (on the upper stage) with interjections by Radames and Aida *Modal harmonies, harp, and flute*

Aida: Triste canto!	Mournful chant!	**Chorus:** Immenso Ftha,
Radames: Il tripudio dei sacerdoti . . .	The priestly rites . . .	del mondo spirito animator,
Aida: Il nostro inno di morte.	Our funeral hymn.	noi t'invocchiamo.
Radames: Nè le mie forti braccia	All of my strength cannot	
Smuovere ti potranno, o fatal pietra!	Move that fatal stone!	Great Ptah,
Aida: Invan—tutto e finito	In vain—all is finished	the world's Creative spirit,
Sulla terra per noi.	For us on earth.	we invoke thee.
Radames: È vero, è vero!	True, it is true.	

DUET: First Aida, then Radames with Aida *With quiet high strings*

Aida and
4.2 **Radames:**

O terra, addio, addio, valle di pianti,	Farewell to earth, vale of tears,
Sogno di gaudio che in dolor svani,	Dream of happiness which vanishes in grief;
A noi *si schiude* il ciel,	The heavens open,
si schiude il ciel e l'alme erranti	And our fleeing souls
Volano al raggio dell'eterno dì.	Escape to the rays of eternal day.

CHORUS (on the upper stage) singing with Aida and Radames
DUET continues: Aida and Radames together (same music) with Amneris and the Chorus

Aida and
Radames: O terra addio, addio valle di pianti,
       Sogno di gaudio che in dolor svani,
       A noi *si schiude* il ciel,
          si schiude il ciel e l'alme erranti
       Volano al raggio dell'eterno dì.

Amneris: Pace t'imploro, salma adorata,
       Isi placata, *Isi placata* ti schiuda il ciel,
          pace t'imploro, pace. . . .

I beg you for peace, beloved spirit;
May Isis, placated, welcome you to
   heaven . . . peace, peace. . . .

Chorus: Immenso Ftha,
       del mondo spirito animator,
       noi *t'invocchiamo.*

Great Ptah,
the world's Creative spirit,
we invoke thee.

Ends with violins playing the "O terra" tune, Amneris singing "Pace, pace," and the Chorus repeating "Immenso Ftha!"

(1813–1883)

Richard Wagner

Chief Works: Early operas, including *The Flying Dutchman, Tannhäuser* and *Lohengrin*

Mature "music dramas": *Tristan und Isolde, The Mastersingers of Nuremberg, Parsifal,* and *The Ring of the Nibelung,* a four-opera cycle consisting of *The Rhinegold, The Valkyrie, Siegfried,* and *The Twilight of the Gods*

Siegfried Idyll, for small orchestra (based on themes from *Siegfried;* a surprise birthday present for Cosima)

Wagner was born in Leipzig during the turmoil of the Napoleonic wars; his father died soon afterward. His stepfather was a fascinating actor and writer, and the boy turned into a decided intellectual. Wagner's early interests, literature and music (his idols were Shakespeare and Beethoven), later expanded to include philosophy, mythology, and religion.

As a young man he worked as an opera conductor, and he spent an unhappy year in Paris trying to get one of his works produced at the influential Opéra there. Wagner's strong anti-French sentiments stemmed from this experience. Back in Germany, he produced the first of his impressive operas, *The Flying Dutchman* and *Tannhäuser,* and wrote *Lohengrin;* the last two of these soon became very popular. Though all three works basically adhere to the early Romantic opera style of Carl Maria von Weber, they already hint at the revolutionary ideal for opera that Wagner was pondering.

This he finally formulated after being exiled from Germany (and from a job) as a result of his part in the revolution of 1848–1849. He wrote endless articles and books expounding his ideas—ideas that were better known than his later operas, for these were extremely difficult to stage. His chief book, *Opera and Drama,* set up the principles for his first "music drama," *The Rhinegold,* the first number of the extraordinary four-evening opera *The Ring of the Nibelung.* He also published a mean essay attacking Mendelssohn, who had just died, and other Jews in music; fifty years after Wagner's death, his anti-Semitic writings (and his operas) were taken up by the Nazis.

Wagner's exile lasted thirteen years. His fortunes changed dramatically when he gained the support of the young, unstable, and finally mad King Ludwig II of Bavaria. Thanks to Ludwig, Wagner's mature music dramas were at last produced (*The Rhinegold,* completed in 1854, was not produced until 1869). Wagner then promoted the building of a special opera house in Bayreuth, Germany, solely for his music dramas—grandiose, slow-moving works based on myths, and characterized by high-flown poetry of his own, a powerful orchestral style, and the use of *leitmotivs* (guiding or leading motives). To this day the opera house in Bayreuth performs only Wagner. For many years his last music drama, *Parsifal* (1882), was allowed to be produced only at Bayreuth, which became in effect a Wagnerian shrine.

A hypnotic personality, Wagner was able to spirit money out of many pockets and command the loyalty and affection of many distinguished men and women. His first marriage, to a singer, ended in divorce; his great oper-

Wagner, Cosima, and their son Siegfried. Named after the hero of *The Ring of the Nibelung,* Siegfried eventually succeeded Cosima as director of the Bayreuth festivals of his father's operas.

atic hymn to love, *Tristan und Isolde,* was created partly in response to his love affair with the wife of one of his patrons. His second wife, Cosima, daughter of Franz Liszt, had been married to an important conductor, Hans von Bülow, who nonetheless remained one of Wagner's strongest supporters. Cosima's diaries tell us a great deal about Wagner's moods, dreams, thoughts, and musical decisions, all of which he shared with her. After the death of "the Master," Cosima ruled Bayreuth with an iron hand.

Half con man and half visionary, bad poet and very good musician, Wagner created a storm of controversy in his lifetime which has not entirely died down to this day. He was a major figure in the intellectual life of his time, a thinker whose ideas were highly influential not only in music but also in other arts. In this sense, at least, Wagner was the most important of the Romantic composers.

2 Wagner and "Music Drama"

Richard Wagner was, after Beethoven, the most influential of all nineteenth-century composers. His strictly musical innovations, in harmony and orchestration, revolutionized instrumental music as well as opera. In terms of opera, Wagner is famous for his novel concept of the "complete work of art" (*Gesamtkunstwerk,* see below) and his development of a special operatic technique, that of the "guiding motive" (leitmotiv).

Unlike earlier innovative composers, it seems Wagner could not just compose; he had to develop elaborate theories announcing what art, music, and opera ought to be like. (Indeed, he also theorized about politics and philosophy, with unfortunate results.) Wagner's extreme self-consciousness as an artist was prophetic of attitudes toward art of a much later period.

His theory of opera had its positive and negative sides. First, Wagner wanted to do away with nearly all the conventions of earlier opera, especially the French and Italian varieties. Opera, he complained, had degenerated from its original form as serious drama in music—Wagner was thinking of ancient Greek drama, which he knew had been sung or at least chanted—into a mere "concert in costume." He particularly condemned arias, which were certainly at the heart of Italian opera, as hopelessly artificial. Why should the dramatic action keep stopping to allow for stretches of pretty but undramatic singing?

The "Total Work of Art"

The positive side of Wagner's program was the development of a new kind of opera in the 1850s, which he called "music drama." Music, in these works, shares the honors with poetry, drama, and philosophy—all furnished by Wagner himself—as well as the stage design and acting. Wagner coined the word **Gesamtkunstwerk,** meaning "total work of art," for this powerful concept.

Since words and ideas are so important in the *Gesamtkunstwerk,* the music is very closely matched to the words. Yet it is also unrelievedly emotional and intense, as Romantic doctrine required. The dramas themselves deal with weighty philosophical issues, or so at least Wagner and his admirers believed, and they do so under the symbolic cover of medieval German myths and legends.

This was another Romantic feature, one that strikingly anticipated Freud, with his emphasis on myths (for example, the myth of Oedipus) as embodiments of the deepest unconscious truths. Thus Wagner employed the old romance of Tristan and Iseult, the saga of the Nordic god Wotan, and the Arthurian tale of Sir Perceval to present his views on love, political power, and religion, respectively.

Strikingly evident in this formal photograph are Wagner's determination and relentless will to succeed—something he liked to flaunt in his well-known luxurious style of dress.

Wagner was one of the first great conductors, and a superb orchestrator. He raised the orchestra to new importance in opera, giving it a new role modeled on Beethoven's symphonies with their motivic development. Leitmotivs (see below) were among the motives he used for this "symphonic" continuity. The orchestra was no longer used essentially as a support for the singers (which was still the situation, really, even in Verdi); it was now the orchestra that carried the opera along. Instead of the alternation of recitatives, arias, and ensembles in traditional opera, "music drama" consisted of one long orchestral web, cunningly woven in with the singing.

Leitmotivs

A **leitmotiv** (guiding, or leading, motive) is a musical motive associated with some person, thing, idea, or symbol in the drama. By presenting and developing leitmotivs, the orchestra in a Wagner music drama guides the listener through the story. Wagner could have found a precedent for this idea in Berlioz's *idée fixe* in the *Fantastic* Symphony, which we examined at the end of Chapter 16. But whereas the *idée fixe* is a full-sized tune, a leitmotiv is a motive—a short fragment.

Leitmotivs were easy to ridicule when they were used mechanically—when, for example, the orchestra obligingly sounded the Sword motive every time the hero spoke about his weapon. On the other hand, leitmotivs could suggest with considerable subtlety what the hero was thinking or feeling even when he was saying something else. Wagner also became very skillful in thematic transformation—the characteristic variationlike technique of the Romantic composers (see page 250). By transforming the appropriate motives, he could show a person or an idea developing and changing under the impact of dramatic action.

And since, for the Romantics, music was the undisputed language of emotion, leitmotivs—being music—could state or suggest ideas in *emotional* terms, over and above the intellectual terms provided by mere words. This was Wagner's theory, a logical outcome of Romantic doctrine about music. Furthermore, the complex web of leitmotivs provided his long music dramas with the thematic "unity" that Romantic composers sought. On both counts, psychological and technical, leitmotivs were guaranteed to impress the nineteenth century.

RICHARD WAGNER (1813–1883)
Tristan und Isolde (1859)

Two major life experiences helped inspire Wagner's first completed music drama, *Tristan und Isolde.* One was his discovery of the Romantic philosophy of Arthur Schopenhauer, and the other was his love affair with Mathilde Wesendonck, the wife of one of his wealthy patrons.

Schopenhauer had made his own philosophical formulation of the Romantic insight into the central importance of music in emotional life. All human experience, said Schopenhauer, consists either of emotions and drives —which he called "the Will"—or of ideas, morals, and reason, which he downgraded by the term "Appearance." He insisted that the Will always dominates Appearance, and that our only direct, unencumbered sense of it comes through music.

Mathilde Wesendonck

For the philosopher, the inevitable domination of the Will was a source of profound pessimism. But a composer could read another message in Schopenhauer's work. It reinforced Wagner's conviction that music was specially privileged for emotional representation, that the deepest truths—those to do with the Will—could indeed be plumbed by music, in a music drama. And what would exemplify the Will better than the most exciting human drive that is known, sexual love? As usual, the story itself would be taken from a medieval legend.

Tristan und Isolde is not just a great love story, then, but something more. It is a drama that presents love as the dominant force in life, one that transcends every other aspect of worldly Appearance. Many love stories hint at such transcendence, perhaps, but Wagner's makes it explicit, on the basis of an actual philosophy that the composer espoused.

Like Wagner's other music dramas, *Tristan und Isolde* derived its story from a medieval tale. In this miniature from the fourteenth century, the ship is sailing to Cornwall.

Background   Written by Wagner himself, though derived from a medieval legend, the story of *Tristan und Isolde* shows step by step the growing power of love. In Act I, when Tristan and Isolde fall in love by accidentally drinking a love potion, the Will overpowers Isolde's fierce pride, which had previously made her scorn Tristan as her blood enemy. It also dissolves Tristan's heretofore perfect chivalry, the machismo of the medieval knight, which had demanded that he escort her safely to her marriage to King Mark of Cornwall, his uncle and liege lord.

In Act II, love overcomes the marriage itself when the two meet adulterously (in the longest unconsummated love scene in all of opera). The lovers' tryst is discovered, and Tristan is mortally wounded—but love seems to negate the wound. In Act III he simply cannot or will not die until Isolde comes to him. Then, after Isolde comes and he dies in her arms, she herself sinks down in rapture and expires also. For both of them, death is not a defeat but an ecstatic expression of love.

At this point (if not earlier) the plot passes the bounds of reality—which was exactly Wagner's point. Tristan and Isolde, representing Schopenhauer's Will, move in a realm where conventional attitudes, the rules of society, and even life and death have lost their powers. Transcendence was a recurring theme of Romanticism; here love becomes the ultimate transcendent experience, beyond reality. Indeed, the opera's transcendental quality brings it close to mystical experience.

Incidentally, Wagner and Mathilde did not live up to their operatic ideals. After a while, Wesendonck—the King Mark in this triangle—put his foot down and the affair came to an end.

Prelude Given Wagner's emphasis on the orchestra in his music dramas, it is not surprising that the strictly orchestral Prelude (or Overture) to *Tristan und Isolde* is already a magnificent depiction of romantic love. Or at least one aspect of romantic love: not the joys of love, but love's yearning.

3 Cassette 2B-2/3 CD 2-7
6 Cassette 4A-5/6 CD 4-5

The Prelude opens with a very slow, fragmentary motive whose ending harmonies create a remarkably sultry, sensual, yearning feeling:

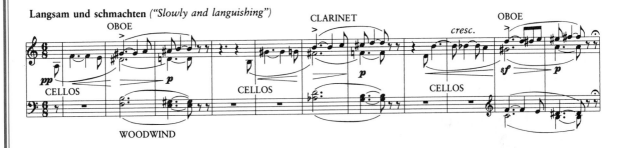

Often treated (as here) in a threefold sequence (see page 31), this motive turns out to be the opera's chief leitmotiv. It becomes associated with a rich compound of meaning, including passion, yearning, and release in death. At the risk of oversimplification, we can label it the Love–Death motive.

This Love–Death motive is an example of a Romantic theme that derives its essential character from harmony, rather than from melody or rhythm. The harmony is dissonant: it does not feel at rest, and we feel it needs to proceed to some other harmony. After the slow opening sequence, the music stretches up and up—still very slowly!—but when the dissonance finally resolves, it resolves in the "wrong" place and still sounds decidedly uneasy. A rich, much more clearly melodic theme follows, played by the cellos:

As new themes emerge—yet are they new, or are they subtle transformations of earlier themes?—we realize that Wagner is never going to let the music rest. A marvelous dark churning of emotion is produced partly by incessant sequences, partly by Wagner's very characteristic trick of avoiding cadences.

The music constantly shifts in key (modulates); every time it seems ready to stop at a cadence, it surges restlessly ahead.

In form, the total Prelude amounts to a gradual, irregular crescendo, reaching a climax with a return of the original threefold sequence on the Love–Death motive. Then there is a hush. The motive is heard again in brooding new versions, growing quieter and quieter, so that when the curtain goes up the orchestra has fallen entirely silent, without ever having come to a cadence.

"Philter" Scene from Act I   A short segment of the action from Act I of *Tristan und Isolde* will show how Wagnerian music drama works, and how it makes dramatic use of previously introduced leitmotivs—in this case, the Love–Death motive and its threefold sequence, featured in the opera's Prelude.

6 Cassette 4A-6/6 CD 4-6

In Act I, a bleak shipboard scene, Isolde is being escorted by Tristan to Cornwall, the kingdom of King Mark. To her maid and confidante, Brangaene, she furiously denounces Tristan, bewails her coming marriage to King Mark, and mutters something about a loveless marriage. "Loveless?" answers Brangaene. "But anyone would love you; and if he doesn't, we have our magic potions."

First, we hear a short solo passage that is as close as Wagner got to writing a clear-cut aria. The music is seductive and sweet, but though Brangaene certainly sings rich melodic phrases, they do not fall together into a tune. Her melody follows the words closely, without word repetitions. Such repetition, which was taken for granted in all Baroque and Classical arias and ensembles, Wagner would have called an "artificial" feature. The orchestra develops its own seductive motive more freely and more consistently than does the singer.

ORCHESTRA   BRANGAENE: Wo   leb - te der Mann, der dich nicht liebte?

Lowering her voice, and glancing meaningfully at Isolde, Brangaene asks her if she has not forgotten her mother's magic love potion. (Isolde's mother was a famous sorceress.) Here her singing line is like heightened recitative. In the orchestra the Love–Death leitmotiv sounds in its sultry way, three times, in a sequence, as in the Prelude. Through the orchestra, Brangaene is hinting about the love potion.

Isolde answers her by imitating or parodying her recitative: no, she has not forgotten her mother's magic; and the Love–Death motive sounds again. But whatever Brangaene was hinting about, Isolde in her despair is thinking instead of the "death philter," a poison. She recalls a special philter that she marked for just such an occasion as this. At the thought (not even the mention!) of death, a sinister new motive emerges in the trombones. And when Isolde actually *mentions* the death philter and Brangaene realizes that she means to kill herself, the orchestra practically explodes. A harsh, intense passage paints Brangaene's horror.

Trombone

Wagner's time-scale is often enormously slow, as we recall from the Prelude. He can, however, move fast enough when he chooses. Before Brangaene can fully absorb the enormity of the situation, she is cut off by a vigorous sailors' sea chantey announcing that land is in sight—the Cornwall so hated and feared by Isolde. The women's moody talk is dramatically interrupted. Tristan's squire, Kurvenal, enters and tells them roughly to get ready for landing.

Again, this passage for Kurvenal is not really a song or an aria. Exactly the same points can be made about it as about Brangaene's speech. Though Kurvenal's song is melodious enough, the main musical idea is an orchestral motive, not the singer's melody; no one will leave the theater humming Kurvenal's music. Yet its bluff accents characterize the man sharply, especially by comparison with the more sensitive, more impassioned women.

(Isolde's suicide never takes place, of course. Brangaene switches the philters, and Isolde and Tristan drink the aphrodisiac, setting the opera's slow, inexorable action into motion.)

Isolde and Brangaene, from a Metropolitan Opera production

TEXT: Wagner, *Tristan und Isolde,* **"Philter" Scene, from Act I**

(Note: The English translation attempts to reproduce the "antique" quality of Wagner's poetry.)

BRANGAENE'S SONG

ORCHESTRA

Brangaene:

Wo lebte der Mann,	Where lives a man
Der dich nicht liebte? Der Isolden säh'	Who does not love you? who sees you
Und Isolden selig nicht ganz verging'?	And sinks not into bondage blest?
Doch, der dich erkoren, wär' er so kalt,	And, if any bound to you were cold,
Zög' ihn von dir ein Zauber ab,	If any magic drew him from thee,
Den Bösen wüsst' ich bald zu binden	I could soon draw the villain back:
Ihn bannte der Minne Macht.	And bind him in links of love.

Love-Death motive, three times

	(Secretly and confidentially)
Kennst du der Mutter Künste nicht?	Mind'st thou not thy mother's arts?
Wähnst du, die alles klug erwägt,	Do you think that she the all-wise
Ohne Rath in fremdes Land	Helpless in distant lands
Hätt' sie mit dir mich entsandt?	Would she have sent me with you?

Love-Death motive, three times

Isolde:

Der Mutter Rath gemahnt mich recht;	My mother's counsel I mind aright;
Willkommen preis' ich ihre Kunst;	And highly her magic arts I hold:
Rache für den Verrath,	Vengeance for treachery,
Ruh' in der Noth dem Herzen!	Rest for the broken heart!
Den Schrein dort bring' mir her!	Yon casket hither bear!

Brangaene:

Er birgt was heil dir frommt,	It holds a balm for thee:
	(Brings out a golden medicine chest)
So reihte sie die Mutter,	Your mother filled it
Die mächt'gen Zaubertränke:	With the most powerful philters;
Für Weh' und Wunden Balsam hier,	For pain and wounds there's salve,
Für böse Gifte Gegengift;	For poisons, antidotes;
Den hehrsten Trank, ich halt' ihn hier.	The noblest draught is this one—

New, ominous motive—
Death motive

Isolde:

	(Takes out a phial)
Du irrst, ich kenn' ihn besser;	Not so, you err: I know a better;
Ein starkes Zeichen schnitt ich ihm ein.	I made a mark to know it again:
Der Trank ist's, der mir taugt!	Here's the drink that will serve me!

	(Seizes another flask)
Brangaene: Der Todestrank!	The death philter!

Sailors (offstage):

Ho, he, am Untermast!	*Ho, heave ho! Watch the lower mast!*
Die Segel ein! Ho, he!	*The mainsail in! Heave ho!*

Isolde:

Das deute schnelle Fahrt.	That tells of a swift journey;
Weh' mir, Nahe das Land!	Woe's me! Near to the land!
	(Kurvenal enters, boisterous and insolent)

KURVENAL'S SONG

Kurvenal:

Auf, auf, ihr Frauen!	Up, up, ye ladies!
Frisch und froh! Rasch gerüstet!	Look lively, now! Bestir you!
Fertig nun, hurtig und flink!	Be ready, and quick, prepare!
Und Frau Isolden, sollt' ich sagen	Dame Isolde, I'm told to tell you,
Von Held Tristan, meinem Herrn:	By Tristan our hero, my master:
Vom Mast der Freude Flagge	The mast is flying the joyful flag;
Sie wehe lustig ins Land;	It waveth landwards aloft;
In Marke's Königschlosse	From King Mark's royal castle
Mach' sie ihr Nahen bekannt.	May our approach be seen.
Drum Frau Isolde bät' er eilen,	So, Dame Isolde, he bids you hasten
Für's Land sich zu bereiten	For landing to prepare you,
Dass er sie könnt' geleiten.	So that he may there conduct you.

3 Late Romantic Opera

Opera continued to flourish in the late Romantic era, in the years after Wagner and Verdi. The orchestra retained the important role it had achieved in the work of both composers. Passages of emotional expression now tend to break down into ever freer and more fragmentary melodic forms, and the distinction between "recitative" and "aria" sections becomes harder to maintain. Wagner's leitmotiv technique was employed in nearly all operas, in one form or another, for its dramatic power was acknowledged by composers and audiences alike.

What composers, librettists, and audiences turned away from, however, was Wagner's mythical, quasi-philosophical ideal for opera. "Music drama" in Wagner's sense gave way to new realistic tendencies. Modern-day subjects were chosen for operas, showing realistic middle- or lower-class characters, rather than kings and queens, gods and goddesses. Typically, librettists emphasized the sordid and violent aspects of life, as far as the censorship of the day allowed.

From a 1984 movie version of *Carmen*

A well-known early example of "realism" in opera is *Carmen* (1874), by the French composer Georges Bizet. Set in contemporary Spain, it is a tale of a fiery, sexually irresistible gypsy girl who works in a cigarette factory and a soldier who loses her to a small-town matador. In Italy, a general literary movement called *verismo* ("realism") extended to opera; here the leading work was *Cavalleria rusticana* (1888) by Pietro Mascagni. A Sicilian peasant girl becomes pregnant, and when her boyfriend deserts her for a married woman, the husband knifes him . . . all very different in spirit from the elevated love-deaths we have seen in Wagner and Verdi.

Giacomo Puccini (1858–1924)

Giacomo Puccini

Puccini was the leading Italian opera composer after Verdi. Several operas that he wrote around 1900 are perennial favorites, thanks to Puccini's special gift for short, intense melodic phrases and his very canny sense of the stage.

Most of Puccini's operas are touched by the new realistic tendencies in late Romantic opera; yet they have important exotic elements that tend to distance the audience from what would otherwise be quite harsh dramatic messages. The locales of his operas range from Japan to the American Wild West, and from eighteenth-century Rome, under Napoleon, to the never-never land of an artists' "Bohemia" in Paris. In these remote, even charming sites, Puccini found it easy to view realistic stories through romantic rose-colored glasses.

Like other late nineteenth-century opera composers, Puccini probed deeper and deeper into psychological depiction with his music. It is not that composers of this generation probed more deeply than Mozart, Wagner, or Verdi; but they did investigate emotions that the earlier composers had never touched. Puccini specialized in intimate, almost voyeuristic emotional analyses of helpless women in hopeless situations. Such is the actress Tosca, propositioned by the Napoleonic police chief as the price for her lover's life *(Tosca);* or the geisha girl Cho-Cho-San, deserted by her cynical "husband" *(Madama Butterfly);* or the poor seamstress Mimi, who is always cold, dying of consumption *(La Bohème).*

While these are not exactly "ordinary" people, they are not remote historical or mythical figures like Aida or Isolde, either. There is no doubt that the shift to more realistic drama makes it easier for audiences to identify directly with Puccini's characters than with those of earlier Romantic opera.

GIACOMO PUCCINI
"Un bel dì," aria from Act II of *Madama Butterfly* (1904)

6 Cassette 4B-1/6 CD 4-7

Puccini's *Madama Butterfly,* derived from a play by the American author David Belasco, has a disturbingly "realistic" story. The composer softened it after the opera's initial unfavorable reception.

In the wake of Commodore Perry's expeditions to Japan in the 1850s, a thoughtless young naval officer, Lieutenant Pinkerton, marries a fifteen-year-old geisha girl, Cho-Cho-San, whom he calls "Madam Butterfly." He then sails away without any intention of honoring the Japanese ceremony. Blindingly naive, charming, deeply emotional, and unaware of the duplicity of Western males, Cho-Cho-San persists against all evidence in hoping he will return to her. When he returns, however, he brings his "real" American wife, and Cho-Cho-San kills herself.

The opera's most famous aria, *"Un bel dì,"* is sung by the unfortunate girl (now a mother) three years after she has been deserted. In response to her maid, Suzuki, who cannot believe they will ever see the day when Pinkerton returns, Cho-Cho-San spins a fantasy about that very day.

From the hills (she sings) they will first see a little wisp of smoke, as the gunboat appears on the horizon. The aria's quiet main theme has a distant, disembodied quality; we can detect a poignant air of fantasy about it:

Andante molto calmo

Un bel dì ve-dremo   Levar-si un fil di   fu-mo Sull'estre-mo confin del mare,   E   poi la nave appare.

But she will not run down to the dock—she will wait on the hilltop; and the music seems to wait as she says this. They will see a tiny figure running up the hill. Is it he? Yes! But Cho-Cho-San will hide—partly, she says, to tease him a bit, and partly so as not to break down completely, not to die of joy, as she puts it, when she hears him calling her all his old pet names.

Madama Butterfly: the publisher's handsome cover for the original edition

Here Cho-Cho-San sings her heart out to the melody of the aria's opening theme—a stroke of almost unbearable pathos, for it dramatizes the helpless growth of her fantasy. Originally linked to the hope that Pinkerton's ship would return to Nagasaki, which could happen (and in Act III, actually does), the theme now expresses her joy at Pinkerton's return to her—which is sheer delusion. Hence, when we hear the theme one more time, played very loudly and emotionally by the orchestra after Cho-Cho-San's last words, it is heavy with tragic resonance.

TEXT: **Puccini,** *Madama Butterfly,* Aria, *"Un bel di"*

Un bel dì vedremo	One day we shall see
Levarsi un fil di fumo	A tiny thread of smoke rise up
Sull'estremo confin del mare;	On the horizon, out at sea;
E poi la nave appare.	And then the ship will appear.
Poi la nave bianca	Now the white ship
Entra nel porto; romba il suo saluto.	Sails into port; cannons roar a welcome!
Vedi? è venuto!	You see? he has come!
Io non gli scendo incontro—io no;	I shan't run to meet him—not I;

Mi metto	I shall come
Là sul ciglio del colle e aspetto,	Up here on the hilltop, and wait,
E aspetto gran tempo,	And wait as long as I have to,
E non mi pesa la lunga attesa.	And not count the hours of waiting.
E uscito dalla folla cittadina	Then out of the crowd down in the city
Un uomo, un picciol punto,	A man—a little speck—
S'avvia per la collina.	Is starting up the hill.
Chi sarà, chi sarà? E come sarà giunto	Is it he? is it he? And when he's come
Che dirà, che dirà?	What will he say? what will he say?
Chiamerà: "Butterfly" dalla lontana . . .	He'll call out: "Butterfly!" from afar . . .
Io senza dar risposta	Without answering,
Me ne starò nascosta	I'll hide myself,
Un po' per celia, e un po'	Partly to tease him a bit, and partly
Per non morire al primo incontro!	So as not to die when we first meet!
Ed egli alquanto in pena chiamerà, chiamerà:	And then he'll be worried and call:
"Piccina mogliettina, olezzo di verbena"—	"Little child-wife! Verbena blossom!"—
I nomi che mi dava al suo venire.	The names he gave me when he was here before.
Tutto questo avverà, te lo prometto!	All this will happen, I promise you!
Tienti la tua paura;	Suppress your fears!
Io con sicura fede l'aspetto!	Full of faith I am waiting!

Richard Strauss (1864–1949)

The most important composer of German operas from around 1900 on, Richard Strauss, was also an important composer of symphonic poems. Sometimes called "Richard II" because of the way he expanded on certain of Richard Wagner's techniques, Strauss was an almost bewilderingly diverse and skillful composer. His dramatic subjects range from everyday realism—his *Intermezzo* dramatizes a fight he had with his wife—to a lengthy mythological-philosophical music drama in Wagner's spirit, *Die Frau ohne Schatten* ("The Woman without a Shadow").

Richard Strauss

Opera composers of his generation, as we have said, probed more and more deeply into unusual psychological states. With Strauss, these extended from the almost physical sense of bliss that one can get when suddenly smitten with love at first sight, in the "Presentation of the Rose" scene in his *Der Rosenkavalier* ("The Knight of the Rose"), to sentiments that had simply been taboo on the opera stage before his time. Such, for example, was the young Princess Salome's sexually tinged eulogy to the severed head of Saint John the Baptist in *Salome,* derived from the then-scandalous play by Oscar Wilde.

RICHARD STRAUSS
Presentation of the Rose, from *Der Rosenkavalier,* Act II (1911)

Richard Strauss's *Der Rosenkavalier* is a brilliant comedy—half sentimental, half cynical—about life in eighteenth-century Vienna. It opens before breakfast in the boudoir of an aging (i.e., thirty-something) field marshal's wife, who is entertaining her very young lover, the handsome Count Octavian. Strauss has him sung by a mezzo-soprano dressed as a man; the idea seems to be that he is so young his voice hasn't changed yet. They chatter about love and transcendence in a very amusing parody of Wagner's *Tristan und Isolde.*

Act II introduces Sophie, the innocent young daughter of a wealthy merchant. She is in a state of almost hysterical excitement at the prospect of marriage to an older nobleman. Now, the custom in Vienna—a custom invented by Strauss's librettist—was that the bridegroom in an arranged marriage would not meet his bride-to-be until a relative had come on his behalf and made a formal presentation of a silver rose. The "knight of the rose" *(Rosenkavalier)* in this case is none other than Octavian. When he and Sophie set eyes on each other they fall instantly, giddily in love.

Strauss catches this feeling with music that seems almost suspended in time, as an oboe winds slowly around beautiful yet restrained melodic phrases. It is interspersed with a kind of magical tinkling, as though Sophie and Octavian were literally seeing stars. Groups of delightfully dissociated chords are played by celeste, flutes, and high strings:

Notice how the singing starts in a declamatory, recitative-like style, when the two exchange formal remarks, and gradually gets more aria-like as they sink into their own thoughts. At the end, their thoughts and feelings merge in an actual fragment of duet. The words, too, grow less "realistic" and more poetic as feelings take over from ceremony.

TEXT: Strauss, *Der Rosenkavalier*, Act II, Presentation of the Rose

(Enter Octavian, bareheaded, dressed all in white and silver, carrying the Silver Rose in his hand. Behind him his servants in his colors, white and pale green. Octavian, taking the rose in his right hand, advances with high-born grace toward Sophie, but his youthful features bear traces of embarrassment, and he blushes. Sophie turns pale with excitement at his splendid appearance. They stand opposite each other, each disconcerted by the confusion and beauty of the other.)

Octavian: Mir ist die Ehre widerfahren, dass ich der hoch und wohl-geborenen Jungfer Braut, in meines Herrn Vetters Namen, dessen zu Lerchenau Namen, die Rose seiner Liebe über-reichen darf.

The honor has fallen to me, most noble and high-born lady and bride, on my kinsman's behalf, by name the Baron von Lerchenau, to present to you the rose of his love.

Sophie: Ich bin Euer Liebden sehr verbunden ... ich bin Euer Liebden in aller Ewigkeit verbunden ...
Hat einen starken Geruch wie Rosen, wie lebendige!

I am deeply indebted to your highness ... I am forever eternally indebted to your highness ... *[embarrassed]*
Oh, it has a powerful fragrance, just like a real rose!

Octavian: Ja, ist ein Tropfen persischen Rosenöls darein getan ...

[Tries to make conversation] Yes, a drop of Persian attar has been put on it ...

Sophie: Wie himmlische, nicht irdische, wie Rosen vom hochheili-gen Paradies. Ist ihm nicht auch?
Ist wie ein Gruss vom Himmel ... ist bereits zu stark, als dass man's ertragen kann! Zieht einen nach, als lägen Stricke um das Herz ...

It's like a heavenly rose, not an earthly one—like the roses of paradise. Do you think so too?
It's like a message from heaven ... it's so strong, I can scarcely bear it! It's like something pulling at my heart ...

Sophie (with Octavian): (Wo war ich schon einmal und war so selig? Dahin musst ich zurück, dahin, und müss ich völlig sterben auf dem Weg. Allein ich sterb ja nicht. Das ist ja weit!
Ist Zeit und Ewigkeit in einem sel'gen Augenblick, den will ich nie vergessen bis an meinen Tod.)

[To herself] (Have I ever been here before? Was I ever so blissful? If I could recapture this moment, I'd be ready to die—but I'm not dying, not yet!
All time and eternity are in this moment, which I'll remember till the day I die.)

Octavian (with Sophie): (Wo war ich schon einmal und war so selig? Ich war ein Bub, da hab ich die, die noch nicht gekannt. Wer bin denn ich? Wie kommt denn ich zu ihr? Wie kommt denn sie zu mir?
Wär ich kein Mann, die Sinne möchten mir vergehn; das ist ein sel'ger Augenblick, den will ich nie vergessen bis an meinen Tod.)

[To himself] (Have I ever been here before? Was I ever so blissful? Up to now I've been just a child, before I saw her. Who am I? What fate has brought me to her, brought her to me?
If I weren't a grown man, I'd go mad. This moment I'll remember till the day I die.)

Chapter 18

The Late Romantics

The year 1848 in Europe was a year of failed revolutions in France, Italy, and in various of the German states. Political freedom, which for the Romantics went hand in hand with freedom of personal expression in life and art, seemed further away than ever. While not all the early Romantics lived in free societies, at least by today's standards, freedom was an ideal they could take seriously as a hope for the future. We recall Beethoven's enthusiasm for Napoleon as revolutionary hero, reflected in the *Eroica* Symphony of 1803, one of the landmarks of nineteenth-century music. And in the 1820s the Romantics thrilled to Byron's personal role in the struggle for Greek independence, then lamented his death near the field of battle.

But the failure of the revolutions of 1848 symbolized the failure of Romantic aspirations. In truth, those aspirations had had little to nourish them since the days of Napoleon. Romanticism lived on, but it lived on as nostalgia.

The year 1848 is also a convenient one to demarcate the history of nineteenth-century music. Some of the greatest early Romantic composers—Mendelssohn, Chopin, and Schumann—died between the years 1847 and 1856. By a remarkable coincidence of history, too, the 1848 revolution transformed the career of Richard Wagner; as we noted in his biographical sketch in Chapter 17, he was exiled from Germany for speeches from the barricades, so that he had no opera house to compose for. Instead of composing, he turned inward and—after a long period of philosophical and musical reflection—worked out his revolutionary musical ideas. Wagner's music dramas, written from the 1850s on, came to dominate the imagination of musicians in the second part of the century, much as Beethoven's symphonies had in the first part.

Romanticism and Realism

It is interesting that European literature and art from the 1850s on was marked not by continuing Romanticism, but by realism. The novel, the principal literary form of the time, grew more realistic from Dickens to Trollope and George Eliot in Britain, and from Balzac to Flaubert and Zola in France. In French painting, there was an important realistic school led by Gustave Courbet. Even more important as regards realism in the visual arts, no doubt, was that powerful new invention, the camera.

Realists in the arts tended toward glum or grim subject matter. The Philadelphia artist Thomas Eakins was so fascinated by surgery that he painted himself in among the students attend-, ing a class by a famous medical professor, Dr. S. D. Gross (*Gross Clinic*, 1875).

We have seen some traces of realism in opera, notably in the "verismo" (veristic) school of Italian opera. On the other hand, the myth-drenched music dramas of Wagner were as unrealistic as could be. And what would "realism" in orchestral music be like? Given music's nature, it was perhaps inevitable that late nineteenth-century music assumed a sort of inspirational and emotional escape function—an escape from political, economic, and social situations that were not romantic in the least.

Perhaps, too, music serves a similar function for many listeners of the late twentieth century. Significantly, concert life as we know it today, with its emphasis on great masterpieces of the past, was formed for the first time in the late nineteenth century.

1 Late Romantic Program Music

Late Romantic program music took its impetus from an important series of works called "symphonic poems," composed in the 1850s by Franz Liszt. A **symphonic poem** is a one-movement orchestral composition with a program, in a free musical form. By using the word "poem," Liszt insisted on the music's programmatic nature.

It is not often that a great virtuoso pianist such as Liszt, who started out composing etudes and other miniatures of the kind cultivated by Chopin and Schumann, turns himself into a major composer of large-scale orchestral works. Liszt's formula was simply to write a long one-movement piece for orchestra associated in one way or another with a famous poem, play, or narrative poem. Though obviously inspired by the earlier genres of program music (see page 269), Liszt departed from them in musical form, as well as in style. Unlike a Berlioz program symphony, a symphonic poem was in one movement. Unlike a Mendelssohn concert overture, it was not written in sonata form or some clear derivation of sonata form.

Although the term failed to gain universal acceptance, perhaps partly because the concept was not altogether original, symphonic poems under that or some other name became very popular in the later nineteenth century.

Among Liszt's symphonic poems are *Hamlet, Orpheus, Prometheus,* and *Les Préludes,* the latter loosely connected with a poem by the French Romantic poet Alphonse de Lamartine. But except for *Les Préludes,* these works are heard less often today than other symphonic poems written by composers influenced by Liszt's example. The most popular of later symphonic poems are those by Peter Ilyich Tchaikovsky and Richard Strauss.

Peter Ilyich Tchaikovsky

(1840–1893)

Chief Works: Symphonies No. 4, 5, and 6 *(Pathétique);* violin concerto; piano concertos

Operas: *The Queen of Spades* and *Eugene Onegin,* based on works by the Russian Romantic poet Alexander Pushkin

Symphonic poems: *Romeo and Juliet, Hamlet, Francesca da Rimini, Overture 1812* (about Napoleon's retreat from Russia in that year)

Ballet scores: *Swan Lake, Sleeping Beauty, The Nutcracker*

Tchaikovsky was born in the Russian countryside, the son of a mining inspector, but the family moved to St. Petersburg (now Leningrad) when he was eight. In nineteenth-century Russia, a serious musical education and a musical career were not accorded the social approval they received in Germany, France, or Italy. Many of the famous Russian composers began in other careers and only turned to music in their mature years, when driven by inner necessity.

Tchaikovsky was fortunate in this respect, for after working as a government clerk for only a few years, he was able to enter the brand-new St. Petersburg Conservatory, founded by another Russian composer, Anton Rubinstein. At the age of twenty-six he was made a professor at the Moscow Conservatory. Once Tchaikovsky got started, after abandoning the civil service, he composed prolifically—six symphonies, eleven operas, symphonic poems, chamber music, songs, and some of the most famous of all ballet scores: *Swan Lake, Sleeping Beauty,* and *The Nutcracker.*

Though his pieces may sometimes sound "Russian" to us, he was not a devoted nationalist like Modest Musorgsky and other composers of the time. Of all the nineteenth-century Russian composers, indeed, Tchaikovsky had the greatest success in concert halls around the world. His famous Piano Concerto No. 1 was premiered in 1875 in Boston, and he toured America as a conductor in 1891 (see page 243).

Tchaikovsky was a depressive personality who more than once attempted suicide. He had been an extremely delicate and hypersensitive child, and as an adult he worried that his dominant homosexual bent would be discovered and exposed. In an attempt to raise himself above suspicion, he married a highly unstable young musician who was in love with him. The marriage was a fiasco; in a matter of weeks, Tchaikovsky fled and never saw his wife again. She died in an asylum.

For many years Tchaikovsky was subsidized by a remarkable woman, Nadezhda von Meck, a wealthy widow and a recluse. She not only commissioned compositions from him but actually granted him an annuity. By mutual agreement, they never met; nevertheless, they wrote intimate letters every day over the thirteen years of their friendship. This strange arrangement was terminated, without explanation, by Madame von Meck.

Tchaikovsky never understood this rejection, and was crushed by it. Three years later he died after drinking unboiled water during a cholera epidemic.

PETER ILYICH TCHAIKOVSKY
Romeo and Juliet (Overture-Fantasy) (1869, revised 1880)

Tchaikovsky wrote several symphonic poems, including one on a subject already used by Liszt (and Berlioz), Shakespeare's *Hamlet*. Rather than "symphonic poem," he preferred the descriptions "symphonic fantasia" or "overture-fantasy" for these works. They are lengthy pieces in one movement, with free forms adopting some features from sonata form, rondo, and so on.

In his *Romeo and Juliet*, Tchaikovsky followed the outlines of the original play only in a very general way, but one can easily identify his main themes with elements in Shakespeare's drama. The surging, romantic string melody clearly stands for the love of Romeo and Juliet. The angry, agitated theme suggests the vendetta between their families, the Capulets and the Montagues —and, more generally, the fate that dooms the two "star-cross'd lovers," as Shakespeare calls them. The hymnlike theme heard at the very beginning of the piece (later it sounds more marchlike) can perhaps be associated with the kindly Friar Laurence, who devises a plan to help the lovers that goes fatally wrong.

Slow Introduction   The slow introduction of *Romeo and Juliet* is already heavy with drama. As low clarinets and bassoons play the sober Hymn theme, the strings answer with an anguished-sounding passage forecasting an unhappy outcome. The wind instruments utter a series of solemn announcements, interspersed by strumming on the harp, as though someone (Friar Laurence?) was preparing to narrate a serious, tragic tale. This sequence of events is repeated, with some variation, and then both the woodwind and string themes are briefly worked up to a climax over a dramatic drum roll.

Allegro   The tempo changes to allegro, and we hear the Vendetta or Fate theme. It is made up of a number of short, vigorous rhythmic motives, which Tchaikovsky at once begins to develop. Then the Vendetta theme returns in a climax punctuated by sensational cymbal claps.

The highly romantic love theme (illustrated on page 245) is first played only in part, by the English horn and violas—a mellow sound. It is halted by a curious but affecting passage built out of a little sighing figure:

VIOLINS, muted

pp   Sighing motive

The Love theme, now played at full length by the French horn, is made doubly emotional by a new accompaniment derived from the sighing motive (marked with a bracket above).

After the Love theme dies down at some length, a lively development section begins (a feature suggesting sonata form). Confronted by various motives from the Vendetta theme, the Hymn theme takes on a marchlike character. We may get the impression of a battle between the forces of good and evil.

The Vendetta theme returns in its original form (suggesting a sonata-form recapitulation). The sighing motive and the lengthy Love theme also return, but the end of the latter is now broken up and interrupted by angry sounds

A famous Juliet of Tchaikovsky's time: Mrs. Patrick Campbell in an 1895 London production of Shakespeare's play

—a clear reference to the tragic outcome of the drama. At one last appearance, the Vendetta theme is joined more explicitly than before with the Hymn theme.

Coda (slow)   A fragment of the Love theme appears in a broken version over funeral drum taps in the timpani. This seems to depict Romeo's pathetic final speeches, where he refers to his love before taking poison. A new, slow theme in the woodwinds is really a transformation of the sighing motive heard earlier.

But the mood is not entirely gloomy; as the harp strumming is resumed, the storyteller seems to derive solace and inspiration from his tale. Parts of the Love theme return for the last time in a beautiful new cadential version, surging enthusiastically upward in a way that is very typical of Tchaikovsky. Doesn't this ecstatic surge suggest that even though Romeo and Juliet are dead, their love is timeless—that their love transcends death? The influence of Wagner's *Tristan und Isolde* was felt here as everywhere in the later nineteenth century.

2   Nationalism

One legacy of Romanticism's passion for freedom played itself out all through the nineteenth century: the struggle for national independence. The Greeks struggled against the Turks, the Poles rose up against Russia, the Czechs revolted against Austria, and Norway broke free of Sweden. All over Europe, people were becoming more conscious of their history and destiny, their national character, and their artistic heritage.

This gave rise to a musical movement, **nationalism** in music. The characteristic feature of this movement is the incorporation of national folk music into concert pieces, songs, and operas. Symphonic poems or operas were based on programs or librettos that dilated on national themes—on a hero of history such as Russia's Prince Igor; a national literary treasure such as the Finnish Lemminkaïnnen legends; or a beloved river such as the Vltava (Moldau) in Bohemia. Such national themes were reinforced by actual musical themes taken from folk song. The result was music that stirred strong emotions at home, and often made an effective ambassador abroad.

LISTENING CHART NUMBER 14

Tchaikovsky, Overture-Fantasy, *Romeo and Juliet*

18 min., 39 sec.

3 Cassette 2B-3/3 CD 2-8
6 Cassette 4B-2/6 CD 4-8

INTRODUCTION (Andante)

	00.00	**Hymn theme**	In the low woodwinds, *pp*
	00.46	**String motives**	Anguished quality; contrapuntal
	01.25	**Strumming harp**	With "announcements" in the high woodwinds
8.2 8.2	02.07	**Hymn theme**	High woodwinds with pizzicato strings. Followed by the string motives and harp; the "anouncements" are now in the strings.
8.3 8.3	03.57	**Buildup**	Ends with drum roll, *f*
	04.31	**Preparation**	Prepares for the main section; *p,* then *crescendo*

MAIN SECTION (Allegro)

8.4 8.4	05.01	**Vendetta theme**	Full orchestra, *f*
	05.23		Development of the Vendetta theme; contrapuntal
	05.47		Reaches a climax: cymbals
	05.58	**Vendetta theme**	Full orchestra, *ff*
	06.18		Relaxes, in a long slowdown
	06.58		Prefatory statement of Love theme (English horn): phrase **a**
8.5 8.5	07.13		"Sighing" theme; muted strings, *pp*
8.6 8.6	07.51	**Love theme**	Form is **a b a,** in woodwinds, with the sighing motive played by the French horn.
	08.51		Harp. Cadences; the music dies down and nearly stops.

Development

8.7 8.7	09.52	**Developmental combination**	Vendetta theme fragments are combined with the Hymn theme, which now sounds more like a march than a hymn.
8.8 8.8	11.06		This works up to a climax, marked by a cymbal clash.
	11.29	**Hymn theme**	Played by trumpets; syncopated rhythm in the cymbals

CYMBALS

Free Recapitulation (abbreviated)

8.9 8.9	11.57	**Vendetta theme**	Full orchestra, *ff*
	12.21		Sighing theme; woodwinds
	12.59	**Love theme**	**a b a;** ecstatically in the strings, with the sighing motive again in the French horn; the last **a** is *ff*.
8.10 8.10	14.01		Fragments of the Love theme
	14.28	**(Love theme)**	Sounds like another ecstatic statement, but is interrupted.
	14.36		Interruption by the Vendetta theme: conflict! Cymbals
	14.51	**Developmental combination**	Vendetta theme fragments combined with the Hymn theme Builds up to *fff*
	15.23		Then dies down, rather unwillingly; ends on drum roll, *f*

Coda (Moderato)

8.11 8.11	15.58	**Love theme**	A broken version of the Love theme, with muffled funeral drums. The music seems to be ending.
8.12 8.12	16.37	**New theme**	Woodwinds; ends with a transformation of the sighing motive
	17.43	**Love theme**	Section **a** in a slow cadential "transcendent" version. The strumming harp of the slow introduction has returned.
	18.17		Final cadences; a drum roll and solemn ending gestures

Nationalism: Finnish myths inspired both the composer Jan Sibelius and his compatriot the painter Akseli Gallen-Kalela. The wounded hero Lemminkaïnen is tended by his mother, who sends bees to fetch a healing balm from a magic fountain.

Though in the nineteenth century political nationalism was certainly a major factor all over Europe, composers in Germany, Italy, and France are not categorized with the musical nationalists. For musical nationalism also strove to make local music independent of Europe's traditional cultural leaders. Nationalist composers often deliberately broke the traditional rules of harmony, form, and so on. They did this both in a spirit of defiance, and also in an effort to develop new, genuinely local musical styles.

Exoticism

Audiences came to enjoy hearing folk music at symphony concerts, whether it was their own folk music or somebody else's. We have seen Verdi write "Egyptian" music, in the priests' hymn in *Aida*. And there are cases of Frenchmen writing Spanish music, Russians writing Italian music, and Czechs writing American music (George Bizet's opera *Carmen,* Tchaikovsky's orchestra piece *Capriccio Italien,* and Antonin Dvořák's famous *New World* Symphony). Such music cannot be called nationalistic, since its aim was not national self-definition. Perhaps the best name for it is "exotic."

Yet even this nonpolitical, exotic music had the effect of emphasizing the unique qualities of nations. In the later nineteenth century, Romantic individuality had become a national ideal, as much as a personal one.

The Russian "Kuchka"

A close group of five Russian nationalist composers were nicknamed (by one of their critic friends) the *kuchka*—sometimes translated as the "Mighty Five," but actually meaning a group or clique. They were an interesting group, with only one trained musician among them, Mily Balakirev (1837–1910). Alexander Borodin (1833–1887) was a distinguished chemist, César Cui (1835–1918) an engineer, Nikolai Rimsky-Korsakov (1844–1908) a navy man, and Modest Musorgsky (1839–1881)—usually regarded as the most talented of the *kuchka*—an officer in the Russian Imperial Guard.

Unit V

The Twentieth Century

This unit, which deals with music from around 1900 on, brings our survey of Western music up to the present. Looking back to 1900, we can recognize today's culture in an early form. Large cities, industrialization, inoculation against disease, advertising, processed food, even the first automobiles, telephones, and phonographs—all were present by the beginning of the twentieth century.

Hence many of the phenomena treated in this unit will strike us as fairly familiar, compared to those of earlier centuries. For one thing, the widespread availability of art to a mass audience—not just to various elite groups, as in the past—is something we take for granted. This change came about in the twentieth century partly from sociological causes and partly from technological ones: as distinctions among the classes of society gradually broke down, this process was hastened by the introduction of the phonograph and movies around 1900, radio around 1920, and television around 1950. We also take for granted the split that has occurred between "art" (or so-called classical) music and popular music. A rift that had opened up in the nineteenth century widened in the twentieth.

We are also aware of the force of American popular music. The characteristic features of this music were formed around 1900, once again. With the evolution of ragtime and early jazz, a vital rhythmic spring derived from African-American sources was brought into the general American consciousness. This led to a long series of rich developments: swing, bebop, rhythm and blues, rock, rap. After World War II, when the United States began to play a larger political role in the world at large, our popular music became a world language.

Modernism and Traditionalism

What was "art" music like in this same period? In America as elsewhere, art music itself experienced a split. On the one hand there was music that we shall call "modernist," on the other hand, music of a more traditional nature.

The term modernist *requires a word of explanation. It is not the same as* contemporary *or* modern, *terms that refer to anything at all that happens to take place in the present; the -ist at the end of the word* modern *gives it an extra twist. The modernists of 1900 were artists and intellectuals who insisted on their modernity—that is, their anti-traditionalism—and who formed a specific cultural movement. Modernism was marked by radical experimentation. Though its roots go back earlier, this movement peaked during the years 1890 to 1918—a period of astonishing breakthrough works by such novelists, poets, and painters as Marcel Proust and James Joyce, Ezra Pound and T. S. Eliot, Pablo Picasso and Henri Matisse.*

The chief composers associated with the modernist movement were Claude Debussy, Arnold Schoenberg, and Igor Stravinsky. Sometimes they are referred to as members of the "avant-garde"; **avant-garde***—"vanguard" —is a military or at least a militant term that has long been embraced by radical artists and intellectuals to denote the forefront of their activity.*

The avant-garde has been a vital force in the arts from the middle of the nineteenth century up to the present. For we continue to use the terms modernism *and* avant-garde *for a new phase of radical experimentation after World War II, associated with an international galaxy of composers such as Pierre Boulez, Karlheinz Stockhausen, Luciano Berio, György Ligeti, and George Crumb. At the same time, some artists found that they could comfortably continue in the general spirit of late Romanticism, or even look back to earlier styles. Though avant-gardists often claimed that the old principles of art had been "used up," we can now see, some years after the event, that this was not so. There was still plenty of potential left in more traditional methods.*

In this unit we shall begin with European avant-garde music of the twentieth century. Though avant-garde music has been the more interesting, if only (though not only) because it has been so innovative, traditional music has continued to exert a broad general appeal. In a final chapter on American music, Chapter 21, we shall see how both innovation and tradition have thrived in our own country—on both sides of the rift, in both "classical" and popular music.

Chapter 19

Introduction: The Modernist Movement

Modernism in art, literature, and music flourished especially from around 1890 to 1918, the end of World War I. It was an unusually brilliant movement. A sharp reaction to late nineteenth-century culture, especially to the accepted rules of art within that culture, modernism found amazing resources within the materials of the arts themselves. It is probably the case that never before have all the arts gone through such revolutionary developments together.

1 Industrialization and Progress

Industrialization is the overriding historical fact of the nineteenth century. Ever since the first so-called age of science in the seventeenth century, technological discoveries had come faster and faster, and industry was transformed. The harnessing of steam power in the eighteenth century was matched by the discovery of electricity in the nineteenth; Europe and America were crisscrossed with railroads, built for the benefit of industry and commerce. In the early twentieth century, automobile and air travel were in their early stages of development, as were telephones, movies, and sound recordings.

Essentially rural societies, controlled by stable aristocracies, turned into urban societies run by self-made entrepreneurs. These changes occurred at

Music (as we have seen in this book) is a popular subject for artists; but few have been so fascinated by music as Raoul Dufy (1877–1953).

breakneck speed, as people saw at the time. Yet no one could have forecast how the stresses caused by such social changes would lead on the one hand to the disturbing artistic-intellectual movement known as modernism, and on the other to the catastrophe of World War I.

On the contrary, "official" nineteenth-century culture was permeated by a sense of confidence in progress. Progress in science and technology, it was thought, would be matched in due time by progress in human affairs. And although there was ample evidence to the contrary—for example, in the terrible conditions of the new industrial poor, as exposed by the novels of Charles Dickens—this evidence was easy to ignore, especially by the rich and powerful who were profiting from technology's advances.

Science and Uncertainty

But another side of progress became evident in the ominous development of weaponry. The deadly novelty of the American Civil War was the rifle, effective over five times the range of previous shoulder weapons. In World War I, tanks, submarines, and poison gas showed technology's terrible potential for destruction. Casualties in World War I have been estimated at 40 million military and civilian dead from war, famine, and epidemic, and 20 million wounded. With World War I, nineteenth-century confidence in progress—a response to the successes of technology—was thrown into question by technology itself.

By this time, however, the groundwork for such loss in confidence had already been laid by science in other areas. Men and women were shaken in their most basic assumptions about life by puzzling advances in physics, biology, and psychology.

> The impact of Einstein's theory of relativity (which later in the century made its own contributions to the technology of weaponry) was at first more philosophical than practical in nature. The idea that things depend on the standpoint of the observer, and cannot be counted on according to the "objective" rules of Newtonian physics, rocked people's sense of certainty.

> For many, this uncertainty simply deepened a crisis in religion that the Victorians had already experienced as a result of scientific theories of evolution. Here the key figure was Charles Darwin. Were human beings created by God in God's image, as the Bible teaches, or were they descended by an impersonal process from animals? The disturbance that this caused in people's sense of stability is still reflected in today's disputes about creationism.

> Meanwhile the psychological theories of Sigmund Freud suggested that in spite of what people thought they were doing or feeling, they were in fact controlled by unconscious drives. The idea of men and women in the grip of irrational forces of their own (or their parents') making was a troubling one. At the same time, the prospect of working out one's "problems" through psychoanalysis gave the new century its paradigm for personality change.

2 The Response of Modernism

If the traditional laws of physics, biblical truth, and psychological certainty could no longer be accepted, it seemed a small enough step to question the rules, conventions, assumptions, and prohibitions surrounding the arts.

Cubism was one of the earliest forms of abstract or near-abstract art; this painting is by the leading cubist, Georges Braque. One can discern the score of *Socrate*, by a leading modernist composer, Erik Satie.

One such assumption was that visual art had to represent something. Once this idea was questioned, and then abandoned, the materials of painting and the other arts could be used for themselves—and a whole world of abstract (or nonrepresentational) painting opened up. This general category includes cubism, abstract expressionism, op art, and other such subcategories.

In literature, the basic assumptions were those of ordinary sentence structure, syntax, and grammar. Freedom from these conditions allowed novelists and poets to move into a whole new sphere of suggestion. Using the so-called stream of consciousness method, James Joyce ended his novel *Ulysses* of 1922 with a famous long section—forty pages, without punctuation or paragraphs—tracking the miscellaneous but not-so-idle thoughts of a character who hadn't even spoken until then, Molly Bloom, as she lies in bed.

In music, the basic assumptions were melody and its close associates harmony and tonality. These assumptions, too, were thrown into doubt. One of the most discussed of all avant-garde compositions, Arnold Schoenberg's song cycle *Pierrot lunaire* ("Moonstruck Pierrot") of 1912, employs a kind of half-speaking, half-singing style that the composer called *Sprechstimme* (speech-song). Ranging from a throaty whisper to a near-hysterical shriek, *Sprechstimme* was an explicit denial of melody—and the entire song cycle of twenty-one songs is written in this style (see page 359).

New Languages for Art

Avant-garde artists developed whole new languages for art—for example, the "languages" of cubism and serialism (discussed on page 336) for communication in painting and music, respectively. If we use the word *language* literally, the most dramatic case is that of James Joyce. At the end of his life, the great Irish novelist wrote *Finnegans Wake* in a language that is part English, part other languages, and part a construction of words he invented.

Schoenberg, once again, provides a striking analogue in music. His twelve-tone method, or **serialism,** developed in the 1920s, replaced the old "language" for music based on harmony and tonality. By arranging the twelve notes of the chromatic scale into fixed patterns, and manipulating those patterns by means of mathematical operations, Schoenberg arrived at a radical new way of composing music—and hearing it, too.

To this day, few people understand *Finnegans Wake* or follow Schoenberg's serial compositions. Perhaps, some day, more people will. Or perhaps these are esoteric art works, the result of artists' concentrating on solving problems for their own sake, rather like "pure" scientific investigation. But if some modernists invented languages to speak to themselves and their followers alone, this was a risk they felt they had to take. Joyce, Picasso, and Schoenberg could no more hold to the old rules than their contemporaries in science, such as Albert Einstein, Niels Bohr, and Marie Curie, could operate within the bounds of traditional physics and chemistry.

However this may be, a good deal of avant-garde art became removed from an audience, and hence abstracted from a base in society. At the same time, intense concentration on artistic materials sometimes led to abstraction of another kind, the abstraction of technique from expression. Some people welcomed this emphasis on technique as a relief from the overheated emotionality of late Romantic art. Especially in the 1920s, "objectivity" was an ideal upheld by certain artists. And their works sometimes struck the public as "abstract" in a cold, dry sense.

Characteristic of this phase of the avant-garde were various experiments with schematic, even mathematical devices in the arts. Later, in the 1930s, the Dutch painter Piet Mondrian made striking pictures out of straight lines at right angles to one another, and juxtaposed planes of bright color. Among composers, Igor Stravinsky was known for his provocative statements extolling objectivity and attacking Romantic music—and certainly the brisk, almost mechanistic rhythms that characterize Stravinsky's style are diametrically opposed to rubato, the rhythmic "stretching" that contributes so much to nineteenth-century music's emotionality.

Several lesser composers, fascinated by "machine" rhythms, even tried to evoke machinery in their works: the American George Antheil *(Ballet mécanique)*, the Russian A. V. Mosolov *(The Iron Foundry)*, and the Swiss Arthur Honegger *(Pacific 231*—a locomotive).

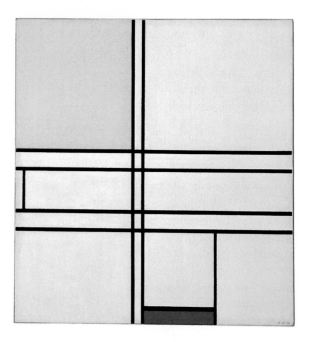

Composition with Blue and Yellow, by Piet Mondrian, 1935

3 Literature and Art before World War I

A significant social development of the avant-garde was the tendency for artists of various kinds to gravitate together in formal or informal groups, both for mutual encouragement and for the exchange of ideas.

Thus Claude Debussy was friends with several symbolist poets. Schoenberg, himself a painter, associated with a group of artists who set forth their ideas in *The Blue Rider,* a magazine named after a picture by the pioneer nonrepresentational painter Wassily Kandinsky (see page 329). Stravinsky and Maurice Ravel belonged to a group of artists and intellectuals in Paris who called themselves the Apaches. With all this interchange, it is not surprising that one can sometimes detect similar tendencies in music and the other arts.

Cover for *The Blue Rider,* a magazine that promulgated expressionist art and music

Impressionists and Symbolists

As we have already remarked, modernism got its start in the late nineteenth century and then peaked in the twentieth. The best-known modernist movement, **impressionism,** dates from 1870s, when people were astonished by the flickering network of color patches by which impressionist painters rendered simple scenes from everyday life (as in Edouard Manet's *In the Boat*). Yet the impressionists claimed that to catch the actual, perceived quality of light on a river, they had to use such a technique. They proudly called themselves "realists," in reaction to the idealized and overemotional art of Romanticism.

In the Boat by Edouard Manet (1832–1883), master painter in the impressionist style among others

Roughly contemporary with impressionism was **symbolism,** a consciously *un*realistic movement. Symbolism began in poetry, as a revolt against the "realism" of words being used for reference—for the purpose of exact definition. The symbolists wanted words to perform their symbolizing or signifying function as freely as possible, without having to follow rules of syntax, sentence structure, and argument. The meaning of a cluster of words might be vague and ambiguous, even esoteric—but also rich, "musical," and endlessly suggestive.

"Musical" was exactly what the symbolists called it. They were fascinated by the music dramas of Richard Wagner, where again musical symbols —Wagner's leitmotivs—refer to elements in his dramas in a complex, ambivalent, multilayered fashion. All poets use "musical" devices such as rhythm and rhyme, but only the symbolists were prepared to go as far as to break down grammar, syntax, and conventional thought sequence to approach the elusive nonreferential quality of music.

T. S. Eliot's *The Waste Land* of 1922 is a major symbolist-inspired poem in English (which quotes from Wagner's *Tristan und Isolde*). Eliot's last great poem even has a musical title: *Four Quartets* (1943).

Claude Debussy is often called an impressionist in music, because his fragmentary motives and little flashes of tone color recall the impressionists' painting technique. Debussy can also be called a symbolist, since suggestion, rather than outright statement, is at the heart of his aesthetic. Famous symbolist texts inspired two famous Debussy works: the orchestral *Prelude to "The Afternoon of a Faun"* (a poem by Stéphane Mallarmé), and the opera *Pelléas et Mélisande* (a play by Maurice Maeterlinck). Especially in the latter, Debussy's elusive musical symbols and Maeterlinck's elusive verbal ones combine to produce an unforgettable effect of mysterious suggestion.

In *Meyerbeer's Opera "Robert le Diable,"* by Edgar Degas (1834–1917), the atmospheric, light-splashed dancers contrast with the gloomy musicians, who are depicted almost photographically. Impressionism and realism were closely related; for all their differences, they can coexist in the same picture.

Les Chaumes à Cordeville,
by Vincent van Gogh, 1890

Expressionists and Fauves

There was also a symbolist movement in painting. In his picture entitled
Music, the Viennese painter Gustav Klimt (1862–1918) used the girl's bowed
head, her mysterious instrument, the sculpted lion, and the mask to suggest
much more in the way of a mood than they actually represent (see page 333).
Symbolism is also the force behind the powerful images in the work of a
much greater painter, Vincent van Gogh (1853–1890); the distorted rooftop
and the almost liquid tree are not there to represent reality, but to symbolize
the artist's disturbing vision of the universe. Even in Van Gogh's most
extreme works, however, the trees are still recognizably trees.

In Vienna and Paris—which were also the great centers of avant-garde
music—two émigré painters pursued separate but parallel paths toward completely abstract painting. The series of "rider" paintings by Wassily Kandinsky
(1866–1944) shows step by step how the process was accomplished. Kandinsky belonged to a German movement in the arts called **expressionism,**
which sought to express the most extreme of human feelings by divorcing art
from everyday literalness. Anguish, even hysteria, could be conveyed by the
harsh clashing of strong colors, irregular shapes, and jagged lines. What seems
to be conveyed is the artist's inner turbulence—completely abstracted, in
Kandinsky's *Romantic Landscape,* from the outer world.

Horses and riders, as depicted by Wassily Kandinsky over a four-year period, show his path toward nonrepresentational painting. In the first picture, the figures are quite clear; in the last, they could be missed entirely. Top left: *Couple on Horseback* (1907); top right: *Blue Mountain* (1909); bottom: *Romantic Landscape* (1911)

Parallel to the expressionists was a short-lived group in Paris who were dubbed *Les fauves,* "the wild beasts." The *fauves* experimented with distorted images bordering on the grotesque; they also employed motifs from primitive art as though in defiance of what they saw as a decadent European culture. In Pablo Picasso's famous *fauve* painting *Les Démoiselles d'Avignon* of 1907 (Avignon is a street in the red-light district of Picasso's native Barcelona), the quality of abstraction is evident in the angular bodies and the African-masklike heads—a complete break with the conventional rules of human portrayal. Picasso took the final step toward abstraction a little later when he turned to cubism (see page 323).

Picasso's famous *fauve* shocker *Les Démoiselles d'Avignon* (1907)

Pablo Picasso, *Les Démoiselles d'Avignon* (1907), oil on canvas, 8′ x 7′8″. Collection The Museum of Modern Art, New York. Acquired through the Lillie P. Bliss Bequest.

There is violence in both Kandinsky's and Picasso's work of this period. Such, at least, was the shocked perception of a generation used to the nonthreatening art of the impressionists—painters of flickering summer landscapes, soft-edged nudes, and diaphanous action pictures of the ballet. Composers, too, courted violence in their music; they sent similar shock waves through the devotees of Wagner, Verdi, Brahms, and Tchaikovsky. The Hungarian composer Béla Bartók wrote a "barbarous" piano piece entitled *Allegro barbaro.* Stravinsky, in his ballet *The Rite of Spring,* depicted ritual rape and murder in the fertility ceremonies of primitive Slavic tribes.

4 Music before World War I

Music never enjoyed (or suffered) a link to the tangible world that was comparable to representation in painting, or to reference in poetry, but it did have its own stable, universally accepted set of principles, its own traditional "internal logic." This rested upon elements that we have discussed many times in this book: tune, motive, harmony, tonality, tone color, and rhythm.

The music of Bach, Beethoven, and Brahms was based on this "logic," and so was the entire stream of European folk songs, popular songs, dances, military marches, and the rest. Avant-garde music moved away from this norm. Like abstract, nonrepresentational painting, music worked out new principles based on the materials of the art itself.

We can lay our main emphasis in music before World War I on developments in melody, harmony, and tonality, for on the whole, these features were the main preoccupations of avant-garde composers in that period. Developments in tone color and rhythm—or, more broadly, musical sonority and musical time—dominated music after World War II.

Experiment and Transformation: Melody

Melody, harmony, and tonality all work closely together. In historical terms, harmony arose as a way of supporting and adorning melody, and tonality first arose as a means of clarifying harmony; then tonality functioned as a more general way of organizing music. Each of these functions was transformed in the early twentieth century.

The Flute, a woodcut by
Swiss artist Félix Vallotton
(1865–1925)

We have seen the Viennese Classical composers bring tunes to the fore in their music, and the Romantics capitalize on tunes as the most emphatic means of conveying powerful emotion. Yet Wagner, despite the melodic quality of many of his leitmotivs, was criticized for the confusing quality of his singing lines, and Mahler's audiences were puzzled and irritated by the bittersweet distortions that he applied to folklike melodies. In his later works, such as his unfinished Tenth Symphony of 1911, Mahler wrote increasingly intricate and difficult melodic lines. The long melodies surge, swoop, and yearn in a strange, painful manner.

And by that time another Viennese composer, Arnold Schoenberg, was writing even more complex melodies that simply made no sense to contemporary listeners. The intense rhythms and the anguished intervals of Romanticism were there, but the actual notes did not appear to hang together at all. This was the melody of expressionism.

The disintegration of traditional melody was accomplished in other ways by French composers. In many (not all) of his works, Claude Debussy used only the most shadowy motives—a constant suggestion of melody without clear tunes. A little later Igor Stravinsky, writing in Paris, seized upon Russian folk songs but whittled them down (or abstracted them) into brief, utterly simple and impassive fragments.

New Scales

The traditional diatonic scale had been used for so long that it was almost regarded as a fact of nature. But composers around 1900 cast a speculative eye over the basic sound materials of music; for the first time in centuries, new scales were experimented with seriously. Thus Debussy and others used the **pentatonic scale,** a five-note scale playable on the black notes of the keyboard. Imported from folk song, this scale was tried in all kinds of music, not only (as before) in nationalist or other folk-derived compositions.

Two further scales are abstract constructions, significantly enough, which anyone can figure out by systematically analyzing the total chromatic scale. The **whole-tone scale** divides the octave into six equal parts—all of its intervals are whole steps; again, Debussy made much use of this resource. The

octatonic scale—a specialty with Stravinsky—fits eight pitches into the octave by alternating whole and half steps. Less used, the **quarter-tone scale** employs all the pitches of the chromatic scale plus the pitches that come halfway between each pair of them.

This mysterious, suggestive image of Music, with her even more mysterious symbolic attributes, haunted the Viennese painter Gustav Klimt; she appears in several of his works.

Does nature imitate art? This snapshot of Debussy (second fom the left) and some friends is startlingly similar in mood to the impressionist painting by Manet shown on page 326.

"The Emancipation of Dissonance"

As melody grew more complex, more fragmentary, or more vague, harmony grew more and more dissonant. The concepts of consonance and dissonance, as we noted on page 37, rest on the fact that certain chords (consonant chords) sound stable and at rest, whereas others (dissonant chords) sound tense and need to resolve to consonant ones. In a famous phrase, Schoenberg spoke of "the emancipation of dissonance," meaning emancipation from that need to resolve. Dissonance was to be free from the "rule" that says it must always be followed by the appropriate consonance.

To be sure, dissonance and consonance are relative matters; there are mild or "low-level" dissonances (play A on the piano together with the G above it) and more tense, "high-level" dissonances (play A and G and all the nine notes between them simultaneously). As early twentieth-century composers explored higher and higher levels of dissonance, they discovered that a kind of resolution could be obtained by proceeding not from dissonance to consonance, but from high-level dissonance to low-level dissonance. Slowly listeners began hearing this, too. Today we accept it as a matter of course.

A whole new range of possibilities opened up in the way chords could succeed one another. This led to new expressive horizons—for the alternation of tension and stability is one of the secrets of music's emotive power. Could one write fully "emancipated" dissonance, requiring no resolution at all? In the early twentieth century, there was no aspect of music that intrigued composers more, and agitated listeners more, than dissonant harmony.

Tonality and Atonality

Tonality is the feeling of centrality, focus, or "homing" that we get from simple tunes and much other music. As melody grew more complex or fragmented, and harmony grew more dissonant, tonality grew more indistinct. Finally, some music reached a point at which no center could be detected at all. This is **atonal** music.

However, just as consonance and dissonance are not open-and-shut concepts, neither are tonality and atonality. Most Baroque music sounds firmly rooted in its key, for example, whereas certain Romantic music seems rather to hover around a general key area. Much early twentieth-century music that was criticized as "atonal" can be heard on careful listening to have a subtle sense of tonality after all.

In fact, tonality had been deliberately and routinely weakened by composers of earlier music—when, for example, they modulated again and again in the development section of Classical sonata form. (At the recapitulation, of course, tonality was restored with a vengeance.) And Wagner's *Tristan und Isolde* shifts tonality almost continuously. This is the very feature that gives the five-hour opera its sultry mood of never-to-be-satisfied longing.

Wagner, as we recall, went further than other Romantic composers in the direction of *chromaticism,* the free use of all twelve notes of the chromatic scale. Since tonality depends on one pitch standing out from the others in the ordinary diatonic scale (for example, C in the C-major scale C D E F G A B), when all twelve chromatic pitches are used freely, the centrality of any single one is automatically diluted. Wagner's technique of chromaticism was a significant forecast of the coming trend toward atonality.

Melody, harmony, tonality: all are closely related. Beleaguered conservatives around 1900 referred to them jocularly as the "holy trinity" of music. The "emancipation" of melody, harmony, and tonality all went together. This joint emancipation counts as the central style characteristic of the first phase of twentieth-century avant-garde music.

5 Between the Two World Wars

Only twenty-one years, from 1918 to 1939, separated the two cataclysmic wars of the twentieth century. It was an uneasy period. The terrible devastation of World War I had stunned artists as well as everybody else, and the sorts of extravagant experimentation that had marked the prewar period no longer seemed appropriate. There was a new tendency toward abstraction, and also a search for standards and norms.

Had atonality gone too far? When dissonance was "emancipated," what else was let out of the cage? Composers began to look back to earlier music, music with a more ordered, stable aesthetic. Without attempting to write music that sounded like Bach or Mozart, they developed modern styles that absorbed some of the older composers' principles and procedures. This movement was called *neoclassicism.*

Musicologists argue about the extent of neoclassicism and debate its different varieties, and nobody wants to push every composer of the 1920s into this category. There were still radical experimenters working at the time, among them a Frenchman who had emigrated to America, Edgard Varèse (see page 410). But the two most influential, trend-setting modernists of music— Arnold Schoenberg and Igor Stravinsky—reconsidered their art after the war, modified their styles, and developed individual neoclassical positions.

> Schoenberg, as has been noted on page 323, developed his twelve-tone method at this time, thus providing a radical new language for music. This important composing method, also known as serialism, which in effect systematized atonality, is discussed further on pages 336–337.

Is this not the height of musical modernism, then? Yes, in one sense. But in another sense, the very fact of systematization counts as an orderly, controlled, "neoclassical" phenomenon. Furthermore, there was a striking change in the kinds of music that Schoenberg now favored. Whereas previously he had pioneered novel kinds of free-form music, he now turned to traditional genres and forms: string quartet and suite, sonata form, and theme and variations.

> Stravinsky was a more obvious case. He went so far as to rewrite older music with his own (sometimes slight, though always telling) modifications: his *Pulcinella* (1920) stays very close to music by the Baroque composer G. B. Pergolesi. More freely, Stravinsky's *Dumbarton Oaks* Concerto (1938) evokes the *Brandenburg* Concertos of Bach (see page 137). Unlike Schoenberg, Stravinsky in the interwar period was never an atonalist.

> In Chapter 20 we shall examine two other modernist composers who are among the most important, Béla Bartók and Alban Berg. The last work written by each—Bartók's Piano Concerto No. 3 (1945) and Berg's Violin Concerto (1935)—are tonal (half tonal, in Berg's case) and even Romantic in spirit.

Serialism

Of all early twentieth-century composers, Arnold Schoenberg (1874–1951) was the most keenly aware of the problem caused by ever-broadening dissonance and atonality. The problem, to put it simply, was the clear and present danger of chaos. In the early 1920s Schoenberg found a way to impose a kind of order or control over the newly "emancipated" elements of music.

This resulted in the **twelve-tone system,** defined by Schoenberg as a "method of composing with the twelve tones solely in relation to one another"—that is, *not* in relation to a central-sounding pitch, or tonic. This method was later known as **serialism.** Serialism was the most important "new language" for music developed by the avant-garde. We cannot go into the details of this composing technique, which has its mathematical aspects, but we should understand the principle behind it, and then listen to an example of serial music.

Schoenberg's "Twelve-Tone System"

Serialism can be regarded as a systematization of chromaticism, the technique developed by the Romantic composers, especially Wagner. None of them, however, would have imagined the kind of systematization applied by Schoenberg.

In brief, what he did was to compose with the twelve notes of the chromatic scale in a *fixed ordering.* An ordered sequence of the twelve notes is called a **twelve-tone row** or **series** (hence the term *serialism*). For any composition, he would determine a series ahead of time and maintain it; the next composition would employ a different series.

Then, with certain carefully prescribed modifications and extensions, Schoenberg composed each of his serial works by writing his notes only in the order of that work's series. As a general rule, he always went through the entire series of twelve without any backtracking before starting over again.

Shown on page 337 is a twelve-tone series, and certain of those carefully prescribed modifications of it (resulting in *retrograde, inverted,* and *transposed* forms of the series, as well as combined forms). The wistful tune derived from this series opens Schoenberg's Piano Concerto, Op. 42, of 1942. CD 5 track 3 (and Cassette 5) contains just the beginning of this concerto—in which the tune is first played by the piano soloist, punctuated by the orchestra. Then comes an interlude, and then the same tune is played by the orchestra (forming an **a b a'** pattern of a quite traditional sort).

The tune includes just a few "free" notes that do not follow the sequence of the series (marked with asterisks), and some note repetitions. Note that the rhythm has nothing to do with the series. Some of the series notes are rhythmically very prominent—they are long notes on the strong beat of a measure. Others go by almost without being noticed.

Serialism and Unity

Part of the point of twelve-tone composition is that each piece has its own special "sound world" determined by its series, and that this permeates the whole piece. The next composition has a new series and a new sound world.

Indeed, serialism can be regarded as the end result of an important tendency in nineteenth-century music, the tendency to seek strong means of unity within individual compositions. We have traced the "principle of thematic unity" in music by Berlioz, Wagner, and others, and mentioned the different "levels" on which it operated—actual recurring themes, thematic transformations, and subtler similarities between motives (see page 250). A serial composition is, in a sense, totally unified, since every measure of it shares the same unique sound world. Thus, on its own special level, Schoenberg's serialism seemed to realize the Romantic composers' ideal of unity.

Rhythmic Serialization

Not many outside of Schoenberg's immediate circle were persuaded of this when he introduced serialism in the 1920s. But after World War II there was an enormous spurt of interest in serial technique. Most composers experimented with it, and many (including Igor Stravinsky, who had once rejected everything Schoenberg stood for) settled on it as a regular means of composition.

Indeed, composers tried to extend the control and unity that twelve-tone technique had asserted over pitch to other elements of music, such as rhythm and dynamics. For each composition, Schoenberg had established a fixed order of the twelve pitches of the chromatic scale, and held to this order (with various modifications) throughout the piece. Postwar serialists of the 1950s and 1960s set up a fixed pattern of note durations, and held to this pattern, again sometimes with certain modifications (running backward, speeding up, and so forth).

The example below, showing such a *rhythmic series*—twelve notes of twelve different durations—is from a two-piano piece by Pierre Boulez called, no doubt appropriately, *Structures* (1951–1952). The numbers below the

staff tally up the number of 32nd-note values in the notes above them. All numbers from 1 to 12 are represented. The pitches, too, form a twelve-tone pitch series.

Rhythmic serialization did not gain as wide acceptance as pitch serialization. Its development was, however, highly symptomatic of a new wave of intellectualism in music. The idea that the increasingly chaotic elements of music needed "controlling," an idea that had been growing on Schoenberg since before World War I, was still of vital concern to a new generation of the avant-garde.

Recommended Listening Alban Berg, Violin Concerto (1935). One of the most approachable of serial works, this concerto was written by Schoenberg's student Alban Berg, to commemorate the death of an eighteen-year-old girl. The series begins with the basic notes of the violin's four strings, G D A E—notes that are easily recognized in their recurrences.

The piece also includes "programmatic" nonserial elements: a folk tune, and a Bach chorale about resignation before death.

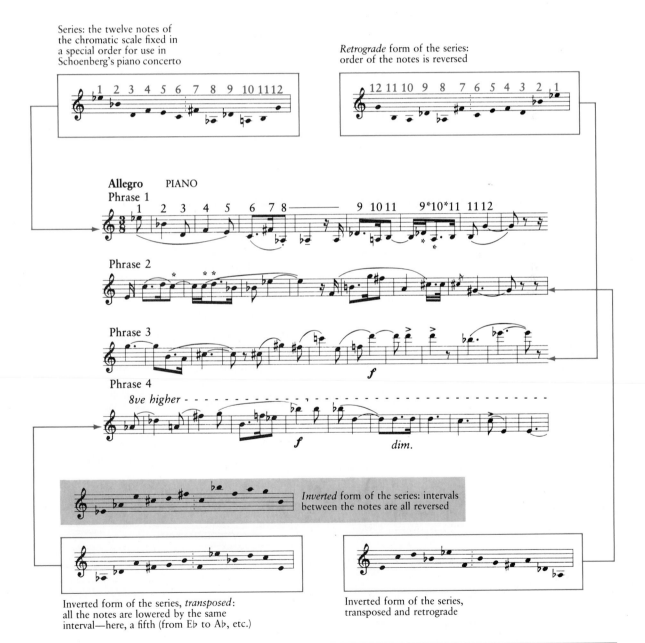

Series: the twelve notes of the chromatic scale fixed in a special order for use in Schoenberg's piano concerto

Retrograde form of the series: order of the notes is reversed

Allegro PIANO
Phrase 1

Phrase 2

Phrase 3

Phrase 4

Inverted form of the series: intervals between the notes are all reversed

Inverted form of the series, *transposed*: all the notes are lowered by the same interval—here, a fifth (from E♭ to A♭, etc.)

Inverted form of the series, transposed and retrograde

6 Music after World War II

For a short time, between the two world wars, Schoenberg's serialism and Stravinsky's neoclassicism stood for the ideals of organization and consolidation. The same could be said for the traditionalism of Berg and Bartók at the end of their lives, and of many other composers—the majority, in fact.

But these ideals were violently undercut by political events. First came the worldwide economic depression of the late 1920s. Then, in the 1930s, the ominous rise of Hitler and the unbelievable (and by many, unbelieved) tyranny of Stalin led Europe to a second appalling world war. With Pearl Harbor, the United States was plunged into this war to an extent that made our involvement in World War I seem minor. The occupation of France, the siege of Leningrad, the bombings of London, Dresden, and Tokyo, the mass murders in the concentration camps, and finally the detonation of atom bombs over Hiroshima and Nagasaki: these events were virtually impossible for human beings (including artists) to take in. History seemed to be showing that all human conceptions or representations of the world were illusory.

In the postwar world, for artists in any medium, all bets were off. For composers, this meant a kind of absolute freedom. While some of them would continue to write music according to the models of the 1930s, or earlier decades, for that matter, a new generation of avant-garde composers invented new systems—or entertained the idea of destroying all systems. In a new age of instant communication, musical experimentation became a truly international movement, no longer centered in the traditional European cultural centers of Paris and Vienna. A second phase of modernism found major figures from Greece to America, and from Poland to Japan (Iannis Xenakis, John Cage, Witold Lutosławski, Tōru Takemitsu, and others).

Two important features of their music can be described in general terms. First, highly intellectual constructive tendencies came to the fore, inspired by Schoenberg's serialism, but going far beyond it. Never before had such complex mathematical theories been advanced to construct and explain music.

Second, composers demanded new sound materials. The ordinary orchestra, even as expanded by such composers as Debussy and Stravinsky, seemed antiquated. Amazing new sonorities were explored, including those produced by electronic apparatus rather than by traditional instruments.

It might seem strange to find the same composers both fascinated by sonority and also preoccupied by construction; the first of these propensities seems sensuous in orientation, the second intellectual. Yet perhaps we can see how they go together. Especially when radical new means become available,

Avant-garde music has made obsolete the old "pitch-time" graph that forms the basis of traditional music notation (see page 23). Composers tend to invent their own notations, as in this excerpt from George Crumb's *Black Angels* (1970) (see page 412).

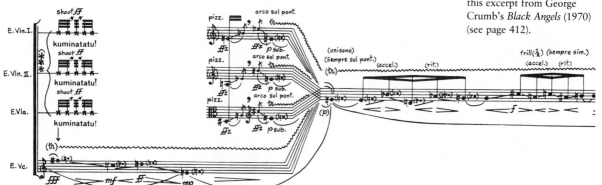

composers need to systematize ways of keeping them under control. Schoenberg had invented the twelve-tone system, indeed, as a "systematic" response to the new sounds produced by "the emancipation of dissonance" and tonality. Much the same concern animated composers after World War II.

New Sound Materials

The search for new sonorities began with an attack on the standard sources of music for unexpected new effects. Singers were instructed to lace their singing with hisses, grunts, clicks, and other "nonmusical" noises. Pianists were told to stand up, lean over the piano, and pluck the strings or hit them with mallets. Using a special kind of breath pressure, clarinetists learned to play chords called *multiphonics*—weird-sounding chords, by conventional standards, but fascinating to those attuned to the new sound universe.

Percussion instruments of all kinds began to be used much more widely than before. Indeed, Western orchestras and chamber music groups had always been weak in percussion, as compared to their counterparts in many non-Western cultures, notably the gamelans of Indonesia. Even more to the point, Western art music had been weak in this respect as compared to jazz. Marimbas, xylophones, gongs, bells, and cymbals of many kinds—percussion instruments that had been used only occasionally in the art music of earlier times—became standard in the postwar era.

However, the truly exciting prospect for new sonorities in music emerged directly out of technology developed during the war: the production of music not by standard instruments, not by standard instruments treated in new ways, and not even by nonstandard instruments, but by electronic means.

Electronic Music

Recording equipment can *reproduce* sounds of any sort—music, as well as the sounds and noises of life. Electronic sound synthesizers can *generate* sounds from scratch—in principle, any sounds that can be imagined, or cal-

A technique increasingly used in modernist art is *collage*, which involves sticking real-life objects onto the canvas—such as a stuffed angora ram with automobile tire, comic strips, and other odds and ends in *Monogram,* by the American artist Robert Rauschenberg (born 1925). Collage can be compared with *musique concrète* in modernist music (see page 340).

Many systems are being devised today to join electronic music making with human spontaneity. The "Biomuse" takes its musical cues from the muscle movements of the imaginary violinist, and from the alpha-wave-sensitive headband of his "accompanist."

culated by using formulas developed by the science of acoustics. A technological breakthrough during World War II, the development of magnetic tape, made it easy for the results of sound generation or reproduction to be stored, handled, copied, and doctored.

> *Musique concrète* This is a term for music employing recorded sounds from life. It is called "concrete" because it is actual sound, as contrasted to the "abstract" products of synthesizers. Traffic noises, waterfalls, heavy breathing, and whale songs can be and have been tape recorded, manipulated in various ways, and then plugged into musical compositions at will.

> *Electronically generated music* Synthesizers can produce any precise pitch, down to quarter tones and one-tenth notes in between our regular chromatic scale notes, if such refinements are wanted. Rhythms, too, can be programmed with a mathematical precision beyond the ability of mere human beings. The introduction of computers into the sound-synthesis process has also made possible the instant production of all overtones (see pages 10–11). Mixed in with the main pitch, they make available an infinite range of tone colors.

Composers of electronic music do not need to rely on a performer to be able to play the exact pitch, rhythm, or tone color that they have in their "mind's ear," or that they can simply calculate in an experimental spirit. What synthesizers should not (indeed, cannot) do is try to duplicate human performance, with its subtle vagaries and tricks, its little inaccuracies of pitch and rhythm—its "personality," as we say. The whole point of electronic composition is that it suggests new sounds, new ways of connecting sound, and whole new areas of sound experience that do not resemble nonelectronic music.

On the Boundaries of Time

Sonority is one of the two areas in which avant-garde music in its second postwar phase made the greatest breakthroughs. The other area was time and rhythm.

To understand one aspect of this development, let us try to contrast two radically different pieces of music. One is a tiny piece by Schoenberg's student and friend Anton Webern, the fourth of his Five Orchestral Pieces of 1913 (see page 361). The whole piece—it is all of six measures long—can be shown on one line of music:

6 Cassette 5A-4/6 CD 5-4

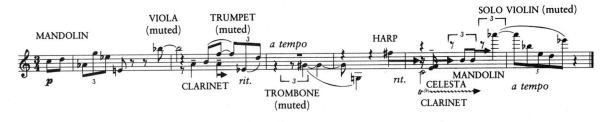

The music feels exceptionally concentrated, because the relationship between the notes is so strained by the "atomized" orchestration and the complex network of pitches and rhythms. Each note somehow becomes a separate little source of tremendous energy. This might be described as a very short time segment of very high intensity.

Contrast this with *In C,* a famous avant-garde work from the 1960s by the American composer Terry Riley. *In C* lasts for about forty-five minutes. During this time the instruments repeat over and over again a set of fifty-three tiny melodic figures that spell out only three harmonies—three harmonies drawn out over the music's total span. The pitches and rhythms are simple, indeed deliberately soothing. This might be described as a very long time segment of very low intensity.

With both Webern and Riley, we measure time (because we have no other way) in the same units: minutes and seconds. Yet the *feeling* of time is very different in the two. It is like the difference between one minute at the end of a tied basketball game and one minute in the middle of an all-night truck run across South Dakota. Such contrasting perceptions of time were now widely explored and exploited by musicians of the avant-garde.

Webern's unique vision of time made him a major influence in the postwar years, even though he died at the end of World War II. Composers were fascinated by his intense, seemingly disconnected note patterns, with their flickering instrumental sounds and their highly complex rhythms. Rhythmic relationships, in particular, were now made more and more complicated. As a Schoenberg student, Webern was a serialist; indeed, his treatment of serialism seemed even more productive than Schoenberg's. We can perhaps better understand the postwar technique of rhythmic serialization, explained on pages 336–337, if we think of it as another radical attempt to restructure musical time.

Chance Music

A striking new trend in music of the 1950s was **chance music,** also called *aleatoric music,* from *alea,* Latin for "dice." This term covers a great variety of music in which certain elements are not precisely specified by the composer, but left to chance—in a way that usually *is* specified by the composer.

The pioneer of this new trend was the American composer John Cage (see page 412); after jazz, Cage's chance music became the first American music to be widely influential all over the world.

In an extreme case, a chance composer would work out a way of throwing dice so as to determine which instruments, which pitches, and so on were to be used in his or her music. Or else the performers might be instructed to do the dice-throwing themselves. In a less extreme case, performers getting to given measures of a piece would be told to play anything at all, so long as it was (for example) loud and fast. Strictly speaking, what would be heard would be determined by chance, but the composer could count on a type of controlled chaos for a limited span of time, a span situated between two passages of fully written-out music.

Whereas earlier modernists had questioned traditional assumptions about melody and dissonance, chance composers questioned even more basic assumptions about musical time. We tend to think of time as linear and goal-directed; time is conventionally plotted on a graph in the same way distance is—see page 23—and a "timer" tells us when to do things. Is time always (chance composers would ask: is it *ever*) actually experienced in this way? Their "timeless" musical vision was like the suspended consciousness that we experience in certain kinds of meditation. This radically new consciousness, a passive sense of time that goes against our goal-oriented culture, lies at the root of chance music.

This chapter has provided a general survey of artistic styles and currents of the twentieth century. We now return to the period around 1900, the first period of consolidation for the avant-garde movement, to examine twentieth-century music in more detail.

Chapter 20

Twentieth-Century Music

The first major phase of avant-garde music began in Paris and Vienna and flourished from around 1890 to 1914. Claude Debussy, Igor Stravinsky (a young Russian working in Paris), and Arnold Schoenberg were the leading figures in this brilliant era. And there were strong echoes of it in Russia itself, Hungary, and the United States (the American composer Charles Ives will be discussed in Chapter 21).

It was a period of rapid development in all the arts, as we have seen, in which the basic tenets of nineteenth-century art were everywhere challenged. In particular, nineteenth-century ideas of melody, harmony, and tonality came under attack. Developments in tone color and rhythm—or, more broadly, musical sonority and musical time—dominated the second phase of modernism, which followed after World War II.

To be sure, musical elements such as melody, harmony, rhythm, and sonority affect each other intimately, and composers hardly ever think of them in isolation. Debussy, Stravinsky, and Schoenberg were all noted for their novel treatment of tone color and rhythm. In terms of historical impact, however, Stravinsky's rhythm, though widely imitated, really worked for him alone, and Debussy's concept of tone color was not fully absorbed until the post–World War II period. It was the revolution in tonality—which went along with a radical reconsideration of melody and harmony—that caught the imagination of the early twentieth-century.

Claude Debussy

(1862–1918)

Chief Works: For orchestra, *Prelude to "The Afternoon of a Faun"* (a famous poem by the French symbolist poet Mallarmé), Three Nocturnes, *La Mer* (The Sea), *Iberia, Jeux* (Games)

One opera (though he began several others): *Pelléas et Mélisande*

Of all the great composers, only one, Claude Debussy, was an out-and-out product of a music school. He studied at the famous Paris Conservatory of Music for ten years, from the age of eleven. As a result of this training, perhaps, Debussy's music was to be accepted by the musical establishment with an ease that was surprising in view of his theoretical innovations and the originality of his style. He was regarded as a radical in the composition classes, but not too radical to win the highest prize (after several attempts), which earned him a three-year period of study in Rome.

Later, Debussy traveled to Russia with Madame von Meck, the eccentric patron of Tchaikovsky. She employed the young Frenchman to play in a trio

For piano: Etudes and Preludes, *Children's Corner* suite, and *Suite bergamasque,* including "Clair de lune"

Songs to poems by Baudelaire, Verlaine

at her home in Moscow. Debussy also visited Bayreuth, home of the great Wagner festivals; at first fascinated by Wagner's music dramas, Debussy eventually turned strongly against them and against German music in general.

Back in Paris, he settled into the city's café life, becoming a familiar bearded figure in his broad-brimmed hat and flowing cape. In his early thirties he seems to have rather suddenly crystallized his musical style, reflecting the influences of the French symbolist poets and impressionist painters. One remarkable work after another was given its premiere, greeted with a flurry of controversy, and then generally accepted by the critics and the public. His one opera, *Pelléas et Mélisande* (1902), written directly to the words of a play by Maurice Maeterlinck, aroused the opposition of the author, who was a prominent symbolist. But today Maeterlinck's play is remembered mainly for Debussy's opera.

Debussy is famous for his innovations in orchestration and in piano writing; his Preludes and Etudes for the piano are the most impressive "miniatures" since the time of the early Romantics. Some would say the same for his songs. One of his later works, music for the ballet *Jeux* (Games), dissolves melody, theme, and rhythm so far that it was taken up as a model by the avant-garde after World War II.

For a short time Debussy wrote music criticism, in which he expressed in pungent prose the anti-German attitudes that were already manifest in his music. Debussy died of cancer in Paris during World War I, actually during a bombardment of his city by the hated Germans.

1 Debussy and Impressionism

Claude Debussy occupies the border area between the late nineteenth- and early twentieth-century styles. His investigation of sensuous new tone colors for orchestra and for piano, his development of new rich harmonies, and his search for ways to express emotion in music—all this reminds us of the Romantics. Yet while in some ways his work seems tied to Romanticism, in others it represents a direct reaction against it.

Thus Debussy's tone colors avoid the heavy sonorities that were usual in late Romantic music, merging instead into subtle, mysterious shades of sound. His harmonies sound strangely vague, and the tonality of his music is often clouded. Debussy's themes and motives are usually fragmentary and tentative, and often draw on the vague-sounding new scales mentioned in Chapter 19. He was also influenced by Javanese gamelan music (see p. 54), which he had heard at the World Exposition in Paris in 1889.

Debussy's orchestral sound differs sharply from that of his contemporary, Gustav Mahler, another great innovator in orchestration. Mahler treated the orchestra more and more contrapuntally; each instrument tends to stand out from the others like a Romantic hero striving for his own say in the world. Debussy's orchestra is more often a single, delicately pulsing totality to which individual instruments contribute momentary gleams of color. One thinks of an impressionist picture, in which small, discrete areas of color, visible close up, merge into indescribable color fields as the viewer stands back and takes the painting in as a whole.

CLAUDE DEBUSSY
Three Nocturnes (1897–1899)

Debussy's *Three Nocturnes,* like most of his works for orchestra, might be characterized as impressionist symphonic poems, though they have no narrative programs. They evoke various scenes without attempting to illustrate them literally.

The title "nocturne" evokes a nighttime scene, the great examples before Debussy being the piano nocturnes of Chopin (see page 265). The first nocturne, *Clouds,* is a pure nature picture. The second, *Festivals,* depicts mysterious nighttime fairs and parades, as we have seen. The title of the third, *Sirens,* refers to the legendary sea maidens who tempt lonely sailors and pull them into the deep.

Clouds   We first hear a quiet series of chords, played by clarinets and bassoons, which circle back on themselves repeatedly. They seem to suggest great cumulus clouds, moving slowly, silently, and inexorably across the sky.

As a "theme," however, these chords do not function conventionally; they make no strong declarations and lead nowhere definitive. This is also true of the next motive that is introduced—a haunting motive that occurs many times in *Clouds,* with hardly any change. (It is built on an octatonic scale: see page 332.) Yet even this muted gesture by the English horn, with its vague rhythm and its fading conclusion, seems sufficient to exhaust the composition and bring it to a near halt, over a barely audible drum roll:

After this near stop, the "cloud" theme begins again, leading this time to a downward passage of remarkably gentle, murmuring chords in the strings —chords all of the same structure (major ninth chords):

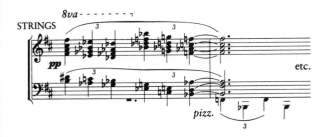

These rich chords slip by without establishing a clear sense of tonality; gorgeous in themselves, they are not "functionally" significant. This use of parallel chords is one of Debussy's most famous inventions.

Clouds might be said to fall into an **A B A′** form—but only in a very general way. Debussy shrinks from clear formal outlines; the musical form here is

LISTENING CHART NUMBER 17

3 Cassette 3A-3/3 CD 3-3
6 Cassette 5A-5/6 CD 5-5

Debussy, *Clouds,* from *Three Nocturnes*

7 min., 4 sec.

	0.00	**A**	**a**	Cloud theme: clarinets and bassoons
	0.18			English-horn motive
	0.25			Quiet timpani roll—music almost stops
	0.43			Cloud theme: high strings
3.2 5.2	0.56			Downward chord passage
	1.10			Further development: strings
	1.29			English-horn motive, with a new echo in the French horn
	2.00			Downward chord passage
3.3 5.3	2.18		**b**	Rising section, more restless: woodwinds added
	2.58			Brief climax
	3.02			English-horn motive (with new even-note rhythm accompaniment) is repeated several times, until it dies away.
3.4 5.4	3.54		**a′**	Cloud theme, with new solo viola counterpoint
	4.10			Downward chord passage
3.5 5.5	4.26	**B**		A new tune enters tentatively, but then repeats itself; flute and harp
	4.49			Tune in strings and solo violin
	5.04			Tune in flute and harp
		(A′)		*Not a real "return" of A, only of selected elements standing in for A*
3.6 5.6	5.23			English-horn motive, with its echo
	5.56			Quiet timpani and low strings—prominent until the end
				Recollection of thematic fragments:
	6.21			Cloud theme: bassoons, then cellos
3.7 5.7	6.40			**B** tune
	6.45			French-horn echo to the English-horn motive

FRENCH
HORN

ENGLISH HORN

much more fluid than that of **A B A** structures observed in earlier music. This fluidity is something to bear in mind when following *Clouds* and other avant-garde music with Listening Charts. By design, avant-garde composers break down the sharp and (to them) oversimple divisions of older musical styles. If they avail themselves of form types such as rondo, sonata form, and so on, they do so in very free, imaginative ways.

In the **A** section of *Clouds,* the return of the "cloud" theme after a more active, restless passage suggests an internal **a b a′** pattern as well. The next idea, **B** (illustrated on page 332), sounds at first like a meditative epilogue to **A**; but when the little tune is repeated several times, it begins to feel like a substantial section of contrast. The "return," **A′**, is really just a reference to some of **A**'s material, notably the haunting English-horn figure. Then at the end the bassoons play a dim, disturbed fragment of the cloud theme, the flute hovers for a moment on the **B** tune, and the drum roll is extended—so as to suggest distant thunder, perhaps.

Festivals We have already experienced this piece as our "overture," in Chapter 1. A more active Nocturne than the other two, *Festivals* also sounds more traditional, with clearer tunes, a clearer structure (**A B C A′**), and a healthy climax in the **C** section. Evidently this **C** section depicts a spectral parade heard from afar, which comes nearer and nearer until it is blaring in our ears (and combining with the busy theme of section **A** in an exhilarating way).

The far-off parade is orchestrated unforgettably with three muted trumpets, while two harps join the timpani and pizzicato strings in beating out the meter. The march tune itself is fairly straightforward in rhythm, but Debussy's harmonies cause a striking distortion of what would be "normal" march music. We shall see distortion employed by avant-garde composers for purposes of parody; indeed, we have already witnessed this in Berlioz's *Fantastic* Symphony and in Mahler's First. But here distortion is used for quite another effect—a fantastic, rich, romantic one.

Igor Stravinsky

(1882–1971)

Chief Works: Ballet scores, including *The Firebird, Petrushka, The Rite of Spring, The Wedding, Orpheus, Agon*

The Soldier's Tale, an unusual chamber-music piece with narrator

An "opera-oratorio," *Oedipus the King; The Rake's Progress,* an opera in English (words by the poet W. H. Auden)

Two symphonies; concertos; *Symphony of Psalms* for orchestra and chorus

Other religious works: a Mass, *Requiem Canticles, Threni* (settings from the Lamentations of Jeremiah)

The son of an important opera singer, Stravinsky studied law and did not turn seriously to music until he was nineteen. Then he studied with the leading nationalist composer Nikolai Rimsky-Korsakov. Rimsky-Korsakov's brand of nationalism served Stravinsky well in the famous (and still outstandingly popular) ballet scores he wrote before World War I for the Ballets Russes, a Russian company centered in Paris.

Stravinsky, drawn by Picasso during the period when they were associated at the Ballets Russes

This enormously dynamic organization, run by a brilliant producer and man-about-the-arts named Sergei Diaghilev, astonished the blasé Parisian public for many years with its exotic spectacles, which combined folklore with the newest and most sensational in dance, music, scenery, and costume design. Among Diaghilev's dancers were Anna Pavlova, Vaslav Nijinsky, and George Balanchine. Famous and soon-to-be-famous painters designed scenery and costumes for the Ballets Russes: Matisse, Chagall, Braque, Rouault, Picasso.

Stravinsky's early ballets were followed by other works in a dazzling variety of styles, forms, and genres. One of the first composers, along with Debussy, to be interested in jazz, Stravinsky wrote *Piano Ragtime* in 1917 and *Ebony Concerto* for Woody Herman's swing band in 1946.

After the Russian Revolution in 1917, Stravinsky made his home in Paris, taking part in the celebrity-studded cultural life there. For an extended period, he practiced a neoclassical style, that is, one which took as its model pre-Romantic composers such as Bach, Handel, Pergolesi, and Mozart.

In 1939 Stravinsky moved to Los Angeles. After World War II his music grew more abstract and formal in style. During the last twenty years of his life, Stravinksy had as his protégé the young American conductor and critic Robert Craft, who helped to manage his affairs, conducted and promoted his music, and introduced him to the music of Schoenberg and Webern. Craft published fascinating books of conversations, in which Stravinsky spoke with extraordinary gusto and dry humor about his long career.

For a quarter of a century people had regarded Stravinsky (and he regarded himself) as the leading neoclassical composer in the French orbit, at the opposite pole from Schoenberg and the Viennese serialists. So he created yet another sensation when, in his seventies, he produced a remarkable group of late compositions employing serial technique.

After some scarifying stays in American hospitals, on which the composer's comments were particularly sardonic, Stravinsky died at his home in New York in 1971. He is buried in Venice, near the grave of Diaghilev.

As a conductor, Stravinsky systematically recorded his own orchestral works, thus leaving a permanent record of how the composer himself "heard" them.

2 Stravinsky and the Ballets Russes

Stravinsky's earliest work followed from that of Musorgsky, Rimsky-Korsakov, and the other members of the Russian nationalist *kuchka* group (see page 305). But in three famous ballet scores written for the Ballets Russes in Paris, Stravinsky rapidly developed his own powerful, hard-edged avant-garde style, a style that can be compared to the contemporary *fauve* style in French painting. These ballets reveal a fascinating progression toward more and more abstraction of folk material. Compare the development of abstraction in art by Kandinsky and Picasso, which we spoke of earlier.

The first ballet, *The Firebird* (1910), spins a romantic fairy tale about the magical Firebird, the ogre Kastchei, and Prince Ivan Tsarevitch, son of the tsar. Its rich, half-Asian setting is matched by beautifully colored folk music and orchestral sound worthy of Debussy himself. But in the next ballet, Stravinsky moved from the steppes to the urban marketplace, to the pre-Lenten fair at St. Petersburg. *Petrushka* (1911), the story of a carnival barker and his puppet, encouraged him to put a hard, satirical edge on his folk material. Then in *The Rite of Spring* (1913), Stravinsky boldly and brutally depicted the fertility cults of prehistoric Slavic tribes. Here Russian folk music, simplified and abstracted, is treated as the source of primitive rhythmic and sexual energy, rather than picture-postcard charm.

The musical style that Stravinsky brought to a head in the *Rite* has many features that struck listeners of the time as "barbaric," apart from its use of deliberately crude folk-tune fragments. The music was "abstract" in the sense that it sounded utterly unemotional, by Romantic standards. It was grindingly dissonant. It emphasized meter in a very heavy, exciting way, and the rhythms themselves were dazzling and unpredictable. Finally, the score is enormously loud: it demands a colossal orchestra, as though the composer wanted to show how he could control—and transform—the chief powerhouse of musical Romanticism. A symbol of prewar opulence in musical terms, the *Rite* orchestra was twice as large as anything Stravinsky ever chose to use later.

IGOR STRAVINSKY
The Rite of Spring (1913): Part I, "The Adoration of the Earth"

The first performance of *The Rite of Spring* caused a riot; the audience was shocked and infuriated by the violent, dissonant sounds in the pit and the provocative choreography on the stage, suggesting rape and ritual murder.

The ballet has no real story, and Stravinsky even said that he preferred to think of the music as a concert piece. However, inscriptions on the score specify a series of primitive fertility rites of various kinds, culminating in the ceremonial choice of a virgin for sacrifice. After this she is evidently danced to death in the ballet's second part, entitled "The Sacrifice."

Introduction   The halting opening theme is played by a bassoon at the very top (indeed, a little past the top) of its normal register. Avant-garde composers strained all the elements of music, including the ordinary capabilities of instruments. The bleating bassoon is joined by odd hootings on other woodwinds, gradually building up an extraordinary texture that is highly dissonant. The instrumental parts sound rather like a static series of preliminary fanfares—or perhaps like the calls of strange antediluvian wildlife.

"Omens of Spring"—"Dance of the Adolescents"   After a brief introduction, in which the dancers presumably "register" an awareness of spring's awakening, the "Dance of the Adolescents" commences with a famous instance of Stravinskian rhythmic irregularity. (Probably this was where the original audience started their catcalls.) A single very dissonant chord is repeated thirty-two times in even eighth notes—but with heavy accents reinforced by short, fat chords played by eight (!) French horns on the most unexpected beats:

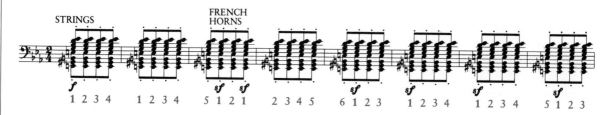

This completely upsets ordinary meter. Instead of eight standard measures of four eighth notes—**1 2 3 4, 1 2 3 4,** etc.—Stravinsky makes us hear **1 2 3 4, 1 2 3 4 5, 1 2, 1 2 3 4 5 6, 1 2 3, 1 2 3 4, 1 2 3 4 5, 1 2 3.** (Try beating time to this passage for a fully bewildering experience.) Yet these irregular rhythms are also exhilarating, and they certainly drive the music forward in a unique way. One really wants to join the dance.

The repeating chords are now overlaid with new motives, derived from folk song. The motives are repeated with slightly different rhythms and at slightly different lengths. This distinctive repetition technique, or *ostinato,* is indicated by brackets on the example below. Like Debussy, Stravinsky tends to concentrate on small melodic fragments, but whereas Debussy soon abandons his fragments, Stravinsky keeps repeating his in this irregular, almost obsessive way.

"The Game of Abduction"   New violence is introduced with this section, a whirlwind of brilliant rhythms, with much frantic work for the timpani.

"Round Dances of Spring"   After a moment of respite, a short, quiet introduction conveys a remarkably desolate, empty feeling (partly as a result of its novel orchestration: a high (E♭) clarinet and low (alto) flute playing two octaves apart). Then a slow dragging dance emerges, built out of the third folk-tune fragment from the "Dance of the Adolescents."

The very strong downbeat makes the meter hypnotic—but one or two added or skipped beats have a powerful animating effect. The dance reaches a relentless climax with glissando (sliding) trombones, gong, cymbals, and big drum. After a sudden fast coda, the bleak introduction returns to conclude the section.

"Games of the Rival Tribes" In this dynamic section two new faster folk-tune fragments are treated in ostinato. The rival tribes vie with one another, each dancing to its own motive. The section ends with a breathtaking passage in which the brass echoes the beginning of the fourth folk-tune fragment.

"Procession of the Sage" Ostinato, we come to realize, is *the* feature of Stravinsky's style that gives it its "primitive" quality: here a lumbering slow ostinato is played by two tubas. A huge masked shaman, the Sage, is carried aloft by half the dancers, while the others leap and gesture around them. The percussion now includes a Cuban güiro—a raucous scraping instrument.

"Adoration of the Earth"—"Dance of the Earth" Slowly the Sage performs a brief ceremony in adoration of the earth. Then, an orgiastic dance. The rhythmic irregularity is more exciting than ever, though in fact this entire dance is built over a regular ostinato, repeated in one of two forms about thirty times.

Notice that all the sections of the *Rite* end by simply stopping, without preparing for cadences in any special way. Particularly in the fast vehement sections, such as the "Dance of the Earth," the music usually gets louder and louder until it is turned off as though by a switch. We may indeed regard this treatment of musical form as elemental, even "barbaric."

What is conspicuously absent from *The Rite of Spring* is emotionality. Tough, precise, and barbaric, it is as far from old-line Romantic sentiment as it is from the more delicate, shadowy vision of Debussy. In Stravinsky's later music the barbarism was tamed, but the dry, precise quality remained, and so did the famous irregular rhythms. Throughout his long career they provided him with a powerful strategy of movement, unlike that of any other composer. Rhythm was at the heart of Stravinsky's "new language" for music.

The ballet for which Stravinsky composed *The Rite of Spring* caused a sensation in 1913. Its choreography, by the legendary Vaslav Nijinsky, was recreated seventy-five years later for the Joffrey Ballet.

LISTENING CHART NUMBER 18

Stravinsky, *The Rite of Spring,* Part 1

Ballet score. 15 min., 56 sec.

3 Cassette 3A-4/3 CD 3-4
6 Cassette 5B-1/6 CD 5-6

	00.00	**Introduction**	Bassoon "fanfare," *p,* twice interrupted by English horn
	01.12		Fanfares in oboe, high (E♭) clarinet, bass clarinet
	01.53		Buildup
4.2 6.2	02.20		New motive in the oboe and E♭ clarinet
	02.56		Stop; return of the bassoon fanfare, *p*
	03.05	**Omens of Spring**	Faster; transition to the Dance of the Adolescents
	03.24		Tempo is established; trill, ♪♪♪♪ rhythm introduced
4.3 6.3	03.30	**Dance of the Adolescents**	Loud rhythmic passage with irregular accents (French horns); various motives are introduced
	04.08		Rhythmic passage again
4.4 6.4	04.17		Folk song fragment no. 1—bassoons and contrabassoon, etc.
	04.55		Return of the introductory "Omens" music
	05.11		Folk song fragment no. 2—French horn, flutes
	05.46		Folk song fragment no. 3—trumpets (triangle)
	06.11		Folk song fragment no. 2—flutes; buildup
4.5 6.5	06.46	**The Game of Abduction**	Faster; frantic rhythms. Brass is prominent, sliding horn calls
	07.41		Ending passage: alternation between scurrying figures in the strings and heavy booms in the drums
4.6 6.6	08.06	**Round Dances of Spring**	Slower; introduction: flute trills, clarinet melody
	08.33		The main slow dance rhythm is introduced; woodwind motive
4.7 6.7	09.12		Folk song fragment no. 3 (slower than before)—violas, *mf*
	10.12		Folk song fragment no. 3, *ff,* with cymbals
	10.38		Climactic passage—brass
	11.01		Short coda: faster, with violent rhythmic interjections
	11.19		Brief return of the slow introduction, *p*
4.8 6.8	11.51	**Games of the Rival Tribes**	Faster; drums, brass; folk song fragment no. 4
	12.24		Folk song fragment no. 5
	12.50		Folk song fragment no. 4; buildup
4.9 6.9	13.21	**Procession of the Sage**	Slow tuba ostinato (with fragment no. 4); trumpets join in later
	14.01		Climax, with *güiro* (Cuban percussion instrument)
	14.19	**Adoration of the Earth**	Sudden stop; quiet sustained chords
4.10 6.10	14.45	**Dance of the Earth**	Faster; drums prepare the furious final dance
	15.13		Quieter, then a big final buildup
	15.46		Violent chords prepare a sudden conclusion.

The next major theme, introduced after a violin glissando, is very regular in rhythm—a feature of contrast with theme 1 that recalls sonata form:

Then a series of three capricious slowdowns has an effect similar to that of a cadence theme in a sonata-form exposition. The music seems to be coming to a close, even though the tonality is quite indistinct and there is no complete stop.

Instead, the strumming starts up again, followed by theme 1 in a rondo-like return. It sounds even more emphatic and rollicking than before.

Development and Trio After a time, there are some abrupt stops; the following section develops several motives from the exposition. But this "development section" is interrupted, surprisingly, by slow music that coalesces into a trio, the contrasting middle section found in traditional minuets and scherzos. A graceful melodic line migrates from one instrument to another, to a lilting guitarlike accompaniment, played pizzicato.

Recapitulation and Coda Soon the fast movement picks up again. A return of the three capricious slowdowns suggests a recapitulation. This time they are followed by extended rhythmic spurts, leading to a whirling transformation of theme 1 with its ostinato in a very fast triple meter. There is reference to theme 2, also in a variant form, more emphatic than before.

Finally, an even faster coda builds up an amazing texture in which the players seem intent on playing fantastic ostinatos with scarcely any reference to the other parts. At the very end of this passage of exciting chaos, Bartók reasserts control. The music grinds to a halt with constant reiterations of the "primitive" features of theme 1:

Hungarian folk dancing

LISTENING CHART NUMBER 19

Bartók, String Quartet No. 2, second movement

7 min., 41 sec.

3 Cassette 3B-1/3 CD 3-5
6 Cassette 5B-2/6 CD 5-7

	0.00	**Introductory motives**	
	0.07	**Theme 1**	Violin 1, accompanied by fast repeated notes in violin 2
			This repeated-note accompaniment always starts prior to theme.
	0.33	**Continuation**	Cello and viola; then viola, *ff*
	0.40		(The introductory motives interrupt briefly, *ff*.)
	0.51	**Continuation**	Cello in the high range and viola, once again, *mf*
	1.10		Transition
5.2 / 7.2	1.17	**Theme 2**	Theme 2 starts after a short glissando (slide); brief and repetitive. (This theme includes one of the introductory motives.)
	1.34	**Cadential passage**	This passage includes three fermatas (brief slowdowns), followed by a motive:
	1.49	**Theme 1**	In the three low instruments; like a rondo return
5.3 / 7.3	2.07	**Continuation**	New, exuberant continuation for theme 1, *ff*
	2.33		Three very abrupt stops!
5.4 / 7.4	2.44	**Development**	Development of theme 2 and the introductory motives. Much stopping and starting.
	3.03		Theme 2 developed with pizzicato background
	3.19		Forceful descending chords, in sequence, prepare for the Trio.
5.5 / 7.5	3.29	**TRIO**	Introduction: short phrases of the coming melody, interrupted by stops and fragments of theme 1, gradually getting slower
	3.46		A long graceful melody moving from instrument to instrument, with guitarlike accompaniment. Slower tempo, *p*
5.6 / 7.6	4.31		Development is resumed, back at the original tempo.
	4.53	**Cadential passage**	Fermatas again; more expansive treatment of the ♪♪♪ motive (with all instruments playing very high)
	5.18		Speedup—using the same motive
5.7 / 7.7	5.26	**Theme 1**	A thematic transformation in fast **3/4** meter, starting in the cello
	5.46		New continuation recalls theme 2.
	5.59		The sequential chords that prepared for the Trio, now in rollicking **3/4** meter
5.8 / 7.8	6.18		Brief recollection of the Trio—two phrases only, medium tempo
5.9 / 7.9	6.27	**Coda**	Fast whirling passage, *p,* made up of tiny bits of theme 1
	7.14		Ends with a clear motive from theme 1, repeated *ff*

Slower

4 Expressionism

In Paris during the first decades of the twentieth century, Debussy's shifting musical shadows and Stravinsky's extroverted gestures were on display nightly at the Ballets Russes. Some analogies can be drawn between these composers in stylistic terms, but primarily what they had in common was their rejection, in their different ways, of the overheated emotionalism of late Romanticism.

In Austria and Germany, however, and especially in Vienna, composers pressed forward with music that was increasingly emotional and increasingly complex. As though intent on taking Romantic fervor to its ultimate conclusion, they found themselves exploiting extreme states, extending all the way to hysteria, nightmare, even insanity. This movement, *expressionism*, shares its name with important parallel movements in art and literature (see pages 328–330).

These years also saw the publication of Freud's first works, with their bold new analysis of the power of unconscious drives, the significance of dreams, and the central role of sexuality. Psychoanalytical theory had a clear impact on German expressionism; a vivid example is *Erwartung* (Anticipation), an important work of 1909 by Arnold Schoenberg. In this long monologue for soprano and orchestra, a woman comes to meet her lover in a dark wood and spills out all her terrors, shrieking as she stumbles upon a dead body she believes to be his. One cannot tell whether *Erwartung* represents an actual scene of hysteria, an allegory, or a Freudian dream fantasy.

Schoenberg was the leading expressionist in music. He pioneered in the "emancipation of dissonance" and the breakdown of tonality, and shortly after World War I he developed the revolutionary technique of serialism (see pages 336–337). Even before the war, Schoenberg attracted two brilliant Viennese students who were only about ten years his junior, and who shared almost equally in his path-breaking innovations. Schoenberg, Anton Webern, and Alban Berg are often referred to as the Second Viennese School, by analogy with the earlier Viennese triumvirate of Haydn, Mozart, and Beethoven.

Nightmarish images recur in expressionist art. This disturbing yet beautiful (disturbingly beautiful?) painting is by the Norwegian artist Edvard Munch (1863–1944).

Arnold Schoenberg

(1874–1951)

Chief Works: An early symphonic poem, *Transfigured Night;* Five Orchestral Pieces; two chamber symphonies, a piano concerto and a violin concerto

Erwartung ("Anticipation"), an expressionist monodrama for one singer and orchestra; the unfinished opera *Moses and Aaron*

Choral works, including *Gurrelieder,* the unfinished oratorio *Jacob's Ladder,* and *A Survivor from Warsaw*

Songs, including *The Book of the Hanging Gardens,* to texts by the German symbolist poet Stefan George; *Pierrot lunaire* ("Moonstruck Pierrot"), a chamber-music piece with *Sprechstimme* singer

Four string quartets and other chamber music

Man Ray, *Arnold Schoenberg* (1926).

The most conscious and self-conscious member of music's avant-garde was Arnold Schoenberg, who grew up in Europe's most intense musical environment, the Vienna of Johannes Brahms and Gustav Mahler. He was largely self-taught in music, though he found a mentor in the conductor and composer Alexander von Zemlinsky, whose sister became Schoenberg's first wife. His second wife, Gertrud Kolisch, was the sister of the leader of an important string quartet—a quartet that featured Schoenberg's music. A man of unusual versatility, Schoenberg produced important books on musical theory, painted (and gave exhibitions of) pictures in expressionist style, and wrote the literary texts for many of his compositions.

His early music—notably the symphonic poem *Transfigured Night* of 1899, still his best-known work—followed from the late Romantic tradition of Brahms and Mahler. But Schoenberg soon came to feel that he was destined to carry this tradition through to its "logical" modern development, by way of increasing chromaticism and atonality. Listeners felt otherwise, and Schoenberg's revolutionary compositions of the 1900s were received with more hostility than any in the entire history of music. At the same time, they attracted the sympathetic interest of Mahler and Richard Strauss, and drew a coterie of brilliant young students to Schoenberg, as we have seen.

Schoenberg's music grew progressively more and more atonal, but he was nearly fifty before he developed the twelve-tone (or serial) system. Of all the "new languages" for music attempted by the early avant-garde composers, serialism was the most radical and also the most fruitful. After World War II, even though some leading radicals rejected Schoenberg's music, they still made use of his fundamental idea of a serial language for music.

As a Jew, Schoenberg was forced to leave Germany when the Nazis came to power, and he spent the rest of his life in Los Angeles. His remarkable unfinished opera *Moses and Aaron* of 1933 is both a Judaic epic and also an allegory of the problem of modernist communication with the public. *A Survivor from Warsaw* was written in memory of the slaughter that occurred in Warsaw's Jewish quarter when the Nazis crushed the uprising there in 1943.

Schoenberg was a remarkable personality: gloomy, uncompromising, inordinately proud, and also highly superstitious. Of all the major composers, he was the first great teacher since Bach; besides his close associates of the Second Viennese School, he strongly influenced many other musicians who sought him out as a teacher. At the end of his life he taught at UCLA. Though only some of his music has won popular approval, Schoenberg is regarded by most musicians as the most significant composer of this century.

The Schoenberg Institute at Los Angeles makes his scores available to students, puts on concerts of his music, and preserves the room he composed in, just as it was, in perpetuity.

6 Cassette 5B, 3–7/6 CD 5, 8–12

ARNOLD SCHOENBERG
Pierrot lunaire (1912)

This highly influential song cycle sets texts by a minor Belgian poet, Albert Girard. Like many artists of the time—poets as well as composers—Girard is not easy to figure out at once. Pierrot is the eternal figure of the sad clown, and hence perhaps also the alienated artist; but why is he called "lunar"? In poems that are dotted with Freudian imagery, we hear about his obsession with the moon, his amorous frustrations, his neurotic aspirations, his pranks and adventures.

To match this, Schoenberg wrote music which utterly lacks the tunes that one might expect to find in a set of songs. The soprano does not exactly sing or exactly speak, but performs in an in-between style of Schoenberg's invention called *Sprechstimme* ("speech-song"). *Sprechstimme* is an extreme example of the avant-garde composers' search through the most basic artistic materials—here, sound that is not even fully organized into pitches—for new expressive means. Through *Sprechstimme,* Girard's strange moonstruck poems are somehow magnified and emphasized, distorted and parodied all at the same time.

Pierrot lunaire calls for five instrumentalists—flute, clarinet, violin, cello, piano—three of whom double on other instruments; that is, the flutist sometimes switches to piccolo, the clarinetist to bass clarinet, and the violinist to viola. Not all the songs involve all the players, so nearly every song has its own unique accompaniment, ranging from a single flute in No. 7 to all eight instruments in No. 21 (the players switching within this one). Schoenberg's dazzling variety of instrumental effects compensates for the inherent sameness of the *Sprechstimme.*

As is often the case in song cycles, there are musical transitions between many of the songs. We will examine the songs from No. 18 to the end.

No. 18: "The Moonfleck" (voice, piano, piccolo, clarinet, violin, cello)   This song begins with a short introduction, or transition from the previous number, for piano solo. Listen to this short passage several times. Dense, dissonant, atonal, and alarmingly intense in its motivic insistence, the passage gives us Schoenberg's uncompromising version of musical modernism in a nutshell.

The song itself is also short, and one of the most fascinating in the cycle from a technical standpoint. Simultaneous fugues and canons are at work, but what the listener perceives is a fantastic lacework of sounds—as if Pierrot were frantically brushing a thousand flickering moonflecks off his tuxedo. Like much later avant-garde music, "The Moonfleck" uses extremely complicated technical means to achieve a unique sonorous effect.

Einen weissen Fleck des hellen Mondes	With a white speck of the bright moon
Auf dem Rücken seines schwartzen Rockes,	On the back of his tuxedo,
So spaziert Pierrot im lauen Abend. . . .	Pierrot saunters off this languid evening. . . .

No. 19: "Serenade" (voice, cello, piano)   The poem of "Serenade" is a parody of the traditional lover's night song, and Schoenberg's long, expressionistic cello solo is a parody of a romantic serenade melody. It begins with very widely spaced, exaggerated intervals—Pierrot's "giant bow," perhaps—in a rhythm that seems like a distorted version of waltz time.

Mit groteskem Riesenbogen	With a grotesque, giant bow
Kratzt Pierrot auf seiner Bratsche,	Pierrot scratches on his viola
Wie der Storch auf einem Beine. . . .	Like a stork on one leg. . . .

No. 20: "Journey Home" (voice, piano, flute, clarinet, viola, cello)   At the end of "Serenade," the other instruments come in to prepare for "Journey Home." The clarinet is prominent in this beautiful song, in which the overall restless, haunting quality suggests Pierrot's rocking boat:

Der Mondstrahl ist das Ruder,	A moonbeam is the oar,
Seerose dient als Boot;	A waterlily serves as a boat
Drauf fährt Pierrot gen Süden....	On which Pierrot journeys southward....

No. 21: "O Ancient Scent" (voice and all eight instruments)   The final song of the cycle is one of the simpler, quiet ones, set to a relatively simple poem:

O alter Duft aus Märchenzeit	O ancient scent from days of fairy lore,
Berauschest wieder meine Sinne!	Intoxicate again my senses!
Ein närrisch Heer von Schelmerein	A foolish swarm of idle thoughts
Durchschwirrt die leichte Luft.	Pervades the gentle air.
Ein glückhaft Wünschen macht mich froh	A happy whim makes me aspire
Nach Freuden, die ich lang verachtet:	To joys that I have long not known;
O alter Duft aus Märchenzeit,	O ancient scent from days of fairy lore,
Berauschest wieder mich!	Intoxicate again my senses!
All meinen Unmut gäb ich preis;	All my depression is cast off;
Aus meinen sonnumrahmten Fenster	From my sun-encircled window
Beschau ich frei die liebe Welt	I gaze out freely on the lovely world
Und träum hinaus in selge Weiten:	And dream far beyond the fair horizon:
O alter Duft ... aus Märchenzeit!	O ancient scent ... from days of fairy lore!

Romantic nostalgia had been made into a specialty by Mahler; Schoenberg seems to strain that sentiment into something unbelievably—almost painfully —exquisite. The opening, for voice and piano alone, is bittersweet with dissonance: the piano covers all twelve pitches of the chromatic scale by measure 2, a good example of the growing chromaticism of avant-garde music:

When the other instruments enter, most of the time they utter sorrowful little comments when the singer-speaker pauses.

In "O Ancient Scent" the same music comes back at the verbal refrains within the poem, making an **a b a′ c a″** form. At lines 7–8, the piano music of line 1 is repeated an octave higher. Then at line 13, the first few notes of line 1 are played in a slight variation by the cello and viola:

Some kind of cadence—however unconventional—was required for the conclusion of a large composition, so Schoenberg emphasized the three notes of the tonic chord (E, G♯, and B: marked with asterisks) in a very deliberate way. One can hear these notes gingerly pick the key of E major out of the wispy pianissimo instrumental sounds, and the singer's final sigh.

Tonality, as we noted earlier, is a relative concept, and this passage would certainly sound atonal by Mozart's standards. But by the standards of the rest of *Pierrot lunaire,* it sounds tonal. Compare the feeling of centrality or finality here with the piano transition introducing song No. 18.

Half troubled and half parodistic, Schoenberg's song cycle about Pierrot and his neuroses ends at a relatively solid resting place—as solid, perhaps, as the twentieth century knows.

5   The Second Viennese School

The two students of Schoenberg who formed with him the so-called Second Viennese School both became his students before World War I, and both followed him in adopting serialism in the 1920s. They were very different in musical personality, and serialism did not draw them together; rather it seems to have accentuated the unique qualities of each man.

Anton von Webern (he later dropped the aristocratic *von*) was an unspectacular individual whose life revolved around his strangely fragile artistic accomplishment. Despite his aristocratic background, he became a devoted conductor of the Vienna Workers' Chorus, as well as holding other rather low-profile conducting positions.

From the start, Webern reacted against the grandiose side of Romanticism, as represented by the works of Richard Strauss and Gustav Mahler. He turned his music about face, toward abstraction, atomization, and quiet: so quiet, that listening to his music, one listens to the rests almost as much as to the notes themselves. His compositions are all extremely short and concentrated (we discussed one of them briefly on page 341). Webern's entire musical output can be fitted on three CDs.

But both Webern's remarkable vision of musical abstraction and his brilliant use of serialism made him a vital link between the first phase of modernism, around World War I, and the second phase. Though he died in 1945, shot in error by a member of the American occupying forces in Austria, his forward-looking compositions caught the imagination of an entire generation of composers after World War II.

Alban Berg, on the other hand, looked back; more than Schoenberg and certainly more than Webern, he kept lines of communication open to the romantic tradition, by way of Gustav Mahler. Indeed, Schoenberg once described Berg to Webern as "our Puccini"—a somewhat snide and envious remark, though perhaps it was meant affectionately. Snide, because Puccini was the outstandingly successful opera composer of the day, known for his sentimental melodies (see page 294)—and emotionality was a quality the modernists tended to scorn. Envious, because Berg's first opera, *Wozzeck,* was an immediate success on a scale never enjoyed by the other Second Viennese composers. His second opera *Lulu* (1935) is now also a classic, though it made its way slowly—Berg had only orchestrated part of it when he died, and both operas were banned by the Nazis.

Berg died at the age of fifty as a result of an infected insect bite. After his death, it came out that he had been secretly in love with a married woman, and had employed a musical code in his compositions to refer to her and even to address her.

ALBAN BERG (1885–1935)   6 Cassette 5B, 8–9/6 CD 5,
Wozzeck (1923)   13–14

Completed in 1923, Berg's opera *Wozzeck* was first conceived in 1917, at the height of the first phase of musical modernism. In general plan, the opera can be described as Wagnerian: it depends on musical continuity carried by the orchestra, makes extensive use of leitmotives, and contains no arias. Its musical style owes much to Schoenberg's *Pierrot lunaire*.

Background   Berg set a remarkable fragmentary play by the German dramatist Georg Büchner, a half-legible draft discovered at his death in 1837. In a series of brief, savage scenes spoken in the plainest vernacular, Büchner presents an almost paranoid vision of the helpless poor oppressed by society. Berg's music for the dialogue is all highly intense, and he kept the tension up by writing continuous orchestral interludes during the blackouts between the scenes.

Franz Wozzeck is an inarticulate and impoverished soldier, the lowest cog in the military machine. He is troubled by visions and tormented for no apparent reason by his captain and by the regimental doctor, who pays him a pittance for serving as a human guinea pig in bizarre experiments. Wozzeck's mistress, Marie, sleeps with a drum major, who beats Wozzeck up when he makes some objection. Finally Wozzeck murders Marie, goes mad, and drowns himself.

Act III: Interlude after scene ii   Scene ii is the murder scene. When Wozzeck stabs Marie, she screams, and all the leitmotives associated with her blare away in the orchestra. It is said that all the events of our lifetime flash before our eyes at the moment of dying.

Blackout: and the stark interlude between the scenes consists of a single note played by the orchestra in two gut-bursting crescendos. Don't turn the sound down if this passage hurts your ears—it is supposed to. (The interlude is also pretty hard on the stagehands, who have less than half a minute for the scene change.)

Scene iii   The lights snap on again. In a sordid tavern, Wozzeck gulps a drink and seeks consolation with Marie's friend Margret. Berg's idea of a ragtime piano opens the scene—one of many signs that European music of the 1920s had woken up to American influences. But it is a distorted, utterly dissonant ragtime, heard through the ears of someone on the verge of a breakdown.

The music is disjointed, confused, shocking. When Margret gets up on the piano and sings a song, her song is distorted, too:

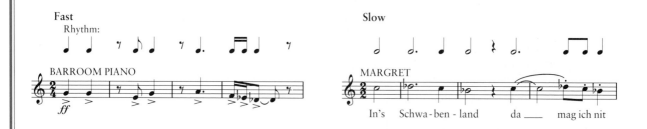

Suddenly she notices blood on Wozzeck's hand. It smells like human blood, she says. In a dreadful climax to the scene, the apprentices and street girls in the inn come out of the shadows and close in on Wozzeck. He manages to escape during another blackout, as a new orchestral interlude surges frantically and furiously.

The whole of scene iii is built on a single short rhythm, repeated over and over again with only slight modifications—*but presented in many different tempos.* This twitching "master rhythm" is marked above the two previous examples, first at a fast tempo, then at a slow one; we first heard it in the timpani in the interlude between scenes ii and iii. Another obvious instance comes when Margret first notices the blood:

Even though this master rhythm may elude the listener in a good many of its appearances, the hypnotic effect of this unusual kind of rhythmic ostinato (see page 351) contributes powerfully to the sense of nightmare and fixation.

Scene iv Fatefully, Wozzeck returns to the pond where he murdered Marie. The orchestra engages in some nature illustration, making strange macabre sounds (so different from the nature illustration in Debussy's *Clouds*!). Wozzeck's mind has quite cracked. He shrieks for the knife (in powerful *Sprechstimme:* see page 359), discovers the corpse, and sees the blood-red moon and the pond, too, seemingly filled with blood. He walks into the water, saying that he has to wash himself.

Wozzeck in the bulrushes

Wozzeck, Marie, and their little child

At this point, his principal tormenters walk by. The Captain and the Doctor hear the vivid orchestral gurgles and understand that someone is drowning, but like people watching a mugging on a crowded New York street, they make no move to help. "Let's get away! Come quickly!" says the terrified Doctor—in plain, naturalistic, prosaic speech, rather than the *Sprechstimme* used by Wozzeck.

In the blackout after this scene, emotional music wells up in the orchestra, mourning for Wozzeck, Marie, and humanity at large. Here Berg adopts and even surpasses the late Romantic style of Gustav Mahler. Our recording fades after a few minutes of this great lament.

Scene v   Berg (following Büchner) has yet another turn of the knife waiting for us in the opera's final scene. Some children who are playing with Wozzeck's little son run off to view his mother's newly discovered corpse. Uncomprehending, he follows them. The icy sweetness of the music here is as stunning as the violent music of the tavern scene and the weird pond music. In turning Büchner's visionary play fragment into an expressionist opera, Berg created one of the great modernist theater pieces of the twentieth century.

TEXT: Berg, *Wozzeck,* Act III, scenes iii and iv

SCENE iii

Wozzeck: Tanzt Alle; tanzt nur zu, springt, schwitzt und stinkt, es holt Euch doch noch einmal der Teufel!

Dance, everyone! Go on, dance, sweat and stink, the devil will get you in the end.
(Gulps down a glass of wine)
(Shouts above the pianist:)

Es ritten drei Reiter wohl an den Rhein, Bei einer Frau Wirtin da kehrten sie ein. Mein Wein ist gut, mein Bier ist klar, Mein Töchterlein liegt auf der . . .

Three horsemen rode along the Rhine, They came to an inn and they asked for wine. The wine was fine, the beer was clear, The innkeeper's daughter . . .

Verdammt! Komm, Margret!

Hell! Come on, Margret!
(Dances with her)

Komm, setzt dich her, Margret!

Come and sit down, Margret!
(Sits her on his knee)

Margret, Du bist so heiss. . . . Wart' nur, wirst auch kalt werden!

Margret, you're hot! Wait, you too will be cold!
(Clasps her—lets her go)

Kannst nicht singen?

Can't you sing?
(She sings:)

Margret: In's Schwabenland, da mag ich nit, Und lange Kleider trag ich nit. Denn lange Kleider, spitze Schuh, Die kommen keiner Dienstmagd zu.

Swabia will never be The land that I shall want to choose, For silken dresses, spike-heeled shoes, Are not for servant girls like me.

Wozzeck: Nein! keine Schuh, man kann auch blossfüssig in die Höll' geh'n! Ich möcht heut raufen, raufen. . . .

No shoes! You can go to hell just as well barefoot! I'm feeling like a fight today!

Margret: Aber was hast Du an der Hand?

But what's that on your hand?

Wozzeck: Ich? Ich?

Me? my hand?

Margret: Rot! Blut!

Red! Blood!

Wozzeck: Blut? Blut?

Blood? blood?
(Everyone gathers around)

Margret: Freilich . . . Blut!

Yes, it is! blood!

Wozzeck: Ich glaub', ich hab' mich geschnitten, da an der rechten Hand. . . .

I think I cut myself, on my hand. . . .

Margret: Wie kommt's denn zum Ellenbogen?

How'd it get right up to the elbow, then?

Wozzeck: Ich hab's daran abgewischt.

I wiped it off there. . . .

Apprentices: Mit der rechten Hand am rechten Arm?

Your right hand on your right arm?

Wozzeck: Was wollt Ihr? Was geht's Euch an?

What do you want? What's it to you?

Margret: Puh! Puh! Da stinkt's nach Menschenblut!

Gross! It stinks like human blood!

Confusion. The people in the Inn crowd around Wozzeck, accusing him. Wozzeck shouts back at them and escapes.

SCENE iv

Wozzeck: Das Messer? Wo ist das Messer? Ich hab's dagelassen . . . Näher, noch näher. Mir graut's! Da regt sich was. Still! Alles still und tod . . . Mörder! Mörder! Ha! Da ruft's! Nein, ich selbst.

The knife! where is the knife? I left it there, around here somewhere. I'm scared! Something's moving. Silence. Everything silent and dead. Murderer! Murderer! Ah, someone called! No, it was just me. . . .

Marie! Marie! Was hast Du für eine rote Schnur um den Hals? Hast Dir das rote Halsband verdient, wie die Ohrringlein, mit Deiner Sünde? Was hangen Dir die schwartzen Haare so wild?

Marie, Marie! What's that red cord around your neck? A red necklace, payment for your sins, like the earrings? Why is your dark hair so wild?

Mörder! Mörder! Sie werden nach mir

They will come look for me. . . . The knife will

	suchen ... Das Messer verrät mich! Da, da ist's!	betray me! Here, here it is.

	So! da hinunter! Es taucht ins dunkle Wasser wie ein Stein.	There! Sink to the bottom! It plunges into the dark water like a stone.
	Aber der Mond verrät mich ... der Mond ist blutig. Will denn die ganze Welt es ausplaudern?!—	But the moon will betray me.... The moon is bloody. Is the whole world going to incriminate me?
	Das Messer, es liegt zu weit vorn, sie finden's beim Baden oder wenn sie nach Muscheln tauchen.	The knife is too near the edge—they'll find it when they're swimming or gathering mussels.
	Ich find's nicht ... Aber ich muss mich waschen. Ich bin blutig. Da ein Fleck ... und noch einer.	I can't find it. But I must wash myself. There's blood on me. A spot ... another....
	Weh! Weh! Ich wasche mich mit Blut! Das Wasser ist Blut ... Blut....	Oh, woe! I am washing myself in blood! The water is blood ... blood.... *(drowns)*
Captain:	Halt!	Wait!
Doctor:	Hören Sie? Dort!	Can you hear? There!
Captain:	Jesus! Das war ein Ton!	Jesus! What a sound!
Doctor:	Ja, dort.	Yes, there.
Captain:	Es ist das Wasser im Teich. Das Wasser ruft. Es ist schon lange Niemand entrunken. Kommen Sie, Doktor! Es ist nicht gut zu hören.	It's the water in the pond, the water is calling. It's been a long time since anyone drowned. Come away, Doctor! This is not good to hear.
Doctor:	Das stöhnt ... als stürbe ein Mensch. Da ertrinkt Jemand!	There's a groan, as though someone were dying. Somebody's drowning!
Captain:	Unheimlich! Der Mond rot und die Nebel grau. Hören Sie? ... Jetzt wieder das Achzen.	It's weird! the red moon, the gray mist ... Do you hear? That moaning again.
Doctor:	Stiller, ... jetzt ganz still.	It's getting quieter—now it's stopped.
Captain:	Kommen Sie! Kommen Sie schnell!	Let's get away! Come quickly!

6   The Postwar Avant-Garde

After World War II, exciting composers seemed to appear like magic from almost every corner of the globe. Among the leaders from France, Germany, and Italy were Olivier Messiaen (b. 1908), Pierre Boulez (b. 1925), Karlheinz Stockhausen (b. 1928), and Luciano Berio (b. 1925). They were joined by the Poles Witold Lutosławski (b. 1913) and Krzysztof Penderecki (b. 1933), the Hungarian György Ligeti (b. 1923), the Greek Iannis Xenakis (b. 1922), the Americans Milton Babbitt (b. 1916), John Cage (b. 1912), and Elliott Carter (b. 1908), and the Japanese Tōru Takemitsu (b. 1930).

Most of these composers are still composing actively—and interestingly—forty years later, in the 1990s. But forty years later, it cannot be said that their music has gained a firm place in the musical repertory, or in the hearts of most music listeners (at least, as far as the United States goes). Modernism's first phase—the phase just before World War I—produced works that now count as "classics": Berg's *Wozzeck,* a fixture in the opera house; Bartók's string quartets, played by every professional string quartet; and Stravinsky's *Rite of Spring,* an all-time favorite in the Schwann CD catalogue, with more than thirty listings. For acknowledged masterpieces written after World War II, however—such as Boulez's fascinating chamber-music work *Le Marteau sans maître,* or Berio's moving *Sinfonia*—similar acceptance has been slow in coming.

GYÖRGY LIGETI (b. 1923)

György Ligeti studied at the Budapest Academy of Music, and as a young man was appointed professor there. Unable to pursue his unique sound visions under the Communist restrictions prevailing in Hungary, he left for the West in 1956. Ligeti was past thirty before his advanced music became known.

Ligeti typifies both the search for new sonorities that occupied the postwar avant-garde and also their new attitudes toward time. His music uses no clear pitches or chords; or, more accurately, while he may start with pitches and chords, he soon adds so many more pitches that all sense of consonance, dissonance, and even the quality of pitch itself is lost. What remain are "sound complexes" that cannot be described (they can only be experienced), sound complexes that slowly change with time.

And in the time dimension, there is no discernible meter or rhythm. Rather there is a sense of gradual, almost glacial surging of the sound complexes, followed by a sense of receding—all the while revealing incredibly diverse new tone colors.

György Ligeti

GYÖRGY LIGETI
Lux aeterna (1966)

Ligeti's *Lux aeterna* is written for sixteen solo singers and chorus; often they sing chords—or rather, clusters—that include all twelve pitches of the chromatic scale. We need a new vocabulary even to talk about music such as this, and some new diagrams—our pitch-time graph on page 23, which indicated melodies by lines, doesn't work for Ligeti's sound complexes. To represent them and show how they develop over time, we have to use nonmusical figures:

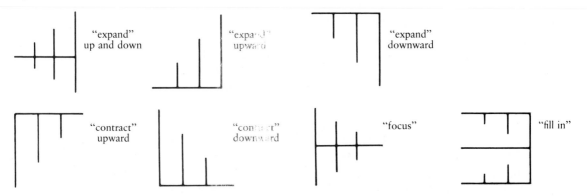

Lux aeterna starts with a single pitch, which Ligeti "expands" both upward and downward by slowly adding a dense mix of pitches above and below it. At other times he starts with a single pitch and expands it upward (adding higher pitches only) or downward (adding lower ones).

LISTENING CHART NUMBER 20

3 Cassette 3B-2/3 CD 3-6
6 Cassette 6A-1/6 CD 6-1

Ligeti, *Lux aeterna*

7 min. 55 sec.

	0.00	**1:** Single pitch, high voices *(Lu)*. The sound "expands," *up and down*.	
	1.42	A high pitch is added.	
	1.59	The sound "contracts" *upward*, ending in . . .	
	2.22	a two-note chord, then a single pitch	
6.2 1.2	2.31	**2:** The high pitch stops, replaced by a chord, in the middle voices *(sanctis tuis)* The sound expands *downward*.	
	3.08	More lower voices; higher voices drop out;	
	3.48	the sound "focuses" to . . .	
	3.58	a two-note chord	
6.3 1.3	4.14	**3:** Complex sound, *f* (with a clear high, low, middle). The sound becomes "filled in."	
	4.34	(New sound added in the middle)	
	4.58	The sound "contracts" *downward* to . . .	
	5.22	a two-note chord, then one note.	
6.4 1.4	5.46	**4:** Complex sound—low voices *(Domine)*. Sound expands, *up and down*.	
	6.16	A high note is added.	
	6.47	The high note is dropped; the sound contracts *downward* to . . .	
	7.36	a two-note dissonant chord.	

Starting with a full-range sound, Ligeti can "contract" it: either downward (by removing notes till only a single low pitch remains), or upward, or to some pitch in the middle—an effect that can be called "focusing," on the analogy of a camera lens. And on one striking occasion, Ligeti starts with a relatively hollow sound consisting of high, middle, and low sounds and gradually "fills it in."

The interest of this music, as we have said, is in the astonishing rich sonorities that are revealed by the slow ebbing and flowing of the sound complexes. Once we have accustomed our ears to this, we can appreciate that the musical form of *Lux aeterna* is simplicity itself. Of the four lengthy sound surges that constitute the piece, No. 1 (going up) seems to be "resolved" by No. 4 (going down). Nos. 1 and 4 are similar, too, in that a high pitch is added half way through—in this music, a very dramatic effect.

The words of *Lux aeterna* are taken from the Requiem Mass, but Ligeti makes sure that they can scarcely be heard and understood. Ligeti has written other "sound complex" pieces employing other forces, such as orchestra—*Atmosphères*, his most famous work, and *Lontano*—and even a string quartet.

Allen derives a novel effect by contrasting "straight" elements—the even-note tune, the stiff trombone melody—with jazzy elements such as the faster counterpoint and the drumbeat (which is getting more and more exciting).

The showcase solos that follow are improvised—solos for *string bass* (Jaribu Shahid: plucked rather than bowed), *alto saxophone* (Steve Coleman: an exhilarating solo with a brilliant percussion background), and Allen's elegant, intricate *piano* solo. The sax solo is terminated by a new descending figure on the melody instruments, and the piano, after its solo, is joined by the curious trombone melody.

"I Sang a Bright Green Tear" is rounded off very effectively by the return of still more music from earlier in the piece—first the jazzy figure, then the even-note second melody. The rhythm slackens to prepare for the vocal (omitted from our recording).

Geri Allen

5 Popular Music in Our Time

Rock, with its strong, driving beat, its electronic sound, and its raucous, miked singing style, is the true characteristic sound of the late twentieth century. The flowering of rock also marked the coming of age of American music. More than jazz or swing, rock represents America's dominance of the world popular music scene.

Modern technology is fundamental to rock, on at least two levels. The actual sound of rock depends on electric guitars and keyboards and massive amplification apparatus. And the distribution and success of rock depend on the enormously sophisticated recording techniques that make recordings and videos possible.

Indeed, there is another side of modern technology that we should credit: the computers in the marketing offices of the music industry. For no other music has been so thoroughly commercialized as rock. At the time of rock's first superstar, Elvis Presley (1935–1977), popular music was driven by the vision of the gold record, the record that sells a million copies. Michael Jackson's *Thriller* sold forty-one million.

Former Beatle Paul McCartney kidding around with electronics

Rock

Rock emerged in the 1950s as a sort of white version of **rhythm and blues,** a slightly earlier genre that had grown up among urban blacks. Once again, as with swing and jazz, music later adopted by an American mass audience emerged from an African-American genre—with the difference that rock has stayed at the center of our culture a great deal longer than swing.

As its name suggests, rhythm and blues brought a faster, heavier jazz beat to the blues, and also a new upbeat mood. Country and western music, then called "hillbilly," was another major influence on early "rock and roll," as rock was originally called. The early white rock artists sang their version of rhythm and blues with a white, "country" accent and with the accompaniment of one or more electric (i.e., electronically amplified) guitars. Later rock has grown more dependent still on amplification and electronic sound manipulation.

Whereas rock began as a strictly American product, once America managed to export it—with great success—it stimulated wave after wave of imports. Some of the most popular and innovative rock groups, in many different genres, have come from overseas: the Beatles, the Rolling Stones, Jethro Tull, the Sex Pistols. There hasn't been such a British invasion since Shakespeare was all the rage in the nineteenth-century American theater.

A very important aspect of postwar popular music is its strong identification with youth culture, and its rebellion against adult values. Rock lyrics have registered adolescent disaffection, anti–Vietnam War sentiment, and a broad urge for freedom. Rock greats from Elvis to Madonna have stood for (and mimed) uninhibited sex; rock and drugs are a long-time twosome. Rock rebellion can even extend to music itself, as when 1960s stars Jimi Hendrix and Pete Townshend of The Who ended concerts by smashing and/or burning their guitars.

Nothing new under the sun: the way the sound box is carved in this bizarre seventeenth-century instrument forecasts today's electric guitars.

Music Videos

Amplification of voices and guitars has reduced the importance of virtuosity in musical performance. It takes less skill ("chops," a jazz player would say) to make music with an electric guitar than with a saxophone, just as it is easier to use a pocket calculator than to do long division. Of course, there are fantastic guitarists who play on the level of an Armstrong or a Parker; but rock as a genre does not depend on them, the way jazz depends on its virtuosos.

On the other hand, image has became more and more important. The unconventional—sometimes outrageous—dress, coiffure, and physical demeanor of popular musicians is matched by the elaborate spectacle of today's rock concerts. A new intermedia form, the music video, combines music with even more elaborate "visuals"—smaller in scale than a rock concert, but infinitely more flexible and imaginative in scope. Indeed, one could say that it was only in combination with music that video technology came of age as an art.

If we are honest, we will admit that all "live" music depends to some extent on how its performers look, as well as how they sound. In the swing era, big-band players in their natty uniforms were picked up by the spotlight when it was their turn to solo. Symphony concerts are not just auditory experiences but spectacles, held in special, imposing spaces and supervised by charismatic leaders (some of whom are known for their "unconventional" podium behavior, too).

Mick Jagger and Keith Richards of the Rolling Stones

Madonna

Bon Jovi

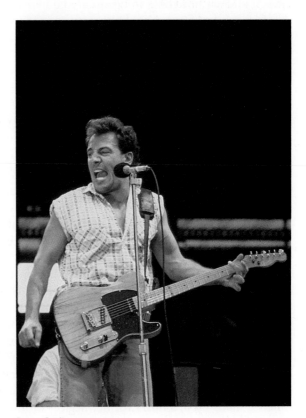

Bruce Springsteen

So, although the extramusical element may be stronger in music video than in other kinds of music—one can scarcely imagine "lip synching" in jazz, for example, or opera—there is nothing fundamentally new about it. Inevitably, in the present age of TV, music has taken a sharp turn toward the visual. MTV is now beamed to dozens of countries around the world, and successful rock videos are inevitably issued for commercial sale.

Rap

Yet in the 1980s, a new genre of African-American music sprang up whose main interest is not so much visual as verbal. *Rap* is less distinctive in strictly musical terms than for its verbal component—fast-moving poems in inner-city argot which are half sung and half spoken, half remembered and half improvised. The verse form, rhyming couplets, recalls the verse form of the blues (page 378), though in its confident, brazen mood, rap could scarcely be more different from the older genre.

The music for rap is often "sampled," that is, pieced together from preexisting recordings, drum machines, and so on, by means of electronic wizardry. No chops necessary here!

The attractions of rapping go beyond the aesthetic pleasure we would probably all experience if we could improvise verse. Poetry has always been a good ("cool") way of saying things that sound drab or awkward in plain prose, and rap is used to comment on a wide range of social, political, and interpersonal issues. In the politically conformist 1980s, during which rock lyrics lost most of their angry bite, rap stepped into the vacuum.

Will rap turn out to be a passing phase in American music, or the basis of a major new wave? That would be hard to say. Predictions in this area are hazardous, and are not going to be attempted here. There is probably only one thing we can feel fairly sure about: between the writing of this book and the reading of it, the ever-changing, ever-vital face of American popular music will have changed again.

6 American Art Music of the Twentieth Century

During the nineteenth century, as we have seen (page 375), conditions were not favorable for the creation of art music in America. European (mainly German) symphonies were played to enthusiastic audiences, but music by native composers lacked a distinctive flavor.

This, it is worth noting, was not a unique situation. England (especially London) was a major consumer of music in the eighteenth and nineteenth centuries, yet by and large, she was content to import music—first Handel, and later Mendelssohn—without producing memorable composers of her own. This was the English way of music, and it was the American way also.

All this changed, however, after 1900. America's growing involvement with Europe, symbolized by our entrance into Europe's two great wars, meant more serious interest in the arts of Europe (all of Europe—not just England), including music. And it meant more attempts to emulate them at home. This was entirely apart from the sudden burgeoning of American popular music: ragtime, jazz, and popular songs by Kern, Gershwin, and others. America made up in a hurry for her neglect of musical composition in post-Revolutionary times.

Charles Ives

(1874–1954)

Chief Works: for orchestra, 4 symphonies and the *Holidays* Symphony, 5 "Orchestral Sets," *Central Park in the Dark* and *The Unanswered Question*

Three Quarter-Tone Pieces for Two Pianos, *Concord* Sonata for piano (movements entitled "Emerson," "Hawthorne," "The Alcotts," "Thoreau")

Variations on "America" for organ (written at age 17; best known in its arrangement for orchestra)

Chamber music—many of the movements having programmatic titles

Church music, choral music, and important songs, among them "General William Booth enters into Heaven"

The output of America's first major composer dates from around 1900 to 1920. He was Charles Ives, the son of a Civil War military bandmaster and music teacher of Danbury, Connecticut, not far from New York City. Ives senior was an extraordinary character, who enjoyed musical games such as playing two tunes simultaneously in different keys. His father's unconventionality—and his association with popular music—left a lasting impression on Charles.

Ives was a church organist as a teenager, and then went on to Yale, where he was a popular undergraduate (with a D+ average; he was a top athlete, too, but his father made him agree not to do athletics in college). Ives absorbed everything that his professor, the eminent composer Horatio Parker, had to teach him. But at that time the American musical climate was basically hostile to modern trends; Parker wrote in a dull, traditional style. For Ives, this was not only dull but somehow also unmasculine. His vision was of a much more vigorous, rough grained, enthusiastic, experimental kind of music.

So when he got his B.A. he hedged his bets and took a job in insurance as well as another church organist position. After a few years he relegated music entirely to his spare time, while pursuing a very successful and innovative business career during the day. He seldom mixed with musicians and for years made little effort to get his works performed or published. (There is an interesting parallel here with the great twentieth-century American poet Wallace Stevens, who also made a good living in insurance.)

All the while Ives was developing his unique mystical notions about music, notions that have been linked to nineteenth-century New England transcendentalism. To Ives, the actual sound of music seems to have counted less than the idea of music making as a basic human activity. As a result, he believed that all kinds of music were equally valid, whether popular or sophisticated, whether simple or wildly dissonant, whether played in or out of tune. What mattered was people's communal joy in music making. Believing also that all musical experiments have equal validity, Ives launched into visionary projects that no other composer of the time would have considered.

Ives' late years were clouded by pathos, for he gave up music almost entirely due to discouragement and bad health. He also, alas, sometimes tinkered with his old music to make it appear even more revolutionary than it was—though the music as he originally wrote it still amazes music historians. For his last thirty years Ives lived in quiet affluence with his wife, Harmony, the sister of a college friend (he had taken her to his junior prom); Harmony seems to have had a strong influence on her husband's ideas about music and life. They lived long enough to see his music admired by a growing number of American musicians before World War II, and rediscovered by the public at large after it.

CHARLES IVES
Second Orchestral Set

6 Cassette 6B-1/6 CD 6-10

A great many of Ives's compositions have American subjects, such as *Central Park in the Dark* and *Some Southpaw Pitching;* he also wrote a *Holidays* Symphony with movements entitled "Washington's Birthday," "Decoration Day," "The Fourth of July," and "Thanksgiving." These pieces regularly employ or quote fragments of American music: folk songs, popular songs by Stephen Foster, gospel hymns, ragtime—sometimes in great profusion. The hymns Ives remembered from his youth are especially favored.

Ives was our first important nationalist composer, then. But he was also more than that: a true American "original," a man with amazingly radical ideas about music, and an insatiable experimenter with musical materials. Ives anticipated many of the most talked-about musical innovations of the early part of the twentieth century—and of the later part, too.

Writing highly dissonant music was the least of it. He also wrote music for pianos tuned to quarter tones. His famous "Unanswered Question" of 1908 employs two uncoordinated orchestras, seated separately, each with its

"Barn door" pictures of this kind were very popular in late nineteenth-century America. The favorite objects shown hanging or pinned to the doors were pipes, papers, dead game, and musical instruments.

A revival meeting and a gospel hymn book of the time, open at the hymn used in Ives's Second Orchestral Set

own conductor. Playing Ives's *Concord* Sonata, the pianist has to use one elbow as well as ten fingers, plus a special wooden block that holds down sixteen notes at a time.

It is something of a marvel of history that, given the musical tradition that he came out of, Ives should have developed many of the same avantgarde ideas that were sweeping Europe at the time. It is an irony of history, too, for while Stravinsky and Schoenberg attracted excited attention in Paris and Vienna, Ives worked in virtual isolation. His music was scarcely played until the 1930s, and not widely appreciated until the 1960s.

No. 2 "The Rockstrewn Hills Join in the People's Outdoor Meeting" (1909)
This orchestral piece is the second of three in Ives's Second Orchestral Set. Ives wrote four symphonies, and his "orchestral sets" can be thought of as informal examples of the same genre. For all its obscurity, the title has a true Ivesian ring: the grandeur of nature joins a human musical festivity, apparently some sort of revival meeting.

The piece begins—after a couple of false starts—with a lively melody that is never completed, for it is twice interrupted violently by the trombones and other instruments. One can sense (without actually identifying them) the reckless superimposition of various melodic and rhythmic fragments. The piano plays a sort of ragtime solo, with irregular snare-drum beats in the background; both of these instruments are prominent in the orchestration.

But like everything else in this piece, the ragtime rhythm is distorted in an invigorating way. The big climax that ensues has something of the quality of Stravinsky's *Rite of Spring*—a work written four years after Ives wrote this one. The climax subsides, and there is a quiet pause.

Next we hear a fragmented trombone melody that sounds like an enthusiastic revival hymn; it works up to a new climax. A second such fragmented hymn, even more enthusiastic—one of Ives's favorites, "I Hear Thy Welcome Voice"—is orchestrated like a march:

Hymn, "I Hear Thy Welcome Voice"

Ives   I am coming, Lord!   Coming now to Thee!   Wash me,   in the blood That   flowed on Calvary.
                                                          cleanse me,

Slow, swinging tempo
                                                                    rit.
                                                                                      (tune fades)

After this collapses, the piano can be heard playing four-note segments of the whole-tone scale (a hallmark of Debussy—but Ives probably learned it from his inquisitive father, not from the French composer). The outdoor meeting ends on an intense but quiet dissonance that is strangely serious, even spiritual—a characteristic Ivesian feature.

The 1920s

Aspiring young American composers around 1920 found more options open to them than Charles Ives did when he graduated from college in 1898. The musical climate was much more favorable to new ideas, partly because the United States had been growing more aware of all things European, including European new music. Like important American writers who lived abroad—Gertrude Stein, T. S. Eliot, Edith Wharton, Ernest Hemingway—composers now associated themselves with European modernism in a way that their predecessors never did.

Our most important composers in the period between the wars were Aaron Copland (1900–1990), a New Yorker; Roy Harris (1898–1979), a Westerner; Roger Sessions (1896–1984), a New Englander; and Virgil Thomson (1896–1990), a proud son of Kansas City who went off to Paris. But the composer who caught the attention of the country at large was a "popular" musician, George Gershwin, who set out to conquer the world of classical music.

A worker, a farmer, and a boss are shown "harmonizing": a political allegory by New York painter Ben Shahn (1898–1969)

GEORGE GERSHWIN (1898–1937)
Piano Concerto in F (1925)

Born in New York, Gershwin received a sketchy musical education. He quit school at sixteen to work as a song plugger or music publisher's agent, hawking new sheet music to singers and band leaders. Soon he was writing his own songs, and he went on to compose some of the finest tunes of the 1920s. His many successful revues and musicals include *Lady, Be Good; Oh, Kay!; Strike Up the Band;* and *Of Thee I Sing.* Gershwin was more attuned to jazz than either of his main competitors, Jerome Kern or Richard Rodgers (see pages 388, 389); he was an accomplished and original jazz pianist.

Ironically or not, Gershwin is remembered more than Kern and Rodgers because of his determination to write "serious" music, concert music that would incorporate jazz elements. While this was a personal ambition, it was also the ambition of a generation. The 1920s was a confident era, and young composers promised a bright new day for American music. A vital, fresh American musical idiom had emerged—the decade from 1920 to 1930 called itself the Jazz Age—and the idea of working jazz into classical compositions was everywhere in the air.

Gershwin wrote a dozen such compositions, including the well-known *Rhapsody in Blue* for piano soloist and jazz band, *An American in Paris,* and finally *Porgy and Bess,* a major opera in popular music idiom.

He also tried a piano concerto, not without some hesitation. Gershwin always regretted his lack of composing technique, and as an adult took lessons on and off with a long list of teachers. (Eventually he even sought out the archmodernist Arnold Schoenberg in Los Angeles, and the two men entered into a somewhat unlikely friendship.) Commissioned by an important American conductor of the time, Walter Damrosch, the Piano Concerto in F was first played by a very nervous Gershwin in 1925.

Last Movement (Allegro) Gershwin followed tradition in making the last movement of his concerto a rondo. His rondo form is a long one: **A B A C A D A E A B A coda.** Most of the tunes past **A** are quoted from the concerto's two earlier movements.

The main theme, **A,** is an open-ended one, built up out of repetitions of a fast, brassy motive with a lively syncopated ending:

Allegro agitato

The jazzy accents grow more exhilarating when the piano takes the theme over from the orchestra. A transition, in which the **A** motive is developed by the xylophone and the piano, leads to the bluesy **B** theme, which is *all* syncopated—a tribute to jazz syncopation that goes beyond the call of duty:

In section **C,** a jaunty new tune is played by a muted trumpet (considered *the* characteristic sound of the jazz bands of Gershwin's time). **C** becomes important in the form, for the next, expanded **A** section is ingeniously blended with the **C** motive. **C** is also the motive with which the piano answers the orchestra in the next two rondo sections, **D** and **E.**

3 Cassette 3B-4/3 CD 3-8
6 Cassette 6B-2/6 CD 6-11

LISTENING CHART NUMBER 21

Gershwin, Piano Concerto in F, last movement

Rondo form. 6 min., 29 sec.

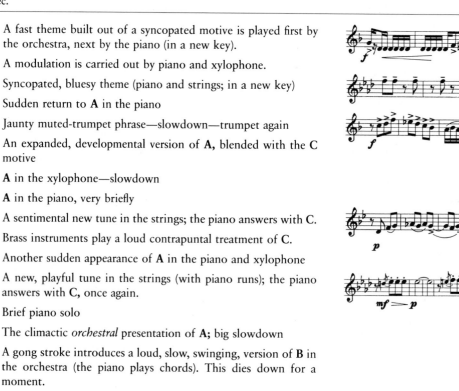

0.00	**Rondo Theme A**	A fast theme built out of a syncopated motive is played first by the orchestra, next by the piano (in a new key).	
0.34	**Transition**	A modulation is carried out by piano and xylophone.	
8.2 11.2 1.01	**B**	Syncopated, bluesy theme (piano and strings; in a new key)	
1.29	**A**	Sudden return to **A** in the piano	
8.3 11.3 1.48	**C**	Jaunty muted-trumpet phrase—slowdown—trumpet again	
2.21	**A**	An expanded, developmental version of **A,** blended with the C motive	
2.34		**A** in the xylophone—slowdown	
2.54		**A** in the piano, very briefly	
8.4 11.4 2.56	**D**	A sentimental new tune in the strings; the piano answers with **C.**	
3.28		Brass instruments play a loud contrapuntal treatment of **C.**	
3.42	**A**	Another sudden appearance of **A** in the piano and xylophone	
8.5 11.5 4.03	**E**	A new, playful tune in the strings (with piano runs); the piano answers with **C,** once again.	
4.20		Brief piano solo	
4.39	**A**	The climactic *orchestral* presentation of **A;** big slowdown	
4.58	**B**	A gong stroke introduces a loud, slow, swinging, version of **B** in the orchestra (the piano plays chords). This dies down for a moment.	
5.47	**A**	The climactic *piano* presentation of **A,** back in the original tempo; orchestral crescendo	
6.04	**Coda**	Nine powerful timpani strokes quote the first-movement theme. The piano winds the piece up.	

Constantin Alajálov, who left unforgettable pictures of the Jazz Age, sketched himself painting George Gershwin in 1932.

When played by the piano, the **C** motive sounds light and whimsical, as though the sophisticated soloist were a bit amused by the orchestra's melodies (which sound like typical Broadway show tunes—sentimental in **D**, more playful in **E**). It is by such means that Gershwin obtained the sense of spirited dialogue that is at the heart of the concerto style.

After **E**, the orchestra returns to **A** once again, this time slowing down into a solo gong stroke—a garish sound. Then the orchestra plays **B** again loudly, at a slow, dragging tempo. After this climax subsides, the piano has *its* last chance with **A**. The loud drum motive heard just before the end is a quotation from the beginning of the concerto's first movement.

Aaron Copland

(1900–1990)

Chief Works: for orchestra: 3 symphonies, *A Lincoln Portrait* (with a speaker), *El salón México* (incorporating South American jazz)

Film scores: *Of Mice and Men* and *The Red Pony* (by John Steinbeck), *Our Town* (Thornton Wilder)

Clarinet Concerto, written for jazzman Benny Goodman

Operas: *The Second Hurricane*, written for high schools, and *The Tender Land*; ballet scores *Billy the Kid*, *Rodeo*, *Appalachian Spring*

For piano: Variations (Copland's outstanding modernist work: 1930), Sonata, Fantasy

A beautiful song cycle to poems by Emily Dickinson

Aaron Copland at a rehearsal

Copland was the son of Russian-Jewish immigrants living in Brooklyn. He received a solid musical education, and at the age of twenty he went abroad to study in Paris. Like many other overseas students, Copland was fortunate to be able to work with a remarkable musician named Nadia Boulanger. Boulanger became an outstanding teacher and mentor of composers, even though she gave up composition herself in deference to the talent of her sister Lili, when Lili died tragically at the age of twenty-four. Boulanger encouraged Copland's interest in Stravinsky, whose avant-garde style influenced him greatly.

Back in America, Copland tirelessly promoted American music in various ways. He organized an important series of concerts (with Roger Sessions) to showcase new American music, wrote articles and books, formed a Composers' Alliance, and taught at the important summer school at Tanglewood, Massachusetts, in conjunction with the Boston Symphony Orchestra. He was one of the first to recognize the importance of Ives. Devoid of the self-centered egoism characteristic of so many artists, Copland was one of the most beloved figures of twentieth-century American music.

From the start he felt that as an American, he should write music that should say something to his fellow Americans. Like many artists and writers of the 1930s, he was attracted by leftist ideology, which insisted that art should "serve the people." But in the way he went about making this happen, Copland differed from Ives or Gershwin. While those men drew on the popular music of their own immediate traditions—hymns and Broadway show music, respectively—Copland reached out for American music of all kinds. In this eclectic attitude we can perhaps trace the influence of Stravinsky, who over his long career also tapped very many musical sources, from Russian folk song to Bach, Tchaikovsky, and Schoenberg.

Thus Copland's early success, *Music for the Theater*, evoked New York in the Jazz Age, and like Gershwin, he wrote a jazz-inspired piano concerto. The ballets *Rodeo* and *Billy the Kid* are western in setting and include cowboy songs. *The Tender Land*, an opera about farm life in the corn belt, includes a big square-dance scene and some country-style ballads. *Appalachian Spring*, a ballet about Pennsylvania in the early 1800s, incorporates a melody sung by a religious sect called the Shakers.

6 Cassette 6B, 3–6/6 CD 6, 12–15

AARON COPLAND
Appalachian Spring (1945)

As a student in Paris in the 1920s, Copland was exposed to all the modernist innovations that had transformed music before World War I. He composed impressive works in a Stravinskian style. However, his growing conviction that his music should speak to the American people meant a conscious decision to make his work more immediately available to the public than the music of the European avant-garde.

The ballet *Appalachian Spring* was choreographed and danced by Martha Graham, a towering figure in American modern dance. She conceived of "a pioneer celebration in spring around a newly built farmhouse in the Pennsylvania hills in the early part of the last century." From his ballet music, Copland arranged a concert suite in seven continuous sections.

Section 1   The ballet begins with a very still, clear, static passage of a kind that Copland made very much his own. It seems to catch the spirit of a vast silent landscape at dawn, perhaps, or just before dawn. Solo instruments play meditative figures in counterpoint; an occasional solemn pulse is heard in the harp.

Section 2   Here "the bride-to-be and the young farmer husband enact the emotions, joyful and apprehensive, their new domestic partnership invited." The celebration of their new house starts with a lively square dance. Soon a new slower melody—something like a hymn—looms up in counterpoint to the dance figures, first in the wind instruments and then in the strings:

Appalachian Spring: Rudolf Nureyev as the Revivalist

Andrew Wyeth, *Christina's World*, 1948, tempera on gesso panel, 32¹/₄ × 47³/₄″. Collection of the Museum of Modern Art, New York. Purchase.

Christina's World, by Andrew Wyeth—like Copland, a conservative twentieth-century artist. The mood conveyed by his sparse figures and barns, empty distances, and reticent lyricism seems to recall the composer's work.

Section 3   This section makes use of a slower version of this new figure, in a new rhythm and with hymnlike harmonies.

Sections 4 and 5   The next two sections pick up the tempo: section 4 evokes another whirling square dance and section 5 is a danced sermon by a revivalist and his followers. Both sections include quiet statements of the hymn.

Section 6   Copland's version of "Simple Gifts," an agreeable Shaker tune, is played by a clarinet and followed by four variations. The Shakers—still to be met with in Pennsylvania—were a religious sect founded in the mid-eighteenth century.

The four variations (indexed 2, 3, 4 and 5 on our CD) are little more, really, than repetitions of the tune with new harmonies, in different keys, and in slightly different tempos. There are brief interludes, or little waits, between the variations. In variations 2 and 3, certain phrases of the tune are heard in imitation.

Section 7   Finally, after some music that the program says is "like a prayer," the hymn and the landscape music return once again. The ballet concludes very quietly. Perhaps the housewarming celebrations have gone on all night, and we are now experiencing another clear gray dawn, a reminder of the many lonely dawns the pioneer couple will face together in the years to come.

The 1950s and Beyond

The period after World War II saw a remarkable flourishing of avant-garde composition, as we have seen (page 367). Composers with similar interests and concerns emerged as if by magic from all over the world—in France, Italy, Germany, Poland, Hungary, Greece, Japan. The main American figures in this constellation are Elliott Carter (b. 1908) and John Cage (1912–1992).

Metrical Modulation

> The music starts in 3/2 time, at a moderate tempo, which is specified exactly by Carter's metronome mark ♩ = 90, meaning 90 half-note beats per minute (the metronome was described on page 22). One minute contains 60 seconds; divide 60 seconds by 90, and we see that each ♩ beat lasts for ⅔ of a second, or 666 milliseconds.

> Next, when the half note splits up into five equal parts, each quintuplet eighth note lasts for 133 milliseconds.

> Switching to 6/8 (a compound meter with two ♪. beats), Carter holds the new eighth note to exactly the same duration as the previous quintuplet eighth.

He has "modulated" metrically to a new, fast tempo, in which each ♪. beat lasts 400 milliseconds. Hence his new metronome marking, ♪. = 150.

Cage, the father of chance music, we shall discuss on page 412. Carter is known especially for his remarkably complex rhythms and his innovations in the area of tempo. Whereas earlier composers had modulated from one tonality to another, Carter devised a way of modulating—not shifting—from one tempo (measured very precisely) to another. "Metrical modulation" is explained in the box above.

Heavily influential on the postwar American scene were two European composers who had immigrated here, Arnold Schoenberg and Igor Stravinsky. Though Schoenberg died not long after the end of the war, his powerful impact as a teacher outlived him. And Stravinsky remained a major figure in American music till his death in 1971.

Also prominent was another foreign-born American composer, Edgard Varèse (1883–1965), who had written what was perhaps the world's most radical music of the 1920s. These works were rediscovered with growing excitement, and Varèse himself took on a new lease of life as an electronic composer.

EDGARD VARÈSE (1883–1965)
Poème électronique (1958)

6 Cassette 1B-11/6 CD 1-24

Though Varèse had started his career in France before World War I, he immigrated to America in 1915 and his first important compositions date from the 1920s. They were marked by an approach to rhythm and especially to sonority that surpassed anything the other early avant-garde composers had attempted. Varèse's *Hyperprism* is scored for seven wind instruments and seven percussion, and *Ionisation* is for percussion alone—thirteen percussionists playing forty-five percussion instruments, including a siren. The manipulation of what had been thought of as "noise" into coherent musical patterns was a heady forecast of modernist music of the post–World War II era.

Edgard Varèse contemplating electronic music equipment of the 1950s

Indeed, it was after World War II that this elderly avant-gardist really came into his own. Around 1930, Varèse had unsuccessfully tried to persuade the Bell Telephone Company to set up a research center in electrically produced music. Now the introduction of electronic composing equipment was a vindication of his vision. His *Déserts* (1950–54), for instruments and tape, was one of the most ambitious early essays in electronic music. And his entirely electronic *Poème électronique* is recognized as one of the masterpieces of the genre.

Poème électronique (ending) Just one part of an extraordinary intermedia experience, Varèse's *Poème électronique* was written for an exhibit at the 1958 Brussels World Fair by the Philips Radio Corporation. The Philips exhibit pavilion was designed by the great modern architect Le Corbusier, who also devised a sequence of colored lights and images to be projected while Varèse's three-track tape was played continuously from 425 speakers.

As visitors entered the pavilion and walked around, the music came at them from unexpected angles. Likewise, as they kept turning corners they kept seeing different parts of the superb building and of the light show. There was certainly an element of chance in the way one got to experience *Poème électronique*—an element that the composer encouraged, as did many of his avant-garde colleagues at that time.

So it is quite in Varèse's spirit for us to take a quick tour of the pavilion, as it were, and hear just the last few minutes of this work, rather than the entirety.

As we come within listening range of *Poème électronique*, a heavy electronic crash is followed by various seemingly random rustles. Then a brilliant section displays a veritable anthology of electronic effects: low sliding groans, rattles, bell-like noises, and watery sounds. Suddenly something human joins these space-age sounds—a short vocal hum. This tells us that Varèse makes use of *musique concrète* in *Poème*: that is, he uses prerecorded sounds from real life, such as humming, singing, bells, and train noises, as well as material that is generated electronically.

Le Corbusier's Philips Pavilion, 1958

The rhythm has been highly irregular. Now it slows down, and a sustained chord appears quietly, grows almost unbearably loud, and then fades. Varèse introduces isolated pitches that appear to be arbitrary, though in fact they merge into another sustained chord. We hear drum rhythms, too, and a *musique concrète* snare drum (remember Varèse's affection for percussion instruments).

Humanity seems to reassert itself in the form of a soprano solo—but this is manipulated electronically so as to shriek its way out of hearing in the high register. Sharp, explosive punctuations decimate the men's voices that follow. A mournful three-note motive (also heard earlier in *Poème*) is played twice with the notes sliding into one another. Then a momentous-sounding siren moves up, falters, and moves up again until it becomes a violent noise, which ceases abruptly and mechanically.

So ends the Varèse *Poème électronique:* for some, on a strange note of unspecified disquiet.

JOHN CAGE (1912–1992)
4'33'' (1952)

The most consistently radical figure of postwar music, here or abroad, was John Cage, the father of chance music (Charles Ives has to count as the grandfather). Cage studied music with Schoenberg, among others, and early developed almost bewildering wide interests—he exhibited specially prepared prints, he toured for many years with the dance company of the famous avant-garde dancer and choreographer Merce Cunningham, and he was a recognized mycologist (mushroom expert). In the 1950s, his study of Zen led him to a fresh attitude toward music, time, and indeed all experience.

Cage posed questions that challenge all the assumptions on which traditional music rests. In words, and also in his compositions, he asked: Why should music be different from the sounds of life? Why "musical" sounds, rather than noises? Why work out music according to melodies, climaxes, twelve-tone series, metrical modulations, or anything else that gives the impression of one thing following another in a purposeful order? Why not leave it to chance? The basic message that Cage wanted to get across was that we should open our ears to every possible sound, every possible sound conjunction.

Often, indeed, the actual sounds produced are less crucial than the "statement" Cage seems to be making about sounds, by means of the ideas he developed for putting his pieces together. This is the case with *4′33″*, perhaps his most celebrated and provocative work (or statement). Any number of players may perform it. They sit silently on the stage for 4 minutes and 33 seconds.

One's first reaction to *4′33″*—a reaction that some people never get over —is that the whole thing is an exasperating hoax. But what Cage is saying is that silence is an entity, too, as well as sound. When did you last really concentrate on silence? (Try it.) In fact, *4′33″* consists not of silence but of little bits of random audience noise, sounds from outside the hall, and the thump of the irate listener's heartbeat. And how does the experience of concentrating on near silence for exactly 4 minutes and 33 seconds compare with concentrating for exactly three minutes, or exactly five?

We seldom really analyze our experience freshly; life is unpredictable and full of surprises. Music should be, too. This is the philosophy represented by Cage and his music. It is a philosophy that has had a major impact on avant-garde composers all over the world.

John Cage collecting
mushrooms

GEORGE CRUMB (b. 1929)

A later representative of the American postwar avant-garde is George Crumb, who teaches at the University of Pennsylvania. Crumb is not a "chance" composer, and he prefers not to work with electronic music, though he makes good use of amplification effects. Instead he has devised new ways of playing an astonishing array of standard and nonstandard instruments. In *Black Angels,* as we shall hear, he asks string quartet players to do things to their instruments that would make a traditional violin teacher turn pale. By such means Crumb obtains a predominantly violent, grotesque quality that could not be achieved in any other way.

George Crumb

In other works (and occasionally in this one), Crumb achieves remarkably delicate effects—quiet, precise, vibrant, a controlled musical kaleidoscope of fascinating elegance. Like many American composers today, he has been much influenced by Asian music; thanks to such composers, Western music has for the first time employed large groups of percussion instruments with something of the subtlety known to the Far East.

GEORGE CRUMB
Black Angels, for Electric String Quartet (1970)

6 Cassette 6B-7/6 CD 6-16

Subtitled "Thirteen Images from the Dark Land," *Black Angels* was inspired by the Vietnam War, if not directly, at least by way of the anguished mood that the war instigated. "There were terrifying things in the air," the composer has said recently; "they found their way into *Black Angels.*"

This highly unconventional string quartet consists of thirteen short (often very short) sections arranged in three groups, of which we will hear the first. A sense of doom is conveyed partly by the titles—"Threnody" means a funeral lamentation song—and partly by various quotations of earlier music with lethal associations, including the plainchant *Dies irae,* already used to macabre effect by Berlioz in his *Fantastic* Symphony (see page 275). But of course it is the music itself that conveys the sense of stress most powerfully.

No. 1 Threnody I: Night of the Electric Insects   The skittery, amplified string playing creates an unforgettable image of menacing insect life, as a deafening clatter alternates with quiet scratching. Against this, the high violins play fast glissandos, or scooping effects. Crumb marks them *piangendo,* "crying."

The scores of Nos. 1, 3, and 4 of *Black Angels* are not written with barlines, and the music has no discernible meter. In contrast, Nos. 2 and 5 project dance rhythms quite clearly, and in No. 2, at least, one can often beat out a regular meter.

No. 2 Sounds of Bones and Flutes   This section evokes Asian music. The players click their tongues and chant "Ka-to-ko to-ko" to illustrate the bones, and imitate a flute by bowing their strings with the back of the bow, that is, with the wood (*col legno*).

No. 3 Lost Bells   A duo for violin and cello, which mimic the mournful, bell-like noises characteristic of electronic music. Fragmentary melodies at the end remind us of the "flute" in No. 2.

Minimalism has proved to be an unusually successful style for American opera: a scene from *Nixon in China* (1987) by John Adams (b. 1947).

No. 4 Devil-music   An extremely vehement solo for the first violin is accompanied by the other players, one of whom also strikes a gong. The violinist produces what can only be called retching sounds; then the cellist, followed by the other players, rasps or grates by dragging the bow very slowly over the strings while applying maximum pressure. Toward the end there are some alarming siren effects, and the electric insects put in another appearance.

No. 5 Danse Macabre   Rhythmic energy picks up again, as the players tap on the wood of their instruments and jiggle maracas. Crumb borrowed the title for this section from a nineteenth-century concert piece by the French composer Camille Saint-Saëns, and he quotes bits of Saint-Saëns's music as well as the *Dies irae*. Isolated phrases of the plainchant appear high in the violin; they are vaguely reminiscent of the "flute" in No. 2 and the ending melodic fragments of No. 3.

The players end up with some mysterious chanting (actually, they count from one to seven in Hungarian).

STEVE REICH (b. 1936)
Tehillim (1981)

One of the most interesting new musical styles to develop in the last twenty years is called *minimalism*. A sharp reaction to the complexities of modernist composition, minimalist music uses very simple melodies, motives, and harmonies repeated many, many times. Terry Riley's *In C*, mentioned on page 341, is an ancestor of minimalism (some say, the first great example of it).

Steve Reich, a philosophy major at Cornell, studied music subsequently and has become the most subtle exponent of this style. A keyboardist, he performs his work with his own special group—a practice, incidentally, that is followed by a number of other contemporary composers.

Tehillim is the Hebrew word for "psalms." Reich has written a long composition in four sections, in which verses from the biblical psalms are sung by a women's choir accompanied by orchestra. The first two sections are fairly fast-moving, the third is slow, and the climactic last section is fast again, almost as though the composer were writing a "symphony of psalms."

Steve Reich

The text for the last "movement" comes from the very last psalm, Psalm 150. And the last *word* in this Psalm, "hallelujah," has echoed down the ages in never-ending praise of God. The word is the same in Hebrew, English, and also Latin (see pages 72 and 155).

Fourth Movement ("Haleluhu")   To begin, the full text of "Haleluhu" is sung by two sopranos in harmony, backed by a steady beat on tambourines. Each syllable of the words gets a single note, and these notes are arranged in lively irregular rhythms. The melody falls into an **a b c c′** form, with verse 3 of the text repeated for **c′**:

Kol han-sha-mah ta - ha-lail   Yah, Ha - le-lu-yah.   Kol han-sha-ma ta - ha-lail   Yah, Ha - le-lu-yah.

With its reiterations of "haleluhu" and "haleluyah," this text seems perfectly suited to Reich's repetitious technique. And internally, the melody is repetitious in its own way; the two "halleluyahs," for example, have exactly the same notes in a slightly different order. This makes for a sort of double cadence, which in conjunction with the words is easy to hear. The many repetitions of this kind *within* the melody, combined with the many repetitions *of* the melody, give this music its feeling of incantation, both static and ecstatic, always changing and yet always the same.

Back of the singing, a few chords are played by the orchestral strings and then sustained for long periods—a solemn counterpoint to the sprightly soprano melody. These strange, irregularly placed chords continue all through the movement, including the orchestral interlude.

Now Reich writes variations on this melody. In Variation 1, two sopranos sing the melody as a canon—that is, one of them starts several beats after the other. The constant melodic intertwining adds new energy and charm. Variation 2, the longest and most complicated variation, is a four-part canon on the original melody. (What is more, each verse is sung several times before the next is heard, so that **c,** for example, comes twenty times. Of course Reich does not expect the listener to hear or discriminate each of these fragments. What we apprehend is a sort of controlled confusion that promises to go on forever.)

Also novel in Variation 2 is that during part **c** the music modulates, for the first time in the movement. After two whole minutes, this is very welcome! Actually, the voices sing as a canon precisely what they had sung before—**c** and **c′**, as shown above—but the solemn, irregular chords that the orchestra plays are new, higher chords, chosen to change the tonality.

Variation 3 starts when the tonality shifts abruptly back to the original key. The melody itself is varied, so as to include sharp, exhilarating high notes for the soprano; the rhythms are somewhat different, too. Variation 4 follows after an orchestral interlude; the string chords grow more intense. Once again, during **c** the music modulates—and returns to the original melody at "Hallelujah," on the highest soprano note yet.

In an enthusiastic coda, extra instruments pile in—two organs, a vibraphone playing along with the tambourines, and bells. United in their joyous ritual, the voices cry out "Hallelujah" again and again, until a final quick, loud "Hallelujah" brings the music to an abrupt close.

TEXT: *Tehillim,* **part 4**

1	Haleluhu batof umachol,	**a**	Praise the Lord with tambourines and dancing,
	Haleluhu baminim va-ugav;		praise him with flute and strings;
2	Haleluhu batzil-tzilay shamah,	**b**	praise him with the clash of cymbals,
	Haleluhu batzil-tzilay taruah;		praise him with triumphant cymbals;
3	Kol hanshamah tahalail Yah, Haleluyah.	**c**	let everything that has breath praise the Lord! Hallelujah.
	Kol hanshamah tahalail Yah, Haleluyah.	**c′**	*Let everything that has breath praise the Lord! Hallelujah.*

LISTENING CHART NUMBER 22

Steve Reich, *Tehillim,* Part 4

3 Cassette 3B-5/3 CD 3-9
6 Cassette 6B-8/6 CD 6-17

6 min., 45 sec.

	0.00	A regular drum beat has accelerated from the previous slow movement.
	0.14	Theme: two sopranos sing the entire text of three psalm verses—**a b c c′** Voices in harmony, percussion. Quiet sustained chords in the orchestra below, shifting at irregular intervals
9.2 / 17.2	0.43	Variation 1: two-part canon **a b c c′**
9.3 / 17.3	1.11	Maracas enter Variation 2: four-part canon; each psalm verse is repeated many times
	1.53	**b**—starts with a very brief punctuation (instruments stop).
	2.18	**c**—starts with another brief punctuation (instruments stop), and then modulates. Each voice sings **c** five times (**c′** is absent).
9.4 / 17.4	2.54	Variation 3: sudden move back to the original key Two voices with clarinets (drums enter a little later) Some new high notes
	3.40	Instrumental interlude. Intense, irregular accents by the strings and electric organ
9.5 / 17.5	4.16	Variation 4: Voices return; from now to the end, they are more intense. New melody. High notes for the soprano
	5.11	Climactic note—higher still—for the soprano
9.6 / 17.6	5.27	Coda: "Halleluyah" repeated again and again. Electric organs, bells enter. Intensity increases.
	5.48	After a punctuation, more "Halleluyahs"; bells prominent
	6.35	. . . plus one more climactic fast "Halleluyah"
	6.43	Abrupt stop (a cessation, not a cadence)

7 Conclusion

Just a few words in conclusion: not so much to this chapter on American music, but rather to our total endeavor in this book as a whole.

We might recall what was said at the end of the introductory unit, on page 61. Our basic goal has been to learn how to listen better, so as to come to understand and appreciate music—music of the European art tradition, mostly, but also other kinds of music. Some musical terminology has been introduced that should help clarify listening, and a rapid trip has been conducted through the history of Western music from Hildegard of Bingen to Steve Reich, by way of Bach, Mozart, Beethoven, Wagner, Stravinsky, and Ellington. The most important thing we've done, by far, is *listen:* listen with some care to numerous individual pieces of music, pieces that have been found rewarding by many people over a period, in most cases, of many generations.

Rewarding is a pale, neutral term that will cover beautiful, fascinating, profound, exciting, blissful, comforting, and any other adjective that may correspond to something deep down in your personal experience. Feelings of this kind about music tend to last for a long time. If you have come to appreciate and love some of the pieces this book has introduced you to, it may be forever. Consider yourself ahead.

Glossary of Musical Terms

The italicized words refer to other definitions in the glossary, which you can look up if necessary. The page numbers refer to fuller explanations in the text.

A cappella (*ah kah-pél-la*): Choral music for voices alone, without instruments *(80)*

Accelerando (*ah-tchel-er-áhn-do*): Getting faster *(22)*

Accent: The stressing of a note—for example, by playing it somewhat louder than the surrounding notes *(18)*

Accidentals: In musical notation, signs indicating that a note is to be played *sharp, flat,* or *natural*

Accompanied recitative: See *recitative (148)*

Acoustics: The science of sound; also, the technology of making concert halls disseminate sound well *(10)*

Adagio: Slow tempo *(22)*

Alba: *Troubadour* song about a knight leaving his lady at dawn *(69)*

Allegro, allegretto: Fast; moderately fast *(22)*

Allemande: A Baroque dance in moderately slow duple meter *(141)*

Alto, contralto: The low female voice

Andante: A fairly slow tempo, but not too slow *(22)*

Andantino: A little faster than *andante (22)*

Aria: A vocal number for solo singer and orchestra, generally in an opera, cantata, or oratorio *(98, 148)*

Arioso: A singing style between recitative and aria *(100)*

Arpeggio (*ar-pédg-ee-oh*): A chord with the notes played one after another in rapid succession, instead of simultaneously (from *arpa,* Italian for harp)

Ars antiqua, ars nova: Contemporary terms for the "old technique" of 13th-century *organum* and the new *polyphonic* music of the 14th century *(73)*

A tempo: At the original tempo

Atonality: The absence of any feeling of *tonality (334)*

Augmentation: The process of increasing the time values of all the notes in a theme at one of its later appearances, thus slowing it down (usually by a factor of two) *(131)*

Avant-garde: In the most advanced style *(320)*

Ballad: A song or song-poem that tells a story, in several stanzas

Bar: Same as *measure (19)*

Bar line: In musical notation, a vertical line through the staffs to mark the measure *(19)*

Baritone: A type of adult male voice similar to the *bass,* but a little higher

Bass: (not spelled "BASE") (1) The low adult male voice; (2) the lowest vocal or instrumental line in a piece of music

Basso continuo: See *continuo (96)*

Basso ostinato: An *ostinato* in the bass

Beam: In musical notation, the heavy stroke connecting eighth notes (two beams connect sixteenth notes, etc.) *(24)*

Beat: The regular pulse underlying most music; the lowest unit of *meter (17)*

Beat syncopation: In jazz, the fractional shifting of accents away from the beats *(378)*

Bebop: A modern jazz style of the 1940s *(394)*

Bel canto: A style of singing that brings out the sensuous beauty of the voice *(277)*

Bel canto opera: Term for early Romantic opera, which featured *bel canto* singing *(277)*

Big bands: The big jazz bands (10 to 20 players) of the 1930s and 1940s *(383)*

Binary form: A musical form having two different sections: **AB** form *(142)*

Blue note: A note deliberately sung or played slightly off pitch, as in the *blues (16)*

Blues: A type of African-American folk music, used in jazz, rhythm and blues, and other forms of popular music *(378)*

Bourrée: A Baroque dance in fast duple meter *(141)*

Break: In jazz, a brief solo improvisation between song phrases *(377)*

Bridge: In sonata form, the section of music that comes between the first theme and the second group, and which makes the modulation; also called "transition" *(182)*

Cadence: The notes or chords (or the whole short passage) ending a section of music with a feeling of conclusiveness. The term *cadence* can be applied to phrases, sections of works, or complete works or movements *(32)*

Cadence theme: In sonata form, the final conclusive theme in the exposition *(182)*

Cadenza: An improvised passage for the soloist in a concerto, or sometimes in other works. Concerto cadenzas usually come near the end of the first movement *(211)*

Canon: Strict *imitative polyphony,* with the identical melody appearing in each voice, but at staggered intervals

Cantata: A composition in several movements for solo voice(s), instruments, and perhaps also chorus. Depending on the text, cantatas are categorized as secular or *church cantatas (153)*

Chaconne (*cha-kón*): Similar to *passacaglia (125)*

Chamber music: Music played by small groups, such as a string quartet or a piano trio *(140)*

Chance music: A type of contemporary music in which certain elements, such as the order of the notes or their pitches, are not specified by the composer but are left to chance *(341)*

Chanson (*shahn-sohn*): French for song; a genre of French secular vocal music *(77)*

Chant: A way of reciting words to music, generally in *monophony* and generally for liturgical purposes, as in *Gregorian chant* *(66)*

Character piece: A short Romantic piano piece that portrays a particular mood *(261)*

Choir: (1) A group of singers singing together, with more than one person singing each voice part; (2) a section of the orchestra comprising instruments of a certain type, such as the string, woodwind, or brass choir

Chorale (*kor-rál*): German for hymn; also used for a four-part *harmonization* of a Lutheran hymn, such as Bach composed in his Christmas Oratorio and other works *(155)*

Chorale prelude: An organ composition based on a *chorale* tune *(159)*

Chord: A grouping of pitches played and heard simultaneously *(36)*

Chromaticism: A musical style employing all or many of the twelve notes of the *chromatic scale* much of the time *(246)*

Chromatic scale: The set of twelve pitches represented by all the white and black notes on the piano, within one octave *(15)*

Church cantata: A *cantata* with religious words *(152)*

Clef: In musical notation, a sign at the beginning of the *staff* indicating the pitches of the lines and spaces. The main clefs are the treble clef (𝄞) and the bass clef (𝄢) *(25)*

Closing theme: Same as *cadence theme (182)*

Coda: The concluding section of a piece or a movement, after the main elements of the form have been presented. Codas are common in sonata form *(183)*

Coloratura: An ornate style of singing, with many notes for each syllable of the text *(147)*

Compound meter: A meter in which the main beats are subdivided into three, e.g., $\frac{6}{8}$ (*one* two three *four* five six), $\frac{6}{4}$, $\frac{9}{8}$, and $\frac{12}{8}$ *(19)*

Con brio: Brilliantly, with spirit

Concerto, solo concerto: A large composition for orchestra and solo instrument *(210)*

Concerto grosso: The main Baroque type of concerto, for a group of solo instruments and a small orchestra *(105)*

Concert overture: An early nineteenth-century genre resembling an opera overture—but without any following opera *(269)*

Con moto: Moving, with motion

Consonance: Intervals or chords that sound relatively stable and free of tension; as opposed to *dissonance (37)*

Continuo (basso continuo): (1) A set of chords continuously underlying the melody in a piece of Baroque music; (2) the instrument(s) playing the continuo, usually cello plus harpsichord or organ *(96, 121)*

Contralto, alto: The low female voice

Counterpoint, contrapuntal: (1) *Polyphony;* strictly speaking, the technique of writing *polyphonic* music; (2) the term *a counterpoint* is used for a melodic line that forms polyphony when played along with other lines; (3) *in counterpoint* means "forming polyphony" *(34)*

Countersubject: In a fugue, a subsidiary melodic line that appears regularly in counterpoint with the *subject (130)*

Courante (*koor-ahnt*): A Baroque dance in moderately slow triple meter *(141)*

Crescendo (*kreh-shén-doe*): Getting louder *(14)*

Cyclic form: A large form, such as a symphony, in which certain themes come back in various different movements *(250)*

Da capo: Literally, "from the beginning"; a direction to the performer to repeat music from the beginning of the piece up to a later point *(148)*

Da capo aria: An aria in **ABA** form, i.e., one in which the **A** section is sung *da capo* at the end *(148)*

Dance suite: See *suite (141)*

Decibel: The scientific unit of loudness

Declamation: The way words are set to music, in terms of rhythm, accent, etc. *(83)*

Development: (1) The process of expanding themes and motives into larger sections of music; (2) the second section of a sonata-form movement, which features the development process *(182)*

Diatonic scale: The set of seven pitches represented by the white notes of the piano, within one octave *(15)*

Dies irae: "Day of wrath": a section of the *Requiem Mass (273)*

Diminuendo: Getting softer *(14)*

Discord: Sometimes used as a term for *dissonance (37)*

Dissonance: Intervals or chords that sound relatively tense and unstable; in opposition to *consonance (37)*

Divertimento: An 18th-century genre of light instrumental music, designed for entertainment *(163)*

Divine Office: The eight daily services, other than the Mass, specified by the Roman Catholic Church *(65)*

Dotted note: In musical notation, a note followed by a dot has its normal duration increased by a half *(24)*

Dotted rhythm: A rhythm of long, dotted notes alternating with short ones *(24)*

Double-exposition form: A type of *sonata form* developed for use in concertos *(210)*

Downbeat: A strong or accented *beat*

Duet, duo: A composition for two singers or instrumentalists *(207)*

Duple meter: A meter consisting of one accented beat alternating with one unaccented beat: *one* two *one* two *(19)*

Dynamics: The volume of sound, the loudness or softness of a musical passage *(13)*

Eighth note: A note one-eighth the length of a whole note *(24)*

Electronic music: Music in which some or all of the sounds are produced by electronic generators or other apparatus *(339)*

Ensemble: A musical number in an opera, cantata, or oratorio that is sung by two or more people *(205)*

Episode: In a fugue, a passage that does not contain any complete appearances of the fugue subject *(131)*

Espressivo: Expressively

Estampie *(ess-tom-pee)*: An instrumental dance of the Middle Ages *(70)*

Étude *(áy-tewd)*: A piece of music designed to aid technical study of a particular instrument *(264)*

Exposition: (1) The first section of a *fugue* *(129)*; (2) the first section of a sonata-form movement *(182)*

Expressionism: An early 20th-century movement in art, music, and literature in Germany and Austria *(328)*

Fantasia: (Usually) a piece of music in a free, improvisatory form

Fermata: A hold of indefinite length on a note; the sign for such a hold in musical notation *(22)*

Figured bass: A system of notating the *continuo* chords in Baroque music, by means of figures; sometimes also used to mean continuo *(122)*

Finale *(fih-náh-lay)*: The last movement of a work, or the ensemble that concludes an act of an opera buffa or other opera

Flag: In musical notation, a "pennant" attached to a note indicating that the length is halved (two flags indicate that it is quartered, etc.) *(24)*

Flat: In musical notation, a sign indicating that the note to which it is attached is to be played a semitone lower (♭). A double flat (♭♭) is sometimes used to indicate that a note is played two semitones lower *(26)*

Form: The "shape" of a piece of music *(56)*

Forte *(fór-tay)*; **fortissimo:** Loud; very loud (*f; ff*) *(14)*

Fragmentation: The technique of reducing a theme to fragmentary motives *(228)*

French overture: A Baroque type of overture to an opera, oratorio, or suite *(142)*

Frequency: In acoustics, the rate of vibration in a string, a column of air, or other sound-producing body *(10)*

Fugato: A relatively short fugal passage within a piece of music

Fugue *(fewg)*: A composition written systematically in *imitative polyphony*, usually with a single main theme, the fugue *subject* *(104, 129)*

Fuguing tune: A simple anthem based on a hymn, with a little counterpoint *(374)*

Functional harmony, functional tonality: From the Baroque period on, the system whereby all chords have a specific interrelation and function for the total sense of centrality *(tonality)* *(96)*

Gavotte: A Baroque dance in duple meter *(141)*

Genre *(zhahn-ruh)*: A general category of music determined partly by the number and kind of instruments or voices involved, and partly by its form, style, or purpose. "Opera," "symphonic poem," and "sonata" are examples of genres *(59)*

Gesamtkunstwerk *(geh-záhmt-kuhnst-vairk)*: "Total work of art"—Wagner's term for his music dramas *(241)*

Gigue *(zheeg)*, **jig:** A Baroque dance in a lively compound meter *(141)*

Glissando: Sliding from one note to another on an instrument such as a trombone or violin *(355)*

Gospel, gospel music: Genre of African-American choral church music, associated with the *blues* *(379)*

Grave *(grahv)*: Slow; the characteristic tempo of the first section of a *French overture* *(22)*

Gregorian chant: The type of *chant* used in the early Roman Catholic Church *(66)*

Ground bass: A short motive, phrase, or theme in the bass repeated again and again as the basis for a composition *(96, 125)*

Half note: A note half the length of a whole note *(24)*

Half step: The *interval* between any two successive notes of the chromatic scale; also called a *semitone* *(16)*

Harmonize: To provide each note of a melody with a chord *(36)*

Harmony, harmonic: Having to do with chords, or the "vertical" aspect of musical texture *(36)*. The term *harmonic* is sometimes used to mean *homophonic* *(35)*

Hocket: The alternation of very short melodic phrases, or single notes, between two voices, used in late medieval *polyphony* *(74)*

Homophony, homophonic: A musical texture that involves only one melody of real interest, combined with chords or other subsidiary sounds *(35)*

Hymn: A simple religious song in several stanzas, for congregational singing in church *(77)*

Idée fixe *(ee-day feex)*: A fixed idea, an obsession; the term used by Berlioz for a recurring theme used in all the movements of one of his program symphonies *(270)*

Imitation, imitative polyphony, imitative counterpoint: A polyphonic musical texture in which the various melodic lines use approximately the same themes; as opposed to *nonimitative counterpoint* *(34)*. See also *point of imitation*

Impressionism: A French artistic movement of the late 19th and early 20th centuries *(325)*

Interval: The difference or distance between two pitches, measured by the number of *diatonic scale* notes between them *(13)*

Introduction: An introductory passage: the "slow introduction" before the exposition in a symphony, etc.; in an opera, the first number after the overture *(186, 198)*

Inversion: Reading or playing a melody or a *twelve-tone series*

upside down, i.e., playing all its upward intervals downward and vice versa *(131)*

Isorhythm: In 14th-century music, the technique of repeating the identical rhythm for each section of a composition, while the pitches are altered *(74)*

Jazz: A major African-American performance style that has influenced all 20th-century popular music *(377)*

Jongleur (*jawn-gler*): A medieval secular musician *(69)*

K numbers: The numbers assigned to works by Mozart in the Köchel Catalogue; used instead of opus numbers to catalogue Mozart's works *(186)*

Key: One of the various positions for the major- and minor-mode scales made possible by using all the notes of the chromatic scale *(40)*

Key signature: Sharps or flats placed at the beginning of the staffs to indicate the *key,* and applied throughout an entire piece, in every measure and in every octave *(27)*

Largo; larghetto: Very slow; somewhat less slow than largo *(22)*

Ledger lines: Short lines above or below the staff to accommodate pitches that go higher or lower *(25)*

Legato (*leh-gáh-toe*): Playing in a smooth, connected manner; as opposed to *staccato (25)*

Leitmotiv (*líte-moh-teef*): "Leading motive" in Wagner's operas *(289)*

Lento: Very slow *(22)*

Libretto: The complete book of words for an opera, oratorio, cantata, etc. *(148)*

Lied (pl. *Lieder*): German for song; also a special genre of Romantic songs with piano *(253)*

Line: Used as a term to mean a melody, or melodic line *(30)*

Madrigal: The main secular vocal form of the Renaissance *(86)*

Major mode: One of the modes of the *diatonic scale,* oriented around C as the *tonic;* characterized by the interval between the first and third notes containing four semitones; as opposed to *minor mode (38)*

Manual: A keyboard of an organ or harpsichord, usually one of two or more on a single instrument

Mass: The main Roman Catholic service; or the music written for it. The musical Mass consists of five large sections: Kyrie, Gloria, Credo, Sanctus, and Agnus Dei *(77)*

Mazurka: A Polish dance in lively triple meter

Measure (bar): In music, the unit of *meter,* consisting of a principal strong beat and one or more weaker ones *(19)*

Medieval modes: See *mode (67)*

Melody: The aspect of music having to do with the succession of pitches; also applied ("a melody") to any particular succession of pitches *(30)*

Meter: A background of stressed and unstressed beats in a simple, regular, repeating pattern *(19)*

Metronome mark: A notation of tempo, indicating the number of beats per minute as ticked out by a metronome; from *metronome,* the mechanical or electrical device that ticks out beats at all practicable tempos *(22)*

Mezzo (*mét-so*): Medium (as in *mezzo forte* or *mezzo piano—**mf, mp**) (14)*

Mezzo-soprano: "Halfway to soprano": a type of female voice between *contralto* and *soprano*

"Miniature": A term for a short, evocative composition for piano or for piano and voice, composed in the Romantic period *(248)*

Minimalism: A late-twentieth century style involving many repetitions of simple musical fragments *(415)*

Minor mode: One of the modes of the *diatonic scale,* oriented around A as the *tonic;* characterized by the interval between the first and third notes containing three semitones; as opposed to *major (38)*

Minstrel show: A type of variety show popular in 19th-century America, performed in blackface *(376)*

Minuet: A popular 17th- and 18th-century dance in moderate triple meter *(106, 141);* also a movement in a sonata, symphony, etc., based on this dance *(175)*

Modal harmony: The characteristically indefinite harmonic style of 16th-century music

Mode, modality: In music since the Renaissance, one of the two types of tonality: major mode or minor mode; also, in earlier times, one of several "orientations" of the *diatonic scale* with D, E, F, and G as tonics *(38)*

Moderato: Moderate tempo *(22)*

Modulation: Changing key within a piece *(40)*

Molto allegro: Faster than allegro *(22)*

Monophony: A musical texture involving a single melodic line and nothing else, as in Gregorian chant; as opposed to *polyphony (34)*

Motet: (Usually) a sacred vocal composition *(73, 86).* Early motets were based on fragments of Gregorian chant.

Motive: A short fragment of melody or rhythm used in constructing a long section of music *(33)*

Movement: A self-contained section of a larger piece, such as a symphony or concerto grosso *(105, 134)*

Music drama: Wagner's name for his distinctive type of opera *(288)*

Music video: Video "dramatization" of a popular song, rock number, or rap number *(398)*

Musical comedy, musical: American development of *operetta,* involving American subjects and music influenced by jazz or rock *(387)*

Musicology: The scholarly study of music history and literature

Musique concrète (*mew-zeek kohn-krét*): Music composed with natural sounds recorded electronically *(340)*

Mute: A device put on or in an instrument to muffle the tone *(273)*

Nationalism: A nineteenth-century movement promoting music built on national folksongs and dances, or associated with national subjects *(305)*

Natural: In musical notation, a sign indicating that a sharp or flat previously attached to a note is to be removed (♮) *(27)*

Neoclassicism: (1) An 18th-century movement in the arts returning to Greek and Roman models *(165)*; (2) a 20th-century movement involving a return to the style and form of older music, particularly 18th-century music *(335)*

Nocturne: "Night piece": title for Romantic "miniature" compositions for piano, etc. *(265)*

Nonimitative polyphony, counterpoint: A *polyphonic* musical texture in which the melodic lines are essentially different from one another; as opposed to *imitation (34)*

Non troppo: Not too much (as in *allegro non troppo*, not too fast)

Note: (1) A sound of a certain definite pitch and duration; (2) the written sign for such a sound in musical notation; (3) a key pressed with the finger on a piano or organ

Octatonic scale: An eight-note scale (used by Stravinsky and others) consisting of half and whole steps in alternation *(332)*

Octave: The interval between a pair of "duplicating" notes, eight notes apart in the *diatonic scale (13)*

Opera: Drama presented in music, with the characters singing instead of speaking *(97, 113, 146)*

Opera buffa (*bóo-fa*): Italian comic opera *(164, 204)*

Opera seria: A term for the serious, heroic opera of the Baroque period in Italy *(147)*

Operetta: A nineteenth-century type of light (often comic) opera, employing spoken dialogue in between musical numbers

Opus: "Work"; opus numbers provide a means of cataloguing a composer's compositions *(105, 136)*

Oratorio: Long semidramatic piece on a religious subject for soloists, chorus, and orchestra *(153)*

Orchestra exposition: In Classical concerto form, the first of two expositions, played by the orchestra without the soloist *(211)*

Orchestration: The technique of writing for various instruments to produce an effective total orchestral sound

Organ chorale: See *chorale prelude (159)*

Organum: The earliest genre of medieval *polyphonic* music *(71)*

Ostinato: A motive, phrase, or theme repeated over and over again at the same pitch level *(350)*

Overtone: In acoustics, a secondary vibration in a sound-producing body, which contributes to the tone color; also called "partial" *(10)*

Overture: An orchestral piece at the start of an opera, oratorio, etc. (but see *concert overture*) *(142)*

Paraphrase: The modification and decoration of *plainchant* melodies in early Renaissance music *(76)*

Part: Used as a term for (1) a section of a piece; (2) one of the *voices* in contrapuntal music; (3) the written music for a single player in an orchestra, band, etc. (as opposed to the *score*)

Partial: Same as *overtone (10)*

Passacaglia (*pah-suh-káh-lee-uh*): A set of variations on a short theme in the bass *(125)*

Passion: A long, oratorio-like composition telling the story of Jesus' last days, according to one of the New Testament gospels

Pavane (*puh-váhn*): A slow 16th-century court dance in duple meter *(88)*

Pedal board: That keyboard of an organ which is played with the feet *(51)*

Pentatonic scale: A five-note scale (familiar from folk music) playable on the black notes of a keyboard *(332)*

Phrase: A section of a melody or a tune *(31)*

Piano; pianissimo: Soft; very soft (*p; pp*) *(14)*

Piano trio: An instrumental group usually consisting of violin, cello, and piano; or a piece composed for this group; or the three players themselves

Pitch: The quality of "highness" or "lowness" of sound; also applied ("a pitch") to any particular pitch level, such as middle C *(12)*

Più: More (as in *più forte*, louder) *(22)*

Pizzicato (*pit-tzih-cáh-toe*): Playing a stringed instrument that is normally bowed by plucking the strings with the finger

Plainchant, plainsong: Unaccompanied, monophonic (one-line) music, without fixed rhythm or meter, such as *Gregorian chant (66)*

Poco: Somewhat (as in *poco adagio* or *poco forte*, somewhat slow, somewhat loud)

Point of imitation: A short passage of *imitative polyphony* based on a single theme, or on two used together *(81)*

Polyphony, polyphonic: Musical texture in which two or more melodic lines are played or sung simultaneously; as opposed to *homophony* or *monophony (34)*

Prelude: An introductory piece, leading to another, such as a fugue or an opera (however, Chopin's Preludes were not intended to lead to anything else)

Première: The first performance ever of a piece of music, opera, etc.

Presto; prestissimo: Very fast; very fast indeed *(22)*

Program music: A piece of instrumental music associated with a story or other extramusical idea *(250)*

Program symphony: A symphony with a program, as by Berlioz *(270)*

Quarter note: A note one-quarter the length of a whole note *(24)*

Quarter-tone scale: A 24-note scale, used in the 20th century, consisting of all the semitones of the chromatic scale and all quarter tones in between the semitones *(332)*

Quartet: A piece for four singers or players; often used to mean *string quartet*

Quintet: A piece for five singers or players

Ragtime: A genre of American popular music around 1900, usually for piano, which led to *jazz (378)*

Range: Used in music to mean "pitch range," i.e., the total span from the lowest to the highest pitch in a piece, a part, or a passage

Rap: Genre of African-American popular music of the 1980s and nineties, featuring rapid, continuous recitation in rhyme *(400)*

Recapitulation: The third section of a sonata-form movement *(183)*

Recitative (*reh-sih-ta-téev*): A half-singing, half-reciting style of presenting words in opera, cantata, oratorio, etc., following speech accents and speech rhythms closely. Secco recitative is accompanied only by *continuo;* accompanied recitative is accompanied by orchestra *(98, 148)*

Reed: In certain wind instruments (oboe, clarinet), a small vibrating element made of cane or metal *(44)*

Registration: In organ music, the choice of stops with which to play a passage

Requiem Mass, Requiem: The special *Mass* celebrated when someone dies

Resolve: To proceed from *dissonant* harmony to *consonance (37)*

Rest: A momentary silence in music; in musical notation a sign indicating momentary silence *(24)*

Retransition: In sonata form, the passage leading from the end of the development section into the beginning of the recapitulation *(183)*

Retrograde: Reading or playing a melody or twelve-tone series backward *(336)*

Rhythm: The aspect of music having to do with the duration of the notes in time; also applied ("a rhythm") to any particular durational pattern *(19)*

Rhythm and blues: Genre of African-American music of the early 1950s, forerunner of *rock (398)*

Rhythm section: In jazz, the instrumental group used mainly to emphasize the meter (drums, bass, and piano) *(378)*

Rhythmic series, rhythmic serialization: A fixed pattern of different note lengths held to throughout a piece; the technique of composing with such a series *(336)*

Ritardando: Slowing down the tempo *(22)*

Ritenuto: Held back in tempo

Ritornello: The orchestral material at the beginning of a concerto grosso, etc., which always returns later in the piece *(134)*

Ritornello form: A Baroque musical form based on recurrences of a *ritornello (134)*

Rock: The dominant popular-music genre of the late twentieth century *(398)*

Rondo: A musical form consisting of one main theme or tune alternating with other themes or sections (**ABACA, ABACABA,** etc.) *(193)*

Round: A simple type of sung *canon,* with all voices entering on the same note after the same time interval *(34)*

Row: Same as *series (336)*

Rubato: "Robbed" time; the free treatment of meter in performance *(244)*

Sarabande: A Baroque dance in slow triple meter, often with a secondary accent on the second beat *(141)*

Scale: A selection of ordered pitches that provides the pitch material for music *(14)*

Scherzo (*scáir-tso*): A form developed by Beethoven from the *minuet* to use for movements in larger compositions; later sometimes used alone, as by Chopin *(226)*

Score: The full musical notation for a piece involving several or many performers *(28)*

Secco recitative: See *recitative (148)*

Second group: In sonata form, the group of themes following the *bridge,* in the second key *(182)*

Semitone: Same as *half step (16)*

Sequence: In a melody, a series of fragments identical except for their placement at successively higher or lower pitch levels *(31)*

Serialism, serial: The technique of composing with a *series,* generally a twelve-tone series (but see also *rhythmic series*) *(336)*

Series: A fixed arrangement of pitches (or rhythms) held to throughout a serial composition *(336)*

Sforzando: An especially strong accent; the mark indicating this in musical notation (**sf** or >) *(18)*

Sharp: In musical notation, a sign indicating that the note it precedes is to be played a semitone higher (♯). A double sharp (✕) is occasionally used to indicate that a note is played two semitones higher *(26)*

Siciliana: A Baroque dance type in compound meter *(141)*

Sixteenth note: A note one-sixteenth the length of a whole note *(24)*

Slur: In musical notation, a curved line over several notes, indicating that they are to be played smoothly, or *legato (25)*

Solo concerto: See *concerto (210)*

Solo exposition: In Classical concerto form, the second of two expositions, played by the soloist and the orchestra *(210)*

Solo sonata: Sonata for one instrument—but in the Baroque period, this usually means a sonata for one principal instrument plus *continuo (140)*

Sonata: A chamber-music piece in several movements, typically for three main instruments plus *continuo* in the Baroque period, and for only one or two instruments in all periods since then *(140, 216)*

Sonata da camera, sonata da chiesa: Categories of Baroque trio and solo sonatas *(140)*

Sonata form (sonata-allegro form): A form developed by the Classical composers and used in almost all the first movements of their symphonies, sonatas, etc. *(180)*

Sonata-rondo form: A form combining elements of sonata form and rondo

Song cycle: A group of songs connected by a general idea or story, and sometimes also by musical unifying devices *(257)*

Sonority: A general term for sound quality, either of a momentary chord, or of a whole piece or style

Soprano: The high female (or boy's) voice

Spiritual: Religious folksong, usually among African-Americans (called "Negro spiritual" in the 19th century) *(376)*

Sprechstimme: A vocal style developed by Schoenberg, in between singing and speaking *(359)*

Staccato: Played in a detached manner; as opposed to *legato (25)*

Staff (or stave): In musical notation, the group of five horizontal lines on which music is written *(25)*

Stanza: In songs or ballads, one of several similar poetic units, which are usually sung to the same tune; also called *verse*

Stop: An organ stop is a single set of pipes, covering the entire pitch range in a particular tone color *(51)*

Stretto: In a fugue, overlapping entrances of the fugue subject in several voices simultaneously *(131)*

String quartet: An instrumental group consisting of two violins, viola, and cello; or a piece composed for this group; or the four players themselves *(213)*

Strophic form, strophic song: A song in several *stanzas,* with the same music sung for each stanza; as opposed to *through-composed song (255)*

Structure: A term often used to mean *form*

Style: The combination of qualities that make a period of art, a composer, or an individual work of art distinctive *(60)*

Subito: Suddenly (as in *subito forte* or *subito piano,* suddenly loud, suddenly soft) *(14)*

Subject: The term for the principal theme of a fugue *(129)*

Subject entries: In a fugue, appearances of the entire fugue *subject* after the opening exposition *(129)*

Suite: A piece consisting of a series of dances *(104)*

Symbolism: A late 19th-century movement in the arts that emphasized suggestion rather than precise reference *(328)*

Swing: A type of big-band jazz of the late 1930s and 1940s *(383)*

Symphonic poem: A piece of orchestral program music in one long movement *(302)*

Symphony: A large orchestral piece in several movements *(197)*

Syncopation: The accenting of certain beats of the meter that are ordinarily unaccented *(20)*

Synthesizer: An electronic apparatus that generates sounds for electronic music *(11)*

Tempo: The speed of music, i.e., the rate at which the accented and unaccented beats of the meter follow one another *(22)*

Tenor: The high adult male voice

Ternary form: A three-part musical form in which the last section repeats the first: **ABA** form *(175)*

Texture: The blend of the various sounds and melodic lines occurring simultaneously in a piece of music *(33)*

Thematic transformation: A variationlike procedure applied to short themes in the various sections of Romantic symphonic poems and other works *(250)*

Theme: The basic subject matter of a piece of music. A theme can be a phrase, a short motive, a full tune, etc. *(33)*

Theme and variations: A form consisting of a tune (the theme) plus a number of *variations* on it *(125, 189)*

Thorough bass: Same as *basso continuo* or *continuo*

Through-composed (*durchkomponiert*) song: A song with new music for each stanza of the poem; as opposed to *strophic song (255)*

Tie: In musical notation, a curved line joining two notes of the same pitch into a continuous sound *(24)*

Timbre (*tám-bruh*): Another term for *tone color (14)*

Time signature: In musical notation, the numbers on the staffs at the beginning of a piece that indicate the meter *(25)*

Toccata: A piece in free form designed partly to show off the instrument and the technique of the player (usually an organist or harpsichordist) *(14)*

Tonality, tonal: The feeling of centrality of one note (and its chord) to a passage of music; as opposed to *atonality (37)*

Tone: A sound of a certain definite pitch and duration; same as *note*

Tone color: The sonorous quality of a particular instrument, voice, or combination of instruments or voices *(14)*

Tone poem: Same as *symphonic poem*

Tonic (noun): In *tonal* music, the central-sounding note *(37)*

Transition: A passage whose function is to connect one section of a piece with another; see *bridge.*

Transpose: To move a whole piece, or a section of a piece, or a twelve-tone series, from one pitch level to another

Trill: Two adjacent notes played very rapidly in alternation

Trio: (1) A piece for three instruments or singers; (2) the second or B section of a minuet movement, scherzo, etc. *(175)*

Trio sonata: A Baroque sonata for three main instruments plus the *continuo* chord instrument *(140)*

Triple meter: Meter consisting of one accented beat alternating with two unaccented beats: *one* two three *one* two three *(19)*

Triplet: A group of three notes performed in the time normally taken by two *(25)*

Troubadours, trouvères: Aristocratic poet-musicians of the Middle Ages *(69)*

Tune: A simple, easily singable melody that is coherent and complete *(30)*

Twelve-tone series (or *row*): An ordering of all twelve notes of the *chromatic scale,* used in composing serial music *(336)*

Upbeat: A weak or unaccented beat leading to a *downbeat*

Variation: A section of music that follows another section (the "theme") closely in certain respects—e.g., in phrase length and harmony—while varying other aspects of it *(125, 189)*

Verismo: A realistic and sensational type of late Romantic Italian opera *(293, 299)*

Vivace, vivo: Lively *(22)*

Voice: (1) Throat sound; (2) a contrapuntal line—whether sung or played by instruments—in a polyphonic piece such as a fugue

Waltz: A nineteenth-century dance in triple meter

Whole note: The longest note in normal use, and the basis of the duration of shorter notes (half notes, quarter notes, etc.) *(24)*

Whole step, whole tone: The interval equal to two half steps (semitones) *(16)*

Whole-tone scale: A scale, used sometimes by Debussy, comprising only six notes to the octave, all at the interval of the whole tone (i.e., two semitones) *(332)*

Word painting: Musical illustration of the meaning of a word or a short verbal phrase *(83)*

Music and Literary Credits

Illustration Credits

84 Mus. Ms. AII, fol. 186, Bayerische Staatsbibliothek, Munich

85 The Bettmann Archive

86 The Bettmann Archive

88 By permission of the Trustees of the Will of the 8th Earl of Berkeley. Photo: The Courtauld Institute of Art, London

89 Giraudon/Art Resource

91 New York Public Library Picture Collection

93 Canaletto, *The Grand Canal*. Photo: The National Trust/Art Resource

97 Museum für Kunst und Gewerbe, Hamburg

98 *both*: Phot. Bib. Nat., Paris

99 The Bettmann Archive

102 The Bettmann Archive

104 The Bettmann Archive

105 *left*: Lauros-Giraudon/Art Resource; *right*: The Bettmann Archive

107 Francesco Guardi, *Gala Concert in the Casino Filharmonico* (detail), Alte Pinakothek, Munich. Photo: Joachim Blauel/Artothek

111 *top*: Pierre Patel, *Carriages Arriving at Versailles, 1688*. Photo: Giraudon/Art Resource; *bottom*: Alinari/Art Resource

112 Domenico Tiepolo, painted ceiling, Residenz, Wurzburg. Photo: Scala/Art Resource

113 G. G. Bibiena, stage set for *Didone Abbandonata*. Photo: Joachim Blauel/Artothek

114 Michelangelo da Caravaggio, *Madonna of the Pilgrims*. Photo: Scala/Art Resource

115 *top*: Jan Vermeer, *View of Delft* (detail). Photo: Scala/Art Resource; *bottom*: Canaletto, *Nymphenburg Palace* (detail). Photo: Joachim Blauel/Artothek

116 *top*: Snark/Art Resource; *bottom*: from Le Brun's *Conférence sur l'Expression*, 1698

118 Oliviero, *Performance at Turin Theater*. Photo: Scala/Art Resource

119 Munari, *Still Life with Instuments* (detail). Photo: Scala/Art Resource

120 Germanisches Nationalmuseum Nüremburg

124 Museo Municipal, Barcelona. Photo: MAS

125 Gaspar Netscher, *The Viola da Gamba Lesson*. Photo: Giraudon/Art Resource

127 © Archiv/Photo Researchers

129 Private collection

130 Lancret, *The Concert*. Photo: Blauel, Gramm/Artothek

136 *left*: Scala/Art Resource; *right*: Vatican Library

139 Museo Municipal, Barcelona. Photo: MAS

141 The Bettmann Archive

143 Thomas Rowlandson, *Old Vauxhall Gardens*, by courtesy of the Board of Trustees of the Victoria & Albert Museum, London

147 Sächsische Landesbibliothek Abt. Photo: Deutsche Fotothek/Loos

149 School of Longhi, *l'Opera Seria*. Photo: Scala/Art Resource

150 *top*: Thomas Hudson, *Portrait of Handel*, 1747, Staats-und-Universitätsbibliothek, Hamburg; *bottom*: Victoria & Albert Museum/Art Resource

151 Metropolitan Opera Press Office. Photo: Winnie Klotz

154 The Bettmann Archive

155 Snark/Art Resource

157 *both*: Giraudon/Art Resource

158 The Bettmann Archive

159 Archiv/Photo Researchers

160 The Bettmann Archive

161 *top*: Österreichische Nationalbibliothek, Vienna; *bottom*: Jean-Antoine Houdon, statue of Voltaire (detail). Photo: H. H. Arnason, by permission of the Comédie Française

162 *top*: Jean-Antoine Houdon, bust of Thomas Jefferson (detail), 1789, marble, Museum of Fine Arts, Boston, George Nixon Black Fund; *bottom*: faïence plaque, *The Magic Flute*, Museum of Fine Arts, Lille. Photo: Giraudon/Art Resource

163 *top*: Thomas Gainsborough, *Johann Christian Bach*. Photo: Scala/Art Resource; *bottom*: Jean-Antoine Houdon, bust of Rousseau (detail). Photo: H. H. Arnason, collection of Edmond Courty

164 The Bettmann Archive

165 *top*: Peter Jakob Horemans, *Court Musician with Stringed Instruments*, Photo: Joachim Blauel/Artothek; *bottom*: Jean-Antoine Houdon, statue of Gluck (detail), National Forschungs-und Gedenkstätten der klassischen Deutschen Literatur in Weimar

166 Gabriele Bella, *Concert in Philharmonic Hall*. Photo: Scala/Art Resource

168 Johann Zoffany, *George, 3rd Earl Cowper, with the Family of Charles Gore*, Yale Center for British Art, Paul Mellon Collection

171 Scala/Art Resource

173 Jean-Antoine Houdon, bust of Mme. Houdon, Louvre, Paris. Photo: Giraudon/Art Resource

174 The Bettmann Archive

175 *top*: The Bettmann Archive; *bottom*: Dance Division, The New York Public Library at Lincoln Center, Astor, Lenox and Tilden Foundations

176 *left*: The Bettmann Archive; *right*: John Hoppner, *Franz Joseph Haydn*, 1791, Royal Collection, copyright reserved to Her Majesty Queen Elizabeth II

177 The Metropolitan Museum of Art, The Crosby Brown Collection of Musical Instruments, 1889

180 *left*: Marie-Louise-Elizabeth Vigée-Lebrun, *The Duchess de Polignac*, 1783, Waddesdon Manor/The National Trust. Photo: The Courtauld Institute of Art, London; *right*: Mather Brown, *Portrait of a Young Girl*, The Metropolitan Museum of Art, gift of Mrs. Theodore Newhouse, 1965

181 Museum der Stadt Wien

182 The Metropolitan Museum of Art, Purchase, Anonymous Gift, Friends of the American Wing Fund, Sansbury-Mills, Dodge and Pfeiffer Funds, and Funds from various donors, 1976

184 *left:* Movie Still Archive; *right:* The Bettmann Archive

185 The Bettmann Archive

189 *top left:* Jasper Johns, *Painted Bronze*, 1960; *top right, bottom left and right:* Monotypes #7, #16, and #4 from Judith Goldman, *Jasper Johns: 17 Monotypes.* Reproduced courtesy Universal Limited Art Editions, Inc.

194 New York Public Library Picture Collection

196 Pesci: *Eszterháza Castle*, Architectural Museum of the National Intendance of Historical Monuments, Budapest. Photo: Gabor Barka

200 The Bettmann Archive

204 Photo: Drottningholm Theater Museum, courtesy Swedish Information Service

205 Holland Festival Press Office

206 Culver Pictures

208 *left:* The Bettmann Archive; *right:* The Metropolitan Opera Press Office. Photo: Winnie Klotz

213 *top:* The Bettmann Archive; *bottom:* © Catherine Ursillo/ Photo Researchers

214 Courtesy Elektra/Nonesuch

216 Museum of Modern Art Film Still Library

217 The Bettmann Archive

221 Library of Congress

222 The Bettmann Archive

223 Jacques-Louis David, *The Coronation of Napoleon I* (detail), Louvre, Paris. Photo: Alinari/Art Resource

224 *top:* Gesellschaft der Musikfreunde, Vienna; *bottom:* The Bettmann Archive

225 *Beethoven Nearing the End* by Batt (Plate 18, *The Oxford Companion to Music*, copyright Mrs. W. A. Barrett) is reproduced by kind permission of the copyright owner

226 Stadtgeschichtliches Museum, Leipzig

230 Beethoven-Archiv, Bonn, H. C. Bodmer Collection

232 The Bettmann Archive

235 Center for Beethoven Studies, San Jose State University, San Jose, CA

237 The Bettmann Archive

238 Rude, *Le Départ des Voluntaires.* Photo: Lauros-Giraudon/ Art Resource

239 *top:* Henry Fuseli, *The Nightmare*, 1771, The Detroit Institute of Arts, gift of Mr. and Mrs. Bert L. Smokler and Mr. and Mrs. Lawrence A. Fleischman; *bottom:* Turner, *The Fall of an Avalanche in the Grisons.* Photo: Tate Gallery/Art Resource

240 Thomas Cole, *Daniel Boone and His Cabin at Great Osage Lake*, 1826, oil on canvas, 38 × 42½″, Mead Art Museum, Amherst College, Amherst, Mass., Museum Purchase

241 *left:* Caspar David Friedrich, *Mountainous Landscape*, c. 1812, Kunsthistorisches Museum, Vienna. Photo: Saskia/Art Resource; *right:* John Martin, *The Bard*, c. 1817, oil on canvas 50 × 40″, Yale Center for British Art, Paul Mellon Collection

242 Turner, *The Music Party.* Photo: Tate Gallery/Art Resource

243 *left:* The Bettmann Archive; *right:* © G. D. Hackett/Archive Photos

244 C. Tellier, *Hornplayer*, c. 1835, Haags Gemeentemuseum, The Hague

247 The Bettmann Archive

248 Wilhelm von Lindenschmit the Younger, *The Music Makers*, 1856, Neue Pinakothek, Munich. Photo: Joachim Blauel/Artothek

249 The Bettmann Archive

250 The Metropolitan Museum of Art, The Crosby Brown Collection of Musical Instruments, 1889

251 New York Public Library Picture Collection

252 Max Klinger, *Beethoven*, bronze, marble, ivory, etc., height: 11′2″, Museum der Bildenden Künste, Leipzig

254 Moritz von Schwind, *A Schubert Evening in the Spaun Drawing Room*, 1868, Historisches Museum der Stadt Wien

256 Julius Schnorr von Carolsfeld, *The Erlking*, 1830–35. Photo: Joachim Blauel/Artothek

258 Robert-Schumann-Haus

261 Archiv/Photo Researchers

263 *left:* Eugène Delacroix, *Chopin*, 1857, Louvre, Paris. Photo: Giraudon/Art Resource; *right:* Eugène Delacroix, *George Sand*, The Ordrupgaard Collection, Copenhagen

264 The Performing Arts Research Center, New York Public Library at Lincoln Center, Astor, Lenox and Tilden Foundations

265 Ludwig von Hofmann, *Notturno*, Neue Pinakothek, Munich. Photo: Joachim Blauel/Artothek

266 Mary Evans Picture Library

267 Mary Evans Picture Library

269 *both:* The Bettmann Archive

271 The Bettmann Archive

274 Goya, *Witches Sabbath.* Photo: Scala/Art Resource

276 Musée du Théâtre, Munich. Photo: Klaus Broszat

277 *left, center left and center right:* Culver Pictures; *right:* The Bettmann Archive

278 Giovanni Boldoni, *Giuseppe Verdi.* Photo: Scala/Art Resource

279 The Bettmann Archive

280 New York Public Library Picture Collection

281 *top and bottom:* New York Public Library Picture Collection; *center:* The Bettmann Archive

285 Richard-Wagner-Museum, Bayreuth

286 Richard-Wagner-Museum, Bayreuth

287 The Bettmann Archive

288 Musée Condé, Chantilly. Photo: Giraudon/Art Resource

290 The Bettmann Archive

291 Metropolitan Opera Press Office. Photo: Winnie Klotz

293 Museum of Modern Art Film Still Library

294 The Bettmann Archive

295 The Bettmann Archive

296 Österreichische Nationalbibliothek, Vienna

299 Thomas Eakins, *The Gross Clinic* (detail), 1875, oil on canvas, 96 × 78″, Jefferson Medical College of Thomas Jefferson University

300 The Bettmann Archive

302 Mary Evans Picture Library

304 Akseli Gallen-Kallela, *Lemminkäinen's Mother*, 1897, tempera, 33½ × 46½″, Finnish National Gallery

305 *top:* Sir Lawrence Alma-Tadema, *Love's Votaries*, 1891, oil on canvas, 34½ × 65¼″, Laing Art Gallery, Newcastle-upon-Tyne. Photo: Tyne and Wear Museum Service; *bottom:* The Bettmann Archive

309 *top:* Scala/Art Resource; *bottom:* Snark/Art Resource

310 The Bettmann Archive

313 *both:* The Bettmann Archive

314 Österreichische Nationalbibliothek, Vienna

315 The New York Public Library, Astor, Lenox and Tilden Foundations

321 Raoul Dufy, *Le Concerto de Mozart*. Photo: Giraudon/Art Resource

323 Georges Braque, *Still Life with Score by Satie*, Museum of Modern Art, Paris. Photo: Scala/Art Resource

324 Piet Mondrian, *Composition with Blue and Yellow*, 1935, Joseph H. Hirshhorn Museum and Sculpture Garden, Smithsonian Insitution. Photo: Joseph Martin, Scala/Art Resource

325 Wassily Kandinsky, final design for the cover of *The Blue Rider* almanac, Städtische Galerie im Lenbachhaus, Munich. Photo: Joachim Blauel/Artothek

326 Edouard Manet, *In the Boat*, Neue Pinakothek, Munich. Photo: Scala/Art Resource

327 Edgar Degas, The Ballet Scene from Meyerbeer's Opera *Robert le Diable*. Photo: Victoria & Albert Museum/Art Resource

328 Vincent van Gogh, *Les Chaumes à Cordeville*, Jeu de Paume, Paris. Photo: Scala/Art Resource

329 *top left:* Wassily Kandinsky, *Couple on Horseback*, 1907, Städtische Galerie im Lenbachhaus, Munich. Photo: Joachim Blauel/Artothek; *top right:* Wassily Kandinsky, *Blue Mountain*, 1908–09, oil on canvas, 41¾ × 38″. The Solomon R. Guggenheim Museum. Photo: David Heald; *bottom:* Wassily Kandinsky, *Romantic Landscape*, 1911, Städtische Galerie im Lenbachhaus, Munich. Photo: Joachim Blauel/Artothek

331 Félix Vallotton, *The Flute*, woodcut, Prints Division, The New York Public Library, Astor, Lenox and Tilden Foundations

333 *top:* Gustav Klimt, *Music*, 1895, Neue Pinakothek, Munich. Photo: Joachim Blauel/Artothek; *bottom:* Debussy, Chausson, Bonheur, and Mme. Chausson on the banks of the Marne. Phot. Bib. Nat. Paris

335 The Bettmann Archive

339 Robert Rauschenberg, *Monogram*, 1955–59, Construction, 5′4½″ × 3′6″ × 5′3¼″, Moderna Museet, Stockholm

340 James Wilson/Woodfin Camp & Associates

344 Giraudon/Art Resource

347 Pablo Picasso, *Stravinsky*, 1920. Photo: Giraudon/Art Resource

348 © Sanford A. Roth/Rapho, Photo Researchers

351 The Joffrey Ballet, Photo: Herbert Migdoll

353 © G. D. Hackett/Archive Photos

355 New York Public Library Picture Collection

357 Edvard Munch, *Angst*, 1894, Oslo Kommunes Kunstsamlinger, Munch-Museet

358 Man Ray, *Arnold Schoenberg* (1926), gelatin, silver plate, 11⅝ × 8¾″, Collection The Museum of Modern Art, New York. Gift of James Thrall Soby. Copyright Juliet Man Ray, 1987

359 Rouault, *The Clown*, Stedelijk Museum

362 Culver Pictures

363 © Reg Wilson

364 © Beth Bergman

367 University of Louisville, Courtesy Mrs. Doris Keyes. Photo: Anderson/Schott Archiv

369 Mark Rothko, *Violet, Black, Orange, Yellow on White and Red*, Gift of Elaine and Werner Dannheisser and the Dannheisser Foundation. Photo: David Heald. Photograph © The Solomon R. Guggenheim Foundation.

370 NYT Pictures

372 © Dr. Detlef Gojowy

374 *top:* Thomas Eakins, *The Concert Singer*, 1892, The Philadelphia Museum of Art. Given by Mrs. Thomas Eakins and Miss Mary Adeline Williams; *bottom:* The Bettmann Archive

375 *top:* From the Collections of Henry Ford Museum & Greenfield Village; *bottom:* The Bettmann Archive

376 The Bettmann Archive

377 Culver Pictures

378 The Bettmann Archive

379 *left:* © Syndey Byrd; *right:* Courtesy of Queens College

381 Culver Pictures

382 *left:* Culver Pictures; *right:* UPI/Bettmann Newsphoto

383 *left:* © Peter Carrette/LGI; *right:* © Ken Frankling/LGI

384 Institute of Jazz Studies, Rutgers

385 © Rex USA

386 © Carol Rosegg/Martha Swope Assoc.

387 Culver Pictures

388 Culver Pictures

389 The Bettmann Archive

390 Barton Silverman/NYT Pictures

391 © Martha Swope

392 © Martha Swope

394 RCA Victor

397 *top:* © Robin Holland; *bottom:* © Rex USA

398 Scala/Art Resource

Illustration Credits

Index